Intramural Director's Handbook

*selected articles from the *Proceedings* of the NIRSA (and NIA) since 1950.

edited by

James A. Peterson, Ph.D.
and
Lawrence Preo, Ph.D.

Leisure Press
P.O. Box 3
West Point, N.Y. 10996

A publication of Leisure Press.
P.O. Box 3, West Point, N.Y. 10996
Copyright © 1977 by James A. Peterson
All rights reserved. Printed in the U.S.A.

ISBN 0-918438-08-X

TABLE OF CONTENTS

✦✦✦

The professional commitment to excellence of the following individuals made this book a reality.

Gary Adams. B. D. Anderson, Frederick A. Barney, Peter R.Berrafato, Larry Berres, Eugene Boyer, Robert T. Bronzan, Edsel Buchanan, Kent Bunker, K. Nelson Butler, Sandra Caldwell, Greg Claeys, Gary Colberg, Nancy L. Curry, Bob Dalrymple, Warin Dexter, Ken Droscher, Charles Espinosa, Louis A. Fabian, E. Moses Frye, Bud Farmer, Larry Fudge, Kathryn D. George, Rodney J. Grambeau, Peter Graham, Paul Gunsten, George Haniford, Linda Hall, Carol Harding, Eugene Hill, Patti Holmes, Peter D. Hopkins, H. Toi Jamison, J. A. Jevert, Joseph Johnson, D. F. Juncker, William A. Katerberg, Paul V. Keen, Nick Kovalakides, Gene G. Lanke, Bernard I. Loft, Gerry Maas, Joe Manjone, William Manning, David O. Matthews, John T. Meyer, Harvey Miller, C.E. Mueller, Alan Murdock, Jim McAvaddy, George M. McDonald, Raymond J. McGuire, Val McMurtie, Jim Nasiopulos, Steve Newman, William T. Odeneal, Harry Ostrander, Mark A. Pandau, Norman Parsons, Jr., David Peshke, James. A. Peterson, Bernard Pollack, Don Poling, Lawrence Preo, Kenneth Renner, John Reznik, Russell L. Rivet, Harvey Rogoff, Francis M. Rokosz, Tom Sattler, Larry D. Schaake, Susan Scheider, Loretta Shane, Steven A. Sherman, Peter Steilberg, Michael Stevenson, Ralph Stewart, Joseph M. Sullivan, David H. Taylor, Bob Thompson, William Thompson, Ross E. Townes, Clifford Trump, Mosby Turner, H. Dutch Usilaner, Tom VanderWeele, Johannes Van Hoff, Hazel Varner, Jim Wittenauer, M. Wayne Wiemer, Janice L. White, and William Zimmer.

✦✦✦

FORWARD

Within the past decade, adminstrators at all levels of responsibility have become increasingly aware of the educational values of the sponsored intramural-recreational sports program. Their awareness has contributed to the growth of these programs through the provision of professional leadership, financing, services and facilities.

An adjunct improvement in numerous individual programs has also been noted. An important contributing factor to their improvement has been the vocality of the participants served. The personalized approach in the administration of the intramural-recreational sports program has resulted from the participants expressing their individual and collective demands for sports outlets to satisfy their physical, mental and emotional needs.

A stereotyped program or one copied after another is usually no longer adequate or professionally acceptable. Rather, the peculiarities of the institution and the need of the participants generally dictate the type of organization, administration and content of the program.

Many volumns and thousands of words have been written about the organization, administration and content of the intramural-recreational sports program. This new *Intramural Director's Handbook* is a valuable addition to the noteworthy works that exist. The editors have assembled in a single volumn, free of frills, the writings of experts. The novice, as well as the professional, will find the materials presented to be professionally stimulating, challenging and an excellent guide for the organization and administration of the intramural-recreational sports program.

George Haniford, Ph.D.
Purdue University

Chapter 1
Organization and Administration

Campus Recreation Department or Division
David O. Matthews
1974 NIA Proceedings, pp. 143-148

The type of administration structure that best suits any particular institution depends upon several factors which are exposited below:

1. *Source of funds*

Each campus recreation director must submit a budget request to some higher authority within the institution. This request should contain rationale for justification of the amounts that are asked for. The closer the director is in the chain of command to the person who ultimately decides what funds will be made available the better the chances are that the amount requested will be approved.

Conversely, the farther away the director is away from the ultimate decision maker the less are the chances of receiving what is asked for.

The rationales that accompany a budget request are sometimes the only opportunity the director has of influencing the decisions regarding the final allocations. These justifications must be clearly and honestly defined. There is always a tendency on the part of directors to ask for more than what is actually needed. This practice is based on experiences that show that the budget requests are usually cut back about ten percent. However, the honest requests will pay off in the long run if higher authorities learn that the director asks only for what he needs and spends no more than is allocated.

The establishing of priorities within a large administrative framework such as that of a Vice-President of Student Affairs Office has a very definite affect on what funds are ultimately allocated to the director. The CRD must compete with many other groups and activities that are housed within that Office. The CRD definitely has to have the opportunity to meet jointly with all other unit heads in the Student Affairs Office to discuss budget needs and problems related thereto.

2. *Priority of facilities*

The establishment of facility usage priorities may or may not be accomplished with the prior consultation of all campus recreation agencies. The CRD can best accomplish his aims and purposes is he is involved in the setting up of priorities on the use of recreation facilities. If the majority of decisions regarding priorities are made by the physical education department or the athletic associations, then perhaps it would be more advantageous for the CRD to be a member of either or both of those administrative units.

It is not unusual for a department to take care of its own needs first and then allocate space to groups and individuals outside of its own administrative structure. An example of this principle is very evident in most schools where intramural sports programs are under the aegis of physical education or athletics. These units will give priority to their own programs before allocating facilities to others. Intramurals will ordinarily rank after physical education classes and athletic team needs. Even so, this third priority ranking gives the intramural director a much needed higher priority than that held by other agencies on campus.

This situation leads one to think that the CRD would best be a part of physical education or athletics. However, if the priorities were set by a combined group consisting of councils coming from the arts, drama, special events, music, athletics, intramurals, physical education, and other concerned groups, the entire campus recreation program would be in a much stronger position to bargain for and attain priority rankings that are quite favorable to the recreation program. Such an all-campus recreation council under the director of campus recreation with final determination of priorities to be approved by the Vice-President of campus affairs could provide a balanced and equitable distribution of the different types of space needed for the total campus recreation program.

In essence, where it is possible, the administrative structure should be so established as to have the CRD in a position where he can exert a great deal of influence in the final determination of space priorities.

3. *Degree of authority invested in the office of the Campus Recreation Director*

In the final analysis, it may not be a critical matter as to where the CRD is located in the line of administrative command. What is more important is the degree of authority that the CRD has in the scheme of things.

The Campus Recreation Director may report directly to the dean of a college, to an athletic director, to a vice-president of student affairs, or to the president of the institution. In any case his effectiveness as an administrator is directly related to the strength of his decision-making processes. If most of his decisions are subject to review and revision by other authorities, there is always a present danger of these other persons to reverse, change, modify, or reject the decisions of the CRD. It is not being advocated herein that the CRD should not be responsible to some other agency or person. What is being advocated is that a maximum amount of freedom should be available to that administrator as he goes about making decisions after prior consultation with his advisory committees.

Someone on campus must be delegated the authority to decide what is best for each individual program as well as for the total program. With the various advisory councils representing the various interests on campus, i.e. arts, music, drama, sports, etc., giving him advice and counsel, the CRD should in almost one hundred percent of the time be allowed to have his decisions stand as being final.

CAMPUS RECREATION DIRECTOR

Major duties of the Campus Recreation Director should include:

1. Acting as general advisor to the Recreation Coordinating Council.
2. Acting as liaison in establishing and maintaining close working relations with all organizations sponsoring student recreation programs and with all staff and faculty concerned with various phases of student recreation.
3. Maintaining continuity in matters related to the coordination of student recreation.
4. Providing professional leadership in matters such as program appraisal and development and recreation leadership training.
5. Carrying out or providing for the accomplishment of all matters recommended by the Recreation Coordinating Council.[1]

Guidelines elaborating the principle that all areas of campus recreation should be coordinated:

1. Coordination should be established among all activities within a given area.
2. Coordination should be established among all areas.
3. There should be a top level coordinating agency for all campus recreation activities.
4. Avenues of coordination should be established through representation from the lowest to the highest levels of organizational structures.
5. Coordinating bodies should function in such a way as to promote satisfying interaction among students, faculty, and administration.
6. There should be both intra-area and inter-area coordination among faculty advisors.
7. Channels of coordination must be open-ended and provide two-way communication.
8. Coordinating agencies should function to insure inter-group awareness and understanding of purposes, problems, and achievements.
9. Coordination should serve to establish a balanced program of activities for all students.
10. Coordination should be concerned with the cooperation of all of those involved in every phase of the activity.[2]

CAMPUS RECREATION COORDINATING COUNCIL[3]

The main objective of the Recreation Coordinating Council would be the achievement of an integrated student recreation program designed to meet the various interests and needs of the students through the complementary development of all resources. Specific purposes might include:

1. Providing a device for horizontal communication of all organizations conducting major areas of student recreation.
2. Providing vertical lines of responsibility which lead ultimately to the Office of Student Affairs or Dean of Students in matters related to both policy and administration.
3. Providing for the coordination of the total calendar of recreation activities and events.
4. Providing for coordination in the use of facilities for recreation activities and events.
5. Providing stimulation and assistance in areas of program appraisal and development, with particular attention to needs such as the current deficiencies in hobby and crafts and graduate program areas.
6. Providing assistance in conducting recreation leadership training programs and services which would be available to all interested groups and individuals.
7. Providing a means of assembling and distributing information concerning the total recreation resources and programs available to students.
8. Providing for operation within established University policy of all phases of the program.

[1]Mary V. Frye, "A Proposed Plan to Coordinate Student Recreation on the Campus of the University of Illinois at Champaign-Urbana" (unpublished master's thesis, University of Illinois, Champaign-Urbana, 1955), p. 116.

[2]Marya Welch, "Guides for the Organization of Campus Recreation" (unpublished doctoral dissertation, Teachers College, Columbia University, 1952), p. 22.

[3]Mary V. Frye, "A Proposed Plan to Coordinate Student Recreation On The Campus of the University of Illinois" (unpublished master's thesis, University of Illinois at Champaign-Urbana, 1955), p. 115.

**Study of the Administrative Structuring and Staffing of the
Intramural-Recreational Sports Programs in the
Member Universities of the Big 10, Big 8, Southwest, and
Pacific 8 Conferences**
George Haniford
1975 NIRSA Proceedings, pp. 197-202

1. Member Institutions

Big Ten	*Big Eight*	*Southwest (SAC)*	*Pacific (PAC 8)*
Illinois	Colorado	Arkansas	U. of Cal., Berkeley
Indiana	Iowa State	Baylor	U. of Cal., Los Angeles
Iowa	Kansas	Houston	Oregon
Michigan	Kansas St.	Rice	Oregon State
Michigan St.	Missouri	SMU	Southern Cal.
Minnesota	Nebraska	Texas	Stanford
Northwestern	Oklahoma	Texas A&M	Washington
Ohio State	Oklahoma St.	Texas Christian	Washington State
Purdue		Texas Tech	
Wisconsin			
Chicago			

2. Official Titles as given on University Contracts and/or payroll changes:

Director, Division of Recreational Sports—Purdue, Texas

Director, Division of Campus Recreation—Illinois

Director of Recreation and Recreation Coordinator—Nebraska, Oregon State

Director of Recreational Services—Iowa, Kansas State

Director of Recreation—Southern California

Director, Colvin Center, Director of Recreation—Oklahoma State

Recreation Supervisor III—U.C.L.A.

Director of Campus Wide Activities—Arkansas

Director of Recreation, Intramurals and Club Sports—Michigan

Director of University Recreation, Intramurals and Women's Inter-collegiate Athletics—Ohio State

Director of Intramural Sports and Recreative Services—Michigan State

Co-Director of Intramural-Recreation—Wisconsin

Director, Department of Intramurals-Extramurals—Minnesota

Director of Intramural Sports and Sports Clubs—Indiana, Northwestern, Stanford

Director of Intramurals—Chicago, Kansas, Oklahoma, Oregon, Southern Methodist, Texas A&M, Texas Christian, Texas Tech, Washington, Washington State

Coordinator of Intramural Sports and Activities—Colorado

Professor of Physical Education and Department Chairman—Missouri

Associate Professor of Physical Education—Baylor

Assistant Professor of Physical Education—Houston, Iowa State, Rice

11

Supervisor of Physical Education, Step IV—California at Berkeley
3. Immediate supervisor of the Director:
Vice President for Student Services/Affairs—Iowa, Kansas State, Michigan State, Minnesota, Oklahoma State, Purdue, Texas Tech, Washington
Associate Vice President, University Community—Oklahoma
Dean, Cultural and Recreational Affairs—U.C.L.A.
Dean, School of Education—Missouri, Texas Christian, Wisconsin
Director of Athletics—Houston, Michigan, Ohio State, Stanford
Dean, College of Physical Education—Illinois
Chairman/Head, Physical Education Department—Arkansas, Baylor, Calif., Berkeley, Chicago, Indiana, Iowa State, Kansas, Northwestern, Oregon, Rice, Southern Methodist, Texas A&M, Washington State
Not Reported—Colorado, Nebraska, Oregon State, Southern California, Texas
4. Name of the department, division or office:
Official Name:
Division of Recreational Sports—Purdue, Texas
Division of Campus Recreation—Illinois
Division/Department of Recreational Services—Iowa, Kansas State
Department of Recreation—Nebraska
University of Recreation Association—Southern California
Recreation, Intramurals and Club Sports—Michigan
University Recreation, Intramurals and Women's Intercollegiate Athletics—Ohio State
Division of Intramural Sports and Recreative Services—Michigan State
Campus Wide Activities—Arkansas
Department/Division of Intramurals and Recreation—California at Berkeley, Oklahoma, Texas A&M, Wisconsin
Department of Intramurals—Extramurals—Minnesota
Division of Intramural Sports and Sports Clubs—Indiana, Stanford
Department/Division of Intramurals—Baylor, Chicago, Colorado, Houston, Northwestern, Oregon (Men), Texas Christian, Texas Tech (Men), Washington, Washington State (Men)
Intramural Office—Kansas, Oregon State, U.C.L.A.
Unofficial Name:
Division of Intramural Sports and Recreative Services—Oklahoma State
Department/Division of Intramurals—Iowa State, Missouri
Department of H.P.E.&R.—Rice, Southern Methodist

5. Directors Term of appointment:
   Academic Year—14 schools
   Fiscal Year—22 schools
6. Directors responsibilities as budgeted:
   100 Per Cent Administrative:California, Berkeley, Colorado, Iowa, Kansas State, Oklahoma State, Purdue, Southern California, Texas, Texas A&M, U.C.L.A., Washington
   100 Per Cent Instructional—Rice
   75-95 Per Cent Administrative Plus Instructional/Research Responsibilities: Arkansas, Illinois, Indiana, Iowa State, Michigan, Michigan State, Minnesota, Nebraska, Northwestern, Ohio State, Oklahoma, Stanford, Wisconsin
   50-74 Per Cent Administrative Plus Instructional/Research Responsibilities: Baylor, Chicago, Houston, Kansas, Missouri, Oregon, Oregon State, Southern Methodist, Texas Christian, Texas Tech, Washington State
7. Directors positions, as currently structured, will or will not earn tenure for successors?
   WILL: (15 institutions) Arkansas, California, Berkeley, Houston, Iowa State, Kansas, Michigan, Michigan State, Minnesota, Missouri, Oregon, Oregon State, Rice, Southern Methodist, Stanford, Texas Tech
   WILL NOT: (19 institutions) Baylor, Chicago, Colorado, Illinois, Indiana, Iowa, Kansas State, Nebraska, Northwestern, Ohio State, Oklahoma, Oklahoma State, Purdue, Southern California, Texas, Texas A&M, Texas Christian, Washington, Washington State, Wisconsin
   NO ANSWER: U.C.L.A.
8. Delegation of administrative responsibilities:
   a. Men's Intramurals: Yes—All Other schools; No—Nebraska
   b. Women's Intramurals: Yes—All Other schools; No—Chicago, Iowa State, Nebraska, Northwestern, Oregon, Rice, Southern California, Stanford, Texas Tech, Washington State
   c. Co-ed Intramurals: Yes—All other schools; NO—Missouri, Nebraska, Southern California, Southern Methodist
   d. Sports Clubs: Yes—All other schools; NO—Baylor, Houston, Illinois, Iowa, Iowa State, Kansas, Missouri, Oklahoma, Oregon, Oregon State, Rice, Southern California, Southern Methodist, Texas, Texas Christian, U.C.L.A., Washington State
   e. Informal Recreation: Yes—All other schools; NO—Colorado, Houston, Indiana, Iowa State, Kansas, Rice, Stanford, Texas Christian, U.C.L.A., Washington

f. Women's Intercollegiate Athletics: Yes—Ohio State, Purdue; No—All other schools
g. Staff Intramurals/Recreational Sports: Yes—All other schools; No—Baylor, Houston, Oklahoma, Rice, Texas Christian

9. Collegiate/university administrative and/or instructional experience of the Directors:

$$
\begin{array}{ll}
0-5 \text{ years} - & 5 \\
6-10 \text{ years} - & 5 \\
11-15 \text{ years} - & 10 \\
16-20 \text{ years} - & 1 \\
21-25 \text{ years} - & 3 \\
26-30 \text{ years} - & 5 \\
31-35 \text{ years} - & 2 \\
36-40 \text{ years} - & 1 \\
\end{array}
$$

Note: Colorado, Nebraska, Southern California and Texas not included

Mean years of experience—16.4

10. Age of the Directors:

$$
\begin{array}{l}
25-30 \text{ years} - 4 \\
31-35 \text{ years} - 4 \\
36-40 \text{ years} - 5 \\
41-45 \text{ years} - 4 \\
46-50 \text{ years} - 4 \\
51-55 \text{ years} - 7 \\
56-60 \text{ years} - 3 \\
60-65 \text{ years} - 1 \\
\end{array}
$$

Note: Colorado, Nebraska, Southern California and Texas not included.

Mean age in years = 44.5

11. Directors salaries—excluding all fringe benefits (e.g. retirement, insurance, etc.):

*Academic Year		*Fiscal Year
4	10,000—11,999	
5	12,000—13,999	3
1	14,000—15,999	2
2	16,000—17,999	4
	18,000—19,999	3
	2,000—21,999	
1	22,000—23,999	1
	24,000—25,999	3
	26,000—27,999	3
13		19

Note: Colorado, Nebraska, Southern California and Texas not included.

*Eight directors reported their actual academic year salary. Mean salary for this group = $15,790.

*Twelve directors reported their actual fiscal year salary. Mean salary for this group = $20,420.

12. Titles that the Directors believe to describe their present positions:

Director of Campus Recreation—Illinois, Michigan, Nebraska, Southern California, Texas Tech

Director of Recreational Sports—Chicago, Northwestern, Purdue, Texas

Director of Campus Recreational Sports—Indiana

Director of Recreational Sports Services—Minnesota

Director of Recreational Services—Iowa, Kansas State, Oklahoma State

Director of Campus Wide Activities—Arkansas

Director of Intramural Sports and Recreative Services—Michigan State

Director of Intramural Sports and Recreation—California, Berkeley, Missouri, Oklahoma, Oregon, Texas A&M

Director of University Recreation, Intramurals and Women's Intercollegiate Activities—Ohio State

Director of Intramurals and Club Sports—Stanford

Director of Men's Intramural Sports—Iowa State, Washington State

Director of Intramural Sports—Baylor, Colorado, Houston, Kansas, Oregon State, Southern Methodist, Texas Christian, U.C.L.A., Washington

Not Reporting: Houston and Wisconsin

13. Number of professional assistants and their responsibilities as budgeted:

No Assistants: Arkansas, Baylor, Northwestern, Oregon State, Rice, Southern California, Southern Methodist, Washington State

One (1) Assistant: Iowa State—80% Administrative, Kansas—50% Administrative, Kansas State—100% Administrative, Oregon—100% Administrative, Stanford—75% Administrative.

Two (2) Assistants: Houston—50-100% Administrative, Oklahoma—50-100% Administrative, Texas A&M—100% Administrative, Texas Christian—10-80% Administrative, Texas Tech—75-100% Administrative, Wisconsin—30-50% Administrative

Three (3) Assistants: California, Berkeley—50-100% Administrative, Chicago, 50-83% Administrative, Illinois—100% Administrative, Indiana, 90-100% Administrative, Iowa—75-100% Administrative, U.C.L.A.—100% Administrative.

15

Four (4) Assistants: Missouri—50% Administrative
Five (5) Assistants: Michigan—83-100% Administrative, Michigan State—100% Administrative, Texas—50-100% Administrative
Six (6) Assistants: Oklahoma State—60-85% Administrative
Seven (7) Assistants: Minnesota—75-100% Administrative, Ohio State—100% Administrative, Purdue—100% Administrative
Nine (9) Assistants: Washington—50-100% Administrative
Not Reporting—Colorado, Nebraska

14. Number of graduate assistants and their total FTE time (using .50 as a normal FTE for a graduate assistantship):
    No Graduate Assistants Employed: Baylor, Chicago, California, Berkeley, Houston, Minnesota, Northwestern, Oklahoma State, Rice, Southern Methodist, Stanford, Texas A&M, Texas Christian, U.C.L.A.
    Graduate Assistants Employed: Arkansas, 8/2.00 FTE; Colorado, 2/1.00 FTE; Illinois, 6/2.00 FTE; Indiana, 3/1.25 FTE; Iowa, 4/2.00 FTE; Iowa State, 1/.50 FTE; Kansas, 5/2.00 FTE; Kansas State, 2/1.00 FTE; Michigan, 8/3.40 FTE; Michigan State, 2/.50 FTE; Missouri, 1/.50 FTE; Nebraska, 3/1.50 FTE; Ohio State, 4/2.00 FTE; Oklahoma, 10/5.00 FTE; Oregon, 2/.45 FTE; Oregon State, 4/.60 FTE; Purdue, 2/.75 FTE; Southern California, 1/.50 FTE; Texas, 11/5.50 FTE; Texas Tech, 4/2.00 FTE; Washington, 8/2.00 FTE; Washington State, 3/1.25 FTE; Wisconsin, 1/.50 FTE.

Centralizing a Men's and Women's Intramural Program
Linda Hall, Loretta Shane, and Val McMurtie
(1976 NIRSA Proceedings, pp. 8-13)

In 1972, I began a presentation at the NIA Conference with the following statement: "When five women armed with clipboards, schedules and file cabinets officially moved into the intramural office two years ago, it was obvious that some adjustments would have to be made." I continued with an explanation of how I felt the intramural program—both the men's and women's—had benefited from the efforts made to centralize the procedures and information that was a part of both programs.

Today, I stand before this session of the NIRSA and continue with an explanation of how I feel the intramural program, all aspects of it, is benefiting from efforts that are being made to centralize the procedures and information that is a part of the total intramural program.

The continuation and the redundancy of thought concerning intramurals reminds me of when one of my college professors told the class of his search for a dissertation topic at a mid-western university. He went to the library at the university to read topics of dissertations that had been written at the school. As he read down the list he came to the following title, "A Study of the Relationship Between the Length of a Field Mouse's Tail and his Jumping Ability". He was amused that anyone would have the need to write a dissertation of that nature. However, continuing the list of topics, he was amazed to find the following title: "A Further Study of the Relationship Between the Length of a Field Mouse's Tail and his Jumping Ability".

I am amazed to be standing before you speaking about what is, in effect, "further centralization" of the intramural program at the University of Florida.

I am amazed because when I spoke in 1972, I felt we were centralized, and we were, as we defined centralization at that time.

Under the previous organizational structure, we felt we were centrally organized and we supported centralization in theory, but in practice we followed different procedures in many areas and maintained separate administrative staffs. Upon review and close inspection, we found we were divided in the same areas in which we thought we were united.

The basic points that were considered in regard to centralized administration at that time were as follows:

1. Facility-wise we were centralized in that the men's program and the women's program were located in the same office.

2. All schedules, results, etc. were posted in one area.

3. Both programs had access to the same athletic facilities.

4. The same publicity director wrote newspaper articles for both programs.

5. Both programs operated out of the same budget.

6. The same policy manual was used for both programs.

7. Many officials worked for both programs.

Today, I would like to share some changes that have occurred at the University of Florida that have helped centralize and unite our program. The following examples are presented, not as the ultimate in organization, but are shared because we feel the changes that have been made toward more complete centralization, and those that will continue to be made, will enable us to better serve all of the university population.

Our program and staff, as yours probably is, is suffering from information overload. All of the competitive leagues grew in size, the questions that had to be answered increased, and the volume of information that had to be distributed increased. In order to help relieve some of the overload, we developed the Intramural Information Book. This book contains information concerning the following areas: phone numbers and office hours of the staff, phone numbers of other offices in the college, the Intramural Calendar—listing all the sports to be played during the year, information concerning approximately 26 clubs, hours the swimming pool is open for recreational swimming, field and equipment room locations, information about the Lake Wauburg Recreational Area, and information concerning all of the leagues that are operated from the intramural office. Everytime a schedule is printed it is put into this book. A book was placed by each phone in the office. It was and still is a valuable aid. It is used constantly. However, we still found ourselves unable to do jobs such as making out schedules, developing necessary rule changes, working with managers and officials, etc., because we were constantly being interrupted in order to give out routine types of information. Even though the information was centralized in a book, we needed a way to free our office staff so that they might do the jobs necessary to conduct the program. This led to the hiring of students receptionists. Depending on the quarter, we have three or four students that come in during the day. They are on duty at the receptionist's desk from 8 a.m. to 5 p.m. The receptionists are expected to greet people as they come into the office, answer the phone, answer questions, receive entry forms and hand out schedules and other information. Since their hiring, the receptionists have become one of our primary sources of centralized information.

Now that the information and the people with the information were in a central location, it became obvious that we were not asking them to know everything about one program, but we were asking them to know everything about two separate programs, the men's program and the women's program. The efforts of consolidate information made us very much aware we were quite separated in our policies and procedures. So, we set about to combine and coordinate as many policies, procedures and rules as possible. Since our programs were governed by constitutions, the first consideration was that of revising those constitutions. We had one constitution for men and a different one for women. Yet, both were in the same policy manual and many articles were the same. Since the women's constitution, however, had information concerning the co-rec league and the all-university special events, it was often confusing to the student and to the office staff. To alleviate this unnecessary duplication and confusion, we categorized information into areas of interests, sport, or convenience rather than "Men's" and "Women's", and combined the constitutions.

Two areas of administration that caused difficulty were: 1) officiating and, 2) different rules for men and women the same in the same sports. These are presented together because they are related in some respects, and the solution to one helped with the solution to the other. Until we trained all officials to use the same procedures and standardized and combined the rules of the sports, we suffered through more confusion than was necessary. Previously, the women's program hired, trained and supervised officials used in the women's and co-rec leagues, and the men's program hired, trained and supervised officials in the men's leagues. Many officials worked for both programs. Working under two systems and two sets of rules for the same sport was confusing for the official, therefore causing us problems. In order to eliminate some of the problems that both programs were experiencing, we combined the officials' clinics and attempted to explain the differences in the procedures and the rules of both programs to everyone at the same time. During the training sessions and through supervision on the field, it became apparent that training them together but under two different systems did not solve the problems. So, we standardized and combined the rules and eliminated all differences in what we expected the officials to do, regardless of the league in which they worked.

Changes were made administratively, also. Up until this time, an assistant program director to each program had conducted the officials clinics. In order to maintain consistency and to allow the assistant program directors to perform other functions, we centralized the tasks, and hired a student to serve as Director of Officials. The responsibilities of this position include conducting the officiating clinics, administering the official's test for knowledge of game rules, assigning the officials to their games, and supervising and evaluating the officials. Previously, we had the league manager assign officials for their particular league games. This often resulted in managers competing for certain officials. It also resulted in mismanagement, as often one manager would need the best official for a championship game or for a game of intense competition, but would find that those officials had already been assigned to officiate a game requiring less officiating experience. Now officials are assigned according to the ability of the official and the status of the game being played. All combinations of officials (2 men; 2 women; one man, one woman) have been assigned to officiate both men's and women's games. If the Director of Officials were to show a preference for one league over the other, he would have to answer for it. Thus, the competition by the managers for the best official is eliminated somewhat because the Director of Officials now decides which officials are needed for the games.

The integration of procedures and the centralizing of responsibility was so successful in regard to officials we began looking toward centralizing other areas of responsibility. Under the previous structure, the men's office director and the women's office director had the same responsibilities. There was much duplication of effort in respect to posting league standings, assisting with scheduling, recording payroll, etc. We centralized the student staff responsibilities into three specific areas and assigned one major responsibility to a student. In addition to their major responsibility, they are expected to assist in other areas of the program, such as answering questions, signing up teams, interpreting rules and policies, and serving as league managers, if they are needed.

Presently, we have a student director, whose specific task is assisting with scheduling for all leagues. This person works with two (2) assistant program directors, but since he has the responsibility for all of the leagues, he has to be concerned that all participants have a schedule and facilities that are reasonable and fair. Otherwise he has partial responsibility to the students to answer for inequalities.

Two examples of how this centralization has benefited the program are as follows:

1. Since the student works with all the schedules, he saves the assistant program director needed time because he knows how heavily the facilities are being used. He has knowledge about previous schedules that another person could obtain only by taking time to look up the information.

2. Part of the student's responsibilities is to have all the materials ready for scheduling at least one day in advance. He checks to see if there are enough rules already duplicated. If not, he gets these ready before time to make the schedule. He also divides the teams into brackets, numbers them, and often makes the draw. Then, he and the assistant program director go over the schedule to check errors. After the schedule is typed he assists in duplicating the information and stapling it together.

To the other student director, we assigned the task of recording the results and participation totals for all of the leagues. We feel that it is important that all statistics are recorded in the same way in order to insure accuracy for play-off games and to determine league winners as well as for all reports that have to be made concerning budgeting and other facets of the program.

The managers of all leagues turn in their score sheets to the same place. The student responsible for statistics records the point standings and posts them on the intramural bulletin boards. Also recorded are the number of games played, the number of games forfeited, and the number of people that participated. One person keeping a standardized recording system has greatly improved the efficiency and accuracy of recording needed statistics. This is very important to our program, as we often have to make presentations and reports to various people and committees on campus. It is not uncommon that these reports have to be prepared in a short period of time. With this system we are constantly up to date. The accuracy with which the wins and losses are recorded is also very important, since an error may keep a team from entering the league playoffs. This happened numerous times under the previous system where the job was one of many for which one person was responsible, and statistical recording was often done in a rush.

We also centralized the tasks of recording the payroll and assigned the responsibility to one student. Previously, one person from the men's program did the payroll for that division and one person from the women's program did the payroll for the women's division. Besides the fact there were two people doing one job that one person could do... there was often confusion because many officials worked in several leagues. Sometimes their working hours were recorded twice; sometimes they were not recorded at all. In addition, we realized that some managers and officials were paid more than others depending on the program in which they worked. Thus, even though the overall budget was common to both programs, there was inconsistency in the criteria used for paying the officials and managers. The inconsistency arose in part because the right hand did not know what the left hand was doing. The student now in charge of the payroll is supervised by the assistant program director, as all of the students are, but that person is the most direct route for information is when there is a question in regard to why an official was paid too little—or too much—or not paid at all.

In another area of student administration, that of league managers, we now have equal expectations in regard to their role to the intramural department regardless of the league they are assigned to manage. Under the previous structure, the managers were assigned differently and their job responsibilities were varied. Now, each manager is assigned to a specific league and all managers must attend combined staff meetings in which the policies and procedures are discussed. Since the managers are often their own supervisors when they are on the field and since they are expected to substitute for each other if needed, it is vital they know the policies and procedures that are now common to all leagues.

Another benefit that occurred from making the staff responsible to both programs is that of a larger number of people from which to draw when a protest board is needed. We now have eight people who are eligible to serve on the protest board rather than four for one program and four for the other. We have found this advantageous for the following reasons: (1) the greater number of people allows us to hear a variety of viewpoints; (2) the same people do not always make the decisions affecting the same leagues; (3) it is easier to get the necessary number of people together as they are often needed to make a decision quickly; and (4) all of the members of the staff now have a responsibility for just decisions being rendered regardless of the league in which a protest was filed.

In summary, we had two programs, often using different policies and procedures through operating out of a centralized office. As the programs grew, it became increasingly apparent that we had to become more efficient. The changes made were gradual and evolutionary in nature. One change lead to another. In retrospect, the two major changes which were of the most significance were: (1) centralizing the major job responsibilities, and (2) delegating these responsibilities to the student staff. We want our program to be student directed. Integrating as many areas as possible has allowed us to do this more effectively. In addition, we expect the intramural staff to take a wholistic view of the intramural program, and to be able to make constructive contributions to solving problems that arise in any area. Each staff member is responsible not only for his specific job but for the image of the total intramural department.

By working as one unit and requiring basically the same expectations of everyone, we feel attitudes have greatly improved and everyone is aware of the important of serving all students equally. Those that had formerly associated with only one program now have a better awareness of the need to provide opportunities for all of the students regardless of their skill or competitive level. There is a better understanding of what intramural athletics is all about.

Now, the task before us is how to best serve the student and conduct a more efficient intramural program. For us the answer seems to be in the phrase—"to get our act together." We are attempting to get our act together and plan to continue to do so.

Prerequisites for a New Intramural Program
Kenneth H. Renner
(1972 NIA Proceedings, pp. 80-82)

Having just seen some pictures of our University in Orlando, Florida, you can realize that we have limited facilities; but, most important, activity has existed on our campus since its beginning. I would like to believe that Intramurals is the most important program on campus, and I hope to see the University's continued financial and administrative support of this program.

Florida Technological University opened its doors with 1500 students in the fall of 1968 and now enrolls over 6500. Since 90% of these students are commuters, we're faced with the biggest of all problems. Just how to administer a program at a commuter's institution with limited facilities, limited financial support, and a fast growing student body is in itself another topic.

In my brief presentation I will present the prerequisites I feel most important when organizing an intramural program at a university or college. Hopefully, each of you will be able to use a few of these ideas in your own program realizing, of course, that every institution differs in many ways and each of us must seek our own way in which to best deal with each situation. Within the next few minutes, I will chat about some *prerequisites* needed within all successful programs:

1. An adequate administrative support
2. Essential facilities and equipment
3. A balanced extracurricular program
4. A director committed to the objectives of the program.

It is important that these factors be present before the Intramural program can break free from the inertia usually associated with the early stages of development in new institutions. I feel that these components have helped build a successful Intramural program at FTU within its first four years. The emphasis at our University is upon excellence and the individual; therefore, Intramurals needs to seek this consideration by utilizing many of its students in the leadership phase of the program, offering a diversity of activities, and being sensitive to student needs.

First, Adequate Administrative Support

In order for our new program to get off the ground it is essential that the administration be fully behind the program. At our University the President stated from the beginning of the University's opening "There will be an Intramural program here on this campus..." which would indicate, of course, that he is much in favor of it and that, ultimately, he will support it. In our situation this program is administratively structured under the Department of Physical Education within the College of Education but financed by Student Affairs. Now with us it has worked out really well although the approach may not be the best situation for you. It means you are fighting dollars within Student Affairs and you are trying to gain administrative support in the academic college. When you have found the proper monies (either from student fees or from the university), then centralized administration of the program should be sought. Most of you have too many administrative chiefs and I know this, too, can offer a delay in success. I feel that it is best to become centralized as fast as possible and to be responsible to only one administrative head.

Second, Facilities and Equipment

Beyond the fact that you have dollars, it is vital that your facilities be adequate and your equipment be plentiful. The kind of program, of course, depends directly upon the kind of facilities you have; and, of course, proper equipment and proper facilities is a definite prerequisite in all Intramural programs. We're fortunate at our University to have had some facilities from the beginning although they've never been sufficient, and as you have seen from the preceding slides FTU is not a Purdue or a University of Illinois. We hope to be able to keep pace with the total University building program and depend a great deal upon the grace of God for sunshine each day until indoor facilities are constructed.

Third, Extracurricular Activities

There should be a very definite balance between all the activities within the school—primarily the intercollegiate varsity sports program, the extramurals sports club program which involves sport activities not recognized to be varsity, the Student Union or Village Center activities, and other related programs. All should remain in good balance and receive equal impetus and support from the University. As you know, there is always a danger in one program competing against the other and in one receiving more impetus than the other. If your priorities are not as high as those of other programs, then I can see your program suffering and the unending battle will commence.

Lastly, You As A Director must be the coordinating factor to the above three points: to *see that* you gain administrative and budgetary support; to *see that* you have proper facilities and equipment; and also to *see that* Intramurals is placed in the proper perspective relative to Varsity Athletics, Extramurals, and Recreation. You must be enthusiastic, you must believe in your job, you must be able to stand beside the best of administrators in the institution, and you must have sound (not argumentative) reasons why Intramurals should receive their favor. You must also believe in those reasons. When we come to a stalemate and cannot have the things we apparently desire and, as a Director, are constantly turned down, it is time for us to re-evaluate first ourselves and secondly the University situation. If you are completely satisfied with the job you are doing now and are not motivated to improve your position or your program, I would suggest that it is time for a move.

In conclusion, many of you will say: "I am not organizing a new program at my place nor am I located at a new institution." I must say that each of you are in essence establishing a new program each year. Never should your program remain the same. You should strive for more administrative support, up-dated facilities, and relate well to the coordinators of all related activities on campus, so that your program will be THE program on campus. *YOU*, as a Director, will be *that* vital factor. There's tremendous potential in directing Intramurals, if the PREREQUISITES are realized, and then properly nurtured.

I hope that this has been beneficial to you, as I have enjoyed presenting this topic. Thank you.

Creating an Atmosphere in Intramurals
Johannes Van Hoff
(1976 NIRSA Proceedings, pp. 103-108)

The specific tasks of any job become apparent in a variety of ways, such as previous background knowledge, a basic idea of the function of the job, mistakes made and necessarily paid for while working, and perception of unique local situations that virtually dictate a certain course of action. The common belief that most people don't care for their jobs is based upon the obvious: most jobs revolve around tasks that are repeated frequently to the extent that whatever challenge existed initially vanishes or becomes meaningless. We in intramurals are lucky. We help to mold a source of activity-oriented enjoyment for a constantly changing populace. Most of us govern voluntary programs in a people-oriented setting, and we *get* to adjust to a whole host of varying viewpoints, challenges, people and atmospheres on a daily and yearly basis. We can many times define our own goals within our programs, and provided that the essence of harmony with students and staff exists, pursue those goals at our self-determined pace. My goal at SUNY-Binghamton evolved fairly early into one of creating an atmosphere in which the greatest number of people could derive a satisfying, enjoyable experience from intramural involvement. Succinctly stated, I began striving for what Bernie Pollack once gently hammered home as "quality in intramurals."

All of this "creating an atmosphere" energy did not receive priority at first. Six years ago, when I walked into the IM office at SUNY-Binghamton for the first time, I was just as bewildered as most of you have been at that stage of your careers. The program in existence had been received well, I was told, so the initial solution was to pattern the program after that of the preceding year. The offerings then were very varied, planned and well-organized by my predecessor, and came accompanied by the usual (at that time) point system, awards, etc. On that first day three students, one Black and two Puerto Ricans—Sam, Juan, and Noel—came up to introduce themselves. Having just come from the University of Illinois, where some tense situations involving blacks

25

and whites had occurred during 1968-70, I was particularly pleased by this ostensible show of friendliness and acceptance. Perhaps it was over the ensuing three months, after Sam had tried to bite off a player's ear in an IM football game, Juan has slapped an opposing player in the face after a baseball game, and Noel had threatened to shove a gun up somewhere in my anatomy and ignite it—perhaps it was then that I first realized that the atmosphere surrounding intramurals was not all that it should have been.

The process of creating an intramural atmosphere began during that first year. The first steps were not wholly positive ones, but they represented necessary progress. The initial steps were to eliminate undesirable facets of the program, those elements that were operating in a manner contrary to the main aims of enjoyment and satisfaction through activity. Falling prey during this eliminative process were:

1) one-man rule—The program had been governed by a director who operated single-handedly in many instances, including the important decision-making process.

2) trophies—If intramural quality was to improve, the idea of eliminating trophies seemed necessary in order to de-emphasize the sometimes fierce need to win.

3) point system—The point system, designed to reward achievement related to winning and probably acceptable in a school where close-knit, permanent living groups exist, was out of place at SUNY-Binghamton. The team and individual point systems, important to so very few participants, were scrapped.

4) league organization—In 1970-71, the competitive units in team sports were dormitory leagues, independent leagues, and social club leagues. One drawback, for instance, was that a friend of dormitory dwellers who moved off campus had to play with a different team. Again, the organizational structure here was at odds with the living arrangements at a public university where fraternities and sororities are outlawed. Ultimately, all such organizational restrictions were scrapped.

5) one-day tournaments—One-day tournaments prior to football, basketball, and volleyball seasons, were designed to help train officials and to allow teams to experience game-type play. Since winners of these single-elimination tournaments were given recognition, the tournaments become pressure-packed one-day nightmares. They were eliminated.

The method of accomplishing these moves involved the decision that has represented my most significant permeating positive step regarding the administration of the program, the establishment of a decision-making Intramural Council. Appointed initially as an emergency measure to deal mainly with behavioral incidents, the Council now has a governing role in all aspects of the program. The difference in the following two statements captures the essence of the atmosphere created by the existence of a decision-making Council: "I have outlawed trophies;" or, "The Intramural Council has voted to eliminate trophies." The Council quickly became the vehicle through which vital changes were made away from a viciously competitive atmosphere toward a cooperative, more recreational one. This Council paved the way for the revamping process as initiated by the elimination of the five items listed above. The response of students to the apparent cutbacks was predictably a questioning of motive, but the reaction to the discontinuing of trophy awards, for instance, was surprisingly mild and infrequently expressed. My feeling in retrospect is that enough of the IM participants at that time realized that something integral was amiss within the program, and were willing to allow someone new to take the lead in restructuring a program with an only partially realized potential. For awhile, it was necessary to explain to individuals the line of reasoning that was being pursued. This process, too, was rewarding in that some of the students who were interested enough to ask questions subsequently became IM Council members, and played an important role in creating diversity in and expanding the program.

Several incidents represented setbacks in this several-year attempt to introduce more mellowness into the program. During the basketball season three years ago a great deal of anger surfaced, enough to make me doubt the advisability of continuing the A League season. In one incident an irate player chased an official out of the gym and down the street, threatening him without restraint. A second episode involved a player shoving an official several times and knocking off his glasses, convinced that the official had purposely ignored a foul. A third incident was a much more personal experience, as a substitute player, without warning, grabbed me and hit me twice in the face just as I entered the playing court area. All of the objectives of intramurals were being worked in reverse. Any contribution that the basketball program was then making to the lives of players and referees was negative. The incident in which I was personally attacked occurred on the last week of the regular season. During the entire weekend, I did a lot of evaluation both of myself and the program. I reached the conclusion that it was not the proper course of action to continue trying to muddle through the tail end of each season, sitting on a powder keg and hoping that nobody got killed. I wrote a short speech, briefly stating that certain incidents had led me to decide that the basketball season was a dead end, I was not proud of it, and that we all shared some sort of guilt for the failure of the season. I called a mandatory meeting of A League playoff team captains, read by statement, and walked out without allowing questions of any kind. The option was left to those in the room to remain and talk about formulating a playoff schedule and officiating schedule on their own, or allowing the season to end right there. My role in the effort was going to be limited to getting court space when it was needed. Predictably, I got some "If you can't stand the heat, get out of the kitchen" reaction. The result of the decision was that team captains had to interrelate in a different and meaningful way. They discovered first-hand how unenjoyable it was to try to pursuade officials to overcome their reluctance to officiate certain games in which abuse was sure to occur. Their efforts succeeded. The season ended in a beautifully played two-pointer between two all-black teams, neither team having had in any way contributed to the near-collapse of the season.

In a football final during the following season, I again ended the action when I felt that, for a variety of reasons, the contest would not end in a satisfactory manner. In this case it was necessary to make a very lonely decision that resulted in a 6-6 tie for the A League championship. This episode represented the final time that I was forced to convey, through a perhaps somewhat unorthodox type of decision, the message that it was not important to me to culminate a season if the absence of cooperation and understanding on the part of participants was leading to a potentially unsatisfying, possibly disastrous experience for those involved.

You cannot simply eliminate elements of an intramural program without using professional knowledge and understanding to offer better alternatives as substitutes. The foundation of the structure was being constructed in two distinct ways, a continuingly more effective IM Council, and getting my own head together. Headway was being made in improving the quality of intramurals, but the pressure-cooker feeling persisted to some extent. Information was needed on how to progress further toward creating the type of atmosphere that would be more conducive to the enjoyment and satisfaction of participants, and to my own contentment. Two individuals provided just that type of information. One member of the IM Council, who had contributed his ideas throughout the very troublesome times, suggested that I not become preoccupied with the occasional flareups that occurred within the program. He felt that, given the number of participants and the emotional involvement of athletic participation, the infrequent behavioral episodes reflected positively on a healthy program, rather than representing a type of flaw in intramurals or in its leadership. He suggested that the incidents would continue to occur from time to time, that they were no "big deal," and that I should deal with these episodes

28

as dispassionately as with other types of problems. The second valuable pertinent suggestion came from my very fine assistant, Jimmy Calloway, who stated that I showed outward signs of distress at times, which allowed the bad actors to realize that they had successfully hassled me. His suggestions was that I do everything possible to retain a calm outward demeanor. Such a demeanor would convey the information that the problem was the students' problem, not mine, and would result in greater confidence in my ability to make correct decisions in tense situations. I immediately incorporated these wise offerings into my personal method of operation to the extent that I have attained greater self-confidence, and have elicited the confidence of the students, in my ability to deal with all problems that arise within the intramural program. With this change in my personal viewpoint, I was finally capable of providing positive leadership in creating the desirable intramural atmosphere.

The atmosphere as it exists now incorporates a good many positive elements that have not occurred by accident. Referring back to the list of five items that were eliminated to expedite this change, the following substitutes have been introduced over the years, all with positive effects:

1) For one-man rule, the thirteen-member University Intramural Council was substituted. All other positive changes have, to some extent, emanated from this most important change.

2) For trophies, no substitute was offered, really, except the option for league winners to purchase copies of a team picture. Recognition is given in the handbook and in the school newspaper, but basically, the emphasis was reverted to the internal rewards of participation.

3) For point systems, which were not applicable to the campus, nothing concrete has been substituted. The absence of trophies and point systems can be referred to as positive absences, in that time formerly consumed in relation to these tasks can now be devoted to the human contact portion of the job, the portion that pays the biggest dividends for all concerned.

4) For social club, dormitory, and independent leagues we have substituted skill level leagues (A, B, C), which has resulted in much more satisfying competitive experiences among players of similar skill levels. No restrictions remain on formation of teams, except that men cannot play on women's teams, varsity players cannot participate in the same sport during the academic year in which they perform as varsity athletes, and the number of sports club performers per intramural team is restricted in that particular sport.

5) For one-day tournaments, which allowed the better teams to play more games anyway, we have substituted practice game time in which

each team has an opportunity for at least a half-hour of court or field space. Officials, prior to being hired, are required to officiate at least one of these contests. In the absence of tournament pressure, the value of these training sessions has been enhanced greatly.

These are the concrete changes, important but not of paramount importance. The most significant changes have been in attitudes toward the program. Frequently, very competitive individuals have undergone a change in attitude, have dropped off of A League teams, and have led teams composed of underclassmen, providing their younger peers with exposure to a "play intramurals for fun" approach. Team captains are now less inclined to play Tommy Heinsohn-type roles in razzing officials, and are more inclined to deal successfully with hot-tempered teammates and to provide a healthy type of restraint. Individuals much more frequently offer spontaneous remarks of appreciation for the program in general, citing it as one of the most, if not the most, enjoyable aspect of their campus lives. Statements and behavior indicate that participants now have more faith in the objectivity of game officials, accompanied by a more realistic expectation concerning the proficiency of officials. Students, convinced that the IM office is receptive to new ideas, have increasingly offered suggestions for new tournaments, two of which were incorporated into the 1976-77 list of offerings immediately. The University Intramural Council and other interested students seem now to be more willing to accept somewhat unusual ideas, such as the Black Brothers Basketball League which was introduced this year and is flourishing. The wide variety of team and individual sports offerings has a positive effect many times, in that the losers of an important game in one sport have perhaps less than a week to wait before embarking on another season of fun-oriented activity in a different sort. Perhaps the most gratifying change has been in the greater involvement and acceptance of the program by black students, whose discontent served as one of the catalysts for the concerted effort to change the intramural atmosphere. To a great extent, those who felt alienated at one time in very recent years now contribute and feel welcome in a program that is better adjusted to their unique needs.

The atmosphere is maintained by paying constant attention to the ingredients that promote mellowness. For instance, an individual who enters the IM office does not confront sheets of point totals, All-University champions, trophies, or records of best performances. He will, instead, hear background music, and look around at posters depicting happiness and friendliness ("It's a Beautiful Day", "Let's Be Friends"). He will be face-to-face with a secretary who personifies friendliness, or with an intramural director who will attach importance to his questions or statements of viewpoint. His subsequent experiences on the field of play may involve interaction with a supervising official who is trained to treat everyone with respect. Rules are designed to reflect what is acceptable and what is not. Since too many fights erupted in indoor hockey two years ago, a new rule suspending fighters for the subsequent game also conveys the message that self-restraint is expected and appreciated. The desired atmosphere cannot be promoted in one area and ignored in another. Only through a continued effort to imbue the participant with a constant feeling for this mellow atmosphere can the results be expected to become relatively all-encompassing.

Such an atmosphere is promoted and maintained by the absence of certain ingredients, also. Although alcohol is allowed on and around campus at SUNY-Binghamton, alcohol is not allowed at IM contests, as the imbiber occasionally reacts by getting unreasonable with officials or opponents. Written rules governing IM participation and contests are not overlooked simply for the sake of avoiding unpleasant situations. The increasing trust in objectivity has resulted in part from this strict adherence to written governing rules. Tournaments are not organized haphazardly, and schedules are always ready on time. The participant is treated appropriately as an important individual, and he is likely to respond in a cooperative manner.

The intramural director should not be secretive about what he is trying to accomplish. I do not want students to have to guess what my approach to intramurals is, I want them to know. Along this line, I would like to finish by reading two paragraphs from the current SUNY-Binghamton "Intramural Sports and Recreation Handbook:"

"The IM program also provides an outlet for creativity. Team captains must recruit teams, assign positions, deal with temper outbursts, and avoid forfeits. The IM Council makes decisions that create new activities, or that provide a new atmosphere for individual IM experience. Each participant, however, is responsible for the ground-level creativity that dictates his approach to and possible benefit from intramurals.

The person who measures his success or failure within intramurals only in terms of wins or losses is non-creative, is overlooking the purpose of the program, and is much more likely to experience frustration than satisfaction. Creating a broader outlook results in a more enriching, beneficial experience for teammates, officials, and opponents. For instance, as much as you might dislike an opponent or opposing team in a contest, how much fun would you have if he didn't appear at all? Creativity, in this instance, reflects maturity and allows the individual potentially to experience fully the joy inherent in real but irrelevant low-key competition."

Intramurals and Recreation in the 1970's
Louis A. Fabian
(1976 NIRSA Proceedings, pp. 114-120)

The 1970's brought with it the need for exanded intramural and recreational offerings for students, faculty, staff and the community. A change of philosophy occurred directing physical education programs toward "activity as a way of life." Oxendine (2) reported this trend at the college level by identifying a marked increase in the number of lifetime activities being taught, increased coeducational offerings, an upsurge of sports clubs, and a decrease in varsity sports. Omitted from Oxendine's survey was descriptive data pertaining to existing intramural and recreational programs at the college level.

This survey attempted to determine the current status of college intramural and recreational programs by identifying specific information pertaining to: general administrative policies, intramural activities and participation, financial considerations of intramural programs, facility use and the status of recreation. Surveys were mailed to 63 colleges and universities on January 7, 1975. As of April 7, 1975, 41 institutions had responded. Major variables considered for selection of the survey population included: enrollment, geographical location, representation by athletic conferences, and academic considerations. The 65% return supplied an adequate number of responses. The number of responses varied for each question because not all questions were applicable to every school.

General Administrative Information

The following responses concern major areas of importance relative to the general administrative policies adhered to on college campuses.

• The Physical Education Department administered 41% of the intramural programs. This amount is significantly greater than the 33% administered by student affairs or student related bodies, 23% by the athletic department, and the 3% by the chancellor's office.

• Eight-five percent of the 36 schools reported men's and women's intramurals were coordinated from the same office.

• Recreation was administered by the intramural department at 28 of 37 schools, (76%).

• A significant number (31) of the 39 schools (76.7%) permitted the rescheduling of intramural contests. Reasons for change were: conflict with classes and/or exams, religious holidays, personal tragedies and weather conditions. In addition, many schools possessed a 24 to 72 hours time limit prior to which notification of changes must be made.

• Complementing these general administrative policies is information pertaining to the staffing and equipment of intramural programs.

• An average of three full-time staff persons (including secretarial) were employed at 36 schools (range 0-13). Accordingly, an average of three half-time staff persons were also employed (range 0-16).

Table I, below, shows the average number of staff members employed at 39 schools with various intramural populations. Statistical analysis revealed a moderate correlation of $r = .61$ between staff size and intramural population.

Table I
Intramural Staff Size

Intramural Population	0-5000	5000-10,000	10,000-15,000	15,000-20,000	20,000-up
Staff Average Per School	1.10	2.50	2.14	3.64	5.00

Most schools provided whatever equipment was necessary for its participants. However, some schools did not supply equipment for tennis, squash, racquetball, and golf. Perhaps this was due to excessive breakage.

• Many schools provided some part of the following equipment for their officials: rule books, shirts, whistles, indicators, flags, and clocks.

• Two methods were employed to insure the return of the equipment. Twenty-two schools employed an average of 15 student activity managers to distribute, observe, and collect the equipment. The remaining 15 schools operated directly through the intramural office with their officials by holding checks, I.D. cards, driver's licenses, or a security deposit.

This information tends to reveal that intramural programs were administered primarily by the physical education department. Recreation, men's intramurals, and women's intramurals were coordinated from the same office. In addition, the intramural departments rescheduled contests and supplied equipment for its participants and officials. Finally, a moderate correlation exists between intramural staff and intramural population.

Intramural Activities and Participation

This section deals with the activities offered by intramural programs and their popularity of participation.

The 37 schools reporting offered a total of 1191 intramural activities: 49.7% were structured for men, 37.7% for women, and 16.9% for corecreational programming.

The 1191 activities represent an average of 32 activities per school.

The greatest number of activities offered was 66 (27 men, 22 women, 17 corec.). The least amount offered was 7 (5 men, 2 corec.).

Table II shows the average number of activities for 37 schools as compared to various intramural populations.

Table II
Average Activities Offered Per Institution

Intramural Population	0-5000	5000-10,000	10,000-15,000	15,000-20,000	20,000-up
Number of Activities Offered per School	20-0	19.0	32.3	35.7	41.5

The 34 schools reporting estimated an average of 36% of their available intramural population participated in their programs.

Men participated most in these team sports: volleyball, softball, basketball, and football. Individual sports for men showing the greatest participation were tennis, swimming, badminton and bowling.

In the competitive corecreational activities of archery, gymnastics, and innertube water polo, females outnumbered males.

Of the 37 schools reporting, 92% (34) offered corecreational competition.

The team sports favoring corecreational participation were volleyball, softball, football and basketball. Dual sport interest centered around table tennis, badminton, tennis, and bowling.

Corecreational participation was greater than male or female participation in the following activities: Two-on-two basketball, turkey trot and innertube water-polo.

Other popular activities offered by most programs were handball, racquetball, horseshoes, weightlifting, and a superstar contest.

An intramural program thrives on participation. The activities offered generally stimulate participation among men and women within the program. This survey revealed a majority of programs thrived on the traditional team sports of volleyball, basketball, football and softball. Tennis was the most popular individual sport. In addition, one-half of the activities offered were structured for men. Lastly, one-third of the available population participate in intramurals.

Financial Considerations of Intramural Programs

This section deals with the source and expenditure of intramural funds, and examines the relationship between intramural population and money budgeted.

Student affairs supplied funds for intramurals at 40% of the institutions. This amount is significantly greater than the 24% which came from physical education, 14.5% from student entry fees, 14.5% from athletics, and 7% with their own budgets. In addition to the six schools supported by student entry fees were eight schools supplemented with $5 to $20 forfeit fees.

A comparison of administrative and financial responsibilities revealed that physical education and athletics administered 64% of the intramural programs, while only funding 40%. Conversely, student affairs administered 33% of the intramural programs, while student related sources funded 54% of the intramural programs.

A significant number of schools, 24 (80%) reported that funds for special projects were not available from extra-school sources. Of the six programs having access to additional monies, two came from state sources, two originated from endowments, one came from special student funds, and one did not specify.

Information pertaining to money expended were supplied by 31 schools. Average figures are shown for each item at various populations in Table III.

Table III
Reported Intramural Budget Figures

Budget Items	Intramural Population				
	0-5000	5000-10,000	10,000-15,000	15,000-20,000	20,000-up
Officials	1,333	4,393	6,364	15,508a	19,744a
Activity Managers	None	2,550	3,833		
Office Supplies	266	328	575	1,433	
Equipment	700	1,053	1,447	3,475	6,897
Trips, Clinics, Professional Organizations	75	None	265	617	982
Total	2,374	8,324	12,484	21,033	27,623

a Breakdown of figures for officials and activity managers not available.

Table III revealed that money spent in each category increases for each succeeding population level. In addition, student activity managers were not employed by schools with an intramural population of less than 5,000. Lastly, Table III shows that the largest expenditure for intramurals was for officials and student activity managers.

Of the 31 schools reporting, 45% indicated they paid their officials between $2.00 and $2.49 per hour, while 37% paid $2.50 or more per hour, and only 18% paid under $2.00 per hour. Activity managers were paid at a rate of $2.50 or more per hour at 46% of the schools, while 38% of the schools paid between $2.00 and $2.49 per hour, and only 16% paid less than $2.00 per hour.

Statistical analysis revealed a moderate correlation of $r = .42$ between money budgeted and intramural population levels.

This section revealed intramural programs were funded primarily by student affairs or student related sources. Administration of intramurals was chiefly handled by physical education or athletic departments. Most of the money spent by intramurals was for officials and activity managers. Finally, a moderate correlation existed between intramural budget and intramural population, while money was not available for special projects by extra-school sources.

Facilities

Information supplied centers around the adequacy of today's facilities, problems leading to inadequate facilities, and a summary of facilities currently needed.

A significant number of 39 schools, 31 (79.5%) reported their present facilities were inadequate to handle the current intramural and recreational populations.

Newer facilities were planned to handle current overload problems, when completed, they were near capacity.

• The costs for material and labor have risen beyond expectations causing initially designed facilities to be constructed for less than total utilization.

• Physical educators have diversified program offerings in the areas of basic instruction, intramurals, and sports clubs; thus placing demands for special facilities. Existing handball courts cannot handle the current rise in popularity of racquetball. Activities such as angleball, team handball and badminton require time and space of the traditionally used basketball-volleyball gymnasium. Separate indoor facilities must be found to accommodate activities such as fencing, golf and archery.

• Priority of facility use appears to be a current concern. Competition between varsity athletics, physical education, intramurals, sports clubs and recreation has produced untenable situations at some institutions.

• The information revealed an urgent need for lighted playing fields, lighted tennis courts, racquetball courts, outdoor swimming facilities, and multi-purpose rooms.

Furthermore, information revealed intramural-recreational facilities at most institutions were inadequate. Problems appeared to have stemmed from increases in populations, insufficient funds for construction, increased program offerings and priority of use. Facilities most urgently needed were lighted playing fields, lighted tennis courts and racquetball courts.

Recreation

Recreation is an ever-growing part of our life. This section describes the administrative policies of recreation on today's college campuses.

• A significant number of institutions (28 or 76.3%) managed intramurals and recreation from the same office.

• The survey revealed three time patterns of facilities designed for recreational use. The first was "continuous use" and was accomplished by having separate facilities with hours ranging from 8:00 a.m. to 12:00 p.m. The second pattern was "allotted use," this was accomplished by sharing facility time equally with physical education, intramurals, sports clubs and varsity athletics. Hours ran from 6:00 or 6:30 a.m. to 12:00 or 1:00 p.m., and 5:00 or 6:00 p.m. to 10:00 or 11:00 p.m. The third pattern was "spot use," only when the needs of everything else were satisfied was recreation considered. Hours varied from 12:00 p.m. to 1:00 p.m., 3:00 to 4:00 p.m. or 5:00 to 6:00 p.m., and 9:00 p.m. to 12:00 p.m.

• A significant number of institutions (30 or 81.1%) deemed it advisable to supply all necessary equipment for its recreators during the above reported hours.

• Equipment provided on a loan basis for team sports included balls, nets, bats, bases and flags. Equipment available for court sports included tennis, badminton, racquetball, handball and squash. In addition, many schools provided specialized equipment for their recreators such as speedbags, jump ropes, tetherballs, tabletennis equipment and billiards.

• Seventy-two percent of the institutions required I.D. cards for the loan of equipment. Other security methods employed to insure the return of the equipment included billing of students, holding of grades, holding requests for transcripts, or preventing registration.

• A significant number of schools (34 or 89.5%) provided locker room facilities for its recreators.

• Participation for recreation at most schools appears to be booming. Figures reported by those schools keeping records are relatively high, and coupled with the fact that many schools report insufficient facilities available to handle their needs would lead one to believe that recreation is "great and growing."

Trends in recreation appear to be the most stable in our profession. Many institutions have placed the management of recreation under the direction of intramurals. Hours for recreation, while extremely limited at some schools, possessed separate facilities at others. Equipment and locker room space were usually in abundance at most times, fostering a great deal of participation.

Conclusions

The preceeding pages have shown the current status and administrative policies of intramural and recreational programs. These concluding remarks describe current trends, emerging within intramural and recreational programs across the country.

A comparison of administrative responsibility and financial sources revealed the trend that physical education and athletic departments administered 64% of the intramural programs, while student related sources financed 54% of the programs.

Fabian and Ross (1) found a significant number of intramural programs reporting sports clubs under their jurisdiction. This study found a significant number of intramural programs administered recreation. From this information it appears that many intramural departments supply structured activity, administered sports clubs and oversee recreation for its population.

This survey revealed the trend that a majority of intramural departments employed student activity managers. Their duties included distribution, observance, and collection of equipment for officials and participants and maintaining the operation of activities whether members of the intramural staff were present or not. The capability and responsibility necessary to maintain this position were generally found in graduate students and upperclass physical education majors.

Recreation is an evergrowing importance to our society. The importance has originated from our need to release tensions and counteract an obsession to save time in our automated society. Recreation partially fulfills our desire for success and hedonistic experiences. This survey revealed that recreation hours at most institutions were geared to avoid conflict with varsity athletics, physical education, intramurals and sports clubs. However, Fabian and Ross (1) found that recreational activity time was scheduled after the needs of the above were satisfied.

In essence, when and where do the students recreate if they are not superior athletes, and if their basic introductory courses in gymnastics, archery, or badminton have ended. We, as proponents of "activity as a way of life," are obligated to provide whatever time, space and equipment are necessary to cope with that which we have initiated.

BIBLIOGRAPHY

[1]Fabian, L. A. and Ross, M. L. "Administrative Trends in Sport Club Programs," National Intramural and Recreational Annual Proceedings, October, 1975.

[2]Oxendine, J. B. "Status of General Instruction Programs of Physical Education in Four Year Colleges and Universities: 1971-72," Journal of Health, Physical Education and Recreation, 43:26-28, 1972.

Chapter 2
Values of Competition

The Quality of the Intramural Experience
Bernard Pollack
(1971 NIA Proceedings, pp. 50-55)

Today, I will attempt to share with you some thoughts I have had about the intramural sport experience. I choose to focus upon the word experience because it defines the active, functional part of the program. I shall be concerned with the *quality* of the intramural experience rather than quantity factors. We have heard repeatedly throughout this conference and past conferences how many teams are in a tournament and how many students are in an intramural sports program, so quantity is emphasized. Directors cite statistics proudly to impress upon various constituencies how successful the program has been. And why not? Certainly quantitative evaluation is a measure of success. Yet, I hope you will agree with me that numbers do not tell the whole story. Surely in all our programs there are students who have chosen not to participate or who have participated and decided not to return because they were not satisfied with some aspect of their experience. Therefore, numbers and percentages will not be emphasized.

Let us examine some barriers that prevent students and faculties from dealing with experiences. These barriers take the form of statements about the value of sports experiences that are slanted by text books and over-zealous teachers to convince the public, students, and faculties that participation in physical competition develops the individual physically, mentally, emotionally and spiritually. Statements that were originally objectives of the total physical education program became through exaggeration inherent values. Cliches about sportsmanship were and are presented as truths. A credibility gap develops when one analyzes what is taken for granted in the name of sports and what is really achieved. What does this mean? If we accept propaganda or public relations' gimmicks as realities, then how can we honestly deal with the quality of the experience?

We must question whether or not there is evidence to support these generalities. Are they facts, assumptions or myths? My hunch is that a few youngsters are helped to develop certain faculties through sports competition; a few probably are hurt and the vast majority are neither aided or retarded by participation in intramural sports programs. I am convinced, however, that to throw around the value of sportsmanship carelessly; its blind acceptance as a glorious product of our programs

Intramurals provide the participant with the opportunity to experience a wide variety of competitive outcomes---joy, despair; individuality, teamwork; challenge, accomplishment.

that is always there; denies what I see before my eyes every day in the intramural program. I do not need a sophisticated study to convince me that experiences I observe such as, players yelling at opposing players; students cursing officials; and teammates berating each other are not examples of sportsmanship.

Is this the fault of the intramural sports program? I think not. Can intramural directors and programs effectively deal with these negative experiences, if we accept cliches about sportsmanship? I think not. It is true that the experiences I have alluded to and others that I and the student panel shall discuss with you cannot solely be considered the responsibility of those concerned with intramural sports programs. These actions reflect values, attitudes and practices that conditioned students and faculty many years before they began to participate in intramural programs. They are an out-growth of teachings and learnings absorbed from society through its vehicle of communication, the mass media. Even with the scale balanced heavily in this direction, we cannot shirk our responsibility for all that occurs in our programs. The real question is, can intramural sports programs create an atmosphere for the development of sound values? I am not sure whether or not we can answer this question at this time, but I am convinced that in order to deal with what is implied, we must be vitally concerned with the quality of the intramural experience.

Presently much of what goes on in intramural sports programs is an imitation of varsity sports. I shall withhold a value judgment as to whether or not this is good or bad. Since students involved in intramural sports programs are a more heterogenous group when compared to varsity participants in terms of level of skill, aspiration, time considerations and interests, creative approaches styled to meet the needs of intramural performers are necessary. In order to provide such elements in a program we must understand the meaning of movement and sport experiences.

The scientists have helped us to explore the meaning of the sport experience but the poets also have contributed. Listen to what Wallace Stevens says about meaning and movement experience:

"A breathing like the wind,
A moving part of motion…
A flow of meaning with no speech
And of as many meanings as of men".

He tells us each individual creates a different meaning but the language of sport is there for all of us to see if we would only work to understand it. When we see a team jumping up and down in victory, or a player purposely striking an opponent or a team using an ineligible player, or the sadness expressed by an individual who considers himself

41

responsible for a loss, we are witnessing experiences that students and faculty need to interpret for their own growth, so that their future involvement in similar experiences will bring forth the most appropriate response for each individual. A sound intramural program will enable participants to explore their actions and judgments rather than to rationalize or suppress them. In order to accomplish this, intramural programs must be structured to provide outlets for the feelings of its participants as well as it does for the procedures and results of its contests. A sound intramural program will recognize that these kinds of experiences and the many not mentioned which you can conjure up before your own eyes are fascinating and should be focused upon in greater detail; because these experiences are what the intramural program is really all about. These experiences challenge students to confront their values and to deal with them. The conflicts that arise force the student to make value judgments derived from his own experience to reach a comfortable solution. If we take seriously the intramural program's responsibility to foster learning, then in the vernacular or our youth," Here is where it's at". Students need resources and tools to deal with experiences in a qualitative manner. An intramural program that encourages the development of individual resources must provide students with choices, give them opportunities to analyze their problems, allow them the opportunity to make decisions and the luxury of committing errors and reevaluating their mistakes.

I suggest that students and faculty reassess their rules and regulations to determine what is the intent of the rules and their actual effect. Is the administrative machinery such, that it encourages or discourages the implementation of new ideas? Can regulations be incorporated that structure an environment that I have outlined above?

Specifically, are simple, qualitative experiences in the program supported by rules and regulations with regard to the following:

1) Time—How long does the student actually play and in how many games?
2) Mood—Is the student happy or frustrated?
3) Motivation—Is he pressured or coaxed to participate or does he partake voluntarily?
4) Winning or Losing—Is he in control of himself after a winning or losing experience?

How can an intramural director understand the meaning of what he observes in the intramural laboratory of experiences? How can he stimulate action on behalf of all concerned with the program to initiate bold proposals to deal with difficult questions and situations?

First, I believe we must be sensitive to the experiences we observe without being too quick to condone or condemn. I am reminded about the story of the Little League baseball game in which the bases were loaded in the last of the ninth inning and the first batter struck out. The second batter struck out also. Finally, the third batter struck out. The fathers of the first and second batters approached the father of the third batter and said "Your boy lost us the game."

Secondly, intramural directors need to examine experiences to understand the real reason for their occurrence. For example, a common experience in life that illustrates this point about understanding underlying factors occurs in the following manner: You make a humorous remark to a colleague and he does not laugh. You inquire as to what is wrong and he tells you a good friend passed away. Immediately, you feel embarrassment at the inappropriate timing of your joke even though you were unaware of his problem. Often intramural directors act in an informational vacuum and without knowledge of the entire circumstances that create problems for student participants.

Thirdly, we have to recognize individual and situational differences and act accordingly. A fight in an athletic contest is a good example of a situation that requires a qualitative approach to an experience. If a fight occurs, do we punish all concerned equally? Is the person who started the fight solely responsible? Should the events leading to the incident be considered? Could circumstances that occurred before the game have contributed to the fight? Can we appropriately evaluate what happened without examining the views and feelings of the participants?

Fourthly, we must be aware of the relationship between the structure and the function of the intramural sports program. What kind of experience does the structure encourage? The following illustrates this point. A teacher administers a "true and false" test that only requires memorization and seats the students in close proximity to each other. He reads the newspaper during the test and cheating occurs. Should the teacher be surprised and indignant? Does he share responsibility for what happened? Did he encourage cheating?

All of you have different answers to these questions, but I hope the situation presented gives you "food for thought". Let us proceed to discuss an intramural sport experience, an experience related to my point about structure, that is closely associated with our work.

An intramural sports rule states that the official should award a forfeit when a team is five minutes late for a game. A softball game is scheduled and after five minutes the umpire declares a forfeit. During the next 30 seconds the other team arrives. The official informs the team that they forfeited the game. The team members argue that a player was delayed because of an examination. The official asks the captain of the team that arrived early if he wants to play the game. He refuses and accepts the win by forfeit. Why did this incident occur? Is not the object of the intramural sports program to play the game? Why did the team refuse to play? A look at other regulations in the intramural program gives us some indication. If a team wins they get points and/or receive an award at the end of the tourney. Sometimes the award becomes more important than the game. Should intramural directors be surprised at what occurred? Did the structure of the program encourage the team not to play in direct contradiction to intramural objectives?

Finally, we must listen to participants describing their experiences and make inquiries that may provide clues that would keep function in closer harmony with form and help to improve our programs. Perhaps we should interview students involved in interesting incidents and keep a log of all that occurred. Maybe our logs of accumulated data will help to resolve present and future problems. This incident in a basketball game occurred a few years ago, but my notes enable me to continue to learn from it. The coach of the team substituted for his best player. The player was enraged and as he left the game he threw his shirt into the balcony and left the gymnasium. The next day I spoke to the coach and player separately in my office. The following is a summary of my conversations:

The player—"I had a poor game. Last year I was the star. I guess I became too involved in myself and intramurals. This year I was the team captain. I felt angry. We were losing. I felt rejection and greater anger when I was removed from the game. I was angry at Herb (the coach) and at myself. I thought I could help if I was in the game. I left the gym and drank some water. I sat on the steps. I feel you're expected to go haywire when you lose. I blamed the official also. After the game I apologized to Herb and other members of the fraternity. A cooling off period occurred and I realized I over compensated. I was embarrassed."

The coach—"I wanted him to rest a minute and view the game from the sidelines. I was surprised at his actions. I didn't expect him to do that. I was embarrassed because of the crowd. I felt the players and the crowd supported me. I felt awkward and our friendship has suffered."

What do we learn by taking the time to become involved in understanding the experience? Certainly one is struck with how important the feelings of the participants are to the quality of the action. Often we focus on the skill displayed by participants and of course on the results of the contest, but rarely do we concern ourselves with the feelings of individuals and how those feelings affect the action. I hope that I have illustrated that feeling and emotion greatly affect participants during and after a game is won or lost. These experiences have a profound affect upon serious problems in intramural sports programs such as, officiating, fighting, and injuries. In my view, student participants and intramural directors must strive to create an atmosphere conducive to expressing and dealing with one's emotion because only through this process can we understand the meaning of sports and improve the quality of the intramural experience. If we desire individuals to be responsive to our programs we must provide them with the resources to discover that sport experiences consist of a series of problem situations and attempted solutions; so that they are not fooled into believing they are successes of failures, if they win or lose. If this task seems to be too idealistic, in closing I remind you of George Bernard Shaw's words often quoted by the late Senator Robert F. Kennedy:

"Some men see things as they are,
and ask why,
I dream things that never were
and ask why not".

An Appraisal of Intramural Activities
Ross E. Townes
(1962 NIA Proceedings, pp. 52-56)

It is the usual procedure with certain types of presentations to begin with a definition of terms. And since the intention of this presentation is to appear scholarly, we begin with the derivation and meaning of the term intramural. The term "intramural" is derived from a combination of two Latin words, "intra" meaning within, and "muralis" meaning wall. Thus, in a symbolical sense, we are referring to sports activities conducted within the imaginary wall of any particular school.

Secondly, since scholarly words usually limit or establish the scope of discussion, we point out the lack of uniformity in title designation of what we shal classify as "intramural activities." We regad as synonymous the terms intramural athletics, intramural sports, and intramural activities. Our purpose here is not to pursue the science of meanings, but rather a scholarly approach to intramural appraisal. While we realize that there may be individuals present who disagree with this position, and while we are quite aware of some of their reasons for disagreement, we are using these terms interchangeably.

It has been said that there are three steps in any evaluative process; namely, (1) definition and appraisal of objectives; (2) determination of status; and (3) judgment of status in light of the established objectives. For example, evaluation of an intramural program merely by the use of picture books, or by recording the statistics of mass participation is not the scholarly approach.

The purpose of intramural activities is to provide students of moderate motor ability with opportunities for satisfaction and enjoyment to be derived from experience in sports. Ideally, these activities should be similar to those constituting the broad base of the physical education program. In short, intramural activity programs offer voluntary participation in the activities whose fundamental skills have been taught in the basic required program.

There is no unanimity in the statement of objectives for intramural activities. At best, our position will be that of condensing, combining, and for the most part, implying objectives. Let us first view some values advanced by colleagues in our profession:

> Intramural activities provide opportunity for students to take part in competitive sports on the field rather than in the stands.

> Intramural activities provide opportunity to play rather than practice.

> Intramural activities afford an opportunity to relieve tensions, improve circulation, clear the mind, and prepare for a better adaptation to academic environment.

In summary, colleagues in the profession content that intramural activities offer the student with ordinary skill a better opportunity to compete. These activities counteract "spectatoritis" in sports events. These activities rule out the "practice grind" necessary to meet acceptable standards of varsity competition. Our colleagues in the profession employ such slogans as "More Sports for More People" and "Better a Second-rater than a Spectator".

According to one authority, "as a people we enjoy, in a rather primitive sense, a contest—not as a clash of wits and strategy, not as an opportunity to applaud skill and fine play, not as a manifestation of excellence and the player's best, but solely to see our side win."

Should one play to win? The answer is in the affirmative. While this does not mean "anything to win," it does question the salt composition of the person who does not play to achieve, to keep the faith, and to finish the course. Winning should not be condemned by the slogan "sports for sports sake". These factors are not incompatible. In short, "sports for the sake of sports" may be admirable or mere nonsense. The former is true if we are stressing false practices of a corrupt nature, the latter true if the contention means victory should not be keenly sought.

Competitive sports have as one value the stimulus necessary to require one's supreme resources, the stimulus to demand solution for the immediate attack, the stimulus to contest the stamina of the foe. The foundation for this stimulus comes from the "roots" of the desire to win. According to Bertrand Russell, "It is difficult to suppress competition completely without destroying individuality."

Athletics in educational institutions should be extensive rather than intensive providing an education in various skills for use in life rather than specialization in one form that is often of no functional value.

Bear with me while I quote directly from administrative officers in institutions of higher education. President Rowland Haynes of Omaha University gave this message to his students in 1914:

"Now that we are seriously looking to the future, I suggest two ways you can each help. One is by supporting the athletic teams which represent your institution. Another is by taking part yourself in intramural sports. Your country needs the habit of loyalty. Your nation needs strong, healthy, young men and women. You cannot become such by sitting on the sidelines. Boost the varsity teams, yes, but also do something on your own."

This message is quite appropriate more than twenty years later, since we are again seriously, even more than in 1941, looking to the future. Loyalty and physical fitness are factors needed by our country and nation.

Nicholas Murray Butler, one-time President of Columbia University wrote:

"The degree A.B. is granted to those young men who meet the prescribed intellectual tests, and the degree of varsity "C" is awarded by competent authority to those who earn special distinction in some one of the manly sports and athletic contests—both represent activity and achievement which are an integral part of education in college."

Norman M. Smith, President of the University of South Carolina said:

"Physical health and vigor are desirable attributes which are likely to increase the mental stamina of our students. Students who indulge in sports are likely to be happier, better adjusted, and better all-around men and women than those who neglect their physical welfare."

Philip Davidson, President of the University of Louisville remarked:

"Such activities, through the promotion of natural rivalries and health competition fosters that all important sense of belonging, increases school spirit, and creates a sense of physical well-being which all of us, athletically inclined or not, can attain this way."

The following statement was taken from the publication "Student Life at Brown":

"Recognizing the interplay of physical, mental, and moral qualities—for nowadays the sound body is conceived as the vehicle and ordinance, and not, as was thought of old, the incumberance of the mind and spirit."

C. Scott Porter, Dean of the College at Amherst said:

"The Amherst student body is a carefully selected academic group, but if this group is to take full advantage of the academic opportunities offered to it, there must be a voluntary intramural program open to all students for purposes of both health and recreation during their four years at Amherst. Academic authorities of the college feel that a sound intramural program is essential for a successful scholastic program."

These remarks by college administrative officers give strong support to the allegations of our colleagues. Scholasticism and asceticism, as guiding philosophies in several institutions, seem to have been supplanted by the "organismic unity theory". That is, separation of mind and body, and separation of soul and body has been replaced by the "unity of the organism" point of view. This shift in educational philosophy has given new support to extra-curricular activities, or co-curricular activities in our schools and colleges.

Shortly after World War I, John Galsworthy wrote:

"Sport, which keeps the flag of idealism flying is perhaps the most saving grace in the world at the moment with the spirit of rules kept, and regard for the adversary whether the flight is going for or against, when if ever, the fair play spirit of sport reigns over international affairs, the "cat-force" which rules there now will slink away and human life emerge for the first time from the jungle."

Intramural activities belong to this heritage of sports. These words of Galsworthy are heatening in these times of internal and external turmoil because they help us to understand democracy just a bit better. Admittedly, some of the current practices in games are not sport and some of those called amateurs play for reasons other than "love of sport".

In mathematics, a proof is a logical chain of deductions starting with what is given and ending with what is to be proved. Let us attempt to make the application. The nourishment of the organism by means of digestion, absorption, and the assimilation of blood, and the elimination of waste by means of the lungs, kidneys, intestines, and skin are basic functions of the living organism. Muscular activity is basic to these vital functions. There exists a close relation between the vital organs and the muscles of the body. For example, muscular activity accompanied by insistent physiological demands maintain organic function. Vigorous muscular activity encourages vital organic participation at a high level. External and internal respiration by means of breathing and circulation of the blood are the result of muscular activity. These foregoing statements are established basic biologic functions. Now that we have the logical chain of deductions, suppose we give the proof.

Studies by Dublin, who concerned himself with athletes at Amherst, Brown, Cornell, Dartmouth, Harvard, Massachusetts Agricultural College, Tulane, Wesleyan, Wisconsin, and Yale show a better mortality, throughout the life span than other men accepted for insurance by companies, and men winning two or more letters in distinct sports were better regarding mortality than other athletes.

A study of the college athlete was conducted for several years under the leadership of the Carnegie Foundation for the Advancement of Teaching. The sample included athletes from Columbia, Harvard, and Princeton. It would seem a fair conclusion from the reports that athletics and scholarship are not incompatible. Recent studies tend to give credence and weight to the organismic theory—the interdependence of mind and body. There is a relationship between wise physical activity and scholastic attainment.

Larson found that forty to fifty per cent of the personnel entering the Army Air Force during World War II did not have a sufficient degree of skill in any sport to desire competition. According to his findings, there was a systematic retrogression in physical fitness with increase in chronological age. The implication here is quite easily detected.

In summary, since this is the general rule for scholarly works, the task of education in this "Space Age" is the teaching of youth skills far beyond present levels and objectives—one's education must help awaken the dynamic forces in culture for decent opportunities for play. Every individual should unlock the attic of his brain and rid it of the stored fears, jealousies, disappointments, and unsatisfied yearnings. If one's brain does not, by some method, rid itself of these "drains" and "strains" eventually they will leak out as what the psychologists call inhibitions, complexes, and maladjustments. Intramural activities may well serve as the laboratory in which these ills may partially, if not totally, disappear.

As a people, we need to cultivate the habit of loyalty. Our country needs the social morality now more than ever. We submit that intramural activities, through this idea of "team membership" can make a major contribution toward the development of this quality.

According to Glen A. Olds, President of Springfield College, "Not only is there no conflict between rational pursuit of knowledge and the rational discipline of the body, but an environment of disciplined freedom on the playing field is essential to the creativity of both.

The unique educative opportunities of intramural activities may be classified in one of the following areas: (1) Socialization, (2) Setting of Standards, and (3) Formation of Attitudes.

In conclusion, physical activity of an enjoyable vigorous nature is of optimum physical, intellectual, and emotional worth. We would suggest intramural activities as the primary extra-curricular activity. The college should extend itself, offering to its studentbody and faculty every enducement and facility for the development of those capacities of mind and body which are designed to enrich and ennoble the present and future.

These activities have been developed in the schools and colleges to supplement the curricular program for the purpose of bringing about a more complete realization of the objectives of education.

Contributions of Intramurals to the Educational Program
Paul V. Keen
(1968 NIA Proceedings, pp. 53-57)

When I was asked to write a paper on "The Contributions of Intramurals to the Educational Program," I though of what a young man who was personnel manager for a large petroleum oil company told me. He said that he learned more about personnel management while he was a senior intramural manager than in any course he took while in the University. I was sure then that intramurals had contributed something to that man's education.

In trying to point out some of the educational contributions of the intramural program to the education of the participants it is first necessary to give a philosophy of intramural sports and how the program has been established.

The first intramural programs were established because some interested students wanted some physical competition in a sport and challenged some other students to a game. This kind of competition became popular, so it grew and as it grew, problems arose. Then the school decided that it needed some direction and supervision, so a teacher was assigned to sponsor the program.

Most of the early sponsors of the intramural programs were assigned on a temporary basis and were promised relief if they would take over for a year or so. Some coaches of athletic teams were assigned to work with the intramural program in their off season[9] just to give them something to do.

It was not until a person was assigned to the intramural program on a continuing basis that the program began to have a coordinated program with a continuing goal.

The first idea of the intramural program was to give the students an opportunity to work off steam and to get some exercise. It was soon discovered that these were not all the benefits derived from the program.

In every high school and college around the country you find that the rallying point for the whole student body seems to be their athletic teams and the traditions built up over the years. I have seen very few people who do not have a strong loyalty to the school from which they have been graduated, and that loyalty is kept alive by following the athletic teams each year.

This loyalty carries over to where the conduct of the students is reflected in every phase of the school.

We feel that this same loyalty is generated by an intramural team, and this loyalty will carry over into the fraternity, university house, club organization, and into all teams that participate in our program.

We also feel that the students learn a great deal about the give and take of living together that will be reflected in their life af er they get out of school.

The first thing that I think the intramural program contributes to the educational advancement of the student is leadership. We have a board of students that has the responsibility of setting the rules and policies of the intramural department so that it does not conflict with the university administration. This experience (dealing with students and student problems) affords them an opportunity to learn to handle problems of leadership; there are also other leaders, such as the unit managers, the captains of each team, and managers of individual sports. These all provide opportunities to add to the leadership training.

We cannot all be leaders, and all leaders have to be followers at times. In intramurals there is an excellent opportunity to teach followership, cooperation and good sportsmanship. Followership is just as important as leadership, and this opportunity to learn cooperation is a very valuable asset that everyone should learn.

There is always a teaching situation in everything we do. If one learns from his mistake and does not repeat that mistake, he has learned. If one makes a mistake and then alibis and makes the mistake again, perhaps he has not learned.

When we speak of education, I think we mean teaching the whole man—the spiritual, physical, mental, social, emotional, recreational, and business ability to make a living and contribute something to his community.

Our intramural department works very closely with the Student Affairs Department and the University Housing Department, so I asked the men in these departments what they felt intramurals had contributed

51

to the educational program of the students.

Dr. Jodie Smith, Dean of Students at the University of Oklahoma said:

First of all it should be understood that an institutional educational program should include all learning experiences, not just those activities related to the classroom and laboratory. If we accept this version of the institution's educational program then these contributions become apparent.

One contribution is the opportunity for young people who have been active in high school athletic programs to continue this interest throughout their undergraduate years. I think it is easy to recognize that when young people are actively engaged in physical recreational programs the health factor alone makes a valuable contribution. Perhaps one of the primary reasons for the worth of an intramural program is the requirement for an individual to become involved in active participation of an event and not to attend just as a spectator.

In summary Paul, I would say that in my opinion, the educational program of the University would be incomplete without an intramural program.

Dean J. F. Paschal, Dean of Men said:

The Intramural program of any major university is more than a slipshod effort to provide a means of students to "let off steam." It has been one of the most effective ways in which resident students at the University of Oklahoma have been able to participate in a concentrated group effort which results in loyalties to themselves, their living group, and to the University. The spirit of competition provides a meaningful outlet for comradeship among independent students which is not available through any other outlet. The non-academic program at the University of Oklahoma is a strong one only as long as the intramural program is a strong one.

The third statement is from Wayne Bodkin, Assistant Dean of Men in charge of mens housing, and the individual who can best see the impact of the intramural program on the students. He said:

Intramural sports' contribution to the educational program is not as easily defined as one would initially think. However, the need for the experience and lessons learned by participating has not changed from that early time when intramural sports were introduced by the British schools.

Intramural sports is an organized program which provides:

(1) the individual participant the opportunity and facilities for an educational experience in competition;

(2) the individual participant experience in participating as an individual and as a contributing member of an organized

group;

(3) the individual participant the opportunity to savor the flavor of winning and the agony of defeat and respond with appropriate discipline and conduct;

(4) the intangible ingredient necessary for the spirit of gentlemanly conduct and esprit de corps;

(5) the individual participant experience in self discipline and responsibility; and

(6) an arena in which each participant is acutely aware of his responsibility to and for his fellow participants.

Intramural sports is an organized program of physical activity which provides the individual participant the opportunity and facilities for educational experience as an individual and a contributing member of an organized group—this program being different from other laboratory experiences on the campus in that participants do not fail, but by the very act of participating are achieving individual satisfaction and achieving the goals of intramural sports.

The intramural program is too many times by too many people erroneously regarded as a means to "let off steam" or as supervised "hell raising." It is a poor program that accomplishes no more than this. Intramural sports was originally introduced by the British schools to provide the learned scholars and future leaders the opportunity to learn sportsmanship in its finest form. The need for this experience has not changed.

The key word is *individual*. Individuals savor the flavor of winning and the agony of defeat. Persons must learn to be graceful winners as well as graceful losers. It is through the individual efforts and attitudes that a group takes on the identity and strength of a team. Team effort is the cumulative effort of individuals humbly sacrificing individual identity.

Intramural sports contribute to educational programs by teaching humility in winning and defeat, the need for participating, and teaching and enforcing the awareness that team effort is the result of individual effort. The things learned on the field of play are applicable in all places of life. Intramural sports is many things to many people but the important thing is the lesson of individual experience.

I asked Miss Bowling, my co-worker for several years as Director of Intramurals for Women, for a statement and she said:

It is an accepted fact the objectives of physical education closely parallel the objectives of education. Intramurals then, as an outgrowth of physical education, certainly contribute to the aim of education—for the physical, mental, social, emotional and recreational well-being of the participant.

An Intramural program:

1. Contributes to the health and welfare of participants.
2. Develops skills and interest for leisure time use, which are more and more needed as a result of more and more cybernation.
3. As recreation, is educationally sound; intramurals offer opportunities for activities with carry-over values, to learn and improve for future recreational pursuits; with increased leisure, there is more need for constructive recreation.
4. Is an emotional stabilizer, relieves tension, helps one to relax and to keep fit.
5. Develops social and ethical qualities, cooperation, loyalty, respect for others, and so forth.
6. Contributes to modern education, which is concerned with developing attitudes. Where better than on a playing field can we develop constructive attitudes and social relationships?
7. Promotes scholarship.
8. Helps develop a self-image (for the unskilled as well as the skilled) that is not usually required through other academic disciplines.
9. Helps satisfy the inherent urge that man has for competition.
10. Is a training ground for leaders; leadership qualities are easily developed through intramurals; the world has never had enough good leaders.
11. Develops physical and mental fitness.
12. Develops student-faculty relationships.
13. Eliminates social barriers, race barriers, and so forth.

No longer are intramurals considered extracurricular. They are co-curricular, because a program built on scientifically sound principles will enrich the curricular program as a part of education.

If the intramural director will coordinate his program with the national cardinal principles found in the administration of his own institution, and follow the principles of the Washington Conference on Intramurals, I am sure his program will be a great contribution to the education of the students of his institution. Nothing is a waste of time if one will use the experience wisely.

Chapter 3
Units of Competition

**Factors Involved in Selecting Units of
Competition for Intramural Activities**
Eugene L. Hill
(1966 NIA Proceedings, pp. 21-23)

Not many years ago intramural directors throughout the nation were in the stage of solicitation. The success of the program was mainly measured by the number of participants that could be induced to take part. This led to the development of many devices, including elaborate point systems, designed to attract student.

This emphasis on quantity gradually became secondary to a new emphasis on quality of participation and the benefits to each individual. Included in the techniques for improving quality were health examinations, training periods, instruction, closer supervision, improved facilities, safer equipment, and better officiating.

However, it is my opinion that two other factors are also of vital importance to the growth and development of quantity and quality intramural programs. These two factors are what I call the "common bond" and "equalized competition." Both of these factors are important and should be considered when establishing units of competition in the competitive phase of the intramural program.

Few, if any, of us at the college level have an opportunity to exert much influence on the method of organizing units of competition because the pattern has already been established. This pattern established mostly by custom includes the fraternal groups and the independents. However, the rapid growth of the junior college movement, the increase in the number of new high schools, and the emphasis now being placed on junior high school programs, gives many intramural people an opportunity to organize and develop new programs in new situations. Thus, these younger men, having the benefit of past experiences, can develop even better programs for the future.

Many types of units for competition are used. The selection of the units depends upon the local situation, which includes staff, facilities, and school administrative organization. Running through whatever units are selected should be the psychological factors of the "common bond" and "equalized competition."

The "common bond" might be defined as that something or feeling that holds a group together. It might also be described as group, school, or team loyalty. Among boys of the junior high school age, the "gang

55

spirit" is at a high level. Boys of this age seem to want to belong to a group. It does not seem to matter much how the group is formed, so long as it is made up of boys of their own age and interests. With this age group most any type of unit for intramural competition will be accepted, and anyone of the so-called "arbitrary" units will work well.

However, as the boys grow older, the "gang spirit" seems to diminish, and their interests and loyalties change to different types of organizations. Thus, the arbitrary units seem to lose their effectiveness due to a lack of common bond which holds them together. College men are more selective when choosing a group or unit with which to participate in sports.

The fraternal organization on most college and university campuses is a natural grouping for college men. Here loyalty to the group is built into the life of the organization, and the common bond reaches a high degree of efficiency. However, the arbitrary unit, having little in the way of a common bond, is likely to be something less than popular with students of this age group.

Thus, the "common bond" is an important factor to be considered when selecting units for competition. In many instances the "common bond" must be built into the organization. In other cases such as the fraternity units and, on occasion, the geographic units, the "common bond" is already present.

The most recent unit of competition to develop to a high degree of efficiency on the college campus is the dormitory unit. Here, there is a degree of "common bondness," but it would behoove the intramural people to capitalize on this whether it be the entire dormitory or specific areas, such as floors within the dormitory. I believe that with adequate development of a common bond, the dormitory units will eventually replace the fraternity as the major unit in the men's intramural program.

A second factor that seems to have received little emphasis in the development of intramural programs is equalized competition. Athletic conferences throughout the country at all school levels are formed with this in mind. When a school finds itself in a conference in which it is too strong or too weak to keep pace with the competition, it seeks another league. Conferences also seek to maintain equality among its members by setting minimum and maximum standards of eligibility.

In the intramural leagues other methods of equalizing competition should be sought. This is a simple matter in those sports such as bowling and golf, which readily lend themselves to handicapping procedures. In team sports, such as basketball, soccer, touch football, volleyball, and softball, handicapping does not seem to be feasible. Thus, other means of equalization needs to be developed.

One of the most common methods used at certain school levels is based upon numbers of students. We all know that numbers alone do not necessarily indicate quality of performance. Hence, one group may contain all the best performers, while another group is almost void of good performers.

The realization of sound educational objectives is more apt to occur in contrasts involving equalized competition. It has been pointed out that courage, cooperation, and loyalty are examples of qualities acquired and demonstrated in closely contested games. A few of the major difficulties presented by unequal competition are forfeits, discipline problems, lack of interest, and poor participation. It is no fun to be obliged to take a one-sided licking; and further, it is no great sport to the winners of this kind of contest. Close competition makes the program more interesting for all concerned.

Various methods of equalizing competition have been discussed and tried, but no one solution has come to be universally accepted. We might mention seeding, classes of flights, combination tournaments, and handicapping. All of these are practices with varying degrees of success.

We have experimented with equating arbitrarily, teams on the junior high school level by means of skill tests and age-height-weight classifications. These techniques bring about equalized competition. By using 7.41 points per game. In 30.6% of the games the score difference was three points or less.

It should be pointed out that the application of a skill test to all intramural participants in a large school at any level involves unsurmountable administrative problems. The various ideas and plans hold much promise, but future experimentation and development is paramount. The profession will do well to devote more and more time to improve the quality of intramural participation through the use of the "common bond" principle and "equalized competition."

Rec Leagues as a Viable Supplement to
Competitive Leagues in Intramurals
Tom VanderWeele
(1975 NIRSA Proceedings, pp. 54-57)

When Michigan State first started the use of recreational leagues, or "B" leagues as we call them, there were probably other schools who had already begun to try this concept. Certainly there are other schools who are now using it. At Michigan State, we did not consider the development of the pure recreational league as an innovation so much as we considered it a natural outgrowth of the standard competitive leagues which were no longer adequate to meet the demands of a majority of our participants. We have defined the "B League" as follows: "A league which is designed for recreational play, where there are no post-season playoffs, and where the emphasis is on enjoyable activity rather than intense competition for a championship." Before I go into the actual structure of our league, perhaps it would be appropriate to explain how this concept evolved.

For more than twenty-five years Michigan State had recognized an all campus intramural champion in the sports of football, basketball, and softball. This later became known as the All-University Championships. At the end of regular league playoffs in the three leagues, the top two fraternity, top two independent, and top four dorm teams would all meet in single elimination play to determine an All-University Champion. Additional awards and recognition were always accorded these champions,and teams were highly competitive in seeking a berth in the playoffs for the All-U's. This competitive intensity was greatly magnified as the games progressed to the championship contest. Teams were using ineligible players, screaming at referees, fighting with other teams and among themselves, and generally losing most of the attributes of sportsmanship in their efforts to win the championship. Fans were no better in their adamant criticism of other teams, abuse and even threats toward referees, supervisions and so forth.

The All-University Championships took between one and two weeks to complete depending on the weather. Since a normal school term ran for nine to ten weeks, we were often hard-pressed to get all our games finished on time. Often dorm teams were forced to play three and four nights in a row in order to finish their leagues championship before the All-U's could begin. Once a team lost, their season was finished. We wondered if there might not be a better way to utilize this time and money rather than on putting it into eight teams who were already gaining quite a bit of recognition. Perhaps it might be better to channel this effort to teams at all levels of play and to emphasize participation rather than competition.

The intramural staff at Michigan State decided to take a philosophical look at the purposes of intramural sports and how well our program fit our stated philosophies. It was determined that the All-University Championships emphasized the "win at any price" attitude and that the "gains" of the eight teams in the championship playoffs did not sufficiently justify keeping such a program. Beginning in the fall of 1971 we no longer had the All-University Championship at Michigan State. They died slowly at first with former champions wearing their award jackets coming in and arguing for their reinstatement. These encounters were few in number, however; and gradually people began to at least seem to understand, if not totally accept, our rationale.

With the demise of the All-University Playoffs, we did find the availability for many more teams to play extra games at the end of the regular season. We weren't concerned with the composition of these teams, only that the teams were able to play as they wished. This was, perhaps, the first origin of what was to later become the recreational league. During the first term under the new system, some fifty teams opted to play at least one game at the end of the regular season.

The following year we made another step toward the elimination of problems caused by increased levels of competition and desire for awards. We eliminated the point structure and the rivalry for all sports championships. We had found that teams were doing almost anything to try to gain points and that most of the recreational and participational aspects of the intramural system were being bypassed. At first, both the residence hall system and the fraternity system wanted to retain the point structure within their own groups and operate through the Intramural department. The residence hall point system folded within the year. The fraternity point system has persisted, but continues to be far and away our biggest source of problems and disputes to this day.

For some time, we had been receiving numerous requests for some type of variety in our league structures. We had continued to operate the three leagues: fraternity, residence hall, and independent. The extra time at the end of our schedule had enabled us to expand our playoff system to take more than twice as many teams into playoffs, but there were still teams who had some desires that were not being met.

In the league structure, as it existed, the teams were divided into blocks of from five to seven teams and played a one-game round-robin schedule during a five week period. The winners, runners-up, and teams with one loss or less went into a single elimination play-off in each league. When a team lost, they were finished for the season. Conceivably, a team could have as few as four or five games. Many of the teams in all of the leagues consisted of merely a group of people who had gotten together to play some ball and have some fun. They were often disorganized; seldom, if ever practiced; and really didn't take the outcome of the games too seriously. This type of team frequently was playing a team which was highly organized, practiced frequently, was very serious about winning and was aiming toward championship play. Most often the organized team would methodically destroy the other team and, although they weren't taking the outcome so seriously, even the most carefree teams could get shaken by being so defeated. It seemed to us that something else was needed.

In the winter of 1974 we organized a B independent league, whose stated purpose was to "provide a league which is designed for recreational play, where there are no post-season playoffs, and where the emphasis is on enjoyable activity rather than intense competition for a championship". We allowed people who played in the other leagues to also play in the B league so that league structure would not be a constraint. This aspect proved so workable in fact that the following term we

59

allowed a player to play for more than one team so long as he was on no more than one team in each league and he met the specific requirements for the special leagues such as fraternity member, dorm resident, etc.

During the first term, we had 88 Independent B teams and 86 Independent A teams in basketball. We had 128 Independent B teams and 163 teams with 97 A teams. The past term we had 120 Independent B teams and 121 Independent A teams in basketball.

We divided the teams into blocks of eight. They played one game each week through the five weeks of regular schedule and two weeks of playoff schedule. We made sure that we spread the games out so that all teams had equal access to all the good gyms, fields, etc. There were no post-season playoffs in the B league. If we still had extra time left at the end of the term, teams from any league were welcome to sign up for extra games. The emphasis was on activity and play rather than on pressure to win. Of the twenty-two people who were ejected from basketball games this past season for any reason, three were from the B league.

The response to the B league has generally been very good. The only problem we have had at all are some increased forfeits with bad weather in softball and football. Forfeits have continually been a problem in all of our leagues. This past term out of 2,448 regularly scheduled basketball games, 68 were originally forfeited for one reason or another. Many of these were later replayed. Of the total games, 840 were in the B league and 1,644 were in one of the competitive leagues. There were 33 forfeits in the B league and 35 forfeits in one of the competitive leagues. In percentages the B league had 3.9% forfeits as compared to 2.1% in the competitive leagues. Percentages would normally be higher in both football and softball because of the weather factor.

This past term we ran a survey of the teams participating in Independent B in order to see what they had expected when they entered the league and how well we were meeting those expectations. Of the 120 teams, 117 responded to the questionnaire. (We handed them out prior to games so we had a captive audience). Copies or the original survey were available as you came in. The results are as follows:

Question 1: More than half of the teams indicated that they wanted some games just for fun. Almost one third indicated they had wanted some extra games and approximately one quarter indicated they picked the league because they thought the competition here best suited their team. Obviously certain teams indicated more than one choice. Nine indicated that either they were using the B league as practice for a competitive team or as a vehicle to let more of their people play.

Question2: Seventy six chose the B league as an alternative to one of the competitive leagues, while 41 did not.

Question 3: Two thirds of the teams felt the level of play met their prior expectations while 14 felt the level was too high and 18 felt the level was too low.

Question 4 and 5: Twelve teams indicated that they had forfeited games with the most common reasons being conflicts with other activities and failure to know about the game.

Question 6: Of the 117 teams who responded to the survey, 116 said that they would like to see the activity continued, while one said to drop it.

Question 7: Suggestions covered a variety of topics including better referees, more games and an even more relaxed attitude. Six teams opted for more equalized competition within the B league and unfortunately four asked for B league playoffs. Evidently, they still wanted the competitive structure, but they didn't want the skill level so high.

From the results of the study, it is evident that although teams jointed the B league for different reasons, most of them were having their expectations met. Although we visualize no changes in this structure for next term, perhaps a follow-up study can lead us to more revisions, enabling us to meet the needs of even more participants at all levels.

It is probably quite evident by the tone of this talk that we have been quite satisfied with the development of our recreational league. It is by no means the second string of our program, but rather seems to effectively be meeting the needs of a large body of individuals. As the title indicates, it is a supplement to the competitive leagues at present.

With the ever increasing pressures to win at any cost and the apparent willingness of some teams and coaches to go to any lengths to achieve such ends, perhaps intramurals is not the place for competitive leagues at all and at some point in the future they may be supplemental to the recreational league.

Chapter 4
Scheduling/Tournaments

Scheduling — Time and Space
Eugene Boyer
(1963 NIA Proceedings, pp. 95-96)

Adequate Time

Adequate time in relation to the scope of the program must be given for the intramural program. Class work, facilities, equipment, and staff are the determining factors in many cases; and, too often, outside interest groups also affect the amount of time available. No program can survive if everything is scheduled before intramurals. The cooperation of the required and varsity programs is needed to coordinate the available time to be devoted to the intramural program.

The times that are reserved for intramurals must be as convenient and favorable as possible for the students. To get the facilities when no one else wants them and the majority of the students are not available puts the program at a disadvantage that can never be overcome regardless of promotion and planning.

Adequate time does not mean that large blocks of time be given to the intramural program for a special few. The use of the time and facilities must be justified by a well-organized and widely accepted program. Time is more valuable than facilities or equipment in many schools, and it must be used wisely. The quickest way to find yourself short of time is to be guilty of wasting it.

Desirable Time

After school, lunch periods, or evening hours may be the best time for the intramural program. Each program must consider the varsity practices, student availability, supervision, equipment and facilities in determining the most desirable time. Some activities by nature are best scheduled after school, while others can only be properly run in the evenings.

Reserve Time

No intramural program can function 100% by the proposed schedule. Time must be available for make-ups, contests that are delayed, postponed or scheduled over by some emergency that could not be foreseen. Reserve time must be saved for tie play-offs, protested contests, and tie games.

Adequate Space

Adequate space to comfortably execute the program is a must for any worthwhile program. Court sizes and field dimensions should not be altered just to save space. An intramural contest should be conducted as nearly as possible to the standard or regulation requirements. Don't shortchange the participants with less than regulation. Adequate space is as valuable as adequate time, use it wisely and maintain accepted standards and regulation requirements.

Desirable Space

Proper playing conditions, adequate lighting, proper lines, adequate equipment, and safe areas are some of the desirable space needs of a program. Once again the satisfaction of the participants will greatly depend upon under what conditions he played and whether he felt he had a fair chance to enjoy and compete in his activity. To crowd or endanger the participant is really shortchanging his chances of enjoying himself and the activity, and the door is open to accidents, injuries, and criticism.

Reserve Space

Reserve space is essential for spectators and reserve players. Space for practice, warm-up, readying equipment, and preparatory essentials of the players must be provided for in addition to the regular space needed to conduct the activity. Any activity becomes more important when it has a following, and there is some reserve space for the non-participating to watch, cheer, and add their enthusiasm. If it is worth your time and efforts to schedule, it is certainly worth watching.

Scheduling for Safety

Many accidents are caused by scheduling time and space unsafely. Adequate, desirable and reserve time and space will mean a safer program for all participants. Regardless of your accident record, safer scheduling, time and space-wise, is essential to your program in the future.

Tournament Calculations Single Elimination
Francis M. Rokosz
(1972 NIA Proceedings, 165-172)

I am going to show you a number of calculations that I can make which aid me in tournament scheduling. The key value in the calculations is that they can be made without the necessity for drawing brackets or rotation columns. They are particularly valuable in those situations where, given a number of entries, the director is not sure what type of tournament he wants to run and would like to experiment with a few figures before making a decision. Calculations can be made for single elimination, double elimination, round robin, and consolation tournaments, but today I will talk only about single elimination.

When we prepare to schedule a tournament, we basically deal with three bits of information, or variables—(1) the number of entries in the tournament, (2) the number of days required to run the tournament, and (3) the number of games that can be played per day (a function of the number of courts or fields available times the frequency of their use). Since there are three variables, three different types of problems can be developed and solved. Given any two of the variables, one solves for the third. The stipulation in all the calculations is that no entry ever plays more than once per day.

Before getting into the actual calculations, some preliminary considerations need attention. Given N, the number of entries in a tournament, the following determinations can be made:

Number of games in the tournament equals: $N-1$

Example: $N = 5$

No. games $= N-1$ No. games $= 15-1$ No. games $= 14$

Number of byes in the tournament equals: (next higher power of two)$-N$

Example: $N = 3$ next higher power of two is 32

No. byes $= 32-N$ No. byes $= 32-23$ No. byes $= 9$

Number of first-round game equals: $N-$(next lower power of two)

Example: $N = 5$ next lower power of two is 16

no. 1st-rd. games $= N-16$

no. 1st-rd. games $= 20-16$

no. 1st-rd. games $= 4$

Number of rounds in the tournament: described by the chart below.

N	next higher power of two	rounds
2	2	1
3	4	2
7	8	3
11	16	4
28	32	5
49	64	6

The most typical problem that we would want to deal with is probably that which involves the calculation of the days required to run a single elimination tournament after we have determined the number of entries and the games that we want to play per day. Problem type I serves as illustration.

The other two types of problems involved calculations which might be used less frequently.

problem type I

Given: the number of entries (36), and the number of games that can be played each day (5).
What minimum number of days is needed to run the tournament?

step (1) Determine the number of first-round games.

$$\text{1st-rd. games} = N - \text{lower portion of two}$$
$$\text{1st-rd. games} = 36 - 32$$
$$\text{1st-rd. games} = 4$$

step (2) Set up the number of rounds and the number of games for each round. Once the number for first-round games has been appropriately designated, start with the last round (one game) and work backwards with multiples of two.

rounds	1	2	3	4	5	6
games	4	16	8	4	2	1

step (3) Determine the number of days needed to play round by round. Start with the last round and work backwards. Eliminate those rounds which obviously take only one day to play (when the games per day are greater than, or equal to, the number of games in a round, place a one under that round).

rounds	1	2	3	4	5	6
games	4	16	8	4	2	1
days				1	1	1

Note: those are not necessarily the only rounds which can be played in one day. Also, since an entry cannot play more than once per day, no two full rounds can be played in one day.

step (4) Start with the first round and determine the number of days required to play each round.
There are four first-round games and five games can be played per day. So, one day is required to play the first round. Since five games can be played in one day, the one remaining game can be used in the second round.

rounds	1	2	3	4	5	6
games	4	16 −1 —— 15	8	4	2	1
days	1			1	1	1

Fifteen games remain in round two, and these require three days to complete. The eight games in round three require two days.

rounds	1	2	3	4	5	6
games	4	16 −1	8	4	2	1
		15				
days	1	3	2	1	1	1

The total number of days required to run the tournament is determined by adding the last line horizontally.

Answer: 9 days to run the tournament.

problem type II

Given: the number of entries (23), and six days are available to run the tournament.

What minimum number of games must be available for play each day in order to run the tournament?

step (1) Establish the number of rounds and the number of games in each round.

rounds	1	2	3	4	5
games	7	8	4	2	1

step (2) Divide the number of days available (6) into the number of games in the tournament ($N-1=22$). This operation results in the first index number, which is 4 (always round off to the higher number). Working backwards from the last round, recognize those rounds whose number of games is less than the index number 4. Those rounds can be played in one day.

rounds	1	2	3	4	5
games	7	8	4	2	1
days				1	1

step (3) Two days have been used to play the last three games. Divide the remaining number of days (4) into the remaining number of games (19). The result is the second index number, which is 5. Still working backwards, recognize those rounds whose number of games is less than 5. One day is required to play each of those rounds.

rounds	1	2	3	4	5
games	7	8	4	2	1
days			1	1	1

step (4) Three days have been used to play the last seven games. Divide the remaining number of days (3) into the remaining number of games (15). The third index number is 5. Five is smaller than the number of games (8) in round two. At that occurrence, the index

66

number becomes the answer to the problem.

Answer: There must be five games available for play each day in order to run the tournament in six days.

problem type III

Given: the number of days available to run the tournament (7), and the number of games that can be played per day (5).

What is the maximum number of entries that can be accommodated within those restrictions?

step (1) Multiply the number of available days (7) times the number of games that can be played each day (5).

$7 \times 5 = 35$ This represents the total number of possible games that could be played under the given conditions.

step (2) Set up the maximum number of rounds and the maximum number of games for each round. The maximum number of rounds is always equal to the number of days available.

rounds	1	2	3	4	5	6	7
max. gms.	64	32	16	8	4	2	1

step (3) Five games can be played each round. Working backwards from round seven, determine the number of wasted games in each round by subtracting from five the maximum number of games for each round.

When the maximum number of games for a round exceeds the number of games that can be played per day, a zero is recorded in the wasted games column.

rounds	1	2	3	4	5	6	7
max. gms.	64	32	16	8	4	2	1
wasted gms.	0	0	0	0	1	3	4

Total games wasted = 8

step (4) Subtract the total wasted games (8) from the total possible games that could be played within the set restrictions (35).

$35 - 8 = 27$ This represents the maximum number of games that can actually be played in the tournament.

step (5) The number of entries that can be accompanied is determined by setting up the appropriate formula.

$$\text{No. games} = N - 1$$
$$27 = N - 1$$
$$28 = N$$

Answer: 28 entries can be accommodated in the tournament.

Chapter 5
Special Event Intramurals

Special Events — A New Dimension in Intramural Programming
David H. Taylor
(1974 NIA Proceedings, pp. 70-73)

Special events at West Virginia University is a new area of programming under Recreation-Intramural Sports which was recently created to encompass many of the activities which did not functionally fall under our current seven program areas: Men's Intramurals, Women's Intramurals, Co-recreation, Sport Clubs, Recreation Center, Unstructured Activity, or Arts and Crafts.

Many times students are most hesitant to add new activities to an already overloaded men's and women's intramural schedule especially if it means adding more activities into the point system. The Special Events area will provide a potpourri of activities which afford students the opportunity to pursue their recreational interests beyond the traditional sports which are most prevalent in men's and women's intramural programs around the country.

The Special Events area will provide the opportunity for many new and before unreached students to become involved in Recreation-Intramural Programming. Many of the students' interest areas can be exploited through a well-designed and meaningful Special Events Program.

The possible selection of activities for a Special Events Program is unlimited. The often used Recreation-Intramural Program slogan, "something for everyone," can truly move closer to reality through a properly planned schedule of activities under Special Events. Let only your imagination establish the limits.

Many new activities have already been conducted and others are being planned to be included in the Special Events area at West Virginia University. The following are only some of the successes realized on our campus with a brief description of each:

One-on-One Basketball—There were 128 participants entered in the tournament the first year. To insure interest the one-on-one was scheduled to commence near the conclusion of the intramural basketball program. Tables were set up at intramural basketball games to promote and recruit for the new activity. A single elimination tournament was employed and each game was divided into nine innings of play. To help compensate for the height difference in players, a maximum of five dribbles were permitted per each offensive attempt unless the defensive man fouled or in some way touched the ball. More than five dribbles constituted a turnover, thus ending the offensive player's half of the inning. The offensive player retained possession of the ball as long as he continued to score. After each successful basket or rebound of an attempted basket, the ball was returned to the top of the foul circle, checked, and put back into play by the offensive man.

Pumpkin Carving Contest — To capitalize on the spirit of the season, this event was co-ordinated on Halloween Day. To insure maximum student participation, the student union was selected as the site for the event. Decorative displays of cornstalks and gourds were utilized to attract attention. Black and orange signs and a masquerade were also used to help depict the Halloween theme. Pumpkins and carving utensils were provided for each contestant. Judges selected the best carved pumpkin and presented the first place prize.

Beginner Ski Night — A site was selected which was conveniently located for the students. Practically any hill will suffice for instruction for beginning skiers. Although many students have a real desire to learn how to ski, they seem most hesitant in getting involved because of the initial high cost of ski equipment, lack of adequate instruction, or lack of ski slopes located near campus. The skiis, boots, and binding poles were provided by the outdoor recreational equipment area of the Recreation Center. Free expert instruction was provided by members of the Ski Club and their racing team.

Frisbee Friday — A site was selected near the student union to take advantage of student travel to and from classes. The event was conducted on Friday afternoon before the annual Homecoming football game, thereby capitalizing on the college spirit of the time. The event combined accuracy and distance (two tosses for each participant) to determine winners in both men's and women's divisions. Prizes were awarded to the top finishers in each division. A total of 582 students participated in Frisbee Friday.

Super Shooter — This event was conducted in conjunction with the intramural basketball tournament. Each player received 25 shots. The five positions for shooting were: corner, 18 feet from basket; foul line, 15 feet from basket; straight-in shot, 5 feet from basket; 45 degree shot, 10 feet from basket; and straight-in shot from top of key, 20 feet from basket. Each player received five shots from each of the five positions. The winner was determined by the least number of misses out of 25 shots.

Tricathlon — This event was conducted in the games area of the student union. Each player entered participated in bowling, billiards, and table tennis competition. A player received points for his specific finish at the conclusion of each of the three activities. Each of the activities were awarded the same point value. The three scores for each player were then added together to determine the overall winner. Trophies were awarded to the top five finishers.

Toboggan Thursday — A site was selected near campus which was easily accessible to students. The event was planned for the first major snow of the winter. Many students had indicated an interest in tobogganing, but were never before presented with the opportunity. Toboggans (2-man, 4-man, 6-man, 8-man) were provided free through the outdoor recreational equipment area of the Recreation Center. Instant publicity was the key to a successful event.

Homerun Derby—This event was conducted in the football stadium and planned in conjunction with the intramural softball tournament. Each participant was allowed nine innings at bat and permitted three outs per inning. An out was declared on anything besides a homerun (foul ball, ground ball, pop up, line drive, swinging strike, called strike, etc.). Fences were equal distance for both right and left handed batters. One neutral pitcher from the Recreation-Intramural Department pitched to all batters. An umpire was also provided to determine balls and strikes. The official 12" intramural softball was used and aluminum and wooden softball bats were provided. The participant with the greatest number of homeruns at the end of nine innings was declared the winner.

Spring Regatta—This event was conducted on a lake approximately 7 miles from the campus. Races in both men's and women's divisions were conducted in heats in the following distances: 100 yards, 200 yards, ¼ mile, ½ mile, and 1 mile. A seventeen foot Grumman Canoe, paddles, and life jackets were provided for each 2-man team. An outside sponsor, Wilderness Canoe Adventure, assisted in promoting the event and provided awards to the first place finishers in all divisions. Over 100 participants entered the Spring Regatta, which also proved to be a great spectator event.

All Campus Individual and Dual Sport Tournaments—All campus individual and dual sport tournaments were conducted in badminton, squash, racquetball, paddleball, handball, tennis, and table tennis. These specific sport tournament was also conducted on a team basis within the men's and women's programs. The all-campus individual and dual sport tournaments provided competition beyond the intramural level. They provided players not affiliated with a point team the opportunity to participate. Players participating for a tournaments was to provide stimulating competition and to determine the best singles and doubles players on campus in the specific sports.

Three very important criteria for insuring a successful Special Events Program are: 1) make the event as attractive as possible 2) select a site which is easily accessible to students and 3) make the event as spontaneous as possible.

The Special Events Program is inexpensive and easy to administer. Contrary to popular opinion we are not doing enough already. Being overworked, underpaid, under-staffed, and short on facilities and time are excuses often used for "statusquoness."

With the addition of this Special Events Program Area, many new and exciting activities can be conducted.

Does your program have "Something for Everyone?"

Unique Events That Succeed
William Thompson
(1972 NIA Proceedings, pp. 147-150)

Sensitivity experts tell us that, "We see what we want to see and we hear what we want to hear." I like to think that Intramural Sports Directors "see it as it is." TOO MANY INACTIVE STUDENTS. All of us in this field should be DISSATISFIED until we have something for everybody.

Some questions to be answered:

1. Are you conducting a *traditional* program of events?

2. Are you concerned with meeting the *needs* and *interests* of your students?

3. Can you agree with the concept that new events can *re-excite* both participants and staff?

If your answer to one or more of these questions is yes, perhaps the solution lies in the following unique but successful events.

The fact that there are only twenty-six events listed is restricted only by the limits of the alphabet.

WRIST WRESTLING—UC, Davis (Gary Golberg)

A great season opener, during the first week of school, while students are still finding classes and generally getting organized. This event is best conducted and weight classes, with divisions for right and left handers, in single elimination tournaments. Equipment requirements include a table and two chairs per weight class with build-up elbow pads. Rules involve keeping both feet flat on the floor and participant's off-elbow and forearm in contact with the table gripping his own bicep.

SIGMA DELTA PSI—UNIVERSITY of Illinois (Ben McGuire)

The national athletic fraternity is comprised of fifteen tests of all-around athletic ability. It can best be described as a "challenge" event in that the individual events in themselves are not difficult. For example, the small, fast, agile man has success in the gymnastic events and the 100 yard dash and difficulty in the shot put and football punt while the strong, powerful man has success in the shot put and football punt and difficulty in the hurdles. Recent reports indicate some problems in administration as this event is generally appointment oriented.

CANOE JOUSTING—Colgate (Francis Plano)

All you need are substantial canoes and two jousting sticks along with a cold lake for participant excitement.

PILLOW FIGHTING—Western Illinois University (John Colgate)

71

A variation finds two players, armed with stuffed pillow sacks, sitting on a balance beam trying to knock each other off.

BATACA—Long Beach City College (Bill Thompson)

A padded, one-handed arm extension with the contest judged by the number of clean blows to the body below the neck.

BIKE RACING—University of Indiana (Otto Berg)

From the "daddy of them all", the "little 500" at Indiana University which started as an IM event and is now a special weekend program in itself with 33 four man teams and 25,000 spectators. Northern Louisiana University (Charles Buck) features variety with sprint racing, slow racing, and tandom coed. Stanford (Dutch Fehring) is proud of their 10 mile race around the dorm complex with all roads blocked presenting outstanding spectator interest.

SABOT SAILING—Long Beach City College (Bill Thompson)

If you have access to a lake or bay and have a sailing club on campus to provide the expertise, this event should be a natural.

TURKEY TROT—UC, Berkeley (Bill Manning)

From a pre-Thanksgiving race at Berkeley with the winners awarded turkeys. Other possibilities include University of Illinois (Ben McGuire) 3 legged sack coed sack race and the football halftime obstacle race at Long Beach City College (Bill Thompson) starring participants going over hurdles, under tables etc.

GUYS AND DOLLS BASKETBALL—Purdue (George Haniford)

Played with 3 men and 3 women with the women shooting anywhere on the floor, and the men restricted from shooting inside the key area. The girls must handle the ball in the offensive end before a shot can be attempted. Sounds like fun to me.

MULTITATHLON—Purdue (George Haniford)

Three men from each organization in 3 activities selected at random in a total performance competition or a competition with a competition.

DRAG RACING—University of Texas (Jim Garrett)

The First Annual Drag Race will be held this year at the Dallas International Speedway, Time trials and handicaps will be used to allow all participants an equal opportunity to win. More important the Speedway is providing the all-important insurance coverage.

FACULTY-STAFF GOLF ASSOCIATION—University of Texas, Arlington (Jim Garrett)

For improved faculty-staff relations, try handicapping and scheduling 4 or 5 tournaments each season followed by a barbecue.

OPEN BOXING—USAFA (Keith Stowers)

If you offer boxing instruction in your physical education program, All-College Championships can very well become one of your stellar events. Expertise in training and control must be exercised.

SKI MEET—Northern Arizona University (Bill Blair)

All you need is a local mountain and some snow for a competitive event. Boston University (Larry Fudge) recommends a Ski Day subsidized by the Students Activities Office and planned by the Intramural Sports Department.

COED PENTATHLON—San Diego State College (Bill Manson)

Five events for total points to include the high jump, long jump, 100 yard dash, 440 and 880 that should prove to be quite a test. I only hope that it doesn't happen all in one day.

TUG-OF-WAR—University of Massachusetts (Pete Graham)

From the famous Beef Pull at the University of Massachusetts to the historic and infamous Frosh-Soph Lake Massasoit Rope Pull at Springfield College exhibits strategy, planning, and excitement at its best.

FISHING DERBY—University of Iowa (Marry Ostrander)

Sponsored by a local sporting goods store with gift certificates for winners in the catfish and walleye divisions. Promising?

BASIC OLYMPICS—University of Illinois, Chicago (Pete Berrafato)

A great all-around interest getter with 5 events to test all the skills with maximum laughs. Events include horse and rider, tug of war, rope climb, mile relay and the hop, skip, and jump.

"21" BASKETBALL—University of Illinois, Chicago (Pete Berrafato)

Three to five men, scoring 2 points from the free throw line and 1 point for the layup with scoring beginning and ending with the long shot.

BROOMSTICK POLO—Cornell University (Scotty Little)

Riding horseback with cornbrooms and a volleyball for thrills and chills. Possibilities even without horses?

KITE FLYING—Boston University (Larry Fudge)

Picture yourself along the Charles River, with your president Larry Fudge, flying your kite in competition for the highest, largest, etc.

FOOTBALL SKILLS CONTEST—USCGA (Nels Nitchman)

A combination of kickoff, punting, placekicks, and passing for accuracy in a senior "pass, punt and kick" competition that is extremely inviting to all football enthusiasts.

FRISBEE—CSCLB (Don Ludwig)

Why not? Using the International Frisbee Rules, a new segment of your campus can be involved.

SPACEBALL—Texas Tech (Edsel Buchanan)

Combining the skills of basketball and volleyball on a trampoline equals action unlimited. Passing the ball through a funnel to the opponent's side is the primary means of scoring.

WATER BASKETBALL—University of Texas, Austin (Sonny Rooker)

Played in deep water with modified water polo rules with a 2 point goal and a 1 point free throw in four 4 minute quarters of exhausting sport.

Makeshift backboards should suffice.

CENTURY CLUB—Long Beach City College (Bill Thompson)

A surreptitious way to fitness. One hundred miles of jogging, swimming or cycling at a ratio of 1:1, 1:4 and 5:1 respectively. A voluntary fitness activity that appeals to students, faculty and staff. T shirts are awarded to successful candidates with trophies to the leading milers. Mileage is submitted to the IM Office on chits provided.

SURFING CONTEST—Long Beach City College (Bill Thompson)

I am proud to report that LBCC conducted the first IM surfing contest in the USA, utilizing quarter, semi and final heats of 5 men each, with USSA judges. If they can do it in Phoenix, it can be done almost anywhere.

3 MAN BASKETBALL—Long Beach City College (Bill Thompson)

A very popular event with our students coming out of the shadows in a commuter school at 3 PM. For the first time, we conducted two divisions, 5'11" and under and 6' and over. The basic rules include scoring team's ball out, change of possession requires the ball to be taken back to the foul line extended, call your own fouls for possession and a general warning system for flagrant fouling by way of a roaming supervisor but no officials. There is nothing quite like watching the little man take his man inside for the hook.

Please feel free to contact any of the resources indicated for more information.

Applications of Rules Modifications in Intramural Sports
Ralph Stewart
(1968 NIA Proceedings, pp. 88-91)

The word "modification" should be stressed when dealing with the topic of rules and regulations for intramural sports. Rules may be divided into three major divisions: (1) rules pertaining to the activity, such as game or contest rules; (2) rules pertaining to participants, such as eligibility rules; and (3) rules pertaining to recognition, such as requirements for point systems or awards. This presentation will deal primarily with rules pertaining to the activity, because for most activities there is a set of generally accepted rules which are prepared by a recognized national authority for use by skilled performers. Eligibility rules, point systems, and awards generally are adapted to local situations.

In intramural sports the rules should be changed to fit the participants, the time, facilities, and equipment at your disposal. Also, some rules may be altered for ease of administration, since official rules were devised for ideal situations and conditions which are rarely available for an intramural sports program. In modifying the rules, however, you should keep the essence of the game. The activity is a part of the voluntary intramural sports program because it is popular, and too much modification will result in a loss of part of the game.

The great majority of the people who participate in intramural sports love to play the game but are not willing to devote the time and effort which are necessary to get into the type of physical condition required for optimum performance for an extended period of time. Since the safety and welfare of the participants should be of primary concern to the administrator of an intramural sports program, the obvious way to alter the rules to adapt the activity better to the condition of the participant is to shorten the amount of time played or the distance covered. In some cases where the activity does not lend itself easily to modification (such as boxing and distance events in track and swimming) it probably is better to eliminate the activity.

TEAM SPORTS

1. Touch Football

Adapt the game to the space available. We have had fields of different sizes, some with five fifteen-yard zones and some with five twelve-yard zones, and the players didn't even notice the difference! They are 120 feet wide rather than the 160 feet found on a regular football field.

Shorten the playing time. We play two twenty-minute halves and stop the clock only for called timeouts, penalties, scores, and unnecessary delays (as determined by the referee).

Ease of administration and *safety and welfare of the players.* To make judgment calls of student officials easier and to help prevent unnecessary roughness, a tackle is a one-hand touch between the shoulder and the knee. This avoid arguments about whether or not the tag was with one or two hands and whether or not the two-hand touch was simultaneous; also, the tag is less apt to be a forceful shove. A game of "one-hand touch" football seems to be a lot less rough than "rag-tag" football.

2. Basketball

Adapt the game to the space available. Shorter courts than the recommended maximum size for varsity basketball is better. You have extra baskets and more courts by playing "cross court."

Shorten the playing time. We play two ten-minute halves and stop the clock only for called timeouts, fouls, jump balls, and unnecessary delays.

3. Bowling

We use four-man teams, bowl three lines, but determine a winner by total pinfall for the team in three lines because the common scoring of four points as used in league bowling is too likely to produce ties.

4. Softball

A game consists of five innings. Games are scheduled one hour apart, including about ten minutes for pre-game warmup and a brief warmup between innings for the pitcher and infield. To conserve time, if competition is uneven and a team has a big lead, a team may elect to forfeit its turn at bat.

The pitch must be a slow pitch (no breaking pitches or curves) with speed enough to travel on a straight line to the batter. "Looper" or "blooper" pitches are not permitted, because they are too difficult for the umpire to judge accurately.

There must be a new pitcher every inning. This provides an opportunity for more players to be more versatile and develop more skills. It becomes a hitter's game with more hits, more errors, more baserunning, more runs, more exercise, and more fun!

No cleated or spiked shoes are permitted.

A catcher with glasses must wear a mask.

Bats must have at least ten inches of tape or cork on the handles.

INDIVIDUAL AND DUAL ACTIVITIES

In individual and dual activities such as handball, table tennis, and tennis, when we have a large number of entries and use a single elimination tournament, we limit the number of entries representing each organization to two men in singles and two teams in doubles, drag them into opposite halves of the tournament, and allow substitution or interchange during the first round. In handball, one game decides a match, the winner plays two matches a day, until the semifinals and finals when the match is determined by the best two out of three games and only one match a day is played. In table tennis, the best two out of three games determines a match until the semifinals and finals when the match is determined by the best three out of five games. In tennis, one set determines a match until the semifinals and finals, when it becomes the best two out of three sets.

1. Track and Field

For the safety and welfare of the participants we do not run any distance greater than the half mile or compete in the discus, javelin, pole vault, and shot put. All running events are run in heats and the winner is determined on a best time basis. No individual may compete in more than three events.

Participants are required to wear basketball or tennis shoes.

2. Swimming

We do not compete at any distance greater than 100 yards. Participants are limited to three events. Races are in heats and finalists are determined on a time basis. The swim meet is run off in four days.

3. Wrestling

Preliminary matches consist of three rounds of one-minute duration. Semifinal and final matches consist of three rounds of one and one-half minutes duration.

Headgear for all competitors is furnished for matches and may be worn.

If administratively feasible, it might be wise to require wrestlers to attend a certain number of supervised practices before competing.

SUMMARY

Game and sports rules are prepared for top athletes in excellent physical condition for activites conducted on ideal fields and courts. Most intramural participants are not top athletes and are not willing to work to get into the type of physical condition required for optimum performance; many intramural fields and courts are far from ideal.

Activities which lend themselves to rules modifications, without altering the activity too much, should be adapted to the condition of the participants and to the facilities which are available.

Iowa State's Cyclone 500
Alan Murdoch
(1971 NIA Proceedings, pp. 109-110)

Each year the Iowa State Intramural Department is host to the "Cyclone 500." This is a fifty mile team bike race. Although it is not unique to American Colleges and Universities our program at Iowa State certainly has aspects which may help many other schools adapt the competition to their own individual needs.

Bicycle History

Iowa State is noted for having a large percentage of students whose major means of transportation on campus has been bicycles. With the new encouragement of environmental conservation, bicycle riding on our campus pathways has increased. The Cyclone 500 was introduced in 1965 and for 5 years the race was held on a quarter mile outdoor track during Spring Quarter. In the fall of 1970, the race was held for the first time on a course around Iowa State's campus.

Race Requirements

Team divisions were mens, womens and co-rec. Each team had 8 riders (co-rec having 4 men and 4 women). The course is approximately one mile long. Each of the 8 team members had to ride a minimum of 5 miles. Pit areas were assigned to each team. It is within this area that repairs were made, rider interchange took place and times and laps were recorded. Any type of bicycle was used.

Equipment in certain instances was quite elaborate. Teams in top contention showed evidence of previous experience in such competition as European racing and Pan American game trials. The special equipment included materials such as crash helmets, special bicycle riding shoes, racing sweat suits, and, of course, specially equipped racing bikes.

A "Grand Prix" start was used for the race. Time trials were held to narrow the field to 12 teams. Random drawings were made to determine the starting order of the race. Team managers held the bicycles while the first team riders lined up 50 yards away. On the firing of the gun all riders sprinted to their waiting bicycles and "the race was on."

Interchanges took place in the 20-yard long pit areas only. The new rider replaced the old rider or started out on a different bike altogether. The first bicycle must be completely past the second bicycle before it can start. Most teams have two team members to stop one bicycle and two other members to push start the second bicycle. Efficiency in this area eliminated needless loss of time.

Each team furnished one timer and two lap counters. One lap counter would count for his own team and one lap counter would count for another team. The timer keeps track of elapsed time and individual lap time which many teams requested. One student supervisor was assigned as head track "marshall." His responsibilities were to check interchanges, keep a master log of laps and time, and coordinate track supervisors around the course. Eight student assistants were posted at strategic positions around the course. Four of these assistants were equipped with walkie-talkies which proved most valuable. An ambulance with qualified medical assistants was also available.

Many teams wore team colors so that they could descriminate their members from others. All riders were required to wear numbers on front and back for the benefit of the lap counters.

Rules of the track prevailed. Track marshall signaled riders with colored flags in appropriate situations: Green—Go, Red—Stop, (Dangerous-Caution), Black—Disqualified, Checkered—Victory. The race was over as soon as the first team has completed 50 laps. All other teams were placed according to the lap and place of their team when they complete the lap they are riding.

RECOMMENDATIONS

1. Have two lap counters per team. (One counter from own team and one from other team).

2. Require every participant on the team to go at least five laps or more. (Get together with these counters at least one hour before the race.)

3. Find out the fastest time for the Cyclone 500 so that the future teams may shoot for the team besides trying to win.

4. There absolutely should be a student trainer present.

5. Any speed of bicycle may be used.

6. Same technical rule on changing riders in the pit areas.

7. Have a list of participants on each of the teams for the participation records.

Chapter 6
Publicity, Promotion, and Public Relations

Communication Principles and Tools for Intramurals
Steve Newman
(1973 NIA Proceedings, pp.101-106)

In many of the sessions of the conference we will be discussing administration, activities and facility coordination all of which apply to program design. But once we determine what our intramural program is, how do we get the message of program opportunities to the participant? It is the purpose of this presentation to discuss basic communication principles and how we, at Illinois State, have used these principles to choose the tools of communication most effective in informing the participant of the intramural opportunities available.

Although the major emphasis of this presentation will be devoted to communicative tools, explanation of basic principles may better explain how we selected the channels to be discussed later.

Most of you are familiar with the basic communication model, the source being the encoder of the message, the channel, how the message is transmitted, the message itself, what is being encoded, and the receiver, the decoder of the message. When the model is specifically designed for our purposes, the source becomes the Intramural staff and the receiver the participant. The message and channel remain the same.

Communication is very effective on this basis; however, another element of the communication model is noise. Noise is distortion which may lead to hindrance or total breakdown in the communication process. Noise may affect either the message or the channel, or both. Some examples of noise which affect communication in intramurals are:

1) Messy bulletin boards
2) Uncomfortable meeting rooms
3) Caller receiving a busy signal when seeking information

There are three methods that may be used to alleviate or work around the noise problem. First pre-planning of communicative efforts in order that the noise factor may be eliminated. Secondly, a multi-channel approach may be used in hopes that the participant may be reached through at least one of the channels employed. Finally lines of communication may be developed which encourage feedback from the participant. When communication is designed to develop feedback and if feedback materializes it is known immediately whether or not the noise factor has affected the communicative effort.

This is a very brief and basic explanation of elementary communication principles. Since theories and principles are only as good as their implementation we shall now move into the tools of communication used at Illinois State to achieve our goal of informing the intramural participant.

At ISU we not only attempt to develop new communication tools, but also make effective use of standard means of getting our message to the student. How to use bulletin boards, student newspapers, departmental publications and other usual channels along with what we feel are unique practices of getting intramural information to the participant are the major emphasis of this presentation.

Our initial effort each year is to inform new students and reinforce returning students of the intramural activities available to them. The approach used is to arrange meetings with students in various campus living units, send a staff members to present an orientation film and offer students opportunities to ask questions and express opinions. The following film is the one we use to kick-off each of these sessions.

As previously mentioned an important aspect of these meetings is the interaction between students and the staff representative. The film is of such a nature as to expose the group to the activities, but not answer specifics of the program with a goal of encouraging feedback and promoting group interaction. Experience has shown that the film serves these purposes superbly.

Another standard practice we all employ is the use of bulletin boards as points of information for our programs. There are basic principles important to successful use of this tool.

Good location of the boards is imperative to quality bulletin board function. Frequently viewed areas and massive campus coverage enhance success of communication. Also attractive, neat and up-to-date boards will increase readership. At Illinois State we employ students to properly maintain over 150 campus bulletin boards. These students work 10-15 hours per week solely up-dating and renovating displays.

Publications are designed each year to provide participants with information needed to take part in ISU's Intramural Program. Our handbook, *Intramural Action,* outlined activities offered,program operations, eligibility requirements and recreation facilities available. These are distributed at all student meetings and are available upon request. Brochures for specific purposes, such as family or Campus Recreation, are printed and distributed massively to various interest areas. Monthly calendars with a day-by-day report of intramural events are posted through our bulletin board program. A yearly list of activities, entry periods and dates of play are also made available through the school year. Activity information sheets are distributed to all entrants and posted on all bulletin boards. These sheets contain all the information necessary for entry and participation in the designated intramural activity.

One of the most successful tools available to intramural administrators is the student newspaper. It is a relevant publication for students, since it is a report on their community. However, as many of us know, it is difficult to receive desired coverage in many of our newspapers. We are constantly fighting for space mainly devoted to intercollegiate sports. At Illinois State we attempted to work around this problem by requesting that articles which report results are the only ones to appear on the sports pages of the newspaper. General activity and facility information were transferred to the Campus News page. Although it did not completely alleviate the problem it did increase chances of publication.

In working with the student press you will find the following techniques can increase acceptance of your news.

Be sure that your request is newsworthy. Constant submission of insignificant news will turn editors off to all of your news. Be your own reporter and writer, making copy ready for print; this requires extra effort on your part but decreases work required of the newspaper staff. At Illinois State we employ a student writer to aid us in better newspaper coverage. Submit pictures whenever possible. Newspapers will lead toward printing news which is accompanied by an action photograph. Know your newspaper's deadlines and meet them. They have to. Stagger the amount of copy you submit; a deluge of copy decreases your chances of publication.

A meeting with the student editor, to get to know him and explain the importance of publicity to your program, and that without the support of the paper your program is less effective. Also a note or call of appreciation for good coverage can increase cooperation. Finally, don't expect all news to be printed, it just doesn't happen.

One of our direct channels of communication employed daily is the use of students as Intramural-Coordinators. These people are volunteers who represent their various living units as information sources for intramural activities. They make up our mailing lists and receive information periodically pertaining to events and details for participation. These students also feedback communication from their floors, whether it be a question of eligibility or a request for a staff member to make a presentation to members of the specific living unit.

A new communicative tool which was made available to our department this year was the student radio station. This medium has provided us with a new dimension in dispensing information to the student.

Each weekday morning Intramural and Campus Recreation news is broadcast to potential participants. A unique aspect of this program is that it is broadcast live, via telephone, from a Recreation Staff member's desk. Information pertaining to that day or important dates coming up are passed on to listeners.

One distinct advantage of this program is that information concerning changes or additions within the department may be announced to students as soon as they are known.

A major effort initiated this year at Illinois State is a five-minute program entitled Rec-Rap. The production is aired Sunday through Thursday evenings at 8:55 and is used to promote various aspects of the Campus Recreation and Intramural programs.

Members of the Intramural staff and student participants are featured in a multitude of programs to explain their particular areas of interest and responsibility. Programming varies from explanations of departmental operations, policies, special events, to promotion of student clubs and organizations.

Rec-Rap is taped a week in advance at a one to two-hour taping session. Tapes are then played on pre-assigned evenings and aired in place of the regular hourly news.

In addition to our regularly scheduled programming, special broadcasts are featured throughout the school year.

Halftime interviews at varsity football and basketball games provide us with an opportunity to discuss special program activities.

Play-by-play reports of intramural touchfootball and basketball playoffs have been initiated in line with increasing use of the student radio station to maximize the university community's awareness of our Campus Recreation and Intramural programs.

The radio has given us another channel to reach our participants by attempting to satisfy their information needs, exposure of their peers' interests, and the reporting of fellow students participating in intramural events.

Another conventional method used to assist our communication efforts is the telephone.

Using the telephone to inform participants of program changes, general information or tournament scheduling is the simplest, most economical method available when compared to the accuracy and guarantee of notification.

Our major goal in handling daily inquiry calls is to satisfy the information needs of the caller. This goal can be more easily attained by having professional staff members handle as many of these calls as possible as well as keeping the general office staff informed of program operations and changes to eliminate misinformation being passed on to the participant.

The telephone has provided an additional communication tool for use at Illinois State, the electronic answering service. The service, entitled Rec-Check, provides the caller with a recorded message of the day's activities, facility schedules, and information on events and meetings coming up.

Tapes are recorded in advance on daily cartridges and inserted by the staff secretary at the beginning of each day.

Rec-Check has proven to be so successful that consideration is currently being made to add another unit to handle the ever increasing number of calls and avoid the problem of a caller receiving a busy signal.

As mentioned previously the greatest communicative success is attained when the communication is two-way, i.e. feedback is channeled back to the source. At ISU several methods are employed to obtain this feedback.

Our major effort is the Intramural Advisory Board which is composed of student representatives from varying parts of the University community. The Board meets, periodically, with Intramural staff members to discuss various problems and recommendations affecting the I.M. program. The Board offers our staff the opportunity to react to student feedback and consider this information when formulating adjustments in the Intramural operations. A very important consideration to be made by the staff is to make the Board feel that they are a real function in the structure of the Intramural program and that their thoughts are carefully judged and appraised by staff members. It is extremely important that the staff be good listeners at these meetings and not mainstays of discussion.

Another channel used by our department is the team captain's meeting held before each team activity. These meetings are not only constructive for dispensing activity information but also for obtaining reactions to the Intramural programs.

Special program presentations by staff members to various living units provide us with yet another method of obtaining feedback. A letter offering each living unit the opportunity to invite staff members to meet with students, at their residence, was sent to all Intramural Coordinators. Meetings of this nature often arise out of a problem which has affected students' participation in Intramurals. This may cause an uncomfortable situation for the staff member; although you need not bring your own "tar and feathers," you should be prepared to seriously question the procedures administered by your office. A sincere effort to understand the group's concerns and provide students with valid reasoning for procedures used to formulate intramural policy will ease the situation and more often than not provide a means for absolving dissatisfaction.

A complaint or protest procedure is yet another tool used to increase feedback to administrators. This procedure is explained to all team captains at pre-season meetings and has proved to be very successful.

All individuals involved are contacted, personally by a staff member, after the report is filed. The facts are compiled and if necessary, the parties are called to appear before the Intramural Hearing Board. It is imperative that all individuals receive immediate reports as to action taken on a complaint or protest filed. If this step is not taken the credibility of the channel will rapidly decrease.

A final major tool used to obtain feedback at Illinois State is an "Open

Office Policy". We encourage all students to feel free to stop by the Intramural Office to meet with any staff member concerning questions, recommendations or reactions to any phase of the Intramural programs.

Despite all the previously mentioned tools used to inform students of the opportunities available in Intramurals at ISU, we are still planning additional programs to better inform the University community. Currently in the planning stages are a weekly newsletter, a bi-semester Intramural newspaper, a centrally located Intramural and Campus Recreation booth and use of the University's closed circuit television system.

That is a look at the communication program at Illinois State. Although few of the tools used are unique, a careful analyzation of the proper tools has given us a well-organized and successful approach to informing the student participant at ISU.

Introspection: Advertising and Promotion
Gary Colberg
(1975 NIRSA Proceedings, pp. 65-72)

Albert Einstein placed more importance on the use of imagination in the creation of new ideas than he did upon intelligence. While intramural directors as a whole (me included) are not pushing the outer limits of ingenuity, it goes without saying, that imaginative publicity next to proper facilities is the most important ingredient in the establishment of a successful intramural sports program. There is no other program in my opinion, that has a more diverse and sought after product than the area of recreational sport. And like McDonalds' Hamburgers, a good product needs constant exposure, emphasizing its desirable qualities, values, and opportunities to its potential users.

Promoting an intramural program properly, involves both enthusiasm and technique as well as imagination. Enthusiasm is completely embodied in the personage of the intramural director. Interests, talents, bias and environment are some of the underlying causal ingredients that result in good or poor publicity. Emphasis, therefore, is not on the promoter, but rather on the numerous techniques that can be imaginatively employed to assist a director's ability toward better publicity.

Many forms of media are available to use as publicity agents in promoting an intramural sports program. Basically, these media techniques break down into four types of formats:
1) The spoken word—person to person communication.
2) The written word—use of journalism primarily.
3) Photography—35 mm black-white pictures, slides.

4) Film production—16 mm film, color production.

The easiest and sometimes most complicated is the spoken word. It's older than prostitution and at times more perverted. Yet, it is the easiest method to expose a program's offerings and if properly used can have the most influence. Let me run down a few techniques I have seen used with a great deal of success.

1. *Freshmen—Transfer Student Orientation Sessions*—being present at many, if not all, of the orientation meetings set up for these new students.

2. *Special Campus Unit Retreats*—an excellent opportunity to share ideas with other directors who are in student affairs business.

3. *Residence Hall Floor Meetings*—at the beginning of each school year contact is made with the numerous resident hall advisors and head residents scheduling meetings with individual floors to explain the intramural program offerings as well as answer any questions students may have.

4. *Ethnic—Minority Functions*—attending and possibly speaking at these special functions such as Black Family Day, Native American Day, etc.

5. *Fraternity—Sorority Meetings*—making contact with the selected intramural representative and talking with members of each individual house.

6. *Faculty—Staff Gatherings*—since most campus intramural programs include staff and faculty members the opportunity to participate in many of its intramural activities, contact at lunch room areas, staff assembly meetings and faculty club gatherings is essential.

7. *Monthly Meetings With The Off-Campus Apartment Owners Association*—contact is made with each apartment owner to solicit assistance in disseminating program information and individual contact with the numerous occupants.

8. *Campus Radio Station*—daily sports show announcements of activity due dates, results and possible play-by-play broadcasts of the all-campus championships. Half-time interviews during intercollegiate events about unique features of the program.

9. *Television Appearances*—highlighting special activities that are new or appearing on a campus perspective show that discusses various aspects of campus activities. Contacting such national personalities as Charles Geralt and his *"On The Road"* travelogue to visit your program, or more local personalities such as Sacramento's Kent Pierce and his *"On The Go"* entourage.

Moving from the verbal communication to the written word or the various forms of journalism is perhaps the technique that most intramural program directors rely upon. It has greater potential to reach more people and can be referred often without taking the director's time as personal appearances do. Consider the following as possible avenues that appeal to the self-interests of potential intramural participants:

1. *Campus Daily Newspaper*—weekly columns on the various intramural events highlighting as many teams and participants. Hiring an intramural

editor whose by-lines might be Dices Delights, Freds Fables, or Glenn's Garbages with its 'trash forecasts'. Features on the infamous team names and of course entry due dates.

2. *Third World Newspaper* — if such a publication is printed on your campus, this can be an excellent media format to reach the various clinic minority groups.

3. *Calendar of Events* — printing several thousand wallet or pocket size calendars of activities, due dates and play begins information or three foot high posters of each quarter's offerings.

4. *Handbooks* — an old reliable method, but very expensive form of publicizing the program is the printing of handbooks. To reduce the involved expense, combined efforts with other non-academic units on campus in a common handbook is another avenue to proceed along. If your program extends into the summer, a completion of information regarding programs and services available for the campus and community entitled Anti-Boredum Manual is yet another tool.

5. *Municipal Newspapers* — special events and interest stories can become very instrumental in promoting the total intramural program.

6. *Billings On Transit Systems* — most campuses today have a bus transit system which carries thousands of students to and from campus. Clever billings on the exterior as well as interior can go a long way in advertising the intramural events offered.

The resources available on any campus are limitless, especially student resource. Couple a darkroom facility fully equipped with a capable photographer and suddenly an exciting promotional technique is available to the intramural director. Photographs are a necessity for use in newspapers, handbooks, activities displays and bulletin boards.

Sports photos are of two basic types: action and individual stills. Both of these types can be used in various combinations in an intramural hall of fame. Teams and individual/dual champions along with the outstanding action shots from those respective sports can be erected on the walls inside of the gymnasium. Students from past years can always return and see a pictorial account of their participation efforts. Present students who view the "wall of fame" are reminded of what is available in the program which may serve as a stimulus for their participation.

Color slides is another technique which can be used to present the program to orientation group gatherings. Slides can also be used at officiating clinics as a learning tool by isolating specific key situations.

The best use of photography today which seems to captivate the viewers' attention the most is 16 mm motion pictures. An entire program can be presented in its entirety through this media. Although expensive in terms of supplies and processing, cinema reproduction is the media of the future. Again the resources on your campus can go a long way in assisting you toward the completion of this exciting media production. Specific themes must be evident in each presentation that develops the action on the screen. A qualified narrator and well-written narration are almost as valuable as the camera person and processing lab. Below are two narrations that were developed on the Davis campus along with the respective motion pictures. Fortunately, the cinematography fits the narration in terms of quality making both films excellent forms of promoting the area of intramural sports.

EVERY DAY OF THE WEEK

Scene No. 1

The University of California at Davis has one of the most active intramural sports programs in the nation. The program sponsors more than 60 team and individual sports from co-ed wrestling to innertube water polo.

By far the most competitive *fall* sport is men's touch football...Basically a passing game, the use of plays like the flea flicker makes the style razzle dazzle.

Though the rules are structured to reduce the possibility of injury, touch football remains very much a contact sport.

Scene No. 2

The men are not the only fall footballers. Powderpuff, as "women's flag" football is called, attracts over 500 eager players each year.

Powderpuffers take their football seriously. Many hours are spent improving skills and working out plays—and the effort pays off.

The exciting playing style of teams like the Chastity Chargers, the Emerson Boozers and Deep Throw draw enthusiastic crowds.

Scene No. 3

1973 marked John Brodie's last and the powderpuffer's first appearance at Candlestick Park.

Invited to San Francisco as part of a "salute to women in athletics," two Davis teams—the D.U. Dolls and the Bod Squad played an exciting pregame exhibition to a packed house. It was the first time most 49er fans had seen women perform on the gridiron without twirling a baton—and they loved it.

The exhibition was so well received that the powderpuffers were invited back later in the fall for a repeat performance.

Scene No. 4

The skill displayed by the powderpuffers inspired the 49ers to trounce the Denver Broncos. Maybe what San Francisco needs is a good woman quarterback to show them how it's done.

Scene No. 5

A touch of inclement weather doesn't drench the intramural spirit—students want to play no matter what.

Scene No. 6

Although the quarters in the gym are cramped and small, the intramural program still provides a great variety of sporting activity in the winter. Scheduling at Davis is difficult as the facilities are shared with physical education and intercollegiate athletics. But the intramural staff somehow manages to accommodate all who want to play.

Scene No. 7

More than 4,000 students and members of the faculty and staff play intramural basketball. Leagues are set up to provide different levels of competition. The goal of the intramural program is to satisfy the player who seeks serious competition, as well as the one "just wanting to have fun."

Scene No. 8

Fans pack the gym for the basketball playoffs and no wonder—players are skillful and the action is fast, and the crowd gets to see what it came for—exciting basketball.

Scene No. 9

Waterballoon warfare has been the traditional signal that spring fever has arrived on the Davis campus.

Scene No. 10

In the spring, softball is king, with over 500 teams keeping 14 fields in constant use—*every day of the week*. Of all intramural events softball draws the broadest spectrum of players. Big and little, fast and slow, young and old, softball offers something for everyone.

Scene No. 11

In an attempt to satisfy those who never seem to get enough, the program offers open tournament play on Saturdays and Sundays. Some people now spend their *entire weekends* on the softball diamond.

Scene No. 12

In addition to softball in the spring, a young man's fancy turns to—water polo.

Scene No. 13

You don't have to swim well to play this brand of water polo. Created in 1969 by U.C. Davis Intramural Director, Gary Colberg, innertube water polo's popularity has grown tremendously, not only at Davis, but across the nation as well. On the Davis campus alone, participation in the sport has mushroomed from 9 teams to more than one hundred and seventy.

Scene No. 15

From mid-April to early June, tube polo keeps the campus' pool facilities busy every night from 5:00 to midnight.

Scene No. 16

Maybe it's the sunshine, or maybe it's the fellowship, whatever—co-ed soccer seems to attract the most ardent participants. Those who play truly love the game. Hundreds of players spend their afternoons kicking not only the ball, but each other.

Scene No. 17

In addition to regularly scheduled play, the intramural program has many special events on its spring time agenda. The first, held in early May, is the annual co-ed swim relay.

Scene No. 18

The co-ed diving, sprint, and relay competition attracts over 300 men and women athletes to the one-day event.

Scene No. 19

These relays allow most swimmers a unique opportunity to swim competitively against the clock.

Scene No. 20

Many campus clubs that engage in off-campus athletic competition are partially funded by the intramural sports program. In this way students have the opportunity to take advantage of competition in sports like rugby, sailing, skiing, skydiving and bicycling.

Scene No. 21

Through the extramural program, the Rugby Club plays many visiting rugby teams. Here, they tangle with EBBA Vale, a tough touring club from Wales.

Scene No. 22

The final activity on the intramural calendar is the annual men's and women's track meet, which has, since 1936, traditionally ended the intramural year.

Scene No. 23

Regular track and field competition, as well as novelty events like the fat man 100 yard dash and the 880 yard walk, attract every caliber of athlete to this season finale.

Scene No. 24

Through the regular school year, more than 9,700 students and members of the faculty and staff take full advantage of more than *60 different activities* offered by the Davis intramural program. *Big time college sports* may dominate at U.C.L.A. and Notre Dame, but at Davis, intramural sports is *where the action is* — every day of the week.

TENTH ANNUAL ALL-CAL INTRAMURAL SPORTS WEEKEND

Scene No. 1

In an age of million dollar sports spectaculars — where every game is bigger and better than the last — where super bowls and matches of the century make headlines—the annual All-Cal sports weekend symbolizes another side of athletic competition—where friendship and fun are more important than bonus offers and gate receipts.

Scene No. 2

This last year, two hundred and seventy men and women from the nine University of California campuses travelled to Santa Barbara for the tenth annual *All-Cal Intramural Sports Weekend*. The All-Cal weekend is financed through the campus interchange program to stimulate the growth of intramural sports throughout the UC system.

Scene No. 3

The competition began almost immediately and, for two days, the university's fields, pools and courts were filled with an atmosphere of friendly and spirited competition...this year each campus sent one team for each of the five All-Cal sports: tennis, badminton, volleyball, water polo and of course softball (the beer drinkers favorite). Students selected to make the trip were chosen on the basis of regular season and tournament play at their respective campuses.

Three years ago in an attempt to deemphasize competition and to encourage cooperation and sportsmanship, the All-Cal weekend went totally and equally coeducational. Now, as every participant can tell you, the games have become more social and competition has become much more relaxed. This year intramural directors made another important change. They decided, in addition to mixing sexes, they would mix schools. As an experiment, some of the games were played by teams which were formed by uniting the men from one campus with the women from another. Here, the Berkeley women and the Davis men teamed up to play UCLA and UC Riverside. In this game, the Berkeley women showed everyone how softball should be played!

Scene No. 4

As the afternoon sun moved toward the Pacific, the action commenced on the green asphalt surfaced tennis courts. Mixed doubles was the game here, and players quickly learned how to mesh their skills with those of their partners. The warm spring sunshine and the clear Santa Barbara air provided the perfect atmosphere for some great court work.

Scene No. 5

Whenever the athletes weren't playing, it seemed like they were eating...and the hosts did a great job in satisfying over two hundred seventy voracious appetites.

Scene No. 6

Meanwhile...back in the Gym...the badminton enthusiasts seriously got down to battering that bird...

Scene No. 7

Innertube water polo, created on the UC Davis campus, has gained national recognition as one of the most popular coed sporting activities. Supported by a used innertube. Now anyone, regardless of swimming skills, can play the fascinating game of water polo.

The highpoint of the All-Cal polo competition was the contest between Davis and Irvine. It would be an understatement to say that water polo is "popular" on these two campuses.

Scene No. 8

Volleyball, whether played on the beach or in the gym, has always been one of California's most popular sports...of all the games played at the All-Cal, it was the one which required the most teamwork and concentration. Here too, in some of the competition, single teams were composed of players from two different campuses. However, the newness of team membership didn't destroy the quality of the game. Competition was filled with many spectacular rallies and great team play.

Scene No. 9

As the final points were played and the weekend drew to a close, the tired athletes packed their playing gear, said goodbye to the many new friends they had made, and headed home — satisfied that the All-Cal weekend was a worthwhile and enjoyable experience.

Mass Media in Intramural and Recreation Programs
Bob Thompson
(1974 NIA Proceedings, pp. 27-28)

Intramural and recreation programs are designed to meet the needs and interests of students through a wide variety of activities. A vital concern of these programs is the communication of schedules, announcements, and sports information. The promotion of an appropriate campus image through various types of publicity is another program essential. In short, public relations is an integral part of any effective intramural and recreation program.

In a society which is functioning at an ever increasing rate, communications have become the key to good public relations. Many methods have been used effectively in intramural and recreation programs throughout the country. Among them mass-communications or mass-media types are perhaps the most effective. Radio, TV, newsletters, and newspapers are obviously among the best methods. All of these are available to program directors who are willing to utilize them.

The intramural program at Oklahoma State University has offered a wide variety of activities designed to meet the needs and interests of the student body for many years. In connection with these programs a number of new and useful public-relations ideas have been developed. One such addition has been the Game of the Week project. This feature highlights one game each week through appropriate communication media. The two teams involved generally include one of last year's winners or a top contender moving up through the ranks. The idea, borrowed from Monday night football and similar television productions, is publicized through the University newspaper, the Intramural newsletter, the campus radio station, and various campus bulletins. Through the cooperation of several broadcasting-communication students, play-by-play commentary is recorded for each game while all contests played indoors are video-taped along with the commentary. Both arrangements provide opportunity for replays at later dates. These recordings are of special interest to the participants along with offering a means of publicizing the program throughout the campus. The heightened interest, increased participation, and publicity gained from the project combine to make it a beneficial program addition.

Newletters have proven themselves as effective means of communication for a number of years. The Colvin Center Courier has emerged recently as such a publication on the Oklahoma State University campus. An attractive orange letterhead gains students' attention as the newsletter is posted all across campus. Bulletin boards in the student union, classroom buildings, residence halls, and all the fraternities and sororities display its announcements. The bulletin is also sent to department heads and administrators throughout the University. Special events, building hours, meetings, and deadlines related to intramurals and the operation of the Colvin Physical Education Center are communicated in the weekly newsletter. The nominal expense and effort required to initiate and maintain the newsletter more than justify its use in conveying intramural and recreation program news.

Both the "Game of the Week" Colvin Center *Courier* have provided avenues for gaining additional publicity through the student newspaper and radio station. These two special projects, combined with extensive efforts to explain and promote the program, have gained regular publicity by these two media. The student newspaper has assigned one reporter to each member of the recreation and intramural staff so that program information could be reported accurately with regularity. This arrangement was the end result of regular reporting and special attempts to cooperate with the sports editor. Initially, scores were reported daily during each major sport. Then written descriptions of newsworthy items were sent each week to obtain added publicity. Telephone reporting of special events was also helpful. All of these efforts have established a good working relationship with the student newspaper. For example, the sports editor frequently supplements his regular assignment by requesting additional information when room is available. Also, the *Courier's* announcements are used on a regular basis and are often repeated as filler items. As a result adequate publicity, comparable to varsity athletics, has served to promote the program while informing students of its activities.

Radio coverage developed and increased following these previous public relations endeavors. A weekly description of the Intramural scene is aired on the campus station. Actualities, or on the spot reports, are also produced frequently. These reports often include taped or telephone interviews with the program directors and supervisors. Every possible effort has been made both at work and at home to provide this assistance. Additional program information has been made available to the student body through this development.

In summary, good public relations is a boon to any intramural and recreation program. The Game of the Week feature has been of particular importance in promoting the program at Oklahoma State University. It has combined with traditional methods of securing publicity through the newsletter, newspaper, and radio mediums to effectively inform the campus community. Cooperation with news personnel has always been a key to good public relations. These experiences have echoed that premise.

Publicity at Texas A and M: The Total Concept
Susan Schleider and Greg Claeys
(1976 NIA Proceedings, pp. 100-103)

As an Assistant Director at Texas A & M, I am in charge of running the individual and duel competitive sports program and publicity. One of my primary functions in regard to publicity is communicating information to the students. You may have an incredible Intramural program, fantastic facilities, superior officials, and the finest staff possible; but, unless the students know what you have to offer, your Intramural program is worthless.

We at Texas A & M have experienced a tremendous growth rate the last three years either because of our communication system or in spite of it. I would like to describe to you how we do what we feel we do best.

First, an overview of our system. We feel that avenues open to Intramural administrators are — (a) paid advertising in the school newspaper, local newspaper or on broadcast media; (b) printed materials, such as fliers, pamphlets, calendars, newsletters, and the Handbook distributed through the Intramural Office; (c) audio-visual presentations; (d) publicity given the program by the campus and local newspapers, radio and television stations; (e) the final and most effective yet least controllable is word of mouth. If people participate and enjoy themselves, they will tell others and before you realize it, Intramural participation will become contagious as well as addicting.

We all know that handbooks, pamphlets, and campus calendars are effective as well as necessary for promoting and distributing information. These printed materials are vital for providing the student with the general information he needs concerning Intramural participation.

A dynamic way of creating an awareness of Intramurals is with slide presentations. See is believing, and we have found slide presentations to be extremely successful in sparking interest. The first type of slide presentation we use gives the viewer general information of our total Intramural program. We show this at student orientations, resident hall advisors meetings, P.E. Majors Club meetings, and wherever possible. It tells people who we are, what we do, and where they can find us for additional information. This general series was prepared professionally by our Media Production Center on campus with the exception of the script, which was written by our staff. It cost us $125.00 for 140 slides. We feel this was an exceptionally good price.

Another type of slide presentation we use is for demonstration purposes. It illustrates and explains the rules of an upcoming sport. This type works unbelievably well for obscure sports such as innertube water polo. This is reasonably easy to do. Take several slide shots of the sport, either posed or actual. Have the slides developed, write a narrative and coordinate the two with music. For $15.00 we have a slide presentation we are proud of. The benefits from doing your own presentation are well worth the time and effort required. This type of presentation is perfect to show at team managers meetings and officials meetings. It adds some spice and variety to an otherwise ordinary meeting.

There is an old axiom, "It pays to advertise". Well, just how much does it pay? We felt to measure the effectiveness of our processes of disseminating information, a study of the campus student population of Texas A & M was needed. A random sample was polled by a telephone survey, administered independently of the Intramural Office. It was undertaken by a senior marketing student. Preliminary results from this study will be used throughout this presentation when discussing various means of advertising.

Sign-up deadlines are a necessary evil to any organized program. For major team sports, it is difficult to inform students when entries open and close. It seems participants know the month a sport begins, but rarely the closing entry date. To combat this, we decided to experiment by placing a quarter page ad in the campus paper three to four days prior to the entry closing date. We did this for volleyball, basketball, and softball. We believe these ads were partially responsible for a netted increase of 40 to 56 per cent. Also, we found that the number of people attempting to enter teams late was significantly reduced. Each ad ran us about $60.00 but these proved so beneficial that we budgeted $1000.00 for this next year.

Sometimes with the quantity of information to be distributed a shotgun approach may be needed. Using diversified channels of communication, a larger number of participants may be reached.

A frequently overlooked approach is through newsletters. Our newsletter, a copy of which is in your packet, is entitled IMPACT and was initiated this past semester. It is published on a monthly basis. In this, we strive to recognize individual and team champions. Face it. There is a little vanity in everyone. People love to see their name in print, especially as being a winner. Also included in the newsletter are participation statistics, IM Tidbits, Watch and Enter, and Special Event announcements. Do not forget that the important features of any newsletter are clarity and conciseness. Our format is geared to the student in a free and easy style. The only limitation in using the newsletter is one's creativity.

Sponsored advertising such as the McDonald's Intramural Highlights Ad has previously been discussed at past conventions but should not go untouched. In the study conducted at Texas A & M, 80 per cent of the students had seen the McDonald's Ad. We attribute much of this to the very broad distribution of our school paper, the *Battalion*. "Repetition is reputation." Since the McDonald's Ad is printed on a weekly basis, many students look forward to reading the ad. We hired a student worker with journalistic and photographic ability to work 25 hours a week on preparing the ad. With awareness of the ad at such a high level, McDonald's now is happy to sponsor the ad, but this was not always the case. For those of you who do not have someone to sponsor your highlights, let me tell you that a selling job is required. Asking an advertiser, in our case for 2,000 dollars, represents a substantial investment on his part. When approaching a potential sponsor, be sure you are prepared with distribution figures, cost of the ad, and above all, stress the advantage the buyer will derive. Being thoroughly prepared is paramount.

If the students on your campus were asked, "What is the last source of information or announcement that you remember seeing concerning Intramurals", what would their answer be? In the study, 40 per cent of the students polled said *fliers!* Since almost every school uses fliers to publicize Intramurals, many times we overlook their importance. They are easy as well as fun to prepare, reach a large group, and cost very little. The thing to remember is to make your fliers "jump out" so the student wants to stop and read it. You need "Fliers with Flash." Here's your chance to let your imagination run wild. Be clever. Use your sense of humor and wit. We have found that caricatures and cartoons on brightly colored paper stand out and are widely read. Now that you have have got their attention, be sure they get your message. The *Who, What, When,* and *How* are required.

At Texas A & M we are blessed to have an agency at our disposal called *Hassle Free!* It is an organization composed of off-campus students formed by the Student Government Service Committee. Their function is to distribute campus information to apartment complexes. The majority of A &

M students live off-campus. A Hassle Free representative comes by the Intramural Office weekly and picks up any information we have and distributes it to the apartment complexes and posts them on bulletin boards, by mailboxes, and in laundry rooms. Hassle Free has done a remarkable job for us. If you do not have a group like Hassle Free on your campus, then it will be well worth your time to approach the Service Committee of your Student Government in an attempt to instigate one. If this fails, you could have your Intramural Council or student workers help in this area.

When shooting indoors, a flash was used only when lighting conditions were excessively dark. Although the flash brilliantly illuminates the subject, the background will become dark because of the diffusion of the light source. Therefore, the flash attachments available — Honeywell electronic models: Strobonar 770 and Strobonar 330 — were used only when necessary. When using a flash, daylight film was used since the flash has the physical characteristics of daylight rather than tungsten lighting.

Our approach to photographing the activities was predicated on the premise of capturing not only dynamic sports' shots, but also crowd reactions and other relevant human interest pictures which reflect the "total latitude" of the intramural program. By the close of the 1969-70 school year, over 1000 slides had been taken.

In order to have the presentation ready for the fall semester of the 1970-1971 school year, work was begun in the summer season. The decision was made to utilize three projectors simultaneously. (The University of Illinois' Department of Architecture, for example, uses six projectors simultaneously in some of their slide presentations on facilities.) The primary objective of our effort was to develop a publicity technique to show to campus living groups: it was found that most campus residences had a room which would accommodate three 70" span screens placed next to each other. In addition, the three slide simultaneous sequence leads itself to certain aesthetic considerations.

Kodak Carousel slide trays — two trays for each projector — were used. Holding 80 slides each, the six trays allowed for the use of 480 slides. Since over 1000 slides had been taken, the better half of our efforts were assured of being edited. When three projectors are operated continuously at a brisk pace with two trays of 80 slides at each projector, the length of the presentation approximates twenty minutes.

The slides were then organized in chronological order corresponding to the yearly sequence of the intramural activity program. As the initial event in the fall semester, football was the first sport illustrated in the presentation. The selection of slides for every sport was accomplished in a multiple of three. For football, for example, 30 slides were selected — ten for each projector. As a result, the slide show included ten football sequences. The three slides for each sequence were randomly selected from the 30

There are a few, and I do mean a few, times during the academic year when a large group of the student population can be reached with relative ease. Since these occurances are rare, be sure to capitalize on them. Registration is one of these times. Since most handouts seem to be 8½ by 11, we put Intramural calendars on 4 by 10 colored sheets. It differentiates itself by shape alone. Do not be discouraged if some end up in the trash cans because it is the beginning of creating awareness of Intramurals. Another excellent location to reach a large portion of students at once is at the friendly campus police station. You are probably thinking that the campus police are an uncooperative bunch. Well, I think our staff keep the police in business; we get our share and more of the parking tickets. But look on the bright side; they do allow us to use their counter as a distribution point for our schedules. Eventually most students pass by the counter the first 10 days of school either picking up a parking permit or paying a ticket. A bit of IM information is usually more appealing than a poster provided by the Department of Public Safety while they stand in line.

Look around your campus. I am sure you have times when concentration of students is inevitable. They will appreciate a little nonacademic literature to pass the time while they wait in line. Who knows how many teams begin here.

The obvious places to distribute information to the highest traffic areas are student centers, dormitories, classrooms, and recreational facilities. But everyone uses these general areas so yours may be overlooked.

First think of your *own facilities*. Mailboxes located in the Intramural Office are pigeon holes for established teams. Team managers may check these on a daily basis. Also equipment checkout counters are a wonderful spot for Intramural fliers.

Strategic location of bulletin boards in your facility and around court areas are effective. For instance, by our handball/racketball courts there are bulletin boards we use to illustrate the current month's activities and deadlines. Apartment complexes, laundry rooms, mail box areas, and around swimming pools are perfect places to catch the attention of the potential participant.

We have found that awarding T-Shirts for All-University provide a walking paid ad. Award ceremonies or steak frys provide additional recognition and everyone has a fun time. You would be surprised how your office and your staff reflect the Intramural attitude. Every aspect of carrying out an Intramural program publicizes your program. Make sure it is an enjoyable and pleasant experience. And here is where word of mouth comes in! Participants will spread the good word.

As you can see there are numerous ways of promoting Intramurals, and I have just briefly touched on a few. Just remember to be creative, try anything once, use your sense of humor, and do not be afraid to really let go.

You are the best publicity your program has. If someone were to pay you to be a walking, talking, breathing Intramural ad, how much would you be worth?

Developing a Multimedia Presentation
James A. Peterson and Harvey Rogoff
(1971 NIA Proceedings, pp. 46-49)

In September, 1969, the University of Illinois' Division of Intramural Activities initiated steps to develop a photographic slide presentation which would serve as a contemporary means to illustrate the many activities in the intramural program. The inspiration for this attempt was provided by a slide show technique used by the Dean of Students' Office to acquaint incoming freshmen with the campus and to orient them to the University way of life. Using several projectors simultaneously, and coordinating the show with music, this presentation had been enthusiastically received by the student audiences.

Recognizing the potential of this technique as a publicity tool for the Division, action was undertaken to "put together" a comparable presentation which would attractively present our program of intramural activities. Beginning with the fall semester, every intramural activity was photographed using a Nikon F Photomic TN camera with a 50 mm f/1.4 lens. A Vivitar 85 mm-205 mm F/3.8 zoom lens was used to capture images two to four times larger than the 50 mm lens. The zoom lens was most useful when photographing outdoor sports which are played on large fields, such as soccer and football.

Kodak High Speed Ektachrome color slide film was used exclusively. The High Speed Ektachrome is available as either an outdoor film called Daylight or as an indoor film designated Type B. Type B is made for rooms with tungsten lighting; that is to say, rooms with lightbulbs or spot lights. Type B has an ASA rating of 125 but can be used with a rating of 320, coupled with a nominal extra development charge when processed by the Kodak Company. The same is true for the Daylight film. It has an ASA rating of 160 but has a potential range of up to a rating of 400 if the user is willing to pay an extra charge. The advantage in shooting film at a higher ASA is that pictures can be taken at either a faster shutter speed to help stop the action, a smaller aperature to increase the depth of field, or a combination of both.

Most of the activities were shot at either 1/500 or 1/100 of a second. These shutter speeds consistently stopped all movement of the human body. For a presentation of this type, however, it is suggested that a blurred arm or leg often does more to imply motion than does a static figure. To achieve this effect, shutter speeds ranging from 1/30 to 1/125 of a second were used.

slides chosen for use. After the ten sequences had been randomly selected, a sequential order for the three slides in each sequence was determined. If, for example, a sequence consisted of a huddle, a quarterback throwing, and an end catching the football, it was determined that the slides would be presented in that order. Subsequently, a script or chart was made for each sequence:

Sequence	Projector 1	Projector 2	Projector 3
1	2	1	3
2	1	2	3
3	3	2	1
4	2	1	1

As in the case of sequence four, it might be best to simultaneously show the slides in projectors two and three and then show the slide in projector one.

By following this chart, it was possible to change the proper slide in the proper order so that a feeling of continuity in time could be conveyed. Further editing of slides from different sequences and from the extra slides in storage produced a sense of continuity for each of the 160 sequences in the show.

After the slides had been edited, the next step was to select and record the music to be played during the presentation. While selection is purely a matter of taste, the pace of the music should approximate the "dynamic" pace of the subject matter and the fast changing of the slides. Although many students enjoy the pulsating beat of hard rock, there are also those that appreciate pop or classical pieces in fast time.

Since the presentation consisted of 20 minutes of slide-action, five musical pieces of about four minutes each were selected. However, the number of selections is primarily a matter of artistic judgement and is completely flexible. After the final musical selections had been taped, notes detailing the length of each song and the exact number of the sequences to be covered by each musical selection were written on the previously mentioned script or chart. This enables the operator of the three projectors to follow the progression of the slides and music with a stop watch so that he can better coordinate the presentation. The football sequences, for example, could be terminated at the end of a specific musical selection.

After the selection of both the slides and music has been completed, the next step was to master the all important audio-visual coordination between the two. It is possible to electronically program three projectors and a tape recorder if the proper equipment were available. The cost and reliability of such an endeavor is, however, quite prohibitive. The alternative method of operation for this type of presentation is to coordinate the technique manually. In this case, it was necessary to practice the presentation *numerous* times in order to establish various audio-visual cues which would serve to eliminate any coordination errors.

It is recommended that projectors having remote control, automatic focusing, and a zoom lens be used for this presentation. The remote control device is a necessity because it enables the operator to control all three projectors from a single spot. The automatic focus, by eliminating the need of the operator to be concerned with the focusing, enables the operator to concentrate on the script or chart for the presentation. The zoom lens enables the operator to adjust the image size on the screen by merely turning the lens rather than by moving the projector, the screen, or both. It is also suggested that the largest screens available be used in order to enhance the presentation by making the projection large.

Student and faculty reaction to the initial showings of this presentation has been highly favorable. The use of this multi-media means of communications offers the intramural administrator a contemporary tool to achieve informational, publicity, and motivational objectives.

Chapter 7
Eligibility Rules

Guideposts for Intramural Eligibility
J. A. Jevert
(1966 NIA Proceedings, pp. 97-99)

It is indeed a pleasure to have been asked to participate in this program and share with you some thoughts on the topic of Intramural Eligibility.

I believe that most of us will agree that a successful program of intramural activities can be operated with very few rules. However, for the protection of the individual participants and the administrative personnel, it is necessary to establish definite rules regarding student eligiblity.

Four years ago when we at Western Michigan University were given the green light to expand our program of intramural sports, one of the first steps undertaken was to write to some of you who are seated in the audience today, who have been involved in the operation of highly successful intramural programs. I received much valuable information from leaders in our field such as Pat Mueller at the University of Minnesota, Earl Riskey at the University of Michigan, Dave Matthews at the University of Illinois, and many others.

Let us take a brief look at four guideposts and consider some of the implications they may have in determining eligibility for use in other programs.

The first and most important guidepost is that of Physical Condition. A student should be allowed to participate in the intramural sports program provided this participation is planned and conducted within the individual's physical limitations. The physical well-being of the student must be considered in the operation of any intramural activity. Many of our leading institutions at one time required health classification cards which had to be presented before a student could be classified as eligible for intramural participation. However, in examining many of the programs from some of our outstanding institutions today, I find that the health examination is becoming less and less a prerequisite for participation in intramural sports.

In my own university, the health classification card which was designed to provide the student with an up-to-date record of his physical condition, determined by a yearly examination, is becoming a thing of the past.

Today, due to the increased enrollments at the majority of our institutions and because of the tremendous growth in the number of participants in intramural sports, a compulsory physical examination once a year is impractical. Therefore, the so-called physical requirements for intramural participation have been amended to read something like the following:

101

Each participant in the intramural sports program should (and I emphasize should) have a physical examination once a year. Participation in intramurals is considered to be verification that the student is in reasonably sound physical condition.

The second guidepost to consider is that of scholastic achievement. The old rule of restricting a person from intramural participation on the basis of scholastic requirements did not appear justifiable and has since been eliminated from the majority of programs in operation today. It does not seem reasonable to deny a student the benefits he may derive from participation in the intramural sports program just because he is failing in one or two subjects. Educators must realize that the intramural sports program is an integral part of the total educational concept, and that participation in such a program can contribute greatly to the individual's total development and education. Other subjects and campus activities, if they are to be educationally worthwhile, must carry their own appeal. Eligibility in intramural sports should not, and must not, be used in any way as a means to force to make the participant pass his academic subjects. It is not conceivable to deprive a student from participating in the intramural sports program because he is failing in freshman reading or chemistry. On the other hand, it would be even more illogical to restrict a student from enrolling in freshman reading who failed to participate in the intramural program.

With the upgrading of admittance standards that most institutions are experiencing today, there is little if any justification in eliminating a student from participation because of his scholastic standing. If he qualified for admittance into the school, he should be allowed to participate. We must keep in mind that the fundamental purpose of our programs is to provide every student the opportunity to compete and participate in an athletic or recreational activity of his own desire and interest.

A third area of consideration that any successful intramural sports program must regulate is the area of individual eligibility. Generally speaking, most intramural programs require first of all that the participant be a student that is currently enrolled in either the undergraduate or graduate program being offered by that institution.

It must be kept in mind that in developing the policies that regulate individual participation, the aim and the spirit in which these rules are upheld is of paramount importance. It is impractical, if not impossible, to devise rules and regulations that will cover every phase of the program. If the students are educated as to the spirit, the aims and purposes, and when they clearly understand the importance of preserving the intramural level of competition for the intramural participant, they will accept more readily the rules which govern the individual's participation.

Except in a very few instances, most intramural sports programs include some of the following individual regulations. No varsity letterman be allowed to compete or participate in that sport or its associated sport in which he has received a varsity letter. In many cases, it is also wise to restrict these letter winners from sports other than those in which they received varsity recognition, due to the tremendous advantage gained through the training and coaching programs available only to varsity athletes. Many people believe, because of their natural ability and the superior coaching, practice, condition and training habits gained through varsity participation, they would tend to dominate the activities in an intramural program. This seems to be more applicable in the areas of track, football, and basketball. In the recreational activities, such as bowling, golf, swimming, and tennis where a more specific skill is required, this philosophy of dominance does not seem to exist. No student should be allowed to participate with more than one team in a specific activity. Many programs interpret this rule to mean that a participant may not transfer from one team to another in the same sport. His first competition with the team in a given sport definitely attaches him to that team for the remainder of the season in that particular sport. Any student who has been declared a professional athlete in a particular sport or its related activity would not be eligible. One of the programs which I have had the opportunity to examine recently, carries this idea further to include the elimination of any student practicing on, or competing with any off-campus, city, or commercial team. Any student who participates under an assumed name would be eliminated from that sport for the remainder of the year and quite possibly, as indicated by some programs, would be expelled from intramural participation entirely for the remainder of the school year. These are just a few of the specific rules and regulations which must be considered regarding individual eligiblity.

The fourth and final guidepost which I would like to mention is that of organizational eligibility. Participating organizations, which should be clearly defined, have additional eligiblity rules that must be met by their members. Such participating organizations might include fraternities, dormitories, and independent clubs.

It is also important in cases of an organization having several teams entered in one sport that the personnel of each team remain stable throughout the active competition in that particular sport. The individual would be eligible only for the organization's team for which he first played.

The problems of eligibility have become even more complicated because of the increase in the amount of unscheduled time the student has while on the campus. Classes are now being scheduled in blocks, where a student attends class fewer days per week for longer periods of time. In some courses the students are given an assignment at the first scheduled meeting of the class and are not required to attend a formal class meeting again until the final exam. Shorter terms, more concentrated course content, year-

103

round operation, all have increased the demand for more comprehensive intramural programs in todays colleges and universities. With this demand, the need for the development of adequate guideposts to regulate the eligibility of the participants involved becomes a greater challenge for us all.

Eligibility Rules: Are They Enforceable?
Gary Adams
(1966 NIA Proceedings, pp. 100-102)

Practically every college and university has a list of eligibility rules for their intramural program. I won't attempt to describe or list the various eligibility rules used in the colleges because each institution usually has its own unique set of rules to serve their own purpose. But, in general, eligiblity rules are set up primarily for the purpose of equalizing the competition. Although an intramural director should be concerned with enforcing these eligiblity rules, it is my opinion that too many college intramural directors place an excessive amount of emphasis and spend too much of their time on checking the eligibility of their participants.

From my own brief experience in intramurals and from the discussions I have had with other college directors who have all used a variety of methods to enforce their eligibility rules, I have learned that eligibility rules **are not**, and, most often, **cannot** be 100 per cent enforceable. In other words, I have yet to discover a practical system which will completely eliminate ineligible players from competing if they really want to do it.

Perhaps the only college that may be able to completely enforce all those eligibility rules necessary to run an effective program is the one with a program consisting of a very small number of participants. For these smaller institutions, the investigation is usually done by sending a list of participants to the Dean of Students' Office where the names are checked to see if the participants are officially enrolled in school, how many units they are taking, and if they have the necessary grades to participate. Besides being time consuming, the intramural staff still may not always learn from the Dean's Office whether a player has lettered in a certain varsity sport at another college nor can they always learn if he belongs to a certain organization. But, even if you could discover all you wanted to know about an individual from the Dean's Office or from any other source and even if there are few participants in your program — is the time and effort spent doing the investigating really worth it? I do not think so.

I do not wish to imply that an effort should not be made to eliminate ineligible participants; on the contrary, I believe wholeheartedly in eligibility rules if they are not too extensive and if they can be made clear to the students. I am merely saying that intramural directors and their staff should not over-emphasize this particular phase of the program to the point where they spend their valuable time acting as a detective agency or a police force for the students. It is my opinion that, regardless of the method of enforcement employed, eligibility rules will be broken and **sometimes** the violators will be "caught" and **sometimes** they will not be caught.

Now I would like to recommend what I consider to be an effective way of checking the eligibility of participants, but, like most other methods, it is by no means 100 per cent effective. Yet, it is not at all time-consuming for an intramural department regardless of staff and participants in the program. Plus, it places the responsibility of checking for violations of the eligibility rules on the students themselves—and this, in college, is where it should be placed. Briefly, I would suggest that a director and his intramural department indirectly enforce its eligibility rules by following the procedures listed below.

1. Publish a handbook which clearly lists all the eligibility rules. Make these rules easily noticeable—do not "hide" them in the handbook.

2. Distribute these handbooks to all intramural managers especially, and to persons representing all of the organizations and dormitories on campus. "Left-over" handbooks may be distributed afterwards to the general student body.

3. Conduct a mandatory meeting early in the semester and just before the first major sport begins for all intramural team managers of that sport and read each eligibility rule—one by one—aloud to them so that any questions they have can be answered and so they understand them.

4. Explain the penalties for individual and team violators of these rules and emphasize that the intramural department will strictly enforce these penalties—make sure the penalty is truly a penalty (if it isn't tough enough, they may take the risk of being caught).

5. Emphasize to all managers that it is their responsibility to check their own roster for ineligible players and that negligence is no excuse if an ineligible player is discovered. (Some institutions include a sentence on each team roster which states that the intramural manager certifies that all players are eligible and that he has checked their eligibility).

6. Invite the managers to do their own "policing" and if they even suspect another team of violating an eligibility rule they should report the case immediately to the intramural office. (It is often a good idea to post the rosters on the bulletin board the first few weeks so that the managers may easily check each other's rosters).

7. When a case is reported to the intramural office, it should be given immediate attention and should be investigated by the department promptly so as to be fair to all teams involved.

8. Consistently enforce the penalties and even publicize the results to all teams (place on bulletin board or in newspaper) so that **they know** you

mean what you say. Once the word gets around that a team was caught and penalized for violating the rules, other teams will become more cautious.

Although, I will admit, that this is not a **completely** effective method for eliminating all ineligibles from participating and that there may be other practical and effective ways of dealing with the problem; however, if an intramural department would follow the procedures stated above **consistently** each year, it will be effective **enough,** and it will save the intramural department considerable time.

So, in answer to the question: "Eligibility Rules: Are They Enforceable?" my answer would be something like this:

Maybe they can be if you want to spend a lot of time at it, but for an intramural department to personally check each participant's records for the purpose of making sure **all** are eligible is, in my opinion, a waste of time and effort and the hours spent for this purpose could be more adequately spent on other more important matters.

Chapter 8
Officials

The Taming and Training of the Intramural Official
John T. Meyer
(1976 NIRSA Proceedings, pp. 80-84)

Officials, referees, umpires, and supervisors all play an important role in Intramural programs. For the sake of clarity I will refer to basketball officials specifically. The principles involved can be applied to officials in all major team sports. I will cover my techniques for recruiting, training, scheduling, paying, and evaluating referees. I'll also include some special "sauces and pickles" regarding officials.

Asking participants of an Intramural program how to improve the program, a common response is, "Get some good refs!" That is exactly the point. Officials can make or break a program. We need to do more to develop good officials. This is not easy, but there are several things that we can do.

It would be ideal to hire trained professional officials. Since this is not always possible, we must recruit a number of people who are interested in the sport as players or spectators. They must then be trained, motivated, scheduled, evaluated, and paid.

RECRUITING

Throughout the year we will lose some officials through self-exclusion or through our own competency cuts. Thus we need to get quantity first. Put flyers out, ads in the paper, contact last years officials, P.E. classes, and team managers. Get as wide a coverage as possible over campus.

Include eye catchers in all publicity. Improvise. We use a trick to catch the potential employee's attention besides showing the pertinent information. Job data includes these: 1) What is the job; 2) What is the pay; 3) When are the meetings held; and 4) Who can answer additional questions. I usually emphasize money in advertisements because that is the main factor that gets people to us initially. Money is not everything, but it buys everything.

CLINICS

Now to get quality, training officials is a necessity. We will probably never reach the point where we are able to do enough, but the point is to do a better job of training each year. Try new ideas and different techniques. Use every trick and aid that you can.

We have formal meetings each week that are the core of our officials training. It's important to us to get everyone there each week. We have a meeting at 7:00 a.m., 7:00 p.m., and 8:00 p.m. each Thursday during the season. They have to arrange their schedules to fit one of these meetings. We pay them for one hour's work to add incentive. The next week's work schedules are handed out at the meeting; an official must be present at the meeting to keep his assignments. The clinics give us the reliability and consistency that we need. The "meat" of the clinic consists of rules, mechanics, procedures, and problem areas. We believe in setting the meeting time at an hour and sticking to this set time allotment.

Our general sample meeting agenda is this:

1) Check in and schedule pick up as official enters room;

2) 30 minutes programmed meeting on specified topics;

3) 15-20 minutes of problems, questions, and answers; (after discussion we give final interpretation so there is no confusion).

4) last 10 minutes for adjusting schedule problems.

Be flambouyant during the clinics to keep their attention. (Showmanship, entertainment, acting.) Make the meetings interesting by being prepared well enough so that you can go over the material quickly and accurately. Of course any audio-visual material that you can use helps to keep interest up.

In a major sport, four to five meetings are a minimum. As many of these as possible should be pre-seasonal for obvious reasons. The following is a sample for five meetings.

1) Procedures and sign up meeting.

2) Special IM rules.

3) Mechanics, position, and signals.

4) Rules 1-5   NCAA or High School   4) Fouls.

5) Rules 6-10   5) Violations.

Motivational techniques are injected into all meetings.

Here are some meeting specifics.

1) Procedures and sign-up: Pass out all the necessary forms and schedule cards. Explain the payroll system and how it works. Go over the schedule and information cards step by step. This is a good time to explain our philosophy of Intramurals and how officials fit into the system. We expect a lot from them and they can expect us to stand behind them 100 per cent. Explain the officials scheduling and what their responsibilities are. These include pre-game, during game, and post game duties. These are all covered on our general procedures hand out sheet.

2) Special I.M. rules. It is of paramount importance for the official to know our special "house" rules.

3) Mechanics, position, and signals. These areas have to become automatic to the official. Supervisors give referees game site pointers so that they can put a fine edge on their mechanics.

Meetings 2 and 3 are excellent for additional confidence and motivation angles. Tell those people how important they are to us. Try to help them to know their business as well as possible. Stress professionalism. Teams

Recruiting, training, and monitoring student officials are critical tasks for the intramural director.

respect an official more if he looks and acts as though he knows what he is doing. Professionalism includes appearance, pre-game conference, no nonsense approach, authority, positiveness, courtesy, and salesmanship. A referee must communicate his call to the players and sell them through his confidence.

4 and 5)   Rules. It is almost mandatory to use slides or film to cover rule sections quickly, accurately, and interestingly. We will not have time to knit pick every point. Association films are excellent if they are available. Slide cassette packages are useful in most situations, but they require some effort to produce. They are used at meetings and by individuals as a review. We like to add some humor and entertainment to these packages. If we can get their attention, they just may learn something.

We have as many additional meetings as we feel are necessary to train the referee. A summary of each meeting topic is included in the notes of the next weeks schedule. The official can refer to his schedule if his memory fails. This keeps policies and rulings as consistent as a case book does.

SCHEDULING

Now that we have the official trained to a finely tuned referee machine, where and when does he work? At the first meeting he filled out a work availability card. (Basketball Official Card and Officials Information for 1975-76 Card.) We transfer these names and the corresponding available work days to master schedule sheets. By using a pencil to mark which people are scheduled to work on particular days, we have a complete picture of how often a referee is scheduled. We also record ratings on this sheet and indicate any partners or officiating teams.

Days of availability can be changed by talking to us before 5:00 p.m. Wednesday since the schedule is made out Wednesday night. Each official gets a copy of the schedule at the Thursday meeting. The first schedule has a page with the names and phone numbers of all officials. Once a person is scheduled it is his responsibility to get any necessary substitute and to report the change to us. Unreliable officials are dropped from the schedule for missing a game or a meeting.

We try to schedule an experienced official with a rookie the first few times. We prefer that everyone eventually finds a partner or a team that he works well with so that they can develop consistency.

PAYROLL

The student must complete University procedure to be cleared for payroll. Our job is to keep an accurate record of the time an individual works each day. The referee must sign the score sheet of each game that he works. We transfer the number of games worked to the weekly officials' schedule. This can then be recorded on the master pay sheets. This way we can observe not only who did work but also who was missing. Pay rates automatically increase with the number of years service. More importantly we can increase an officials pay after he has demonstrated his reliability, game experience, and improved skill.

EVALUATION

Evaluation includes a rules test and many supervisors written critiques of officials in game situations. Tests are all right and should be given; but remember their limitations. The test is more of a learning tool for the official rather than an evaluative device. To evaluate, there is no substitute for watching them in action.

The main purpose of evaluation is to assist in training the official. This has to be done largely by supervisors in order to reach every official each time that he works. A general numerical evaluation is all right to determine who is fair, average, or excellent; but written notes are used to indicate what specific areas an individual does well or needs to improve.

At the end of the game the supervisors talk to each crew of officials. We stress the positive approach. First, hit the official with the things that he is doing well, to help his confidence and to insure he will continue to do these things. Secondly, give him a few of the most urgent things that he must work on to improve. Officials will do things consistently wrong if we let them practice bad habits. Video tape would be excellent to use in showing the official just what he is or is not doing. We must rely on the supervisors to call the problems to the attention of the official.

We check the supervisors out on their rating system. They must all rate the same way for it to be valuable. The supervisor and I both watch the same game. He then tells me exactly what he will tell the official after the game. I can then tell the supervisor what I might say or how he might approach the official in another manner.

I want to emphasize that these evaluations are to a large extent confidence builders and motivators. Use that positive approach. Officials can come into the office at any time to review their ratings and to discuss what they can do to improve.

SAUCES AND PICKLES

I would like to list a few of the ideas that I am currently working on regarding intramural officials training. Add your own modifications or ideas to these so they will be applicable to your situation.

1) I.S.O.S. — Intramural Sports Officials Association. Establish a criteria for necessary meetings attended; test score; and evaluations. Award a Velcro I.S.O.A. patch to be worn on the officials uniform shirt. Communicate as much as possible with your officials. A weekly newsletter is a method of corresponding attitudes and situations in an understandable manner. The association puts more responsibility on the officials to help each other. It becomes a professional attitude booster.

2) Non-paid rap meetings. Find a coffee house or some other place to hold these optional meetings. Announce what specific rule the meeting will

concentrate on and suggest that everyone bring a "stumper" question.

3) Be an information library for officials to join other officials associations. These can be city, state, or regional associations.

4) Develop a rapport with your officials. Know your people by name. Sure we are all busy, but we are never too busy to talk to an official. Shoot straight with them while being as tactful as possible. All our dealings have to be based on honesty and fairness.

SUMMARY

There is no problem with being a Zebra as long as you are always right. The third team, the officials, are an integral part of the game. They are as involved as the players, but the referees are not allowed any mistakes.

The official must be mentally ready for the sort of things that are likely to happen. The unusual will happen. He must develop the confidence to challenge the teams to violate a rule rather than to hope that they will overlook his presence. The official can not guess. He must know. When in doubt, a quick positive decision will suffice.

Officiating is not an easy sport. Referees can make it easy on themselves by being prepared. The ingredients of good officials are these: 1) Desire; 2) Confidence; 3) Rules; 4) Mechanics; 5) Practice; and, 6) Consistency.

Teams win in spite of us and lose because of us. We help the official to realize that he alone can evaluate himself objectively and thus feel that he has done a good job.

Officiating Is the Answer
Louis A. Fabian
(1976 NIRSA Proceedings, pp. 89-95)

"Improve your officiating! The officials stink! The official was for the other team!" Have you ever heard these or other cliches about your intramural program? Chances are you have, and are continually trying to do something about it. Most intramural administrators would probably agree that the success or failure of an intramural program rests with the quality of officiating. Rokosz (3) stated good officiating is a key to successful intramurals. Mueller (2) commented that numerous unhealthy protests are avoided by good officiating. Fabian (1) found a significant number of intramural departments employed student activity managers to oversee intramural activities, whether or not a member of the intramural staff is present. It is our belief that proper supervision coupled with good officiating may best achieve an enjoyable intramural experience.

The purpose of this article was to gather information pertaining to intramural officiating and supervision. Material included was concerned with: salaries of intramural officials and student activity managers (supervisors), usage of officials, the female's role in intramurals, training methods for officials, and suggestions for administrative handling of officials and supervisors.

Surveys were mailed to 105 colleges and universities on December 5, 1975. Close-out date for the survey was February 10, 1976. As of that date, 86 surveys were received and used for statistical analysis. The 82% return supplied a usually high response and further indicated to the writer the importance of the topic. The number of responses varied for each question because not all questions were applicable to every institution.

Officials and Supervisors Salaries

All of the institutions contributing estimated an average of 36% of their overall budget was spent for officials and supervisors. The mean salary for officials at 78 institutions was $2.60 per hour. Salary range varied from $1.50 to $6.00 per hour with a mode of $2.50 per hour for 12 institutions. Supervisors' mean salary at 48 institutions was $2.45 per hour, with a range of $1.60 to $4.00 per hour, and a mode of $2.50 per hour at 10 institutions.

Only two-thirds (58) of the reporting institutions gave their officials or supervisors raises. Salary increases for officials and supervisors varied in amount and reason from institution to institution. Salary increases varied from 2 to 16 percent per hour, and approximately one half of the institutions gave raises every year. The remainder kept their salaries constant for two to four year periods. Reasons for increases centered around availability of university funds, an individual's ability to officiate, changes in minimum wage or cost of living, credit hours earned, and duration of an individual's employ.

How Many Officials are Needed

Some concern should be given to the number of officials adequately needed to officiate one regular season contest in various sports. Table I, following, indicates the number of institutions reporting, an average number of officials per contest, recommended officials per contest based on those averages, and recommended officials per contest suggested to Rokosz (3).

TABLE 1
Officials Used in Regular Season Intramural Contests

Sport	Reporting Institutions	Average Officials Per Contest	Recommended Officials Per Contest	Rokosz Officials Per Contest
Football	83	2.71	3	3
Basketball	83	2.22	2	3

Officials

Soccer	55	1.69	2	2
Softball	80	1.58	1	1 or 2
Volleyball	78	1.38	1	1

The Women's Role in Intramurals

Many intramural programs are experiencing extensive and rapid growth of some activities. Perhaps this is due to an upsurge of women's participation both individually and corecreationally. To accommodate this increase in activity, many intramural departments have felt the need to hire more women as officials and supervisors. Eighty-two schools reported on the disposition of women within their programs as officials. Eleven schools (12.5%) did not employ any women as officials, while 71 schools employed an estimated average of 13% women officials. The number of women employed as supervisors was much greater than the women employed as officials. Thirty-eight of forty-five institutions reported employing an estimated average of 35% women supervisors, while the remaining 15.5% (7) did not employ any women supervisors. Perhaps the reasons for more women supervisors than officials result from a majority of activities in most programs being male-oriented, for that reason a female is more likely to function adequately as a supervisor than an official.

Training of Intramural Officials

Virtually all intramural departments employ some form of educational technique or information document to inform and train their officials. The following are descriptions of instruments employed by various institutions with different size programs. The instruments described below were not the only ones received with the survey, however, they represent what the writer considers the best available.

Educational Instruments

1. General course description for Intramural Officiating. (University of Massachusetts — Schmitt, T. A.) The officiating course is perhaps the best means for an intramural administrator to train competent officials for his or her program. The course allows the individual director to adapt oddities and specifics within sports unique to his or her program, while reeducating and organizing officials to function correctly for the purposes desired.

2. Rules Test — Basketball

(University of Texas at Austin — Thompson, B.A.) A well-constructed rules test would be valuable for officials to develop self-confidence prior to the actual season. It should include rules of the game, mechanics of officiating, common game situations and decision-making problems. An elaborate series of officiating rules exams, meeting these criteria, have been developed by Daniel L. Allen, University of Minnesota, Twin Cities.

In addition to officiating courses and rules tests, some intramural departments show films on officiating, supplied by state or local officiating organizations, give practical tests through the medium of scrimmage games, and bring in guest speaker who specialize in officiating specific sports.

Information Documents

1. Officials Contract

(University of Minnesota, Twin Cities — Allen, D. L.) The contract acts as a legal binding document between both parties and spells out exactly what is expected of each individual official and in turn, the responsibilities of the institutions.

2. Officials Administrative Procedures

(University of Maryland — Kovalakides, Nick) The official's procedure sheet is more thorough than the contract in that it spells out exactly what the official is to do on a daily basis in the performance of his or her duties. In addition, information is supplied informing the official what to do in case of rain, protests, injuries, etc.

3. Intramural Officials Guidebook — Football

(Michigan State University — Sierra, Lawrence) The guidebook is a thorough explanation of an institution's intramural program for one or multiple sports. It supplies the officials with all information covered by a contract or procedures list in addition to the following: philosophy and objectives of intramural program, intramural eligibility, rating system, and specific rules and game situations relative to the sport in season.

4. Intramural Staff and Officials Information Sheet

(University of Maryland — Kovalakides, Nick) The information sheet should supply the intramural departments with all necessary and relative information about a prospective official or supervisor. Information included should cover personal demographic data, availability for work, preferred times and sports, and previous experience.

Evaluation Forms

1. Officials Evaluation Form — Basketball

(Ohio State University — Frederick Beckman and B. L. Maurer) The evaluation of an official's capability while performing under game conditions is the best indicator of the qualify available to us. It not only tells what areas need improvement and which officials are most reliable in pressure situations, but it gives us an indication of the success of our program. A form which may be filled out by the intramural staff should include: pre-game duties, official's judgment, mechanics, reaction time, poise, attitude, and knowledge of rules.

2. Supervisors Evaluation Form

(University of Pittsburgh — Fabian, L. A.) To coincide with the official's evaluation is an evaluation of the student activity managers. While skill is not a necessity for supervision, the manager acts as a liaison for the intramural department and should reflect the attitudes, philosophy and judgment of the intramural director. Students should be evaluated on their relations with others, judgment, ability to learn, attitude, dependability, quality of work, attendance and punctuality.

The aforementioned instruments for training of officials, information documents, and evaluation forms are to some degree a necessary part of most intramural programs. They provide valuable information to officials, supervisors, and the intramural staff as to their duties, effectiveness, ability, and improvement. It should further be understood that not all methods are practical for every institution. The size, philosophy, structure, and goals vary with each institution and the needs of the program may be evaluated best by each intramural director.

Sources of Officials and Supervisors

Where to look for qualified officials and supervisors is a constant challenge for the intramural director. Generally speaking, a good pool of officials and supervisors comes from the following sources: physical education majors, varsity athletes, and individuals with a high interest in a specific sport. Desirable qualities of leadership, dependability, knowledge of the game and performance under pressure are inherent in these individuals and aids in maintaining a pleasant atmosphere. In addition, consider the use of women as officials and supervisors. Our staff employs women as both officials and supervisors and has witnessed firsthand a phenomenon which should be brought to your attention. Their observation was that female officials and supervisors tend to have a euphoric effect upon intramural and recreation participants. It appears that boisterous, domineering trouble-makers tend to be subdued by a "Sir Galahad Syndrome" brought forward by other participants within a group structure when a female is in control. This permits the female to make decisions without too much harassment, and maintain a low profile of excitement for the participants.

Tips for Administering Officials and Supervisors

1.   Ask your prospective employees for all available working time, their preference for time and job, and how many hours a week they can handle without taxing their schedule.

2.   Permit the better officials to work more than the power officials. We employ a system whereby after our first officials' rating, we classify our officials in the categories previously mentioned and then reassign hours for the following week: Best Officials — 10 to 14 hours, Good Officials — 6 to 10 hours, Satisfactory Officials — 3 to 6 hours, Unsatisfactory Officials — look for another job.

3.   Consolidate the number of days each week an individual comes to work. This allows more flexibility in their schedules for other activities and will minimize the number of times you will have to find replacements.

4. As previously stated, you may have to find replacements. To accomplish this, have a phone list of all your officials arranged by ability and showing availability. This enables you to find a satisfactory replacement quickly.

5. Avoid taxing your officials with too many contests in one evening. Four contests for even your best official is a good day's work. Due to a facility crunch at many institutions, intramural scheduling calls for consecutive five game evenings and six or more on weekends. When this situation occurs, the following suggestions have helped us. On a five or six game schedule, have a swing official for every two fields. When six or more contests are scheduled consecutively, split your shifts and spread the wealth.

6. Only the best officials should work playoffs and should be compensated accordingly. Time and a half for preliminary playoff games and double time for championship games.

7. Do not put undue pressure on your people by undermining their authority with your presence. When you're on the scene, keep in the background, avoid jumping in when a decision has to be made. Permit the officials and supervisors to handle it. Intervene only if they cannot resolve the problem.

8. Go with what you've got and do not worry about it. This situaton arises when your best officials are not available for your championship game. If the situation arises (as it did for us) that our best officials were unavailable for all of our playoff games, then it's time to look back and determine what mistakes occurred during the regular season causing them to be unavailable later.

9. Supervisors should supervise only. A supervisor who is repeatedly or permanently asked to officiate cannot function properly in both jobs. There are obvious losses in crowd control, evaluation of other officials, and organizational duties. Also, if something should require his or her arbitration elsewhere, you have four miserable teams. Fabian (1) reported 7.16% (136) of 190 institutions polled, never (or only rarely—as an alternate) asked their supervisors to officiate.

10. The previous suggestions might be more effective if the following is a part of your lifestyle as intramural director. If an official, supervisor, or participant comes to you with a problem or suggestion to improve a situation, do you take time to listen? Nine times out of ten, the program will benefit from the outcome. After all, the program services the needs of the people within it.

CONCLUSIONS

Few patterns appeared when investigating intramural officials and supervisors; perhaps, it is safe to say that each school is situationally specific with regard to the needs of their program. However, certain trends seem to be remaining constant. Salary levels for officials and supervisors were above minimum wage, with two-thirds of the institutions giving their officials and supervisors raises at regular intervals. Over eighty percent of the institutions employ females as supervisors and officials. Virtually all intramural departments use educational methods to improve the quality of the officiating in their programs.

COMMENTS

Intramurals across the country are growing in participation and program offerings. To accommodate growing pains experienced through expansion, intramural directors are seeking ways to successfully improve various aspects of their programs. This survey examined one such aspect, officiating and supervision of intramural contests, with the hope that improving this area will benefit the participants' intramural experiences.

An enjoyable experience for the intramural participant is a prime objective of our intramural philosophy. The intramural participant goes away from a contest remembering the officiating experienced. Only upon occasion does a losing team comment the officiating was good. When this occurs you may be sure there is a diamond in your coal bin. Good officiating should be cultivated and rewarded.

Bibliography

Fabian, L. A. "New Directions in Intramurals and Recreation," *National Intramural Recreation Association Newsletter,* June-July, 1976.

Mueller, Pat, *Intramurals: Programming and Administration,* Ronald Press Company: New York, 1971. 4th Ed., 342 pp.

Rokosz, F. M., *Structured Intramurals,* W. B. Saunders Company: Philadelphia, 1975, 306 pp.

Innovative Procedures for Rating and Retention of Intramural Officials
William E. Katerberg
(1976 NIRSA Proceedings, pp. 87-88)

Regardless of the sport involved, one of the most critical visual areas of intramurals is the officiating. Often as a result of its success or failure, the intramural program is justly or unjustly measured. This method of judgment and its identification and stigma is not limited just to intramurals, but it is the visible standard from junior high athletics through intercollegiate and professional competition. Evidence of this is the multitude of game protests, chair-throwing displays by "dignified" coaches, tennis rackets broken in protest, and fan riots during international soccer games.

In an attempt to minimize situations such as these from occurring in our intramural program, we carefully surveyed other intramural, collegiate, and the professional programs. From these observations, we selected the best devices and procedures and incorporated them into our intramural program.

(1)   Philosophically, it is believed that both in practice and theory, intramurals should be first and foremost for the participant, rather than the spectator — a basic difference between intramurals and professional or collegiate sport. With this in mind, it should be obvious that the individuals most interested in intramural programs are in all probability those who are participating in it.

Students who play are encouraged to consider working as officials. This principle serves a two-fold purpose. First, the participant who is competing under the same regulations as he is officiating tends not only to elicit greater respect but also tends to be less critical when participating, which can also serve to influence team reaction. Secondly, since the majority of the intramural funding comes from student fees, students are provided an opportunity to recover a portion of their fees.

(2)   Varsity athletics are not our prime source of officials. Unfortunately because of their high skill and limited time, varsity athletes are often disinterested with the lower level of competition found on the intramural level. Many varsity athletes have proved not only to be intolerant of intramural games, but also lacking a knowledge of rules and play situations.

(3)   Prior to a sport's competitive season, the intramural program extensively advertises for officials. Rather than contacting just interested individuals from the athletic groups, past officials, or the physical education's officiating class, fliers are mailed off campus and posted over the entire campus, soliciting students' help. This method allows the intramural program to be almost self-contained; when the teams complain about the level of officiating, they are often condemning themselves. It allows for the comment, "Next year if you think you can do a better job, come out and give it a try."

(4)   In order to officiate in our program, each interested individual must attend one training session, which ranges from one to two hours, depending upon the sport involved. This is mandatory. At the training session, the topics discussed include philosophy of service, officials' ratings, pay, assignments, etc. The majority of the session covers a capsulized explanation of rules and situations involved during the games. The final portion of the clinic involves theoretical play situations as well as a question and answer period.

(5)   For each major team sport, the intramural department has developed a series of slides for individualized study and improvement. Each slide series not only deals with rules and interpretations, but also with an actual game situation. The Illustrated Case Books, which are published by the National

High School Athletic Association, as well as the National Collegiate Athletic Association guides, are excellent sources if one wishes to begin to develop such a series. Although the student official is not required to participate in this learning situation, he is encouraged to do so, and a written record is made of those who do take advantage of this opportunity. The intramural office also provides current rule and case books for study and perusal, available through the office on an in or out-check basis.

(6)   Officials Rating Charts have been developed for all major sports activities. Not only does this written form provide feedback to the intramural office in evaluating the officials, but it also allows for the individual himself to receive some positive or negative feedback from his task. Adaptations from those formats used by collegiate conferences and professional teams have been utilized. The rating system allows for not only the elimination of weak officials, but also for objective rationale in assigning certain officials to the positions which they work most competently. The actual rating is done by the intramural supervisors. The rating charts are made available to each official 48 hours following the game, thus providing him with an opportunity to see where his strengths and weaknesses are. Data collection is obtained immediately following each game. It is important to provide positive feedback—demonstrating to the official what he has done well, not merely his errors.

(7)   Based on the results of the officials' Rating Charts, officials are scheduled and assigned. It is important that officials' assignments are not made for the entire season in advance. Each official attending the training clinic is assigned for a minimum of one week, but after that, the only way to establish themselves is through the ratings. Assignments are made on a weekly basis throughout the season. This provides some prestige and motivation in officiating. When making assignments, the entire intramural staff should be involved, since verbal input tends to humanize the rating scales. This input is necessary to make the process work smoothly.

SUMMARY: This presentation, illustrated by means of audio-visual aids, demonstrates not only the need for establishing procedures for rating and retention of officials, but also the definite benefits derived from the implementation of such an instrument. In the program where these techniques have been employed, there has been a significant decrease in problems related to officiating. In addition, it has been noted that the competency standard for officials in general has conspicuously improved, as is evidenced by both the intramural staff and participants themselves.

21 Ways to Develop Esprit De Corps Among Your Student Officials
Nick Kovalakides
(1976 NIRSA Proceedings, pp. 84-86)

No matter how many sports you offer or how big you make your trophies, the success of your intramural sports program will, by and large, lie with the caliber of student officials you provide for your team sports — the backbone of your program.

Student officials are hard to come by at best. Good student officials are a rare breed, unless you are able to develop an atmosphere where students are as anxious to become a part of your "team" of officials as they are to become a part of a traditionally successful varsity team.

To be top drawer in anything, aptitude and attitude are essential ingredients. Aptitude in officials can be enhanced through clinics and on-the-job training. However, the attitude of the officials is a little more difficult to nurture. Here are 21 ways to develop esprit de corps among your officials:

1. Emphasize at your pre-season rules clinics that you expect the students to be signing up as officials in your program for *more* than just the money. They must realize that they have volunteered to help you provide first-class, professionally-run tournaments *for the intramural athletes.*

2. They must be convinced of the fact that you will back them 100% in their judgment calls.

3. They must be shown that you will not tolerate their being physically nor unduly, verbally abused by players, coaches or spectators. You would show this support while supervising the games. Furthermore, this would be a major point of emphasis to be made during your pre-season organizational meetings with the coaches of the teams.

4. Pay your officials well. A minimum wage is not very attractive in view of the tremendous responsibilities and errorless efforts which will be expected of them.

5. Institute an incentive pay program wherein officials returning for their second, third and fourth years would be paid more (perhaps 25-50 cents) per game than that of the rookie officials. The proficiency of your officials is in direct proportion to the number of veterans available. Present an "Intramural Staff" nylon jacket, sport shirt or T-shirt to an official who is serving in your program for the third year or more.

6. Provide them with professional-looking referee's shirts. Help them look the part. Improvised striped shirts or pinnies only serve to hinder the image of the officials. By the same token, the officials should be expected to wear clean trousers or shorts to complement the shirts. You should also have the shirts laundered regularly.

7. Provide each official with an NCAA rulebook so that he can study the "gospel" and be able to carry it with him during his game.

8. Observe and evaluate your officials frequently, if not daily. Criticize them privately. Praise them publicly. Compliment an official on his strong points before pointing out his weaknesses. Emphasize that your criticisms are for his benefit — to help him improve as an official.

9. As an incentive, let it be known that through your evaluations the better officials will be assigned more often. (This may prevent the slow-improving official from gaining experience, however, most intramural athletes are not very patient with late-blossoming officials.)

10. Encourage your officials to form "crews" whereby the same two or three officials would work together on each of their games. Better teamwork will result sooner than if they were assigned to different officials on each game. (This is the same system used by officials in professional sports.)

11. Never assign all rookie officials to the same game. Always have at least one veteran on the crew. The rookies will appreciate it.

12. Avoid competition among the officials such as "Official of the Week", "Best Official", etc. No matter who makes the ratings — players, coaches, fellow officials or yourself — the officials will always second-guess each selection. Furthermore, why make one official happy while making the rest of them mad. Your mortality rate may increase accordingly.

13. Reward the officials you consider best by assigning them to the championship games. However, when assigning the officials for that final game, list twice or three times as many alternates and make a notation that "each official listed—regular or alternate—is considered qualified to handle the championship game, but unfortunately, only three could be chosen." You should also announce that "those not selected should regard is as a challenge to return next year to demonstrate marked improvement."

14. Assist your officials in getting paid officiating assignments in local recreation, boy's club, or church leagues. Be certain, however, that these outside games are not scheduled in conflict with your program.

15. Inform your officials that upon their graduation from college you would be most happy to recommend them to their local commissioner of officials if they want to continue officiating as a "moonlighting" profession.

16. Devote a full page in your intramural sports handbook to recognition of your officials. This could be picture of them as a group or a list of their names along with the sports which they handled and how many years that they have been on the officials' staff.

17. When taking the picture of your team champions for next year's handbook, include the game officials. And, of course, add their names to the picture's caption.

18. Encourage your more administratively-sounding officials to serve as

tournament directors in your other team and individual sports. Tournament directors should also be well paid, receive a staff jacket and be included on the official's page in the handbook as well as in the pictures of the championship individuals and teams.

19.   Include your student officials and tournament directors in your Table of Organization as depicted in your handbook or on your intramural bulletin board.

20.   Initiate and encourage informal gatherings of your officials in your office, lounge area, or local hangout where officiating experiences can be shared, rules can be discussed and interpreted, and field/court mechanics can be reviewed. Foster a club or fraternal atmosphere.

21.   Love your officials as if they were members of your own team — because they are.

Intramurals Without Officials
Peter D. Hopkins
(1972 NIA Proceedings, pp. 51-54)

Have you ever heard an official complimented?

How many times have you heard players, coaches, fans chastise that "blind ding bat in the striped shirt" for ineptitude?

How many protests did you have this year over officiating?

How many fights or temper flair-ups did you have this year in your program, let alone injuries?

Did you have a problem even getting officials besides worrying about their quality?

How much time do you spend recruiting, training, evaluating, selecting, placing, reprimanding, justifying and backing officials?

Have you ever been phoned at home informing you that the "beep beep" officials haven't shown up, and the game has to be replayed?

Have you ever had your referee-in-chief in basketball thrown out of a game for fighting?

Have you ever had an official swear at a player, and the player return with a short blast of profanity, and then the official throw the player out for swearing?

How many of your officials have the proverbial "rabbit ears"?

Have you ever asked yourselves—is there a better way?

I'm a firm believer that there is a definite "officials syndrome" in our society—a hate syndrome. Regardless of the nature of the activity, or the level of competition, no one likes officials, no one thinks they are rational, intelligent, companionable human beings. Instead they are "homers" or "awayers," deaf, blind, stupid, and on and on with other more uncomplimentary adjectives.

We have all tried to improve officiating by recruiting normal individuals, held numerous clinics, gone to elaborate rating systems, increased their money, gone to non-student officials, etc.

While we may have improved the quality of officiating, have we improved peoples attitude towards officials?

I'm not sure if you ever can.

This does not mean I'm down on officials. At the University of Waterloo, I hire 400 plus students as officials, convenors, referees-in-chiefs, lifeguards, etc. a year. Our Intramural budget is in excess of $10,000 for officials alone. For the most part they are highly reliable students that make a valuable contribution to the program.

I've always been a firm believer in 2 basic concepts:

(1)   Involve as many students as possible in the organization and administration of your program and it will be successful.

(2)   Only hire student officials, therefore putting student money back in the pocket of students.

Officials help your program in many ways:

(1)   as supervisors of equipment;

(2)   as input with ideas on rule changes;

(3)   reporting scores, conduct, game reports and the like.

However, for a variety of reasons, we are experimenting with a different concept—activity without officials.

Some of the reasons are:

(1)   increasing student attitude, rejecting authority and rules;

(2)   increasing cost of officials;

(3)   lack of officials;

(4)   deep concern over continually poor attitude toward officials and the game itself.

Our program goes beyond the voluntary competitive definition of Intramurals. We view Intramurals as "a voluntary, internal program of physical activity based on the needs and interests of the community the program serves".

Consequently, Intramurals at the University of Waterloo has 4 basic levels—competitive, recreational, instructional and Athletic Clubs.

Our competitive level is the traditional Intramural program with unit structure, points, awards, officials and all sorts of team, individual and dual sports. This serves approximately 20-30% of the population involved in 33 activities.

Our largest area is the recreational Intramural program. Here there are 3 program areas: free time, individual scheduled activities and recreational team sports.

In this latter area, recreational team sports, we have no officials. Now some of you may say, that's because of the nature of this recreational level, without units, points, awards, etc., there is no need for officials. You may have a point. But, if the question is rhetorically asked—Do you only have officials because "something is at stake"? I question the need and the program.

Do young children playing sandlot softball use officials or even need officials? Do young children use or need officials to play street hockey or football? No—it is a peer influence directed toward self discipline with an adaptation and simplification of the rules.

Why, as we grow up and become mature, responsible individuals do we impose a vast complicated set of rules enforced by officials?

Why as soon as we are mature, responsible adults do we suddenly need officials to play the game? Why not act as our age indicates by being mature and responsible individuals and discipline ourselves in team activity?

If we have a social objective in our program, are we reaching it under the present system with officials? Or are we hindering the social objective by laying the blame on others—namely officials—for our own inability to control ourselves. We must impose authority in order to play.

Most of us are really trying to put "fun" back into activity to create an enjoyable atmosphere or environment in which to play an activity. Are your activities fun, or are they highly competitive, fight-filled, injury ridden?

We have tried to look at these things and have come up with the—no-official-concept which has added a tremendous impetus to our program.

Our recreational teams are: floor hockey, ball hockey, touch football, hockey, co-ed broomball, co-ed volleyball, co-ed inner tube waterpolo, softball, and basketball. Many of these activities are contact in nature, rule oriented and elevated in skill. Yet we play 700 games a year, involve over 1800 students in 200 or more teams, with very few problems—no protests, few defaults, no fights, few injuries, and increased playing time.

Can you imagine playing floor hockey with its body contact, its speed, its intensity without officials?

It has taken 3 years to develop this approach or attitude to activity. It has come to the point where students request the "recreational level" rather than the competitive one. Why—simply, it is more fun.

We have all had problems with student interest on our campuses. Who participates in this program—the freaks, the radicals, the yippies, the long-haired wierdos. Those that control your student federations, your newspaper, who criticize your athletic programs. They are activists, but in Intramurals.

In conclusion the benefits of an area of your Intramurals—without officials are as follows:

(1)   It is economical—saves money while involving double the people in

your program.

(2) It teaches self-discipline.

(3) It is an area of program for the radical element on campus.

(4) It reduces the "competitive" aspect in your program in that "win at all cost" attitude that does exist in Intramurals.

(5) It reduces injury, fights in activity.

(6) It creates a proper atmosphere for co-ed activities which are more social in nature.

(7) It makes you think about your philosophy of Intramurals.

(8) It makes you think about your rules, awards, points—what adjustments have to be made when there are no officials.

(9) Great area for faculty/staff involvement in your program.

(10) Increases playing time—no delays for official decisions like foul shots, penalties.

(11) Simply—puts fun into activity.

It is a tremendous experience to see students laugh during an activity. Let's become children again, they seem to have so much fun.

Chapter 9
Co-Rec Intramurals

Co-Rec Intramurals — Emphasis Fun
Sandra Caldwell
(1974 NIA Proceedings, pp. 43-44)

The slogan "An Activity for everyone, and everyone in an Activity" is probably the underlying theme in most intramural programs. But, each season as the number of teams increase, the desire to win becomes a motivating factor in forming teams. Expert performance, good techniques and the competitive spirit are becoming essential characteristics in forming the best dormitory teams, the best Greek teams, and the best club or independent teams.

The spirit of play and the desire to participate are still important to intramural existence, but often are not enough to insure participation. The intramural program needs something to offer those who are not highly skilled, who do not have the time to practice, or to those who just want to play for fun. Some type of program is needed where the emphasis can be placed on wide-spread participation and enjoyment, rather than on competition and all-university titles.

Nation wide trends indicate that Co-Recreational programs are growing faster than any other type of intramural activity. The numerous sports activities which can be enjoyed by mixed groups might be incorporated into such a program.

The activities offered by the creative intramural director are important to the overall effectiveness of the program. But, the uniqueness of the Co-Rec program seems to be keyed in the effectiveness of the rule modifications. It is important to keep the rules simple, while equalizing play among men and women. Often the rules are unique to certain regions, and need to identify with the interests of the students.

The rules and techniques for many of the individual team sports are the same as in regular doubles programs. The only difference is each team is made up of one male and one female. The team sports that involve personal contact are suitable for Co-Rec programs with a few adjustments to the rules. The established physical differences necessitate the adaptation of the rules to avoid male domination. Simplicity must be maintained, while equalizing play—still insuring an enjoyable activity for everyone. The rule modifications often add to the enjoyment and add challenge to the game. The truly recreational aspects of sports activity are probably more emphasized in the novelty programs.

A well-organized and published Co-Rec program can almost offer an Activity for everyone and stimulate everyone to join an Activity.

CO-REC PROGRAM**

Golf	Flag, Touch Football	Arm wrestling
Badminton	Basketball	Field goal kicking
Archery	Volleyball	Free throw
Tennis	Softball	Frisbee softball
Ping pong	Water polo—inner tube	Frisbee football
Fencing	Basketball—inner tube	
Racketball	Volleyball—inner tube	
Squash	Field hockey	
Putt-putt	Track & field	
Billiards	Swimming meet	
Bowling	Kickball	
Novelty bowling	Dodgeball	

**As for the rules, use the imagination and create your own. Students are great for coming up with strange ideas, and most of them are fun!

Co-Intramural Sports
Kathryn D. George
(1975 NIRSA Proceedings, pp. 59-62)

The process by which programs come about is common in any area of work. It starts with a need or interest for services; followed by organization of programs; then, the experience of staff in carrying out programs uncovers common problems and gradually, one gets tested results to deal with these problems. Our intramural programs have developed along similar lines and it is clear we have accepted intramurals as a function to be performed or a service to be rendered. But there seem to be areas beyond men's and women's intramural sports that we have included in our programs during the last ten years. One of these areas is co-intramural sports.

In the 1970 NIA proceedings are listed the results of a survey dealing with trends that have been incorporated in intramural programs from 1960 through 1969. Bill Wasson, the author of the survey, researched the NIA annual conference *Proceedings* for some inherent trends and prepared a survey which included 18 areas. He then sent the survey to 100 members of the NIA who were asked to indicate which trends they had adopted in their program.

During his research, the only references he found to co-intramurals as a program area were in the 1971 and 1962 conference proceedings. In each instance the survey results showed that administrators were indicating an increasing awareness of the need to include co-intramurals in the total program of intramural activities. However, no further information was provided in regard to actual application of this belief.

Although the reasons for participating in co-rec activities vary from student to student, one constant factor almost always exists for the players------AN ENJOYABLE TIME

Then, in the 1969 NIA proceedings, Charles Buck provided results of a survey he designed to determine whether or not co-intramurals was a national trend or just a topic among collegiate intramural directors. Again the members of the NIA were considered to provide a representative cross section of collegiate institutions. Of the 377 surveys sent out to collegiate intramural directors 178 were returned. Buck summarized the results of his survey in the following way:

This investigation did not find a majority of the recipients increasing the number of coed activities being offered in their intramural program. The majority of the coed activities were being offered during free-play programs or open house activities. This was evident since only a minority of the institutions indicated that they had formal coed programs. Also, the majority of the intramural directors neglected to utilize a special council for the coed program and submitted a minimal amount of carry-over from the coed to the regular intramurals in such areas as participation points and point systems. The coed program was not generally included in the annual intramural activity schedule, nor was it included in the published intramural handbook.

This investigation did reveal a considerable amount of coeducational recreation taking place on the collegiate campuses across the country, but it was generally of an informal nature. Therefore, the suggestion that a national trend toward increased coed activity in intramural programs was rejected.

Since 1969 there have been many other inferences to co-intramurals as a national trend in programming. As a result of my responsibility on this panel, I developed an informal survey to obtain information on attitudes toward co-intramurals on various campuses. I selected fifty members of the NIA who I felt would provide a representative cross section of the collegiate institutions in the United States. Of the 50 surveys sent out 41 were returned. I feel that the results of this survey provide the necessary information to indicate current trends that have developed or are developing in the area of co-intramurals. Unlike the position taken by Buck, I feel that co-intramurals have become a recognized and vital part of the total intramural program. For the sake of brevity, I will not read through the surveys but will be happy to make them available to anyone upon request.

A review of the return revealed an overwhelming majority of the institutions currently offer co-intramural programming. These institutions also indicated they have seen a tremendous statistical increase in the popularity of the program on their campus. A majority of the institutions also plan to increase the number of activities offered in their co-intramural program during the 1975-76 school year.

The previous information may be related to a trend toward having a staff position for co-intramural programming as was revealed by the survey results. The survey results also showed that awards are being offered by a majority of the institutions. The fact that an overwhelming majority of the institutions consider the co-intramural program on an equal basis when scheduling facilities for intramurals is another indication that this area has become a recognized part of the total intramural program.

There was also a tremendous response indicating a greater emphasis on enjoyment and sportsmanship within co-intramural programs rather than winning, league standings, or awards. But perhaps the most interesting information was the frequency that sociability was cited as being emphasized in these programs. Although many people participate in activities because of an interest in the sport, there is evidence that sociability is a predominant factor in bringing and holding them to the activity. It does not seem too fantastic, then, for us to be concerned with ways in which we organize and our methods of grouping people in co-intramurals so as to contribute to sociability. This may be especially true since the transience of modern society reduces the change for meaningful and lasting relationships.

It is evident that as the movement for incorporating co-intramurals into our programs grew, the first concern was in determining the activities to offer. Today, we still look to one another for new activities that add diversity to our programs. Perhaps the greatest innovation in thinking though has come in the realization that it is not the activity alone that is important. It is also the human relations in which it is set. For example, we have seen that a particular kind of sport situation can be enjoyable or painful to a particular person according to his acceptance in the gang. We also know that a sport experience can mean one thing to a shy woman if it is so designed as to give her confidence and quite another to the "star" who builds up her ego by dominating her team. There are countless other situations indicating human relations as a significant part of what sport experiences mean to people.

As we being trying to understand these situations our place as program leaders becomes more significant. Hopefully, as we become more sensitive and knowledgeable in the area of human relations we might make our co-intramural programs a more satisfying experience. This will happen, however, only to the extent that we look at co-intramurals as something more than structure, awards, tournaments, and competitions. When viewed in the larger perspective of their contribution to our participants, co-intramural programs can provide opportunities for social interaction between men and women that is meaningful. They can produce situations for participation in orderly social pressures, opportunities where men and women can learn to appreciate one another's needs, and opportunities where men and women can learn to respect differences in interest and abilities.

I think current trends indicate that co-intramurals have become a recognized part of our administrative responsibilities. I also think there are trends in co-intramurals toward sweeping away the stereotyped programs, reliance on awards, and imposition of programs on participants. We should be putting in more flexible, more personalized programs to make enjoyment available to more people in more meaningful ways.

References

Wasson, William N., "A Survey To Determine The Trends Which Have Been Incorporated In Intramural Programs During The Past Ten Years", *NIA Proceedings,* Los Angeles, California, 1969, pp. 54-55.

Buck, Charles R., "Coeducational Intramurals: Trend or Topic", *NIA Proceedings,* Los Angeles, California, 1969, pp. 54-55.

Coyle, Grace L., *Group Experience and Democratic Values,* The Woman's Press, New York, N.Y., 1947, p. 72.

Co-Recreation and Intramural Sports
George W. Haniford
(1963 NIA Proceedings, pp. 19-21)

Administrators of intramural programs are becoming increasingly aware of the need for the inclusion of co-recreational sports in the total program of intramural activities. College men and women students are becoming more demanding in their requests for activities which are new in character, which will provide them with outlets for the satisfactions of their recreational desires, and which will further provide them with the opportunities to express themselves. These outlets help them learn to get along together as members of our democratic society. The conscientious director, realizing the importance of co-recreational activities, will attempt to include them in his program.

Co-recreational activities should not be inaugurated until careful consideration has been given toward the solution of the several problems which effect administration of the program:

First, there needs to be understanding and cooperation established between the personnel of the men's and women's departments. This is a necessity, as no co-recreational program can be successful if there are too many existing differences of opinion in the following area of administration:

1. The activities to be included in the co-recreational program.
2. The rules and regulations governing play of the participants.
3. The amount and kind of supervision necessary. Sex of the supervisors.
4. The use of areas and facilities.
5. The safety procedures to be followed.

Second, careful consideration must be given to existing college or university regulations pertaining to the administration of activities for college men and women. The administrative policies to be used in governing the co-recreational program should be discussed with the Dean of Men and the Dean of Women.

Third, an administrative co-recreational council should be established. The Intramural Director of the men's program might serve as council chairman, with other members of the council representing the: (1) Women's Physical Education Department; (2) Women's Athletic Association; (3) Intramural Managerial Association; and, (4) Student Union Board. This council, in joint cooperative effort, shall plan and administer the policies of the co-recreational sports program. Particularly, in the area of program, students need to be given every opportunity to express themselves as to their choice of activities and the methods to be used in their administration.

The co-recreational program will, of course, be vying for the participation of as many men and women students as possible. However, the intramural director must constantly remember that the purpose of co-recreational activities is not to detract from the **regular** program of intramural activities. Rather, one should strive to enlarge the total offering, and, at the same time, provide the participants with increased enjoyment. Consideration must be given to the existing intramural programs for both men and women. Co-recreation activities should not be scheduled in direct competition with the activities of the regular intramural program.

The co-recreation program should be well-balanced and offer opportunities in the following several areas: (1) competitive team sports; (2) competitive individual and dual sports; (3) informal activities; (4) non-competitive activities; (5) social activities; (6) clubs; and, (7) outing activities.

The competitive program should only include activities which are approved by the director of physical education for women. The administrator must also realize that he is expected to abide by the rules governing the participation of women students as established by the NSGWS (National Section for Girls and Women's Sports). This section has recognized and accepted standards pertaining to health, participation, leadership, and publicity. One of the stipulations of this group is, that "college women shall not participate either with or against men in activities not suitable to competition between men and women such as basketball, hockey, lacrosse, soccer, speed-a-way, speedball, and touch football".

Emphasis should not be placed upon the winning of the contest, but rather upon the enjoyment and understanding that comes as a result of the participation. The rules and regulations governing mixed participation in many of the competitive sports must be modified to insure the safety, health, and physical and mental well-being of the woman participants.

Informal activities should be an integral part of the total program.

Facilities should be available at scheduled times for groups and/or individuals desiring to participate in the free-play type of activities. Directors must recognize that many men and women students do not enjoy scheduled activities, but rather want the opportunity to participate informally as their desires and interests demand satisfaction.

Non-competitive activities such as recreational swimming, roller skating, dancing (folk, square, round), ice skating, toboganning, boating, etc., are important and should be included in the well-rounded program. Perhaps, the greatest obstacle to overcome in these areas of the program is the shyness and hesitancy of youth. The director must realize the importance of this obstacle and be prepared to use all the known methods of psychology in an attempt to overcome the problem. The need for trained, qualified personnel is particularly important in these activities.

Social activities certainly are a part of the total co-recreational program. They have been, and will continue to be, recognized as very important phases of campus life. These activities, in many instances, are, may be, or have been promoted under the auspices of other existing campus agencies. The intramural department should not necessarily let this fact discourage the inclusion of these activities. Duplication is sometimes necessary in order to meet the needs of the total student body. It is recommended, however, that there be careful joint planning between the intramural staff and these other campus agencies. The personnel of the intramural departments should always be ready and willing to assist other campus agencies in the coordination, selection, promotion, and conduct of social activities. In this area of the program one needs to have a thorough knowledge of the University policies pertaining to chaperones, hours, conduct, etc.

The desire of students to participate in various activities by functioning as a sports club must be recognized. The intramural department should encourage the growth of the club movement. Each club should be allowed to become as self-sufficient as possible. Members should write their own constitutions, select their own officers, organize their own meetings, etc. Each club should have a faculty sponsor and abide by all the rules and regulations established by university or college authorities. Extramural events have been one of the outgrowths of the sports club movement. In many schools extramural events have been used to enrich and complement the intramural program.

The primary function of the intramural department in the area of co-recreational outing activities is to encourage the students to participate, thereby leading them to an understanding and appreciation necessary for optimum use and conservation of our natural resources. Most of the popular activities in this area can be conducted quite simply. Many times all that needs to be done is to purchase the necessary equipment for check-out.

Supervision in this area of the program is relatively simple unless one is involved in the outing club movement.

In closing, I quote the statement pertaining to co-recreation activities written and adopted by the delegates to the First National Intramural Sports Meeting for College Men and Women held in Washington, D.C. in October 1955. "The program should include as many activities as lend themselves to efficient and meaningful participation. Men and women should have an opportunity to play together, to develop an understanding and appreciation for differences in interests, skills and limitations, and an opportunity to develop mutual interests which carry over to adult life. Experiences in co-recreational activities contribute to and enrich both personal and family living."

Status of Co-Recreational Intramural Sports
Joe Manjone
(1976 NIRSA Proceedings, pp. 141-145)

The following are the results of a survey on co-recreational intramural sports mailed to the 254 institutional members of the National Intramural-Recreational Sports Association on January 15, 1976. Two hundred and twenty-eight responses were received. For various reasons, questions on all questionnaires were not answered, so the number of responses will vary for each question.

A. *Extent of Current co-recreational intramural sports programs*
1. 193 (84%) of 228 schools offer a formal program of co-recreational intramural athletic programs.
2. 226 (99%) of 228 schools offered a men's intramural athletic program.
3. 223 (98%) of 228 schools offered a women's intramural athletic program.

B. *Activities*
1. 34 (19%) of 184 schools offered more than 10 co-recreational intramural sports activities.
2. 99 (54%) of 184 schools offered at least five, but not more than ten co-recreational intramural sports activities.
3. 51 (27%) of 184 schools offered less than five co-recreational intramural athletic activities.
4. The various activities offered and the number of schools offering them are listed below:
    a. Volleyball — 150
    b. Tennis — 119
    c. Softball — 108
    d. Football (flag & touch) — 102

  e. Basketball — 98
  f. Bowling — 91
  g. Badminton — 88
  h. Inner-tube water polo — 61
  i. Racquetball — 60
  j. Swimming — 57
  k. Golf — 51
  l. Track & Field — 41
  m. Soccer — 25
  n. Bicycling — 18

C. *Administrative Structure*
 1. Departments that administer co-recreational intramural athletics: (193 replies)
  a. Intramural Department — 105 (54%)
  b. Student Activities Office — 38 (20%)
  c. Others, including physical education department, athletic department, recreation department — 50 (26%)
 2. The intramural director is also: (190 replies)
  a. The men's intramural director — 123 (65%)
  b. The women's intramural director — (57%)
  c. A faculty member — 94 (49%)
  d. A student — 10 (5%)

D. *Financing*
 1. The following sources of funding were indicated: (162 replies)
  a. Student activity fees — 88
  b. Institutional budget — 46
  c. Monies budgeted for Physical Education — 22
  d. Monies budgeted for varsity athletics — 12
  e. Entry fees — 8

E. *Awards*
 1. Awards are presented to co-recreational intramural athletic participants in the following manner: (183 replies)
  a. No awards are presented — 27
  b. To league champions — 107
  c. To league runner-ups — 44
  d. To tournament champions — 128
  e. To tournament runner-ups — 54
  f. To consolation winners — 9
  g. To all-year point champions — 37
  h. To all participants — 6
 2. The types of awards given are as follows: (156 replies)
  a. trophies — 90

    b. t-shirts — 62
    c. certificates — 33
    d. medals — 18
    e. plaques — 16
    f. photographs — 14
    g. pennants — 5

F. *Publicity*
    1. The following methods of promoting and publicizing the co-recrea-
        tional intramural activities were utilized: (185 replies)
        a. School newspaper — 168
        b. Posters — 144
        c. Bulletin Board — 141
        d. Intramural Handbook — 134
        e. Mailed announcements — 81
        f. Picture board — 59
        g. Radio — 50
        h. Telephone hotline — 43
        i. Television — 22

G. *Officials*
    1. The following are statements made concerning officials: (190
        replies)
        a. Do not use officials — 18
        b. Pay officials 0 - $1.00 per contest — 11.6%
        c. Pay officials $1.01 - $2.00 per contest — 18.6%
        d. Pay officials $2.01 - $3.00 per contest — 55.8%
        e. Pay officials $3.01 - $4.00 per contest — 11.6%
        f. Pay officials $4.01 + per contest — 2.4%
        g. Give course credit for officiating — 9.9%
        h. Utilize only male officials — 4.1%
        i. Utilize only female officials — 2.3%

H. *Injuries*
    1. Respondents were requested to rank the top three injury causing
        co-recreational intramural athletic activities at their school and the
        results are as follows: (175 replies)

	First	Second	Third	Total
Volleyball	27	23	14	64
Basketball	20	32	11	63
Football	45	8	4	57
Softball	17	19	19	55

I. *Problems*
   1. The problems encountered while scheduling co-recreational intramural athletic contests were listed as follows: (182 replies)
      a. Lack of interest by females — 114
      b. Lack of outdoor facilities — 99
      c. Lack of indoor facilities — 94
      d. Conflicting extra-curricular activities — 90
      e. Conflicts with other intramural contests — 65
      f. Lack of interest by males — 64
      g. Conflicting classes — 55
      h. Lack of funds — 52
      i. Lack of equipment — 30
      j. Lack of entries — 20
   2. The largest problem faced by the co-recreational intramural athletic director was: (182 replies)
      a. Lack of facilities — 37.3%
      b. Lack of participants — 33.6%
      c. Lack of staff — 11.5%
      d. Lack of funds — 9.6%
      e. Others — 10.0%

J. *Evolution of Co-Recreational Intramural Sports*
   1. Co-recreational intramural athletics evolved through: (193 replies)
      a. A staff decision — 170
      b. Some pressure from the student body — 59
      c. Some pressure from school administration — 33
   2. Reasons for inaugerating co-recreational intramural athletics included: (193 replies)
      a. Need for more female participation — 105
      b. Socialization of the sexes — 96
      c. Other schools had co-recreational programs — 65
      d. Conform with Title IX regulations — 45
      e. Need for more male participation — 20

K. *Beliefs Concerning Co-Recreational Intramural Sports*
   1. The following reflect the beliefs of respondents concerning co-recreational intramural athletics: (201 replies)
      a. Co-recreational intramural athletics should not be included in a collegiate intramural program — 8 (4.0%)
      b. Co-recreational intramural athletics should be offered in a collegiate intramural program, but should not be considered as important as the men's and/or women's program — 30 (14.9%)
      c. A collegiate intramural program should contain a co-recreational, a women's and a men's athletic program, but the co-

recreational athletic program should be considered most important — 31 (15.4%)

d. Co-recreational intramural athletics should be an integral part of the collegiate intramural program, and should share the same status as the men's and/or women's program — 121 (60.2%)

e. All activities in a collegiate intramural program should be co-recreational; there should be no separate men's and women's intramural activities — 11 (5.5%)

L. *Effects of Title IX Legislation on Co-Recreational Intramural Sports*
   1. The following are the beliefs of respondents concerning recent Title IX Legislation and its effect on co-recreational intramural athletics: (224 replies)
      a. Title IX legislation will not affect the present co-recreational intramural athletic program — 149
      b. Title IX legislation will cause more women to be involved in leadership roles — 74
      c. The number of co-recreational intramural athletic programs will increase — 70
      d. The co-recreational intramural athletic budget will be increased — 64

It is my firm conviction that this philosophy applies equally as well to our university communities. It is our job to foster and develop these programs for faculty and staff and their families and, if necessary, to convince the administration of our institutions of the importance of this phase of our programs.

I would like to conclude by saying that we, as intramural directors, receive many rewarding experiences through working in our various programs. We certainly don't stay because of the pay!! In my experience working with the faculty and staff program at the University of Michigan, I have not only found it to be a rewarding experience, but I have also found it can be extremely beneficial in terms of gaining administrative support for the entire program.

Chapter 10
Faculty-Staff Intramurals

Faculty-Staff Intramural Programming
Rodney J. Grambeau
(1970 NIA Proceedings, pp. 137-143)

The responsibility of the intramural department for providing a varied program of leisure time pursuits for the faculty and staff of our universities and colleges has become clearly defined. At last year's National Intramural Association Meeting in Los Angeles, Russ Rivets, Assistant Intramural Director at Michigan State University, presented a paper entitled "New Directions in Faculty Participation." He reported that, in a survey conducted among members of the Big Ten Conference Intramural Directors, he found that six of the nine schools responding favored a philosophy or policy of developing faculty intramural or recreational programs, and six of the nine schools also indicated that their administration felt that they had a responsibility to provide a faculty program, including programming for faculty families.

The University of Michigan is one of the schools that wholeheartedly supports the concept of a faculty intramural and recreational program. The basic philosophy of the University Intramural Department is that it is as necessary to adequately provide for faculty participation as it is for student participation. A specific portion of the overall facilities usage are programmed for faculty participation. In planning for new facilities, the faculty program is included as an integral part of the total program. We feel that there is need for greater faculty involvement in intramural sports, just as there is a need for greater student involvement.

It is understood that not all college and university administrators and intramural directors accept this responsibility for faculty programming, and that many in charge of the various programs sometimes find it difficult in terms of budget and facility to adequately provide for this segment of the university community. However, it is my personal conviction that we, as the specialist on our campus in the area of recreational needs of the university community, have a responsibility to develop, in every possible way, this phase of the program.

While the intramural program is usually responsible for the greater share of faculty-staff programming, we should keep in mind that there may be other departments or areas within the university or college which may be in a better position to offer certain services to the faculty and staff than the Intramural Department. Intramural departments may only become involved on a consultant basis, or on a publicity basis when and if needed. The important thing is that the job is getting done. As I describe some of the programming at the University of Michigan, you will note that different facets of the University, as well as the community, are involved.

With this philosophy in mind, I would like to describe some of the programming which we do at the University of Michigan for faculty and staff, in the hope that it may stimulate your thinking for your own program. I am sure that many in attendance here are conducting as good, or even better programs than we are at the University of Michigan.

Size and Scope

There are approximately 8000 faculty members at the University of Michigan. This includes all academic teaching, research, administrative, and fellowship appointments. Of this number, approximately 1000 obtain permanent lockers at the Intramural Sports Building.

The faculty intramural program is divided into a competitive program, a sports club program, an instructional program, an informal program, and a Faculty-Student Competition Program.

COMPETITIVE PROGRAM

The competitive program focuses around leagues and tournaments in twelve different sports, involving approximately 2500 participants.

Eligibility

All faculty, administrative staff, research assistants, and teaching assistants are eligible to compete in the Faculty Division Program.

Fees

A $10.00 fee, payable at the time of entering, is required of all softball, football, volleyball or basketball teams. Each team pays the fee only once and this covers it for all subsequent sports. If a department enters two or more teams, each team must pay a separate fee. Golf and bowling have special greens and lines fees respectively. There is no fee for entering other singles and doubles competition tournaments.

Equipment

Equipment may be supplied by the player or team or may be checked-out at the equipment cage. There is a rental fee and/or deposit required on some items. Expendable items may be purchased at the equipment cage.

All-Sports Points

Points are awarded to teams (usually representing a department) for their finish in the competitive program sports. Sports organized as a league followed by playoffs have a range of 50-150 points; sports organized as either a league, meet or an elimination tournament have a range of 35-100 points. Interim point values are determined by the number of teams and/or places in the competition. Only one entry per department may earn points in any given sport — the one advancing the highest. In the event of a split

141

double entry, i.e., two partners from different departments, the point total earned will be split equally among the two departments. The department earning the highest number of points at the end of the year is crowned the All-Sports Champion for the division.

Awards

Individual or team trophies are awarded to the members representing the winning team in each sport. The Intramural Department selects one faculty member each year to receive a Faculty Intramural Honor Award. The individual is selected on the basis of sustained interest, athletic ability, participation, and leadership in the Faculty Intramural Program. The winner of this award last year had completed 24 years of intramural competition in both softball and volleyball. During this period, behind his pitching and his leadership in softball, his team won thirteen faculty softball championships and numerous volleyball championships.

Participation

Approximately 50 different academic and administrative departments are represented in the faculty competitive program. Several of the departments field more than one team in many of the sports.

Senior Division

A Senior Division for faculty players 45 and older was recently introduced in the tennis, handball, paddleball, and squash competition. An individual eligible to enter the seniors competition may also enter the open competition if he wishes.

SPORTS CALENDAR

First Semester
1. Softball
2. Tennis (Singles)
3. Golf
4. Touch Football
5. Bowling
6. Badminton (Singles)
7. Paddleball (Doubles)
8. Squash (Singles)
9. Handball (Singles)
10. Volleyball

Second Semester
11. Basketball
12. Volleyball
13. Bowling
14. Tennis (Doubles)
15. Handball (Doubles)
16. Paddleball (Singles)
17. Badminton (Doubles)

Sports Club Program

Faculty-staff members are eligible to join any of the many sports clubs active at the University. Clubs which have the largest faculty-staff membership are the Faculty Tennis Club with 49 members, Faculty Squash Club with 35 members, and the Sailing Club with approximately 60 faculty-staff members. A Faculty Water Polo Club has been playing three days per week for the past forty-two years in the I. M. Building Pool. This group competes annually against the students in Student-Faculty competition.

Instructional Program
Faculty may enroll without charge in any of the elective programs offered throughout the year by the Department of Physical Education. These include courses such as Skin & Scuba Diving, Skiing, Tae Kwon Do (Korean Karate), Golf, etc.

Informal Program
Many individuals work out informally in many activities including jogging, swimming, conditioning, paddleball, handball, squash, basketball, volleyball, badminton, tennis, golf, and many other activities.

Faculty-Student Competition
For the past eighteen years, highly competitive matches between faculty and student representatives have been scheduled in several different sports. In each sport, top performers from the various I. M. tournaments throughout the year are selected to represent both the faculty and the students. The matches are selected to assure both a high skill level as well as an equal match for the participants. In scoring, one point is awarded to the winner of each match and no points are given to the loser. The total points are then tabulated to determine whether the faculty or the students have earned the higher overall score. Competition is held in tennis, softball, golf, paddleball (singles and doubles), basketball, billiards, water polo, badminton, rifle shooting, and volleyball.

PROGRAMS OFFERED BY OTHER UNITS OF THE UNIVERSITY
As mentioned earlier, there are a number of programs for faculty that are offered by other units of the university. Examples of some of these are:

1.   The Department of Physical Education for Women offers a faculty-staff family swim night twice a week during the regular school year and once also during the summer session.

2.   The U. of M. Radrick Farms Golf Course is a faculty-staff eighteen hole championship golf course, developed primarily as a faculty-staff facility, through land and funds donated by alumni. Membership costs are $100.00 per year for a single membership, $150.00 per year for a family membership, $300.00 per year for an alumni membership with a $5.00 per round fee. There are 260 regular members and there are only golf facilities. Tournaments are provided throughout the year by the course management. The operation of the course is under the Vice-President for University Relations.

3.   The University Club, located in the Michigan Union and managed by the Union, has a membership of 400 at a fee of $15.00 annually. It provides a

game room for billiards, pool, cards, chess, etc. and a spacious reading room. Membership in this club is limited to ranks of assistant professor and above.

4. Camp Michigania, a summer camp located in Northern Michigan, is operated by the Alumni Association for alumni, faculty and staff. They offer weekly programs for ten weeks throughout the summer. Faculty forums are held each evening by selected members of the University faculty who are invited as guests of the camp. The Alumni Association also sponsors numerous faculty-staff foreign travel opportunities throughout the year.

5. A faculty-staff bowling league is operated by a community bowling alley, with approximately thirty faculty-staff teams.

6. The University of Michigan Athletic Department provides numerous services for faculty and staff. In addition to providing special faculty rates for the use of the U. of M. Golf Course, also an 18 hole championship course, both mens and womens golf leagues are operated by the course management throughout the season. Other benefits include special rates on all intercollegiate athletic tickets, faculty representation on the Board-In-Control and the use of inter-collegiate facilities such as the track, tennis courts, and ice skating rink for faculty and staff.

Conclusion

One of our programs this morning centered around the idea of "borrowing from business". If you will look at some of the larger and the more successful businesses, you will find that the recreational and leisure time needs of their employees is of utmost importance to them. Millions of dollars are spent by these industries in developing and promoting recreation for their employees. They have accepted and believe in the philosophy that greater efficiency and output can be obtained from employees are who provided with recreational opportunities.

It is my firm conviction that this philosophy applies equally as well to our university communities. It is our job to foster and develop these programs for faculty and staff and their families and, if necessary, to convince the administration of our institutions of the importance of this phase of our programs.

I would like to conclude by saying that we, as intramural directors, receive many rewarding experiences through working in our various programs. We certainly don't stay because of the pay!! In my experience working with the faculty and staff program at the University of Michigan, I have not only found it to be a rewarding experience, but I have also found it can be extremely beneficial in terms of gaining administrative support for the entire program.

New Direction in Faculty Participation
Russell L. Rivet
(1969 NIA Proceedings, pp. 56-59)

Faculty participation in sports and recreational activities is experiencing change. New demands are calling for investigation and new directions. The extent of some demands seems beyond reality. Greater emphasis on fitness has led students and faculty to the extent of jogging in hallways and up and down parking ramps. Some institutions add to this situation by promising intramural and recreational opportunities to recruit new faculty members.[2] Student demands on intramural facilities and administrators are making faculty participation most difficult. Intramural directors are finding it impossible to continue to serve the student interest and still provide facilities for faculty activity.[5]

There are trends the writer believes significant which are giving rise to new directions and attempts to meet this challenge. These trends for faculty participation are: summer programs, sports clubs, informal and family activities and faculty clubs.[1] Recognizing these trends, let us discuss their value and desired outcomes.

The first and most defined trend is summer programs for faculty participation.[11] During the summer, student programs are minimum, outdoor facilities are available, and the demands on the faculty are relieved.

Organized summer faculty programs in softball, volleyball, tennis and golf can be very successful. Faculty participation in informal and family summer activities of swimming, tennis and golf is well substantiated.[2]

The desired outcomes of summer faculty programs are increased faculty participation and some decrease in the faculty pressure for facilities. In summer programs, students and faculty may participate together in more activities.

Faculty participation in sports club programs is increasing.[11] There are several reasons for this trend. Clubs permit intramural as well as extramural activity. Clubs allow the faculty to participate in club work and associate with students.[6] Faculty members have a voice in scheduling and conducting club activities. Finally, clubs receive more consideration regarding facility allocation. Sports clubs contribute to many desired outcomes. They aid in scheduling for the maximum use of facilities, they have educational value, and they can develop good student-faculty relations. The faculty are very active in sports clubs for bowling, swimming and tennis.[12]

The current and most significant trend to appear in the Western Conference and numerous other institutions is toward increased informal faculty participation. From a review of collected intramural handbooks one realizes that faculty members are not entering organized scheduled activities as much as one might suspect; this may indicate that faculty want to set up their own schedules, make their own arrangements for facilities and compete with colleagues, students and friends.[10] In groups of two or four they will play paddleball, handball, tennis, badminton and golf. They form larger groups for informal participation in basketball, volleyball, bowling and softball. Many faculty members are involved in fitness, weight-lifting, judo, karate, steam rooms, pools and other facilities on an informal basis. They join in with the students in the use of these areas when their schedules permit. Some faculty members may appear as early as 8 a.m. and others may arrive as late as 9 p.m. to use facilities informally.[1] These are all effective towards increasing informal participation. However, I must point out that this trend is following a pattern.

The informal trend is usually found at schools blessed with good-to-excellent intramural facilities and programs.[2] Most institutions place student participation before faculty participation.[11] In institutions with inadequate facilities, the faculty have little to no opportunity to participate.[11] Organized faculty programs are more successful under crowded conditions, because the only way for the faculty member to obtain facilities is to enter tournaments. In schools with adequate services and facilities, informal participation is increasing and organized or formal activities are decreasing.[10] Only the organized activities that faculty are interested in and are willing to initiate and conduct are remaining.

Intramural departments experiencing increasing informal participation are providing more services. Hours for use of facilities are being extended. Reservation systems are necessary.[1] Injury procedures are carefully planned. Lockers and towel services are provided on a more permanent basis. Needed sports equipment is issued upon individual request and all play areas are requiring more supervision. Women's informal participation is growing.[7] Women faculty, staff and faculty wives are increasingly using the pool, steam rooms and fitness room. The trend for informal participation is becoming big business to many intramural programs.

The trend towards family participation is evident.[2] Faculty members are asking for recreational opportunities which include their families. At present, intramural departments are only providing token services.[11] The faculty are very much aware of their situation and are searching for ways to promote their interests.

Faculty clubs are beginning to take independent action.[3] Most major colleges and universities have faculty clubs. The main purpose of a faculty club is to promote the intellectual, professional and social interests of the academic community.[4] Faculty clubs do provide some recreational opportunities. These usually include: table tennis, billiards, card tournaments, outings and other activities their club room facilities will allow. North Carolina State and Michigan State are leading a new trend in faculty clubs:[8] the development of recreational facilities for the faculty and their families. North Carolina State's Faculty Club now maintains excellent clubhouse and recreational facilities. Michigan State's Faculty Club will soon start construction of a clubhouse and facilities which I believe will lead to a model program.

The Michigan State Project is an exciting new direction in faculty participation. The Michigan State University Faculty Club began their effort with a survey to indicate the interest of the faculty in supporting clubhouse facility. The results were positive and plans were made to facilitate the project. To date, the progress is outstanding. One thousand faculty members have incorporated as a non-profit organization, purchased necessary property and planned a $2 million construction program.[9]. The construction will include a clubhouse with meeting, dining, activity, locker and shower rooms, an outdoor pool, tennis courts, and a slope for beginning skiing and tobogganing.[13] The site is located adjacent to the University Golf Course. Construction will begin this April. The outdoor pool is scheduled to open in May of 1970 and the Clubhouse in September, 1970.[3]

The membership dues are unique. An initial deposit of $225 is required with present annual dues of $10. After the operation begins, the annual dues will be approximately $240. To ease this seemingly high cost, members have stock or share options up to $2,500 at 6% dividends. This means such an investment will partly pay a member's annual dues. The Club then, in effect, may borrow from its membership and avoid the higher interest rates of lending institutions. Dr. Lawrence Bogar, Professor and Chairman of the Department of Agricultural Economics at Michigan State University is the president of the Faculty Club. Further information may be obtained from the progress report and the constitution and by laws included in the reference section or by contacting Dr. Bogar. The Club anticipates serving approximately two thousand faculty members. In effect, this is a dynamic project sponsored by the Michigan State faculty, truly expanding a new direction.

Finally, in summary, faculty participation is relative to each local situation. Intramural directors must decide upon their own faculty activities. The trends presented may or may not be helpful to you. But let us consider that the faculty are in changing times. They want more freedom in selecting their recreational activities. They want "to do their thing." If we realize this and assist them, we'll be doing our thing.

Serving Student Wives
Linda Hall
(1974 NIA Proceedings, pp. 77-79)

In an attempt to serve the population of approximately 22,000 students and 2,250 faculty at the University of Florida, the Intramural Department is offering opportunities to participate in 25 clubs, a faculty staff program, a co-recreational program, a special events program, a men's program and a women's program. We had ten leagues and we thought we were serving every one.

Each college at the University of Florida has an organization called Dames. The membership is comprised of wives of students within the college. Thus we have Business Dames, the Engineering Dames, the Education Dames, etc. They are fairly well organized in that they elect officers and have regular meetings. In addition to meeting one night a week for activities such as a ceramics class, and a book club, they decided to meet once a week for an exercise class or to participate in some type of sport. They attempted to do this, but found that it was difficult to do. The difficulty was due not to lack of interest but due to lack of facilities and equipment, lack of knowledge and skill of the sport by many of the ladies, and lack of leadership. I had the opportunity to present an exercise program to the Dames and consequently became aware of the problems they were having in carrying out a sport and exercise program.

In order to try and meet the needs of this group, we decided to form the Dames league and provide scheduled activity once a week for them. At the beginning of the next quarter we contacted the president of each Dames group and promoted a bowling tournament. Within 3 weeks, we had 24 4-lady bowling teams. Since the league was new, unique, and successful, the campus newspaper gave us good coverage. We felt great about our new league and felt that surely we were now reaching everyone. Student wives who were not members of Dames called wanting to know how they could participate; the president of law wives called saying that even though they, as a group, had withdrawn from the Dames, they wanted to be involved in the intramural programs; and the office of Married Housing called asking how wives who are not Dames may participate. In order to solve this problem and really try to serve everyone, we changed the name of the league to the Student Wives League.

The major difficulty in working with student wives is communication. In order to facilitate communications with student wives other than the Dames, each married housing village had an Intramural Chairman who served as a liaison between the Intramural Department and the residents in the village. In addition, the Division of Married Housing assigned one of their staff to publicize the intramural activities, tournament winners, etc. in a newspaper that all married students received. Communicating with the Dames is the easiest as they are reasonably well organized and have regular meetings. They also elect an Intramural Chairman and the Intramural Chairmen are very good about calling the Intramural Office for information. They call us; we seldom have to call them. We also work closely with the Dames Board of Directors.

From our point of view and from the participants' point of view, the Student Wives League is one of our best leagues. They really have fun. Although a tournament is conducted and a "champion" is declared, the league is more recreational than competitive. We offer this as a "ladies night out" and they arrive at the courts eager to get started and enjoy the activity. An indication of whether or not the participants are having fun might be measured by the lack of complaints and by the frequency of the participant's return. We have virtually no complaints, and many of the same ladies compete in every activity throughout the year. The Dames were sponsoring several different kinds of activities — ceramics, book club, sewing class, Intramural Program, etc. Due to expense in both time and money they took a vote to determine which activities they should continue to schedule on a regular basis. The Intramural Program received the most votes to be continued. Now it is the only activity that the Dames have scheduled on a weekly basis.

From our stand point, the success of the league is in part indicated by the following things: (1) Since they enjoy the program, we have had to deal with very few complaints, (2) Part of the program is instructional in nature in that we offer clinics before each activity, and our students have the opportunity to instruct as well as serve as manager and officials, (3) Many students request to work out with Student Wives' League, therefore, we have no difficulty in getting help, (4) Other students and staff are often introduced to the Intramurals Program by Student wives who tell friends and co-workers at the University, (5) The success of the league has given Intramural Department good publicity with the University Administration. Last year president of Dames sent a letter to the president of the University praising the program, and (6) We receive our operating budget from Student Government. They seem to be pleased that we were one of the few organizations on campus that seek to serve the student wives. The Student Government Budget Committee was interested enough to question as to why we do not have a "Student Husbands" League.

Some of the reasons for the success of the program include:

(1) There is a need for the program.

(2) We give clinics before each activity and have students at each game who have volunteered to help.

(3) We furnish equipment for all sports, and there is no cost involved.

(4) We spend a large part of our budget alloted for bowling on this

league. We conduct the bowling tournament at the beginning of fall quarter and free bowling attracts a lot of participants.

(5)   We make it convenient for them. The Dames decided that Monday night was the most convenient night for participation, so we reserved Monday night for them and are careful to make sure they have the facilities. This often means that larger and more active leagues have to be scheduled around the student wives league.

The activities that they seem to enjoy participating in are bowling, badminton, racquetball, volleyball and deck tennis. They also have access to the exercise room and may attend exercise classes. In order for them to be able to participate in activities that are not offered in their league, they are eligible to participate in the Co-Recreational League, the Women's Independent League and the Special Events Program.

We get a lot of pleasure out of providing activities for the Student Wives.

Chapter 11
Women's Intramurals

Women's Intramurals — Past, Present, and Future
Janice L. White
(1973 NIA Proceedings, pp. 73-82)

Birth...the beginning. Life...a gift. Our world of joy and wonder filled with miracles, some unique and different, while some are universal and the same. A baby's cry, a tiny smile, a mother's love, a child's play...all ever-present- birth, action, change, play...yes, all life and it is here in life itself and in man's innate and strong desire to play that we find the beginning of unorganized sport and thus eventually of physical education, intramurals and athletics. The growth of popular intramural and recreational sports in the United States has emerged like a river with its course adapting itself to the nature of the country through which it flows, the mainstream continually augmented by tributaries and the very river bed itself ever growing both deeper and broader.

In the early period, this river was little more than a trickle, forcing its way through forbidden terrain in a world where survival depended on work; yet, it forged onward gathering volume and flowing quietly and steadily. Initially to school officials, unorganized play was only something to be tolerated as a necessary evil but finally they were forced, due to increasing enthusiasm and popularity, to adopt this early play into their curriculum in the form of physical education. From the beginning, women faced cultural barriers that made their river of recreation deflect into narrowly defined channels. Prior to 1870, they did not even continue their education beyond elementary school since it was believed that the pursuit of higher education would result in the loss of their health and feminine qualities.

Meanwhile, men's intramural programs got a head start growing up on the intermediate ground between the intercollegiate athletic program and the required physical education program. The required program at this time was entirely formal and completely unconcerned with the out-of-class recreational pursuits of the students. At the same time, the varsity athletic program for men was primarily concerned with the so-called major sports and devoted its entire time to those students skilled in these activities. These two programs of varsity athletics and required physical education left the majority of students with no organized recreational sports and it was eventually this lack which resulted, through student demand, in the voluntary intramural program. Ideally, this program was comprised of activities using the skills acquired in the physical education program and provided the opportunity to the masses to practice voluntarily for the sheer

151

joy of participation unmarred by commercialism, professionalism, or false pressures. As early as 1913, Dr. Mitchell was appointed Director of Intramural and Recreational Sports at The University of Michigan and in 1928 was housed in the first intramural sports building. Women, meanwhile, were busy seeking the right to exercise—but it was in exercising their right to vote rather than their bodies that their chief interest rested. Yet, little by little, as they gained educational opportunities and legal rights, women broke away from many stifling restrictions including corsets and hooped skirts and short-skirted and bare-legged, in dress that would have horrified their Victorian ancestors, played tennis as much and as well as men. They then remained on the courts far beyond the age at which the concept of "feminine delicacy" had previously dictated the pursuits of china-painting and embroidery. Adopting the slogan "a game for all and all in the game," they inaugurated intramural programs which they felt must provide "sports for all" and from which participants should derive moral, physical and social benefits. Playing tennis, swimming and seeking a dark sun tan, women had indeed come a long way from the slender, delicate, ideal female whose pale, fragile form with its sallow and waxen complexion had been seen and admired for so long. Still time and culture worked against any great advances since intense physical training was thought to lead to strain and nervous tension. Many women felt that the disadvantages so far outweighed any advantages that it was pointless to even consider a recreational program.

Even then, however, consideration was given to the ideal of democracy in education which Dewey has defined as:
1) The maximum development of all students.
2) Equal opportunities for all and
3) Special privileges for none.
While idealistically sound, cultural reality prevented women from realizing all their potential. Modesty, differentiation, and the mere "Female" or "feminine" concept kept them within the confines of a separate program with different needs, facilities and finances.

The men's program enlarged to offer a wide variety of activities and to attain democracy in the education of men. These programs were autonomous and while viewed as an integral part of the education of the whole man, were recognized as important in their own right without subservience to physical education or athletics.

Perhaps because of separate facilities, modesty, or those individuals who had dared to break from cultural tradition and find value in sport, the women's intramural programs became an important phase in the administration of the women's physical education department. Leavitt and Duncan (16) found that the national trend in 1931 was for the intramural programs to be one *phase* of the departmental program in conjunction with the Women's Athletic Association (W.A.A.). These programs had thus

The number of women in competitive intramural programs has grown tremendously since the early 1970's.

progressed up until this time from a recreation program sponsored, directed and financed by students, through interclass activities supported by the physical education department; to programs sponsored, administered and financed to a large degree by the department of physical education. Thus in 1931, 70 of 90 schools stated (16) that intramural responsibilities were a cooperative function of the W.A.A. and the Department of Physical Education, while, now one held intramurals as separate, with special needs, individual importance, and a specially selected staff. Leavitt and Duncan further learned that staff assignments usually included a staff advisor to the W.A.A. and a faculty member for each activity. Faculty sponsorship of such an activity could mean that the W.A.A. elected the head of all intramural sports or that 1 or 2 girls were either appointed or elected to take charge of all intramural activities. Thus, the roots of women's intramural sport programs were planted deep in physical education serving as a laboratory for the required instructional classes and taking its place as one phase of the physical education program.

As early as 1940, Daniels (8) stated that the education of the leisure no longer belonged in the hands of casual agencies but rather such education belonged with agencies of deliberate education including colleges and universities. Daniels believed that even at this time there was reason to believe that some universities were doing "something" along the lines of self expression and development, but there was no way to ascertain the extent to which the intramural offerings were meeting the needs of the student body. He went on to predict that the next few years would see the acceptance of the idea of providing for the general students' recreation as a "legitimate college function."

Not only has recreation been accepted as a legitimate college function but this quiet, steady river has exploded in a riotous torrent, breaking through all barriers, carving out new and fresh channels and sometimes seeming to sweep all else aside spreading in a full flood over a vast territory. This change has come quickly. For men, the intramural programs which evolved from the limited offerings of highly competitive team sports have swept up all sports and activities for which there is student demand. They now encompass team, individual and dual sports and outings, social and creative activities. For both men and women, deep cultural changes have occurred. Our nation has become health conscious; yet, individuals are trapped in increasing stresses and less activity. Thus, the national health trend and misuse of leisure time have led to the realization of the necessity of some regular form of mild exercise. In a student generation of social and intellectual activism, in which contemporary students are filled with a desire for the truth, for knowledge, and personal understanding, for ways in which they can and must effect their own destinies and searching for something to "relate to," many have come to realize that what could be more relevant than good health, for without this, nothing else is possible. Getting high on health has replaced artificial trips. For many, L.S.D. has come to relate to running and to mean long slow distance. The whole individual with a hard workout becomes absorbed with the physical act of moving through a spiritual universe with the finish line or game the goal. This feeling knows no limit as to sex or age, yet, women have not naturally sought or learned to enjoy such feelings. For years, women have faced a double standard in which they were expected to be active, healthy and co-ordinated while still being dainty, fragile and feminine. Janet Seidler (21) wrote in 1963 that as a physical educator she faced the problem that the majority of women that she tried to educate "physically" shuddered in fear of being typed as "athletic." Seeking to motivate women to move, she felt confident that once they began they would find activity relaxing and enjoyable and thus would continue. Yet, Mrs. Seidler, like so many other women physical educators of that time, found her job difficult and felt that beyond the point of the classroom teaching of a skill, she had not been successful. For of what value is a skill if it is not mastered with pride, then used and enjoyed? Yet, how can we expect women, many of whom have never been encouraged to exercise and many who have come from poor high school backgrounds, to suddenly get up and exercise and enjoy it? Girls, until the age of about twelve participate with boys in the most active games, enjoying them and totally capable of good performance. Suddenly, under the wing of society, young girls in the past disappeared from the playing field to learn to be "feminine" —physical activity became secondary. A decade later with the added complexity of body development she is just as suddenly expected to be physically fit and to be as active as her male counterpart who had never stopped exercising, playing and training. While males are expected to go through an awkward age, they all allowed to trip through it gradually adjusting to both growth and development changes. Such has not been the case for women who exercising little have suddenly found themselves with all new tools with which to work—a lower center of gravity, changes in size, shape, proportions and basic form. She may plainly not know how to run or move. Running may be a painful experience—for while it has been found that men with high athletic skill have gained high social acceptance and thus adjustment (21), such has not been the case for women. Encouragement and praise can not be expected to provide motivation. Thus, the apparent "lack of co-ordination" may be in reality "lack of practice." Mrs. Seidler asks for help—help in the motivation of women and help has come! The cultural continuum with femininity on one end and athletics on the other has narrowed. The ideal female has become a physically fit one. Exercising is "in" and suddenly the sports woman is daily eating right, exercising and covering 5 miles a day needing only the right deodorant. In ten years, we have arrived! In the past women's physical education has been bound by cultural problems to be sure but we have sought the easy way out for too long. Certainly we have been limited by culture, facilities and finances but often all too readily we have accepted these limitations. As Jonathan Livingston Seagull sought to learn about flying only to fall and become discouraged...

"a strange hollow voice sounded within him. There's no way around it. I am a seagull. I am limited by my nature. If I were meant to learn so much about flying, I'd have charts for brains...I must fly home to the flock and be content as I am, as a poor limited seagull...He vowed he would be a normal gull...there would be no ties now to the force that had driven him to learn, there would be no more challenge and no more failure. And it was pretty just to stop thinking and fly through the dark toward the lights on the beach."

It appears to me that we have been coasting peacefully through the dark for too long; yet, like Jonathan Seagull, this does not have to be our fate. He soon realizes that...

"such promises are only for gulls that accept the ordinary. On who has touched excellence in his learning has no need for that kind of promise."

Neither do we—! We have our ancestors and women's physical education to **thank for giving us the strength and desire not to accept the ordinary and for helping us touch excellence.**

For Jonathan a discovery was made as is apparent in his statement, "How much more there is to living! Instead of our drab slogging back and forth to the fishing boats. There's a reason to life. We can lift ourselves out of ignorance, we can find ourselves as creatures of excellence and intelligence and skill. We can be free! We can learn to fly!

The time is now for there is much more to recreation than a laboratory for physical education. Motivation is no longer lacking. Women want to exercise. They want a total program of organized competition, informal drop-in activities and sports clubs. We can find ourselves, build total programs and "learn to fly."

The late professor, Carl Becker, stated that, "We cannot recover the past, but we can, within the limits set by nature and history and our own intelligence and resolution, make the future...We make the future in any case, it is better to make it by not letting things ride, but by having some idea of where things ought to go and then doing whatever possible to make them go in that direction." To be sure we find ourselves in many stages of development but that is not important for in the words of Oliver Wendel Holmes "The great thing in the world is not so much where we stand, as in what direction we are moving." We have taken the easy way out for too long. We must now rise above idealistic planning and move toward the development of quality programs. Like the seagull we must realize that "the gulls who scorned perfection for the sake of travel go nowhere, slowly. Those who put aside travel for the sake of perfection go anywhere, instantly."

...the trick was to stop seeing themselves as trapped inside a limited body that had a forty-two inch wing span and performance that could be plotted on a chart. The trick was to know that his true nature lived, as perfect as an unwritten number, everywhere at once across space and time."

Thus, we must scorn programs which are not quality programs. We must consider our students as unique and individual and aim to satisfy their needs. We must stop seeing ourselves as trapped inside the limited body of physical education with limited staff time and secondary importance and know that our true nature lives now — in our importance, in our unity, and in our ability as administrators.

Shakespeare once stated that "there is nothing either good or bad but thinking makes it so." Thus, responsibility for our programs rests with each of us. Nothing is inherently good or bad. It is only in our thinking and careful evaluation with consideration for our own unique students and local situation that we may determine the positive or negative aspects of a policy or program. Thus, point systems and awards are not always bad for they can give added inducements to some students to participate and without participants our programs, regardless of their quality, are nothing. To view them arbitrarily as negative we are not moving toward an ideal, we are admitting to poor administrative capabilities since it is our responsibility to have the insight to carefully evaluate such policies and change then as needs demand.

It is just as narrow to view officials as good because they are women and bad because they are men. We must have the best officials possible and should evaluate them all on their officiating capabilities. We must take the responsibility of developing good women's officials who will then officiate because of their own merit as officials not just because they are women.

Too much time has been spent in the differentiation and delineation of differences between men's and women's programs, needs, rules, etc. We must ask ourselves "why?" Women are demanding equality. Give it to them! Modify based on need — not on principle.

While each school has a way of doing things, it is apparent that we should be constantly evaluating our programs in an attempt to better them. According to Dr. Grambeau (10), "Because we have been doing something in a certain way does not mean that it should not be altered, changed, discarded, or retained intact." All of us, both men and women, have an obligation to dynamic and positive leadership. What is sacred about keeping the women's program within physical education? If this affords the best method of achieving the best possible program then and only then should it be accepted, but as George Haniford (11) pointed out in 1965, changes seem to be occurring, finding a relocation of the intramural office with the office of student services. More and more schools are combining personnel to obtain the best possible professional staff to meet the intramural and recreational needs of men and women alike.

Women for the first time are appearing as intramural administrators in their own right, not as physical educators with a secondary interest in intramurals. This should not be viewed as a negative thing for only emphasis separates the two fields. To view such a separation as negative is like a general practitioner training a new doctor and then disowning him and resenting the fact that he decides to specialize in surgery. We have just chosen to express our knowledge and enthusiasm for physical education through the medium of recreation.

The physical education program provides the skills necessary to participate and enjoy some form of recreation. Intramurals (competitive, informal and club) then provide the voluntary opportunity to the masses to recreate regularly. The varsity athletic program completes the picture providing recreational opportunities to the highly skilled. Thus, rather than dividing ourselves up into factions, we, and this is especially true of women, must restrain from commissioning ourselves into more and more committees, standards and policy boards, etc., or we will commission ourselves to death. Rather we must unite and together look at the students and ask ourselves, "Am I offering the best program possible?"..."Am I meeting the needs of my unique students?" For these students are becoming more and more demanding in their requests for program offerings. They expect quality and demand many outlets for the satisfaction of their needs. We must realize that no longer can their physical, emotional and social needs be met in one stereotyped program. Rather diversification and enlargement is necessary as can easily be seen in the growing co-recreation programs as well as the men's and women's. Yet, such movement is not possible without administrative commitment. Student athletic associations cannot be expected to meet these needs. We live in an age of professionalism and as such must develop professional programs. While students must have education and personal life as top time priorities and faculty advisors with demands in the required physical education curriculum may find conflicts of interests, trained women's intramural administrators will enable all of us to work together, to present our own needs and interests on an equal basis and through a trained eye and in short to provide the stability, continuity and consistency necessary to build a sound, quality program, establish tradition and meet the needs of *all* students—without emphasis toward physical education majors.

It is far too easy for all of us to point out the negative, the injustice of the past, to react to change because it often brings fear and temporary insecurity. Unity is the answer. Together we have an amazingly strong, justifiable and accountable program.

John Heffernan (13) in reference to the joining of the northeast and southeast sections of the N.I.A. paraphrased the president of Morgan State saying, "it was a wonderful thing that a new group was coming into the meetings...there was a need for new blood and new ideas...with both groups working together he was positive that the N.I.A. would leave its mark in the university and college field." Hopefully, the same holds true today for our strength is in our unity. We must speak together with authority and take a back seat to no one. Ours is a vital mission and we hold a golden opportunity. We must believe that the glory of flight awaits us if only we open our eyes and see. We must look with our understanding. We must find out what we already know. We must realize that each of us is an unlimited idea of freedom and that quality programs are a step toward expressing our real nature. Together we must move and then and only then we'll see the way to fly.

REFERENCES

1. Beeman, Harris F. "An Analysis of Human Relations in the Administration of Intramural Sports Programs of the Western Conference," *N.I.A. Proceedings 1960*, 27-29.

2. Buchanan, H. Edsel, "The Relationship of Intramurals and Physical Fitness," *N.I.A. Proceedings 1962*, 61-66.

3. _____ . "Point Systems, Awards, and Records," *N.I.A. Proceedings 1963*, 50-53.

4. _____ . "Current Trends — Personal and Program Requirements," *NCPEAM 1964*, p. 11.

5. Clark, Don. "The Present Years. 1962-1968," *N.I.A. Proceedings 1968*, 72-74.

6. Clegg, Richard. "Methods of Involving Students in College Intramural Programs," *N.I.A. Proceedings 1966*, 87-90.

7. Curtis-Bennett, Sir Noel. "Youth and Leisure: The Importance of Recreation," *Journal of Health and Physical Education*, III, No. 9 (November, 1932), 18-19.

8. Daniels, Arthur S. "Report on National Survey of Student Recreation in Colleges and Universities," *Research Quarterly*, XI, No. 3 (October, 1940), 38.

9. Gaither, A. S. "Jake." "Sports Contribution to the American Way of Life," *N.I.A. Proceedings 1965*.

10. Grambeau, Rodney J. "The Relationship of Physical Education to Intramurals," *N.I.A. Proceedings 1963*, 103-106.

11. Haniford, George W. "The Changing Complexion of the School Intramural-Recreational Program," *N.I.A. Proceedings 1965*.

12. _____ . "Co-Recreation and Intramural Sports," *N.I.A. Proceedings 1963*, 19-21.

13.   Heffernan, John. "The Middle Years," *N.I.A. Proceedings 1968*, 69-70.

14.   Higgins, Joseph R. "Intramural Sports and New Dimensions in Residential Education," *N.I.A. Proceedings 1966*, 82-86.

15.   Jones, Grace E. "An Intramural Organization for Girls," *Journal of Health and Physical Education*, II, No. 8 (October, 1931), 29-31.

16.   Leavitt, N. M. and Duncan, M. M. "Status of Intramural Programs for Women," *American Physical Education Association Research Quarterly*, VIII, No. 1 (March, 1937), 68.

17.   Lee, Makel. "The Case For or Against Intercollegiate Athletics for Women and the Situation Since 1923," *American Physical Education Research Quarterly*, (May, 1937), 68.

18.   Luibrock, Philip. "Publicity and Public Relations," *N.I.A. Proceedings 1963*, 47-49.

19.   Means, Louis E. "Health and Physical Fitness Needs at all Academic Levels," *N.I.A. Proceedings 1963*, 117-121.

20.   Oglesby, R. R. "Speech to N.I.A. Luncheon," *N.I.A. Proceedings 1965*, 21-24.

21.   Seidler, Mrs. Janet. "Viewpoints on Intramurals," *N.I.A. Proceedings 1963*.

22.   Stumpner, Robert. "Philosophy of Intramurals—Indiana University," *N.I.A. Proceedings 1960*, 5-8.

23.   Townes, Dr. Ross E. "Play With a Purpose—A Resolution," *N.I.A. Proceedings 1964*, 2-5.

24.   Vattano, Dr. Frank J. "Psychological Implication of Participation to the Student Engaging at the Intramural Level," *N.I.A. Proceedings 1964*.

25.   Wagner, M. M. "Intramurals and the Women's Athletic Association," *American Physical Education Association Research Quarterly*, II, No. 1 (March, 1931), 206.

Women's Role in Society
Patti Holmes
(1975 NIRSA Proceedings, pp. 258-260)

I think it is essential to examine our social system and how, over a long period of time, our society has trained us for specific roles. Therefore, a brief background of the history of women's roles is necessary to understand women's roles today.

Our society programs all of us in certain roles in order to maintain itself. In primitive tribal cultures, a classless society is described by Engels in his book, *Origin of the Family, Private Property and State*. This communal society has certain characteristics which gives us essential information for understanding the evolution of the mother role, a role where *most* women find themselves today.

In *Origin of the Family, Private Property and State* a description of this collective society is given in depth. The people in this primitive society work collectively together for a collective end. All people in the community were provided for on an equal basis. The members of the tribe or clan were self-governing and all were equal. This was considered a matriarchal society where women were held high in respects and were the core of the commune, producing both children and material necessities of life. No individual family exists and all adults regard themselves as social parents of all children. The system of Kinship was through clan or tribal connections.

So, as you can see, we are dealing with a classless society, collective work for collective ends, group marriage and a time when women occupied a high position, enjoying freedom in contrast to today's situation.

Then eventually comes the breakdown of the original collective system. Brotherhood of men is no longer the basis for social relations. The society changes with the introduction of large scale agriculture and stock raising. Tribal communes begin to breakdown, first into separate clans, then to farm families and eventually into today's "nuclear family". People became property orientated and there is a need for the individual family so man can transmit his property to his son. Male domination and the beginning of the father-family order changes the social order not from any superior attributes of males over females but from a new social economic force—property ownership and its transmission through the patriarchal line.

Through this social change, class differentiation of work and life style becomes apparent, the patriarchal institution of family, private property and eventually the downfall of the female sex comes into the limelight.

Men become the principal producers and property holders. The institution of monogamous marriages serves to fulfill the needs of landlords.

It is extremely interesting to see the development of this major social change. This is when women find themselves in the homes, as a result of a society which develops around an economic base.

Woman, today, is still found in the home, her economic function easily becoming that of the principal consumer. There are many other roles which women have. Women are secretaries, consumers, sex-pots, community volunteers, teachers, clerks, homemakers, professionals and many other roles as a result of social programming. But women do have a great deal more potential. There is a need to create a new society where women don't have to play roles that force them into positions where they never reach their fullest potential.

All people, not just women, need to understand how society has programmed us. We need to analyze this institution which created our present situation. Eventually, this system of social programming will undergo great changes but only if we devise methods and join together to create conditions so that all people can develop to their potential. Women are not the only ones stifled by this present social order, but we are the majority and it is necessary to determine what action needs to be taken to change the system that allows little or no growth.

Woman's Place in Sport
Carol Harding
(1975 NIRSA Proceedings, pp. 260-261)

Sport has been a man's world and women have always had a segregated place in this world, far removed from men's sportsworld. Even men's sports were not originally for all men, but for white men; eventually sportsworld allowed black men. Sport was racist and now we view clearly that sport is sexist. Wilma Rudolph, Olympic track star, had double the problems of Jack Johnson or Jackie Robinson. Her discrimination has been racist and sexist and she still remains unknown. Until the 1960's, there was an order to our culture that held people less equal to others, and sport still remains a microcosm of that old culture or class structure.

Because this country is committed by doctrine to equal opportunity, women should not have a separate place set aside for them. Instead, women should be fully included in sportsworld. Separate has in no instance meant equal in this society.

Elizabeth Janeway, noted sociologist, clearly indicates women's place is not any single place in our culture. She is not solely in the home, business, education or politics—in fact, she is the original "moonlighter," with multiple jobs and roles. Her interest in sport and fitness has been met by resistance and a campaign or a crusade is underway in having the freedom to choose, freedom to change and freedom to participate in sport. One of the most significant areas of women's interest has been in recreational sport and women continue to participate in remarkable number.

Discomfort and discouragement has been prevalent amongst women interested in sport: all women do not have the opportunity to participate in sports; sports administrators in schools, colleges and universities were not responding to the needs and increased sports interest of women students; facilities and administration of sport for women was not keeping pace with women's sport interest or anywhere near the investment in men's sport.

Women's place in sport in many institutions has been to have them: use the old men's gym or an area without enough facilities; use used equipment; be housed in inferior locker rooms and shower areas; have no priority in use of existing men's fields or courts; suffer a variation in pay scales for men and women—officials, supervisors and professional staff and inadequate budget for effective administration.

Now, we see difficulties and discomforts in sport administration falling away to new solutions and resolutions. Title IX will extend far beyond the immediate situation. The transition period in the acceptance and implementation of Title IX will show people that: sports are sexist, and if they are less sexist at particular institutions, all colleges and universities will now pay the price for existing sexism in sport wherever it occurs; women want a piece of the sports action; it is economically and philosophically feasible to serve all people, and this expansion of sport will lend further emphasis on need of better sport facilities, equipment and administration.

The popularity of men and women participating in sport has not yet crested and it is the work of IM administration to prepare the way. This organization, the N.I.A., has been responsive to all men in sport with a fine tradition and we want the same commitment for women.

Women's Role in Intramurals
H. Toi Jamison
(1975 NIRSA Proceedings, pp. 261-262)

Women intramural administrators represent women who have aspired to achieve in a traditionally and predominantly male domain. Although this domain presents unparalleled opportunities for women, much has yet to be accomplished in our achievement of professional status.

As administrators, the role is leadership and our job is to provoke people into doing things they may or may not want to do. However, this is an "aggressive" and "assertive" quality, and we should be aware of the negative societal attitudes toward such qualities in women.

Whether or not we succeed will depend upon how well we play our role and how aggressive we are. We must begin by realizing the vital need for women's involvement in the total intramural program on all organizational levels. The responsibility to provide quality and equal sports services for all students must be our commitment.

We have met as members of this organization and discussed the various problems in women's programs. There appears to be basic functions we must perform in our role as leaders. We must exercise our rights and our obligations to develop quality programs. We must expose, condemn and stop discriminatory uses of budgets and resources that diminish the quality of and prevent the equalization of women's programs. This relates to unequal pay for equal and superior work, discriminatory practices in fringe benefits and promotions, and inferior support systems in terms of office space and staff.

There is an imperative need to establish training programs to provide leadership opportunities for women in intramural administration, and a need to seek financial aid for women to enter professional preparation in intramural administration. There is a definite need for women to assist in planning areas of professional preparation to provide sports services for women and men.

The need for sensitivity to and concern for problems and needs in programming women's activities is long overdue. It is imperative that we create an affirmative climate that is receptive to women's utilization of all facilities. The problems involved in scheduling activities and open recreation for women in places which were previously considered male facilities are real and should be a major concern of everyone at this conference.

We cannot afford to accept these kinds of inferior situations if we expect to achieve professional status. We must believe that we have the right and the duty to develop quality programs and fight for the chance to display our abilities. We must become cognizant of our potential and be willing to accept the full responsibility of our leadership role.

Chapter 12
Public School Intramurals

Intramurals/Elementary Style
Mark A. Pankau
(1976 NIRSA Proceedings, pp. 70-72)

Often times in the elementary school program the actual organizational segment of the program ranges from mediocre to poor (if organization is actually sought) but through no fault of the person in charge, necessarily. If that phrase seems confusing, let me clarify by stating that if a stronger intramural program is sought, regardless of the level, proper steps should be taken to ensure ease in organization (Intramural Newsletter, Sept.-Oct., 1974), regardless of the desired results. If on the other hand, general values of play are stressed, then less organization is obviously needed. Additional points of interest will arise throughout the article in defense of the above statement.

Pertaining to my personal situation, many of my experiences came about as an undergraduate student staff member and later as a graduate director while working on my masters degree. The period of time when I grew wings, came about through the campus newspaper and a concerned sports writer. Our program was condemned as being the corner stone of the "Lombardi Theory"; meaning, "winning isn't everything—it's the only thing". Even though major changes were underway to correct this feeling, it seemed to be late in arriving for some individuals. By major changes I am referring to co-rec leagues, faculty-graduate student leagues, free play, additional measures of publicity, and so on.

All of this trivia leads to a very fine article in the October 13, 1975 issue of *Sports Illustrated* magazine, concerning Dr. Bill Harper's dream at work, the *PLAY FACTORY,* of Emporia Kansas State College, Emporia, Kansas. Through Bill's approach to this topic I have discovered that he is satisfied to continue to experiment with his creation without much fanfare. I was so impressed with the idea in the article that I have taken up my own crusade to publicize Dr. Harper's efforts every chance I get. Many of his ideas and philosophies work well in my situation as I am sure they would in yours, to some degree.

The idea at hand is how to have fun and still compete, play and still play fair, win and lose gracefully. It is of serious importance to realize that children are involved and such things as a major trophy or awards system, and the desire to win at all costs can be detrimental to their social growth. All too often the great invention of the media, television, depicts the wrong side of sports as they occur, and knowing how many hours are logged by children in front of the screen, the young spartan perceives a distorted view of play.

From an elementary level, let us consider the flight of the miniature Pete Rose of the Olga Korbut. In this instructor's first year with elementary intramurals I found an opportunity to experiment, change, expand and delete various social ideas revolving around the aspect of play. All of the assumables were left intact; teams, rules, standings, tournaments, et cetera.

The most interesting occurrence came about following our soccer tourney and preceeding the basketball competition. I announced to the students that the system of referees for their games would no longer exist (NIRSA Newsletter, Jan.-Feb. 1976) and that instead a system of fair play would be experimented with. The shock occurred when a fourth grade boy quizzed, "but how will we play?" At that point, I decided it was time for my young gladiators to start thinking for themselves again. It was announced that each person would call his own fouls, settle his own disputes, and hopefully, play just for the fun of playing.

Not to this instructor's surprise, but to the students' it worked! I remained in a capacity of supervisor to post scores, set up the next weeks games, and act as mediator through confusing situations. I have found the students to be more strict with themselves than I had been in the past. The type of play did an about face and our slogan, "Friendship first, competition second", was off to a roaring start.

Before this approach was implemented a lesser number of games took place, due to the need of my services as the referee. I could not be on two or more fields at the same time which thereby limited the number of games in a specific sport. Due to such things as weather and time factors, some teams played each other but once, in order that other sports might be scheduled. In my situation most of the schools have the space and interest to play at least two games at a time. By decreasing our time standards, in certain situations, from one hour to one-half hour, more activities were being incorporated. This allows the children to play against everyone else more often, which is exactly what they seem to do best.

Our weekly program is set up for team sports. A new program entitled "Super Saturday" Intramurals is concerned with approximately thirty individual and dual activities and held on Saturday mornings through the same channels mentioned earlier for participation. The girls come for one hour, then the boys come the next hour. Each session we flip-flop the times for variety. This approach is new this year and the students are still warming up to the idea of competing against themselves instead of becoming lost in the regular pack. However, interest is continuing to climb positively.

Methods of motivation can range from nothing to everything, depending on your philosophy of play. In my program, I publish an intramural newsletter four times a year for the homerooms, which includes high point scoring, team standings, up-coming events, and the like. A bulletin board in the gym posts about the same information. I use a different type of trophy

system that is based on:
1) Outstanding athlete per sport activity — however
2) In order to achieve the trophy such factors in physical education program, extra-curricular activities and citizenship are some of the other culminating factors. Our program encourages the students to participate even though they might not be athletically inclined, and awards all students through physical means or social needs.

A very fine teaching associate of mine had little luck with an organized approach and has reverted to the purest form of play imaginable—that of choosing sides from those who show-up and allowing everyone to come out a winner. I am sure you will agree there are pros and cons to both styles of play, however, the main concern is the children.

In evaluating this type of approach, "play—just for the fun of it", I find the students general outlook on their friends and classmates attain new levels of friendship and happiness. We now have more students participating and enjoying it. As part of my philosophy I have adopted the words of a one-time member of a foreign sports federation. This gentleman stated, "a game lasts only for a few moments, but a friendship lasts long, much longer...". I hope you have been able to distinguish parallels between my program and yours, for my ideas have come from yours. With the elementary approach to intramural play, this instructor feels it is the most important aspect of play, and life itself.

High School Intramurals: The Need and Meeting It
M. Wayne Wiemer
(1969 NIA Proceedings, pp. 156-159)

We read and hear much about student violence and unrest today in our colleges. Perhaps, it has occurred at your campus.

Some incidents of student unrest are beginning to develop in the high schools too, sit-ins and other defiances or disregard for the so-called "educational establishment." Part of this unrest in the high schools is being generated by "underground" newspapers which are supplied by outsiders and adapted to the local situation by students enrolled in such schools. Drug abuse and drinking are also becoming serious problems at the high school level.

Let's not kid ourselves. These are not temporary problems; they are difficulties that will increase in intensity. Let's not kid ourselves. Students do not spend all their time studying and working; they need wholesome recreation; they need to release tensions; they need meaningful, healthy activity.

Two of my sons attend a high school neighboring the school in which I teach. These two boys are busy with their studies, interscholastic basketball, baseball and intramural football. When they are asked about unrest, drinking, drugs, and underground newspapers which exist at their school...they know little about these degrading activities; they are involved in wholesome, worthwhile, meaningful activities. Intramural and interscholastic sports and recreation play an important part in their young lives.

Many colleges have been offering elaborate intramural programs for years which is to the credit of you gentlemen; meanwhile, however, the "seeds" of dissatisfaction and disruption have been germinating in many of the high schools throughout this land.

Intramural sports is not, of course, a "cure-all" for all the social ills of our country, but intramural sports can do much to give high school students an outlet for their frustrations and excessive energy. High school intramural sports can direct students into wholesome, meaningful, relevent recreation that can have desirable post high school carryover values for college and adult life.

Perhaps part of the college campus unrest is a result of no or poor recreational services at the high school level and, therefore, too little opportunity for self-identity and recognition outside of the classroom. Perhaps these students who have not participated in high school intramurals do not avail themselves of the opportunity in college, and their excessive energies explode into questionable activities. Maybe this is an area in need of investigation as to the correlation between participation and non-participation in intramural sports as it relates to student dissatisfaction and unrest.

The National Intramural Association's membership is comprised of the real pros in intramural sports. Because this is so, I appeal to each and every one of you to get involved; to make yourself available to provide leadership and consultation to the high schools of your state. I further recommend that this organization set up a committee in each state to develop state associations throughout this nation. These state associations, upon meeting reasonable minimal requirements, should be permitted to be affiliated with the National Intramural Association.

I make this appeal to you for no selfish reasons, for I am fortunate to be directing an I.M. Sports program at a high school district where the board of education, the administration, the faculty, the students and the citizens of the community are sold and committed to intramural sports...but, I make this appeal for the millions of high school students who desire and need part of the sports action as a participant!

I believe that school officials will welcome intramural sports with open arms: when they realize that the majority of students will participate on a volunteer basis; when they realize that an efficient program can be offered for less than five dollars per student per year; when they realize that this service can provide for student leadership involvement and development in a wholesome, meaningful, relevent activity; when they realize how much students' morale can be substantially improved; when they realize the public relations value that intramural sports can provide. You know, of course, that many high schools throughout the country are in a financial dilemma. Many school bonds and educational referenda have failed over the past few years. But, no matter how you cut it, a major part of school financing is and will be dependent upon local community financial support. The willingness for self-taxation is based primarily upon the quality of education, services and public relations.

High school students are wanting student rights and responsibilities; for example, they resent following a rigid study hall plan. They want the option of attending the Instructional Materials Center, visiting and studying with friends in a student commons area or to have a place where they can participate in recreational activities.

Many high schools claim they have an intramural program. Their intramural sports activity mainly consist of throwing out a basketball at the noon hour to occupy the time of some of the students until the bell rings and they have to return to class or to a study hall.

The high school where my boys attend began to give more serious attention to intramurals last year. They appointed an Intramural Director, gave him a grand total of one hundred dollars, and told him to organize and operate an I.M. Sports program. Upon hearing this at one of the Dads' Club meetings, I approached the newly appointed I.M. Director and the Athletic Director and explained, in part, what we do in our school intramural sports program. Almost instantly, they became enthusiastic about the potential of this activity. Later, I talked to one of the board members with whom I had a passing acquaintance. He too, became enthusiastic. So this year, the Intramural Directors' budget has been increased substantially and he has an official meeting place and an office where he and the student leaders organize and carry out many of their activities. Participation is high in over fifteen activities which he, thus far, is able to offer.

And so you see, it is not really too difficult to get programs organized at the high school level. All they need are the facts...the product will sell itself!

I conclude with this question: Is this organization willing to dedicate itself to the leadership necessary to provide direction to this sorely neglected activity in the high schools throughout this nation?

High School Intramurals: The Decade for Decision
Frederick A. Barney
(1966 NIA Proceedings, pp. 103-106)

First of all let me thank you as an organization for inviting me to act as a representative of the various high schools in this most important conference. When I received the letter of invitation back in November from Sonny Rooker asking me to speak at this program, it read in part "your recommended subject is in the area of how college and university programs can assist high school intramural programs. Please suggest a definite title when replying to this letter, as you will be providing information requested by the members of our profession." I suspect that those of you who requested that we discuss this problem may have taken your cue from the business meeting of this organization which was held in the spring of 1964 in Denver. If you remember there were constitutional changes proposed which would make this organization exclusively one for college intramural directors. I said at that time, and I still feel, that this organization can be instrumental in improving the number and quality of high school intramural programs throughout the land. I say this because this is the only organization that I know of which is concerned wholly with intramural sports, and equally important, it is probably the only organization which is concerned with intramural sports that is not influenced to a large degree by people whose primary interest is in a winning season.

I would say that at the present time high school intramural sports programs are quite pathetic. There are many schools who say they have intramural programs and on paper you might see something, but in actual practice there is very little. Very few schools have an intramural director or some other person charged directly with the responsibility of organizing and administering the intramural program. Since this meeting was to be held in Oklahoma I wrote to Mr. Henry A. Vaughan, Director of Physical Education of the State of Oklahoma. His answer in part is "your request is a bit embarrassing since the intramural programs are so scarce in this state. In answer to your first question we probably have no more than ten or twelve schools with a good program in intramurals."

Now I am not one of those people who thinks that our high school athletic program is bad and needs drastic revision. I believe that those boys who get into our interscholastic programs derive many benefits from them. I do feel, however that our athletic program is in part short-sighted. Let me make this point by example. Suppose you have a son who is in high school and he is an average student with no major problems of any kind. As he prepares his high school program he is told by the counselor that he is not permitted to take any lab course at all and the reason given for this is that he is not in the upper percentile of his class. In other words he is not a gifted student. He is told that this type of course is reserved specifically for those who have greater ability. Now I think that if this happened to you, you would be quite angry. You might argue and say that your son deserves to take this course and that you pay taxes just the same as the parents of the more intelligent children. But when you stop to think about it, isn't this just what we have been doing for a long time in athletics? We don't say it this way. We say we will let anyone try out. Sure, the poor ones can come out and be neglected all season long. Maybe they will get something out of it, but most kids aren't going to do it. They drop out on their own accord. Then we say they just didn't want to pay the price. I wonder if every kid would be willing to pay the price if we would keep them on the team.

One might say at this point, why don't you high school people exert an influence to change the athletic program. Perhaps we need to review the various influences upon high school athletics. First of all, the high school curriculum and the various facets of supporting activities are determined by the community through the school board. As far as the athletic program is concerned, there are probably more people who are interested in this, than any other phase of the school program. The superintendent and the athletic director will certainly have a major responsibility in shaping the style, intensity, and content, of this program. The booster club will have no little say in this matter; fathers of outstanding athletes are to be reckoned with; the local sports editor has a major influence; and certainly interested faculty members seeking to field winning teams are going to have an impact on what type of athletic program is sponsored by the high school. Gentlemen, these are pretty strong influences and the high school intramural director who is able to be heard above all this clamor is a rare bird indeed.

Perhaps this is where we need to say something about the influence of the various colleges and universities. First of all, let me say this. There are very few high schools who can do a lot in the way of planning the curriculum and the various programs within the school. The larger schools, like the one I am in, have qualified people with many administrators who have time allotted for this, but there are few schools in that category. Most of the smaller schools are actually organized according to what other schools are doing, or what is recommended by the colleges. When one comes right down to it, much of our growth and enrichment, not only in the extra-curricular activities, but of course, in the academic fields, are spawned to a large extent by research. Much of the enrichment of all these phases in high school programs has come from colleges. This is obviously true in the various sciences, mathematics, literature, art and in physical education. Certainly, if there is going to be any change we need the same type of leadership in athletics. Colleges have had fine intramural programs for decades while high schools have not. Physical education and athletic men coming out of colleges are not interested in intramurals. We have very few physical education and athletic people that visit our school who are really interested in what we are doing in intramural sports. However, they are vitally interested in the rest of the program. Almost no physical education majors display an interest to work in intramural sports. While physical education majors are required or given the option of taking courses in how to coach track, football, basketball and almost any other sport, few seem to be required, or indeed given the opportunity, to take a course in intramural sports. Perhaps besides requiring majors to take a course which includes at least one paper or major project involving intramurals, every course should almost **hammer home** the philosophy that no athletic program which caters only to a few is really complete. And perhaps we should insist that all physical education majors do some intramural work in high schools.

Perhaps the various colleges, or at least the major universities, could provide some sort of assistance to the high schools through their supervising teachers; organizing clinics for high school intramural directors; and by sending literature on the various phases of intramurals to the high schools. Perhaps this association could do a great deal to further high school intramurals by working through state membership chairmen to invite high school intramural directors to join or at least to invite those in nearby areas to this conference. Many of you know about the new Intramural Council of the AAHPER. It is my feeling that this association could do much to influence this new council. And perhaps most importantly, this organization should take some steps to provide speakers for the various conventions and conferences of the superintendents and principals associations.

In the spring of 1964 the athletic institute invited some 45 to 50 experts, teachers, and consultants to Michigan State University to prepare three pamphlets on intramural sports for the senior high school, junior high school and elementary school. I was fortunate enough to participate in this conference along with some of your members including Frank Beeman and Dave Matthews. Considering what I might say here I thought back to this conference and wondered why the athletic institute had sponsored it. And when I asked Ted Bank the president of the Athletic Institute why this was done and why some 15 different organizations were asked to sponsor it, he answered, "For many years I have been an advocate of greater participation in competitive sports, even to the extent of having more than one inter-school competition in each sport. In other words I think it would be wonderful if every boy and girl in the United States could enjoy the thrills of competition." With regard to why he asked various organizations to sponsor this conference he said, "Actually my hope was that they would then help the promotion of intramural sports, not only in the schools but in recreation departments, volunteer agencies like the Y.M.C.A. etc. Specifically, I had hoped that the National Federation of High School Athletic Associations would help push and promote intramural sports in the same way that they have promoted the expansion of a number of sports activities for inter-school competition." After reading this I contacted Cliff Fagen who is the executive secretary of the National Federation of High School Athletic Associations and asked him some similar questions. To partially quote his letter he said, "I am certain that the per cent of high schools that have good intramural programs is much smaller than we would expect," and he further stated that "the Natonal Federation has no direct responsibility in the area of intramurals. We do encourage this program. We give suggestions and try to motivate, but we have no jurisdiction relative to them." Without in any way directing any criticism at Mr. Fagen, for whom I have the utmost respect and confidence, here we have **THE ONE** organization which undertakes the promotion of athletics in high schools almost completely ignoring intramural sports.

I was very gratified to read a speech given to this same national federation by Supreme Court Justice Byron "Wizzer" White on June 27, 1965. I would put this on a required reading list of every intramural director and every college physical education major in the United States. He masterfully describes how the Greeks in the 5th and 6th centuries BC had the utmost respect for a combination of athletics and the arts, and how this was completely misunderstood by the Persians as signs of weakness and which eventually led to the Persians downfall; but how in the long run the athletics corrupted the Greeks as they over-specialized and sought to win at any cost, and it finally developed into bribery and weakness. These comparisons with our present day program are masterpieces. While I feel that his entire address is very important I will quote but a little. "—that athletics carry the seeds of their own destruction and without sound direction a suicide will almost surely occur." He further stated, "no one can justify a school program which benefits only a few and neglects the many. No one can defend a system which discourages the many who cannot compete with the best and see no reason, therefore, to compete at all. No one can fairly close his eyes to those many young people who do not put athletic skill high on their priority list, but who urgently need and would enjoy athletic participation, given more inviting conditions. Is it really necessary for the schools to choose between the athletic team on the one hand and no athletics or no physical fitness programs on the other? The answer is clearly in the negative." He went on to tell this conference that, according to their handbook, athletics are to be an integral part of the secondary program and that athletics are for the benefit of all youth, and that the aim is maximum participation in a well-balanced intramural and interscholastic program. He also went on to explain that there is no mystery about what the group's problems are, that since their goals are reasonably clear the difficulties lie in closing the gap between principle and practice, between theory and reality.

I have never heard these principles stated more clearly nor more forcefully to any group. But in addition, to make these statements to **this** particular group he displayed courage which you and I can envy. Gentlemen, we have a problem which has been with us long enough. **Now** is the time for some positive thoughts, positive actions, directed at the proper groups. What you do in the future years is going to have an effect on many young men. Many young men who are going to be getting out of school and sitting at desks doing jobs which haven't even yet been created. These boys need carry over sports and they need patterns of activity set for later years. These are things which intramural sports can do and **must do.**

Intramurals in Adams Middle Schools
Mosby Turner
(1975 NIRSA Proceedings, pp. 148-149)

I am delighted to be given the opportunity to chair this session at this year's conference because I have been trying to figure out a way to contact others with elementary and secondary level programs. This conference provides an ideal sounding board for all those with similar problems to get together and be mutually helpful. Youngsters between the ages of 9 and 13 are bursting with energy and ready to play anything and everything that comes their way. It's very satisfying to me to see a field of 100 to 150 kids hard at work in their game situations which are well supervised. An interesting intramural program is good medicine for the urban or suburban child.

Our program in Holliston services Grades 5 thru 8 and is open to the entire 1200 student enrollment. Well over half of these students participate in at least one activity each year. Our program is run five days a week and some youngsters are involved in some activity as often as three of the five days. We try to provide as varied a program as possible with a $4,500 budget. We average between 17 and 20 activities a year, part of which are strictly competitive, such as cross country, ping pong, or team sports such as flag football and softball; others are non competitive but teach a skill or art form; in this category are cheerleading and folk singing. We also offer some activities in which competition is optional. Gymnastics is a prime example of this type of activity. The participant may opt to compete in the meets, help stage an exhibition for the student body or just to come to learn what floor exercise and apparatus work is all about.

There are many problems inherent in getting a program going on any level. The toughest is selling the idea to the administration. It helps if some are pro intramurals but often many were never exposed to intramural programs as school boys and feel that interscholastic athletics is the only way to go. Unfortunately, our High School falls into this trap. There are 22 teams competing on various interscholastic levels, but no intramural programming. The 1000 odd students have no choice but to compete with the highly skilled or become a spectator whose ranks are dwindling rapidly in our area. Often in such situations, an interested person must start the ball bouncing with some sure-fire activity in which there is lots of interest. More often than not there will be no compensation other than the fact that some of these would-be spectators are now a part of the action. Let the action grow a little each year until help is needed to handle the program. If careful records are kept, it might be hard to justify not subsidizing this maverick program.

Help may come in the form of volunteers, paid faculty, and students eager to preserve their program. Volunteers are least desirable because 100% dependability is a rarity and more often than not absence occurs without prior notice. A small number of paid faculty who are dependable gives the best results. Students help tremendously by serving as officials. On the Middle School level, the only compensation is the fun and satisfaction in being a part of the program mechanics. There must be good communication with the officials and periodic training sessions to insure continuity.

In Holliston, we rely heavily on a small nucleus of 8 to 10 paid faculty supervisors and students from our official's club. The paid personnel are veterans of at least 5 years and are 100% dependable. They are essential not only to good supervision throughout the year but also help develop the leadership qualities of the youngsters in their charge.

We have had to solve a few problems with the varsity coaches as far as time and space were concerned. It's really quite nice to have an administration that agrees that intramurals come first immediately after classes for 1½ hours everyday, and then varsity teams may use our facilities for as long as necessary thereafter. The varsity coaches don't particularly care for this arrangement, but working mothers love it and so do the kids.

Chapter 13
Community/Junior College Intramurals

Junior College Intramural-Recreational Programs:
A Survey and Analysis
John W. Reznik
(1973 NIA Proceedings, pp. 164-170)

The American junior college movement has experienced an astonishingly rapid growth since the turn of the century. Only eight two-year institutions conducted classes in 1900 while today, there are over 800 junior colleges throughout the United States. The literature repeatedly implies that junior colleges will continue to grow both in terms of numbers of new institutions and increased enrollments within the next ten years.

The growth of intramural-recreational programs in the United States has been equally impressive in recent years. From a haphazard beginning in the mid-nineteenth century, the intramural movement has refined and broadened its program to encompass team, individual and dual sports as well as social, creative and outing activities.

While intramural-recreational programs in four-year colleges and universities are presently enjoying a period of growth and popularity, little is known concerning the status of intramurals at the junior college level. This survey attempts to provide insight into the status of such programs.

Purpose: The main purpose of this study to investigate and ascertain the general nature and extent of intramural-recreational programs of junior colleges throughout the United States in the following areas: philosophy and objectives, organizational structure and personnel, administrative practices, program content, facilities and equipment, and finances.

Methodology: The descriptive survey method of research was utilized. A research instrument was developed and contained both closed and open ended questions. This questionnaire was a modification of two instruments used to appraise and evaluate college and university intramural programs.

One of these instruments, known as the "Criteria for Appraisal of Intramurals in Colleges and Universities," was based on the recommendations made at the 1956 National Conference on Intramural Sports for College Men and Women in Washington, D.C., and the other was a questionnaire utilized in conjunction with a doctoral dissertation completed in 1969 by Ralph Pink.

The research instrument was sent to 336 junior colleges selected at random from those listed in *The Junior College Directory* 1971. Fifty-six institutions were chosen from each of six geographical districts as set-up by the American Association of Health, Physical Education and Recreation.

Since it is generally agreed that the nature and extent of intramural programs vary according to size, the colleges were further sub-divided into three categories based on school enrollment, i.e., small schools with 599 students or less, medium sized schools with 600 to 1999 students and large institutions having an enrollment of 2000 or more.

The statistical analyses employed in this study included the analysis and comparison of junior college intramural-recreational programs in terms of percentages, means and numerical rank. The type of statistical method used was contingent upon the nature of both the question and response. A brief analytical discussion was included for each item and tables were presented to aid in the clarification of the data.

Findings: A summary of some of the more pertinent findings relative to the current status of the surveyed junior colleges is presented according to the major areas of the research instrument.

General

Questionnaires were mailed to 336 junior colleges with a response of 236 or 70.2 percent of the 336 schools returning questionnaires, 177 or 75 percent reported they conducted an intramural program while 59 or 25 percent indicated they had none. The number and percentage of institutions having intramural programs increased as the size of the student enrollment increased. The sole or contributing factor which accounted for the absence of programs in 43 or 72.2 percent of those junior colleges not having intramural programs was either inadequate facilities or equipment.

Philosophy and Objectives

1. The majority of the schools had their intramural philosophy and objectives in writing and in harmony with the overall educational objectives of their institution with only 26 of the surveyed schools not having written objectives.

2. Size of institution was relatively unimportant in terms of the degree to which colleges had their philosophies and objectives in writing.

3. The major objectives of the intramural-recreational programs of all schools combined were directed toward the recreational values of the students were well above *To A Degree* in terms of the appraisal criterion.

Organizational Structure and Personnel

1. Only six schools had full time directors, and 171 had part time directors.

2. Only six directors employed a full time secretary while 90, or 50.6 percent, reported having part time secretarial help.

3. In addition to administering the intramural program the directors in 124, or 75.8 percent, of the institutions taught classes; 83, or 46.9 percent, of the directors coached varsity teams; and 72, or 40.6 percent, conducted intramural programs in addition to coaching and teaching.

4. The size of the school had no effect on the size of the additional work load assigned the directors.

5. Of the schools surveyed, 138, or 77.8 percent, of the intramural directors had Master's degrees.

6. Over one-half (55.6 percent) of the directors held their highest degree in physical education while only 5.5 percent held their highest degree in recreation.

7. Nearly three-fourths (72.9 percent) of the directors reported they did not have any assistants with faculty status.

8. Nearly all of the junior colleges surveyed (96.6 percent) used students to assist in the administration of their programs both on a paid or voluntary basis with medium and large schools employing a higher percentage of paid personnel.

9. While 62.2 percent of the intramural directors favored an intramural council, only 37.8 percent had one.

10. Regardless of the size of the school the primary function of the intramural council was to determine intramural policy.

11. In the majority of the colleges, 110, or 62.6 percent, irrespective of size of student enrollment, officials were selected by the intramural directors with clinics the primary method utilized to train them.

12. According to the administrative lines of authority, the men's intramural director tended to be responsible to the dean, director, or department head of physical education in 33.3 percent of the schools; to the dean, assistant dean, or coordinator of student affairs in 32.7 percent of the colleges and to various other college administrators in 34 percent of the junior colleges.

13. According to administrative lines of authority, the women's intramural director was primarily responsible to men's director in 70.5 percent of the schools.

14. Standards in the schools regardless of size relating to staff qualifications applied equally to both intramural staff and college faculty members slightly above *To A Moderate Degree* on the appraisal criterion with a mean of 3.24.

15. Duties assigned to intramural staff members on the same basis as class instruction, departmental assignments, and administration were credited to their work loads slightly above *To A Moderate Degree*.

Administrative Practices

1. There was very little acceptance of the appraisal criterion concerning medical examinations as a requisite to participate in the intramural program and the giving of subsequent examinations when necessary. The mean was 2.28 ranking it slightly above *Very Little* acceptance.

2. According to the appraisal criterion, guidance and counseling as an integral part of the program had a mean of 2.77 ranking it slightly below *To A Moderate Degree*.

3. Intramural sports are played under approved rules by students and

faculty well above *To A Moderate Degree*. The mean was 3.72.

4. Certified and bonded transportation provided by the school for intramural program participants had a mean of 2.86 ranking it slightly below *To A Moderate Degree*.

5. Prescribed safety and health standards were observed by the junior colleges very slightly below *To A Great Degree* with a mean of 3.98.

6. The time of day during which intramural activities were conducted varied from school to school with the small and medium-sized schools conducting their programs most frequently at the close of the class day and the large institutions utilizing the time period between 11 a.m. to 2 p.m. most often.

7. Slightly over 83 percent of the junior colleges allowed protests in their programs with the larger institutions providing greater opportunity for protests.

8. The intramural director was the individual primarily responsible for deciding protests and forfeits regardless of school.

9. The trophy was the type of award most frequently presented with the average cost of the awards by all schools was $3.42.

10. Sixty-five percent of the schools did not have a point system.

11. Posters and bulletin boards, the school newspaper, word of mouth, school publications, and class announcements, in rank order were the five most commonly utilized methods of publicizing the intramural program.

12. Participation records and observation were the two most frequently utilized methods of program evaluation in all schools regardless of size.

Program Content

1. The junior college intramural programs stressed individual and dual activities for the purpose of developing life-long leisure time interests well above *To A Moderate Degree* according to the appraisal criterion and the mean was 3.78.

2. The intramural programs of the colleges surveyed provided opportunities for participation for individuals and groups whose limitations required particular attention slightly below *To A Moderate Degree*. (Mean — 2.79).

3. The programs of the surveyed schools provided opportunities through co-recreational activities to develop mutual interests in activities acceptable to both men and women somewhat *To A Moderate Degree*. (Mean — 3.41).

4. Competitive intramural programs were offered by 95.5 percent of the schools, co-recreational activities by 67.8 percent and faculty-staff programs by 53.1 percent.

5. Round robin and elimination tournaments were the most popular types of tournaments found in 80.2 percent and 70 percent of the junior college intramural programs, respectively.

6. Independent units were the most frequently employed units of

competition in 83.6 percent of the schools regardless of school size.

7. Eighty different activities were offered in the men's program, seventy-one in the women's program, sixty-two in the co-recreational program and forty-two in the faculty-staff program.

8. The most frequently offered activity regardless of school size in the men's program was basketball and the women's program was volleyball.

9. Volleyball was the most frequently offered activity in the co-recreation programs of medium and large institutions while bowling was most frequently offered in the small schools.

10. Volleyball and basketball were the two most frequently played in the faculty-staff program.

Facilities and Equipment

1. The facilities of the colleges were slightly above adequate *To A Moderate Degree* for the large schools (Mean 3.13) and slightly below adequate *To A Moderate Degree* for the smaller and medium schools. (Mean — 2.74).

2. The most frequently utilized methods of financing the intramural program were: a) Separate Intramural Budget (40 percent); b) General College Fund (13 percent); c) Student Activity Fees (12.4 percent); d)Athletic Gate Receipts (1.1 percent); and e) combinations of the above (33.5 percent).

3. The total annual budgets for all schools ranged from $100 to $18,000.

4. The total budgets of the small schools ranged from $100 to $2,350 with an average of $1,094.19; of the medium schools from $100 to $18,000 with an average of $1,738.79; and of the large schools from $300 to $10,000 with an average of $2,484.90.

5. The minimum hourly rate of pay for student employees excluding officials ranged from $1.00 to $2.50 with an average of $1.56 per hour and the maximum rate of pay ranged from $1.35 to $3.50 with an average rate of $2.02 per hour.

6. The minimum hourly wage for student officials ranged from $.50 to $5.00 with an average rate of pay $1.62 and the maximum hourly rate of pay ranged from $.50 to $5.00 with an average rate of $2.03.

General Discussion of Findings

The findings of this inquiry suggest to the investigator that the status of intramural-recreational programs in junior colleges of the United States is generally below par in terms of meeting the varied needs of the participants. There is a decided discrepancy between the written philosophical aims and objectives of the programs and the actual policies and practices being implemented. The intramural directors of these programs cannot be held fundamentally responsible for this situation, however. It appears, instead, that minimal budgets, inadequate facilities, lack of administrative time and personnel and the general characteristics of the junior college student body, i.e. working and commuting, contribute heavily to the existence of this theory-practice gap.

It is evident that the majority of directors, in spite of all obstacles, have adopted an enterprising and creative approach in the implementation of their programs, attempting to provide suitable activities by drawing to the fullest extent upon the limited resources available to them. The best programs, however, will evolve in part from a genuine concern and interest on the part of the junior college administrations in terms of providing adequate budgetary resources, good facilities, and the appointment of intramural directors and assistants whose primary duties are in the area of intramurals.

Recommendations for Improvement and Further Study

In light of the findings of this study improvements to the intramural-recreational program of its junior colleges surveyed should be made not only in the areas which revealed an obvious weakness, but also in those areas reflecting only a moderate degree of agreement with the appraisal criteria of the research instrument.

Some of the recommendations stemming from this investigation are:

1) Schools having no written philosophy and objectives should formulate a statement in writing.

2) Intramural directors should be freed from additional responsibilities not related to intramurals.

3) Directors should obtain degrees either in physical education, recreation, or related areas.

4) Adequate finances should be obtained from reliable sources. Programs should be conducted preferably through a separate intramural budget.

5) Secretarial help, preferably full-time, should be provided for all programs.

6) Assistants with faculty status should be employed to assist intramural directors of schools having large intramural programs.

7) Certified and bonded transportation for intramural participants should be provided for extramural events.

8) Medical examinations should be required where feasible for participants.

9) More activities should be provided for individuals with restrictive physical handicaps.

10) Provision should be made for some type of guidance and counseling of students participating in the intramural program.

11) Stronger faculty-staff and women's programs should be provided with respect to amount and diversity of activities offered.

12) Provision should be made for future expansion, maintenance, and improvement of intramural facilities.

13) In-depth studies should be conducted in the areas of:

    A) Financing junior college intramural programs.

B) Patterns of participation in junior college intramural programs.
C) Qualifications and training of personnel for administering junior college intramural-recreational programs.
D) Administrative problems peculiar to the administration of junior college intramural-recreational programs.

An Innovative Unit Competition for a Community College
H. Dutch Usilaner
(1976 NIRSA Proceedings, pp. 52-53)

An intramural program is only as successful as the time spent by the Intramural Director in trying to reach the students not already participating in the program. We feel that this two year community college with a student enrollment of approximately 10,000 students has a very adequate program. Our participation is very high and the interest is likewise. Our extramural program with 14 colleges is an added incentive.

Our main objective at the present time is to reach our freshmen students to help them achieve a sense of belonging in their new environment.

At the present time, our teams are composed of students and staff. They are on their own, which usually brings forth an interested group or individual who will act as captain and try to recruit other students. They assume the role of captain and submit entry forms, distribute schedules and attempt to keep their newly formed teams informed at all times.

To make our freshmen students feel at home, we attempt to develop interaction with other freshmen through the intramural medium. Competitive games are not the only area in which we stress the importance of the overall objectives of our program. We try to stress that the students, including the freshmen, will develop skills and strengthen their sense of community through encouragement and understanding. We believe that our freshmen students should be committed to developing community attitudes toward recreation.

In order to achieve these objectives in a two year community college we feel that a home base is necessary. This would be similar to a fraternity, dorm or social club. This home base will rarely have the same students for more than 2½ years.

We will try to develop geographic units of competition. At the present time, we merely have a recruiting type of competition. In developing a program under these circumstances we have not been able to establish a traditional home base. As each named group was born, it soon died as the recruiters graduated.

Our question to the group is — how can we develop a unit of organization or competition that will perpetuate a name after the recruiters have gone?

With the help of our Office of Institutional Research and Analysis, which is headed by Dr. Robert Gell, we evolved the following plan: Dr. Gell was our expert and he guided us to a plan that we hope meets our needs and objectives.

The following demographic model was evolved: We have 18 high schools that are geographically located in our county. This means 18 different neighborhoods, ethnic groups and economic groups. When our freshmen students are registering at the college, the Registrar or Director of Admissions has a card punched out for all new students. He has our Data Processing Department develop a set of labels with addresses and a printout. This will include the high schools (a number-seen in sample). When this is completed, we mail out our questionnaire (see sample) to every freshman student in a stamped window envelope. The student receives and fills out the questionnaire and sends it back to the college. The return questionnaire will have the student's name tag. We then enter his social security number on the questionnaire (by hand). The questionnaire is then sent to Data Processing. Data Processing will keypunch and print it out in two ways — we can ask for the activity and the high school or the reverse, or we can ask for a count for each activity and a printout with the high school and all the activities from that high school. Having all this information, we hope to group the high schools and keep them as a perpetual group. New students coming to our college in later years will inevitably gravitate to their own high school group. If an activity at one of the high schools does not have enough participants in an activity, then we will combine it with the nearest geographic high school.

After these groups are assigned, they will be on their own. We will assign them a permanent meeting area for the school year. The only restriction for the groups will be that they have a minimum of 15 participants for all team activities.

We hope that other two year community colleges will try our plan. We hope, too, that others can build on what we intend to do. An exchange of new ideas is what this Intramural Convention is noted for.

Promotion Plus Motivation Equals Involvement in Intramural Sports for the Community College Student
Bud Farmer
(1976 NIRSA Proceedings, pp. 53-54)

In order to develop participation and maintain a quality Intramural Sports Program in the Community Colleges, the Director must constantly seek new avenues to get students involved.

Most Directors recognize the importance of promoting the program and motivating the student; however, many fail, or simply do not have the time, to sell their program to this all important buyer.

Intramural Directors must be alert for new and exciting activities for their program. They must be open to input by the student body—they are the buyers of our product.

The Daytona Beach Community College, serving Volusia and Flagler Counties, has an open door policy with lower division transfer courses, technical, occupational, adult, and non-credit community programs. They support a philosophy of student and community involvement. Their aim is to create a climate conducive to student and community participation in their various programs. The total enrollment is approximately 20,400.

Listed below are a few promotional and motivational techniques we use at Daytona Beach Community College.

PROMOTE AND MOTIVATE WITH:

1. Special Activities
2. T-Shirts
3. Evening Coed Activities
4. Bulletin Board with pictures of winners
5. Student newspaper insert with schedules, deadlines and intramural office location and phone number
6. Promotional desk during the Fall and Spring Registration
7. Student Coordinators discussing Intramurals at Freshmen orientation
8. Student newspaper survey of activities most desired by the student body
9. Bulletin board in strategic places across the campus
10. Student newspaper coverage of every individual contest
11. Student assistants available to give information, rules, equipment, etc. to the students.
12. Activity period
13. Weekend activities
14. Flexibility in scheduling
15. New activities — while they are "new"
16. All star teams in all activities
17. Extensive photography coverage
18. All star contest and exhibitions at the half of a varsity game
19. Assign two student assistants to write for the newspapers
20. Personal touch
21. Student coordinators
22. No entry fee
23. Community and private facilities
24. Extramurals
25. Physical Education Classes

Chapter 14
Urban/Commuter College Intramurals

Important Issues for Commuter College Programs
Tom Sattler and Larry Berres
(1974 NIA Proceedings, pp. 129-132)

INTRODUCTION

Eight years ago, a commuter college section was established in the National Intramural Association to deal with problems associated with this unique type of institution. The uniqueness is found in the type of student enrollment.

The commuter college student emerges predominantly from an urban environment. The pennant waving enthusiasm for school functions and activities does not achieve the proportions commonly found on residential campuses, because the commuter students must budget their time for travel, class attendance and employment. It has been reported that as many as 86% of a student population in a typical midwest commuter institution are employed.[1] In the same institution, the median number of hours that all students remain on campus is twenty-seven. Seventeen of these hours are spent in classes and laboratory experiences, five hours are spent in the library and the remaining time is spent in the student union.[2] It should seem obvious from these statistics that the amount of time available for recreational activities is minimal. This is the major problem confronting the commuter college intramural director. As a result, efficacy of program operation is essential in appealing to the interests of the prospective participants.

PROCEDURE

Each year, prior to the intramural conference a survey form is sent to directors of commuter college institutions. The purpose of the survey is to ascertain which topics will be discussed at the upcoming session. During the actual session of directors, the membership is divided into four groups. A group leader and recorder are selected for each group to generate discussion on the four topics which have been selected from the survey. At the end of the discussion, each recorder provides the membership with a five minute summary of the group's deliberations. The topics selected for this particular conference were research, motivational techniques, innovative activities and scheduling.

DISCUSSION OF RESULTS

Research

When we speak of research for intramural sports, we are not gearing our efforts to a process of elimination approach. In other words, if we try something and it doesn't work, then we will try something else. Research must be considered as three dimensional in scope. It pertains to the past, present and future. Historical research tells "what was." Descriptive or survey research tells "what is" and experimental research indicates "what will be."[3]

Historically, we are concerned with past achievements based on facilities which were available and school enrollments. If we find that participation for an activity has grown in proportion to the growth of student population and the expansion of facilities, then it has earned a place of merit. If the reverse is true, then its feasibility is questionable and a substitution or complete elimination is recommended. After carefully weighing the merits of each activity based on their past achievements, most significantly in participaton, student enrollment and facility availability, we are ready to concern ourselves with conditions and relationships as they currently exist.

Suggestions for enriching our programs through the descriptive or survey method are motivation research, exposure through interclass competition, follow up studies and the co-educational survey.

In motivational research, we are attempting to solicit the reasons why a student has participated hoping that we will uncover motives that aren't normally obvious. We can use these underlying motivations to sell our program to students in the future. The sale of an activity to a student can be based on the awakening of an unconscious motivation for a need. Secondly, by working with a cooperative staff and administration, we can promote an intramural activity through the physical education classes teaching that activity. With additional cooperation in scheduling of classes, one hour may be set aside two afternoons a week for intramural competition among the various classes. (This has proven to be the lifeline for many commuter college intramural programs.) The competition will not only compliment the program of instruction in the physical education class, but will also provide another avenue for intramural exposure. The third approach is the follow-up study. This is best accomplished by maintaining a card on each student listing the activities he entered during the school year. The cards will provide us with total student participation for our end of the year summary, participation in each activity (a cross check of strengths and weaknesses in our program) and student contact for the following year. All entries can be made by one student manager from the entry blanks for each activity after the tournament is completed. Lastly, we must not overlook the co-educational survey. Distribute a form among all the students listing the activities by quarter or semester and request a check mark for each activity they would like to participate. All forms will have a place for the student's name, home address and telephone number.

In experimental research we are concerned with an exposure to the unique activities which may enhance our programs in the future. The unique activities would be judo, karate, sailing, skiing, etc. By providing instruction in activities which are foreign to our students, new interests may be developed and eventual competition in intramurals can be justified.

Motivational Techniques

In the previous section we have discussed motivational research as a tool in detecting underlying causes. This section is devoted to techniques which may inspire participation. Some suggestions are:

1. An insert sheet into the newspaper containing schedules, deadlines and results.
2. Publish a top 10 of the leading contestants and teams.
3. Organize competition according to ability groups.
4. Some schools are using male managers and coaches for female activities to entice women to participate.
5. Utilize extensive photographic coverage.
6. Establish a written or visual presentation for the game of the week.
7. Develop all-star competition.
8. One school has used a horse with large notices attached to bulletin board on either side.
9. Start each school year with a special event and add a novelty event each quarter.

Innovative Activities

Most commuter colleges have established a wide array of competitive athletics. However, more students are expressing a concern, through their actions, for activities of a non-competitive import and modifications of traditional sports and games which introduced new elements of competition. Some activities you may wish to consider are:

1. Orienteering$_4$ — This sport is competitive navigation of the countryside with map and compass in search of control markers which have been spotted on prominent terrain features in advance of the meet.
2. Offering unusual activities such as curling, golf basketball, broom ball, pickle ball, shower volleyball or push ball.
3. One-on-one basketball competition.
4. All-star athlete of the year competition based on the "Superstar" competition held on national television.
5. Archery turkey shoots prior to a holiday.
6. Tandem bicycle derbys patterned after the "Indianapolis 500."
7. Special event nights for special groups. e.g. Ladies night. All activity would consist of make up games.
8. Development of state play days. Two or more universities within a certain geographical area could merge for recreational activity.

Scheduling

There are two major problems which perpetually antagonize scheduling efforts of intramural events. First, it is recalled that students spend a minimal amount of time on campus. Second, is the age old problem of conflicts with the varsity athletic programs. In both cases the schedule should be flexible enough to provide varying opportunities which will appeal to the convenience of the commuter student. Some considerations are:

1. Vacation or holiday tournaments.
2. Incorporation of activity hours into the daily academic program.
3. Scheduling around physical education classes when facilities are not in use.
4. Out of season scheduling. e.g. Basketball in the spring.
5. Short tournaments immediately after physical education classes.
6. Events based on time or distance instead of head to head competition.
7. During the last half of a physical education class if no other times are available.

CONCLUSION

In order to develop and maintain a quality intramural sports program in a commuter institution the directors must be perpetually vigilant to the minimization of negative effects and the adoption of successful approaches being utilized in other colleges and universities. The commuter college section in the National Intramural Association has provided the avenue to deal with the latter. The task of identifying obstacles is the responsibility of individual directors. It is suggested that research tools be developed. They are important for two reasons. First, many negative effects of program operation will be high-lighted. Second, program offerings can gain a more substantial basis for accountability.

BIBLIOGRAPHY

Best, John W. *Research in Education.* New Jersey: Prentice Hall, Inc. 1959.

Crane, Lawrence R. "Orienteering: A Most Natural Sport," *Fitness for Living.* November-December, 1972, p. 55.

Klassen, Peter P. *Commuter Students in an Urban University.* Chicago, Illinois: University of Illinois at Chicago Circle, 1971. pp. 40, 51.

---

[1]Peter P. Klassen, *Commuter Students in an Urban University.* Chicago Illinois: University of Illinois at Chicago Circle, 1971, p. 40.

[2]Ibid., p. 51.

[3]John W. Best, *Research in Education.* New Jersey: Prentice-Hall, Inc. 1959, p. 12.

[4]Lawrence R. Crane, "Orienteering: A Most Natural Sport," *Fitness for Living,* November-December, 1972, p. 55.

A Community Within A Community — The Urban University

Warin H. Dexter and Steven A. Sherman
(1973 NIA Proceedings, pp. 44-48)

American universities and colleges have inescapable responsibilities for student recreation opportunities. These responsibilities stem from the primary educational mission of institutions of higher learning and from their nature and function as communities. Although they are communities of a special type and unique nature, nevertheless, life needs characteristic of any community must be met. Provisions for meeting the recreation needs and interests of their citizens have been accepted as basic responsibilities of community agencies and institutions. Thus, responsibility for student recreation opportunities devolves upon colleges and universities as a corollary of their community nature and function (SPRE, 1972). In other words, we as intramural and recreation directors must insure the availability of adequate recreational opportunities for students, and other individuals, during their years of university residence.

The initial intent of this paper was to present a defense of a laboratory or field experience in recreation services and intramurals at an urban university as a means for learning about the total scope of providing recreational services in other settings. This would involve in depth experiences in administration, supervision and programming.

Preliminary research and endless dialogue led us to believe there was something more relevant, and more vital, that needed to be brought to the attention of people in our growing field. There appears to be an urgent need for us to expand our horizons. The present scope and definition of intramurals must now be made to include ideas for total leisure service planning at institutions for higher education. We must do it before someone else does. Is it not our responsibility to help prepare people in our community for life in a leisure-oriented society? Responsibility for the effective delivery of services, formulation of policy, and development of programs is caste upon us as recreation and intramural directors. Of course, the responsibility, to be most effective, must be assumed by university personnel at all levels—policymakers, administrative and instructional staff, students, and at least in an advisory capacity, the representatives of the larger community.

The university is a multi-faceted, complex, unique type of community which must be properly and effectively serviced for leisure. One might question what our basis was for this opinion. Our reply would be in two parts. Looking first at the definition of the word *community,* we see it referring to things, to people, to ideas and to a place; all in common with a university. The university is greater than the mere sum of the people and buildings which comprise it. Community can also mean an idealogy, a social philosophy, or a goal to achieve, an implication of commonality among people. (Baizerman, 1972) The second means of viewing the university as a community is that all phases of university life appear to parallel that of any community, in that both provide for the health, education, welfare, shelter and recreation and leisure opportunities of its citizens. In addition, each has its own form of government, system of informational services, body of consulting services, security forces, maintenance departments and the like. In short, the university can be viewed as a microcosm of the so called outside world to which it ideally must relate. Who said that we in the university are dealing with the ideal, the unreal or the impractical? In the urban-centered universities of today, we in recreation and intramurals must be real and very practical for we deal with very real problems. It must be our responsibility then, in our urban community to help restore some of the lost sense or spirit of community on our campuses.

Literature in this area of the university as a community all seems to point toward the idea that higher education's involvement is not only a process of educating for leisure but providing opportunities for it as well. Part of this emphasis has been placed in renaming university leisure services to Campus Recreation or the Department of Recreational Services with intramurals being one part of this organization. We feel that the title is not important but that the service is. There is a need to equalize these types of programs with other phases of the university in terms of administration.(Berg, 1969; Berrafato, 1971; Matthews, 1969) The expansion of recreational services in the urban universities has also been parallel with a growing awareness of the metropolitan surroundings and the immediate environmental conditions. (Berrafato, 1971; Jordan, 1971; McGuire, 1971; Pollack, 1969)

Consideration needs to be given to university location in planning programs and facilities. In reality this has affected the nature of the programs and facility offerings at such urban universities as Temple, Columbia, and Pennsylvania. Temple University, for instance, has found it most appropriate to establish their old athletic and physical education building as a separate center to service the major part of their involvement in providing recreational opportunities for their surrounding community. It is staffed with a full-time recreation professional, part-time personnel, and students involved in field experiences in recreation and leisure studies. It is also evident that many urban universities are now supporting summer programs for neighborhood youths. This is not an entirely new role for universities as they have supported 4H Clubs' youth programs, enrichment programs and training sessions all geared to bettering rural life. (Jordan, 1971:2). It is a more recent phenomenon of the cities and their social plight that we have seen an awakening of the urban universities and their involvement in urban areas. Other literature relevant to this total concept of the university-community, looked at it from the perspective of the provision of social functions, the arts, etc. is being included in total leisure services. Miller (1969) believed that the provision of leisure services helped to reinforce the overall educational objectives of an institution (its arts and sciences) as well as to add vitality to campus life, mainly through the interaction of people. A unique insight into this idea was presented by Frederick Law Olmstead, designer of Central Park in New York in 1858, and several college campuses, who thought universities should reflect and plan for an ideal of communality, a total community.

Thus, the feeling is that we need not question the fact that we are providing and will continue to provide recreational services, but rather to what extent. What will our commitment to this concept of total leisure services for the university community be? What means can we avail ourselves of to reach a commitment from the administrative powers of the urban universities? What special considerations need we make for the commuter citizens of our communities? How do we get them more involved? We must help to provide a stable, enriched and creative environment not only for education, but recreation as well. The best way to accomplish this end is to make the university citizen feel more like a member of the community in which he or she participates. To do this, many of us will have to remove the shackles of a definition. From the narrow focus of sports and game programs, we must move to a total program of leisure services. This would include the arts, entertainment and the aesthetics of passive recreation and leisure. Campus recreation must establish itself as a vital, equal cog in the total realm of university-community services, with a responsibility for providing input into related areas which affect leisure time opportunities. The change in direction will not be easy. Within the rigid university structure, services will always place third behind research and credit hour production. However, we feel, if viewed as a community, we can then take our place as a recognized function or service equal to any. Involvement and commitment are not limited only to the planning and supervision of programs but include the creation of facilities and areas from buildings to quiet lounges, to game rooms, to grassy areas, campus scenery and lighting, to entertainment, trips and outings. The future of the urban university is bright not only in terms of its educational locale within the city, but because of its recreational opportunities too. Urban universities are important and vital communities, which we as professionals must serve, and in the process develop, along with the rest of the university.

The role of the intramural and recreation professional in the urban universities is one of vast importance, evidenced by the fact that there is widespread misunderstanding and ignorance about the importance of leisure in our society. These conditions exist in colleges and universities as well as throughout our society. This creates major roadblocks for obtaining the necessary financial, intellectual and moral support for directing our efforts toward fulfilling the promise of the wise use of leisure time.

This presentation has sought to increase the awareness and understanding of the responsibilities and functions of higher education in relation to leisure and the vital role intramural, recreational professionals must play, in order to reach this goal. If the needs of our community are to be served, then those individuals in colleges and universities must recognize that our members must be made more aware of leisure and its implications, and also be prepared to deal with it.

We realize that we have only touched base with many of the real issues confronting us and our urban universities today. If we have created a feeling or an awareness of the great complexities of the urban university and the tremendous role we must play then this paper has been a success. It is our sincere hope that this presentation will continue to stimulate questions and debate, as well as action, and that we as campus recreation professionals will adapt to the changing needs and new concepts in our urban universities.

Questions to be Answered

1. What should your commitment to the concept of total leisure services for the urban university community be?
   a. What means can we avail ourselves of to reach a commitment from the administrative powers, to this leisure concept?
2. As administrators of recreation and intramurals in urban universities, what input have you had in overall campus planning—in such areas as security, the environment, facilities, space allocation, curriculum, and outdoor recreation?
3. What is your commitment to the community outside the insulated walls of the campus?
   a. What are some of the pressures you have had to deal with?
4. What special considerations need we make for your university citizens?
   a. How do you get them more involved?
   b. What is the universities responsibility in providing them with greater leisure-time opportunities?
5. What role do we need to play in coordinating with the general aims and goals of higher education and the education for leisure within our metropolitan areas?
6. Have we as recreation and intramural professionals considered the available leisure resources of the urban areas within which we reside to complement our own program.

REFERENCES

Baizerman, Michael, 1972. "The University and the Community". *Center Quarterly*, Vol. I, No. 4.

Berg, Otto. 1969. "Future Trends in the Administration of Intramural

Sports at the College Level." *Proceedings of the Twentieth Annual NIA Conference.* UCLA, Los Angeles, California.

Berrafato, Peter. 1971. "Community Recreation in the Commuter Institution." *Proceedings of the Twenty-Second Annual NIA Conference.* Virginia Polytechnic Institute, Blacksburg, Virginia.

Goodall, R. 1970. "The Urban University—Is There Such a Thing?" *Journal of Higher Education.* XLI, No. 1, January.

Gusfield, Joseph; Kromis, Sidney; Mark Harold. 1970. "The Urban Context and Higher Education." *Journal of Higher Education.* XLI, No. 1, January.

Jordan, J. Robert. 1971. The University and Its Role with the North Philadelphia Community, mimeographed. *Temple University, Philadelphia, Pennsylvania.*

Fein, Albert. 1972. *Frederick L. Almstead and the American Environmental Tradition,* Braziller, New York.

Matthews, David. 1969. "The New Look in University and College Intramurals." *Proceedings of the Seventy-Third Annual Conference NCPEAM.* U. of Illinois, Chicago, Illinois.

McGuire, R. J. 1971. "Communiversity Programming" *Proceedings of the Twenty-Second Annual NIA Conference* Virginia Polytechnic Institute, Blacksburg, Virginia.

Miller, Norman P. 1969. "Recreation at the University of California at Los Angeles." *Campus Recreation,* AAHPER, N.W. Washington, D.C.

Pollack, Bernard. 1969. "The Student View of Intramural Sports at an Urban College." *Proceedings of the Twentieth Annual NIA Conference.* UCLA, Los Angeles, California.

Society of Park and Recreation Educators. 1972. "The Role of Higher Education for Leisure, and in Education for the Leisure Service Professions." *Communique.* April, p. 21.

Whisnant, David. 1971. "The University as a Space and the Future of the University." *Journal of Higher Education* XLII, No. 2, February.

Chapter 15
Rec-Sports Programming for the Community

Community Recreation in the Commuter Institution
Peter R. Berrafato
(1971 NIA Proceedings, pp. 19-21)

Traditionally the American University has perceived itself of having three major missions: teaching, research, and public service. The public service mission has always been important and it seems clear that it will gain more importance. "Higher education is becoming increasingly socialized, public-oriented, publicly aided, and public-policy conscious."[1] It is vested with a public interest as never before.

Most commuter institutions because of their geographic locations enjoy a unique advantage in the area of public service. *They are where the action is!* Inescapably, they are part of their respective communities. As a part of the community the commuter institution must use its resources to contribute to the improvement of life in the community with the emphasis on the immediate university neighborhood.

Not the least of the public services which the commuter institution can provide is the augmentation of recreational opportunities for its "clientele." Working cooperatively with the community we must try to provide an enjoyable, on-going, and meaningful program for all groups in the university community.

The establishment of such a program may not be an easy task. In fact under adverse conditions it may be a monumental task. However there is reason to believe that it can be done provided that the planning is initiated and developed in a spirit of cooperation and an atmosphere of mutual respect between the institution and the community.

The steps necessary to the initiation of such a program may not be an easy task. In fact under adverse conditions it may be a monumental task. However there is reason to believe that it can be done provided that the planning is initiated and developed in a spirit of cooperation and, an atmosphere of mutual respect between the institution and the community.

The steps necessary to the initiation of such a program are listed below. It is recommended that nine to twelve months be reserved for the planning.

1. A preliminary meeting with representatives from the following offices:
   a. Chancellor and/or Vice Chancellor for Neighborhood Relations (2)
   b. Neighborhood Relations (2)
   c. Physical Education (1)
   d. Intercollegiate Sports (1)
   e. Intramural Sports (1)
   f. Student Union (2)

g. Neighborhood Agencies (2 or 3)

h. Student Affairs (4 including 2 or 3 students)

This preliminary meeting is primarily to develop broad guidelines and to select a "working committee." The working committee (University Community Recreation Program Committee), should include at least one representative from each of the above offices.

2. The University Community Recreation Program Committee should do the following:

a. prepare a budget

b. hire a director

c. develop the philosophy, the goal, the objectives, specific guidelines, methods of procedures, etc. etc.

d. make its individual and collective "expertise" available to the director

e. consult with and advise the director

3. The director, with the help of the Neighborhood Relations office personnel, would:

a. Consult with the neighborhood agencies and other neighborhood groups

b. With the help of the Physical Education, Intramural and Athletic Department personnel ascertain the availability of university physical resources: gymnasiums, pools, courts, fields, etc.

c. Ascertain the availability of human resources: committee members, recreation and physical education faculty, recreation and physical education majors, neighborhood persons, etc.

d. Survey the existing neighborhood facilities

e. Develop agency priorities by need. That is, those agencies that have some facilities would have low priorities.

f. Ascertain the needs and interests of the potential participants

g. In consultation with the committee develop "divisions of responsibility."

h. Develop a set of forms to be used: registration, identification, report sheets, etc. etc.

i. Develop a tentative program. This should include a detailed, hourly, daily, weekly, etc. program of scheduled activities.

The committee would then review the tentative program. If the tentative program were approved the committee would proceed to implement the program.

Additionally the following comments may prove to be helpful:

1. Make every effort to secure adequate funding for the program.

2. Develop a set of priorities for the use of physical education and recreation facilities (physical education classes, intramural sports program, intercollegiate sports program, community recreation

program, etc. etc.)

3. It may be wise to initiate the program with a comparatively few activities
4. Accept the fact, and try to make others understand, that the university cannot meet all the recreational needs of the neighborhood
5. Provide the necessary arrangements, when applicable, for the control of spectators.
6. When possible and feasible make admission for spectator events available to the community at no cost or reduced cost.
7. Insist that all personnel be dressed in an appropriate manner for each activity.
8. Frequent review and evaluation of all phases of the program.

REFERENCES

University of Illinois, *Extension and Public Service in the University of Illinois;* Phase I Report, November, 1968.

University of Illinois, *Extension and Public Service in the University of Illinois;* Phase II Report, August, 1968.

University of Illinois, *Provisional Development Plan, 1971-72 Through 1980-81,* September, 1970.

The Extended Day, Community Recreation and Title IX As They Affect Commuter Institutions
Tom Sattler and Jim Nasiopulos
(1975 NIRSA Proceedings, pp. 252-256)

In an age of increasing specialization and technology in which the virus of research, federal mandates and undergraduate programming has affected nearly every college and faculty, the aftermath of change directly alters the student's life on campus. More specifically, any transition will affect the curriculum as well as the extracurricular. Since we are primarily concerned with effectively providing a generous variety of intramural and recreational sports activities for the student populace, we must be perpetually aware of any changes which will ultimately confound the efficacy of our programs which are classified as extracurricular.

Administrators in all institutions of higher learning must apply creative imagination in order to successfully adjust to demands of new pressures, but the problems are compounded in commuter colleges and universities due to their uniqueness. The uniqueness is based on the mission of commuter institutions, the composition of the student population and the communicative difficulties of a non-residential setting.

In terms of mission, the commuter institutions are charged with the responsibility of wearing the "urban halo". Simply stated, every energy must be directed toward meeting the needs and adjusting to a deterogeneous population from the encompassing community. Students in attendance represent a cross section of wealthy suburbanites, high rise apartment dwellers, sons and daughters of blue collar workers and inner city youth consisting primarily of minority factions. The majority of students only spend enough time on campus to attend class and "grab a snack" before departing to afternoon and evening jobs. Communication is difficult because the students are not housed on campus and the buildings are widely dispersed to accommodate parking facilities for the commuter students.

Since periodic change is inevitable, extracurricular programs must be consistently evaluated and adjusted. In an attempt to meet these new challenges, a commuter college buzz session is provided at each yearly conference of the National Intramural-Recreation Sports Association. The purpose of the session is to identify topical issues of mutual concern and to then register suggestions by various commuter directors throughout the country to effectively establish new methods for programming. During the Twenty Sixth Annual Conference in New Orleans, the three issues cited as deserving the most attention were the extended day, community recreation and Title IX.

THE EXTENDED DAY

The extended day is not a night school, but rather an extension of day programs and day faculty into the evening hours. The purpose is to provide opportunities for the campus to serve a much wider range of people, and to tap new potential student populations if the campus is to increase or even maintain its enrollment. The projected decline in the college-age population by the early 1980's as a consequence of the declining birth rate is dramatic. The Carnegie Commission Reports:

"The number of students added to enrollment in higher education is likely actually to be slightly larger (5.0 million) than the number added in the 1960's (4.7 million). But the rate of increase over the decade as a whole (59 percent) will be markedly lower than the exceptionally high rate of increase in the 1960's (124 percent). The picture in the 1980's will be very different because those entering college will have largely been born from 1962-63 to 1972-73, a period of generally declining absolute numbers of births as well as of a decline in the birth rate."[1]

In order to assess the potential demand for the Extended Day at the University of Illinois—Chicago Circle, the Survey Research Laboratory was authorized, in April 1973, to conduct an extensive demographic survey of Cook County with a goal of quantifying the enrollment demand. The results of the survey suggested that there would be a strong demand and that there would be two major groups of students interested in the extended day. The first would be those who would transfer from the day program and the second would be comprised of several sub-populations who would be new to the campus. Essentially, it was viewed as possible and probable that an Extended Day would increase the total enrollment by several thousand and would provide University access to many people not currently served.

Commuter college and university directors in NIRSA who feel that they will be affected by the Extended Day have cited the following points for consideration:

1. Expansion of intramural-recreation sports scheduling in harmony with the hours offered for the extended day.

2. Assistant Directors may need to be reassigned to afternoon and evening work loads.

3. Increase in budgetary considerations for longer hours of program operation.

4. Incorporation of activity hours into the daily and evening academic program.

5. Facilities in some cases may be drastically limited. Intramural and recreational sports programs which had been traditionally conducted during the evening could be curtailed due to the need of facilities for the extended day academic program.

6. Interclass Intramural Competition could be strongly revived (Interclass is defined as various sections within one activity which compete against one another.)

COMMUNITY RECREATION

Universities, colleges and Junior Colleges nationwide are experiencing the added dimension of servicing the academic and recreational needs of their immediate residential communities. In the past, institutions of higher learning have directed their programs toward teaching, research and service. The service component of an institution's mission is most directly related to the programs discussed at the 1975 NIRSA "Buzz Session", namely community recreation programs.

For the sake of clarification, a community recreation program provides for services rendered which compliment and supplement the recreational needs of the encompassing community. Programs existing within this description range in scope from "Open Door" policies to "Restricted" admittance.

The preliminary decisions for program implementation involve the University or College Administration, Student Government, Athletics, Intramurals, Recreation and Neighborhood Agencies. All the concerned parties should meet and discuss what is needed. Failure to include concerned parties can result in half-hearted support from the university and less than expected participation by the community.

Commuter, as well as residential institutions are experiencing an increase in demand for their recreational programs and facilities; however, the commuter campus is realizing a greater demand due to the fact that many commuter institutions are located in urban metropolitan areas. In this respect, the potential commuter campus has a superior density in correlation to the residential campus. The following are items which have been presented as legitimate concerns during the "Buzz Session". Some apply universally to all institutions while others seem unique to the commuters:

1. Problems have been encountered regarding the priority of facility usage. Where do community recreation programs stand on priority ladders? The general consensus would seem to indicate that physical and fiscal restrictions dictate the priorities.

2. What population or parameter is considered to be the "community"? Boundary lines must be established!

3. Should institutions be required to provide total financing for community programs? How can federal or state funds be secured? Should fees be charged to the participants?

4. The increased utilization of facilities and the expanse of expanded programs has been used by some institutions as a justifiable means for sizeable budget increases.

5. Some schools were actually forced to "play down" or discourage community involvement. So far the ramifications of the decisions within those schools have not been felt.

6. Many schools have placed emphasis on community programs during the summer months. The advantages of this approach are numerous:

   a. Funding has been provided by the NCAA and state youth agencies.

   b. Summer employment opportunities have been made available for staff members.

   c. Facility conflicts have been drastically reduced.

TITLE IX

Title IX of the Education Amendments Act of 1972 is a mandate enacted to insure sexual equality in educational programming. The critical text of this Congressional action states, "No person in the United States shall, on the basis of sex, be excluded from participation in, be denied the benefits of, or be subjected to discrimination under any education program or activity receiving Federal financial assistance."[2]

In the absence of any specific guidelines, Title IX proves to be a frustrating and confusing document. As a result, the mandate is very difficult to enforce. Proposed rules governing the implementation of Title IX have been drafted and have appeared in the *Federal Register* on June 20, 1974. Subsequent to that date, several regional interpretive sessions have been conducted by H.E.W. in an attempt to assist educators who are concerned with the wide-ranging effects of Title IX. Faced with a situation of pending legislation and loosely structured guidelines, program administrators at all institutional levels are coping with a dilemma. Are present programs in compliance? If not, should modifications be enacted?

So far, Title IX has had, and will continue to have, broad ramifications directly affecting our vested interests in intramural and recreational sports. The effects of Title IX are not restricted to the programs on a residential campus, a commuter campus, two or four year campuses, mega-universities or hill top colleges.

Through formal programming and informal conversation, Title IX literally dominated the Twenty-Sixth Conference of NIRSA. The subject was also selected as timely topic for consideration by those present at the commuter "Buzz Session". The following are some concerns and observations voiced by directors relating to the pending enactment of Title IX. In general, comments apply to Title IX as a universal phenomenon; however, several directors expressed unique concerns for commuting institutions:

1. The opportunity for equal participation has always been available. Therefore, the transition between present programs and those mandated under Title IX guidelines will be easy to implement.

2. Co-rec activities seem to be the most appropriate vehicle available for directing women into "all" women activities.

3. There is a growing conflict at commuter institutions between women's intramurals, women's sports clubs, and women's athletics. They respectively require increasing commitments in actual time and in physical dedication. The commuter, upon weighing this time commitment carefully, may be more apt to engage in intramural or informal recreation.

4. An informal poll was taken to determine the percentage of women participants in existing programs. The range was from 1% to 20%. Of various reasons cited for this low figure, the primary reason centered around commuting and its ramifications.

5. Due to security problems, some schools, especially urban inner-city, have little success attracting women participants, even though attractive programs are offered.

6. The general consensus was that the intent of Title IX is equality in opportunity and that "drag in" tactics for increased participation by women are not within this intent.

SUMMARY

The topics considered by the commuter college "forum" have the potential to substantially alter existing intramural-recreational sports programs. As stated previously, program administrators are charged with the responsibility of constantly monitoring needed changes and then efficiently and completely implementing such changes. Insensitivity in inaction should not be tolerated. Through the medium of a "Buzz Session", those present enriched themselves and contributed for the benefit of others. These comments hopefully clarify the problems and expand the possible solutions so that the Extended Day, Community Recreation, and Title IX have become somewhat less abstract entities.

[1]Carnegie Commission on Higher Education, A Digest of Reports and Recommendations (New York: McGraw Hill Inc., Sept. 1967-Oct. 1971) p. 88-89.
[2]Education Amendments of 1972, Public Law 92-318, *U.S. Code Congressional and Administrative News,* (St. Paul: West Publishing Co., 1972) volume 1, p. 444.

Sports Club Development — The 70's Community Involvement
D. F. Juncker, B. D. Anderson, and C. E. Mueller
(1975 NIRSA Proceedings, pp. 144-147)

Widespread professionalism in varsity sports, limited sports opportunities available to the highly skilled student athlete, and perhaps most importantly, the substantial increases in the desire for sports involvement, has produced a large scale movement in colleges and universities toward sports clubs. Most of the developing clubs have structures similar to European sports clubs which emphasize learning through self-government and sports programming, as well as the learning of new sports skills. A club may be defined as any groups of individuals organized about a particular sport or activity for the purpose of furthering interest in sports participation and socialization. In practically every case within the United States, the formation and guidance of such clubs in the university of college setting has fallen under the jurisdiction of intramural-recreation department programs.

Starting from a brief historical review of the formation of sports clubs and the rapid growth which appears to have resulted from student activism during the '60's, a development of the increasing role that the community has assumed within campus sports clubs in the '70's is presented. A report of the preliminary survey data on sports clubs taken in 1974 is also included.

BRIEF HISTORICAL REVIEW
Sports clubs have been in existence almost as long as formal intramural programs have been offered. Although somewhat obscured by rather hazy records, sports clubs have been identified in the literature as early as 1905. Very little formal writing exists concerning the development of sports clubs until the 1940's. Through the medium of the NIA Proceedings, we can gain some knowledge of sports clubs programming since World War II. Perhaps the best known early program was in operation at Purdue University where the emphasis was to provide an opportunity for all students to engage in "self-expression and self-involvement" recreational activities. One key

aspect of the success of this program was the degree to which club members were allowed to be involved in much of the decision-making pertaining to their club. Another positive note in the Purdue situation was the willingness of the administration to deal with the concepts which differentiate club sports from other phases of recreational sports programming. Other examples of rather successful early sports club programs which have been publicized include the University of Tennessee, Michigan State University, and the University of Washington.

CLUB SPORTS PROLIFERATION

Among the reasons given for the main growth of sports clubs during the 1960's are the increase in the number of younger graduate students who wished to continue their sports experiences (some of which had been at the varsity level in their undergraduate days) and an increasing number of students who were unable to make intercollegiate teams, either because of the need for greater skill level or because of the fact that no intercollegiate team existed. In addition, many students chose not to try out for the varsity teams for personal reasons related to their conceptualization of what sport activities meant to them.

In 1969 a sports club survey was reported by Richard Jamerson, of North Carolina University, in the 72nd Annual NCPEAM Proceedings (p. No. 41), in which 78 "selected" educational institutions participated. Jamerson found that the number of sports clubs per institution ranged from 0 to 40, with most campuses showing 3-8 clubs. A total of 75 different sports with club status were represented. Of the 8 most popular club sports listed (soccer, karate, sailing, skiing, judo, fencing, gymnastics, and rugby), six are individual sports and all eight fall within the currently accepted lifetime sports category. This emphasis on a wider choice of sports activities and participation in sports which can be continued throughout one's lifetime was also reflected in later surveys.

COMMUNITY INVOLVEMENT

The '70's brought a slight change in emphasis which we felt in Minnesota, and which was indicated by Peter Berrafato, University of Illinois-Chicago Circle, in the NIA Proceedings, in 1971 (p. No. 19): In short, educational institutions were beginning to be evaluated by the communities in which they resided. Existing programs utilizing community involvement grew and began to be emphasized by school administrators. Higher education, as Berrafato reported, "was becoming increasingly socialized, public-oriented, publicly aided, and public-policy conscious."

Within this framework, sports clubs enjoyed a distinct advantage and again proliferated. For years most clubs had been based on one, two, or a few graduate students, or interested faculty members for volunteer coaching, travel, scheduling, etc. Now, increasing emphasis on community involvement resulted in the participation of greater numbers of interested community volunteers in sports club activities, mostly at the advisor, coach, etc. level. Typical club structures included groups of men and women, generally from the professional community-at-large who banded together for purposes of team teaching, fund raising, and travel assistance for undergraduate teams. Some of these undergraduate teams chose to become the intercollegiate representative of their schools.

At this point I'd like to digress a moment...we do not wish to undermine our main goal as intramural/recreation personnel: that is, providing sports experiences for as many students as possible. However, we are investigating the exciting and many times surprising support of sports clubs by students, the community and the institution. It is this setting which permits the participating student to learn and perform administrative skills as well as develop advanced physical proficiency.

In a more recent survey (Mueller, Anderson, Juncker—Spring '74) a preliminary mailing was sent to 2,011 educational institutions in Canada and the United States to ascertain sports club proliferation and to locate coordinator addresses on the various campuses. Of the 1,022 returns (51%) received by February of this year, 77% (790) of the schools indicated sports clubs of some type on campus. There were an average of 6-to-8 clubs per institution with one school reporting over 60. If this sample is representative of the entire 2,011 schools, there may exist at this time over 10,000 sports clubs in North American educational institutions alone. A more extensive survey will be mailed this year.

EDUCATIONAL BENEFITS

In review, community involvement has aided the undergraduate sports club program by providing the impetus and initiative for forming many new clubs, often by supplying leadership and expertise in a given sport. On the Minnesota campus, one volunteer instructor, a corporation president, turned out to be a former Hungarian national coach in the sport which he assisted. In addition, because community members are often more permanently located, year-to-year continuity in scheduling league competitions fund-raising activities and transportation are more easily maintained.

Community volunteers have, by their involvement, come face to face with the problems and ramifications associated with professionalized varsity sports programs and intramural programs and have carried the differences in emphasis and philosophy back to the community. The effects are beginning to be felt at the administrative level by increased pressure from inside and outside the University on evaluation of sports programs for their educational and community service content. Funding distributions may soon begin to reflect these pressures!

Finally, faculty and community personnel now engaged as volunteers in the sports clubs at the University of Minnesota are beginning to think in terms of expansion of the sports club concept to lifetime community sports clubs programs, the hiring of full time coaches by the club and community, buildings associated with the educational institutions and park systems, and corporation-community funding for their programs. One club at Minnesota has hired a full time coach whose salary comes jointly from the University and the community. Indeed it will be most interesting and exciting, we believe, to follow the sports club movement these next few years.

Chapter 16
Facilities

Game Plans for Getting the Facilities You Need
Robert T. Bronzan
(1972 NIA Proceedings, pp. 9-14)

Introduction
Intramural sports has entered a new, bright era. Never has the interest and enthusiasm in intramural sports been shared by so many students and university administrators. Reasons for this phenomenon are not with the perview of this discussion, but one can safety say that a new set of life's values, held by students, is a dominant cause.

Whatever the reasons for this new emphasis, all of us agree that the signs are good.

It seems to me that one of our primary responsibilities is to make certain that we provide *imaginative* and *positive* leadership to assure the availability of facilities at least equal to current interest and enthusiasm.

Many of you have fortunately inherited facilities which are adequate to satisfy this huge wave of student participation; others of you have been instrumental in obtaining fine facilities. One should then ask: is there an urgent need for more and or improved sports and recreational facilities at most four-year institutions and community colleges?

Definitely YES. Surveys of facility needs, conducted on a national scale, reveal clearly that there is a severe shortage of adequate, modern facilities to meet current demands.

Acceptance of these findings leads one to ask: what are the chief obstacles to obtaining adequate, modern facilities?

The *apparent* obstacle to providing desirable facilities is the lack of funds. In a majority of cases, the *real* obstacle to providing desirable facilities is the lack of insight by those charged with conducting activities, which would use these facilities. Wherever facilities are grossly inadequate, several contributory factors are likely to be present. Most common of these are:

1. Failure to properly acquaint administrators and students with the concepts of *multi-use* facilities, their potential uses and contributions to campus life, and the values of sports and non-sports related events.

2. Failure of administrators or responsible persons to understand the necessity for a concerted plan and effort, by *all* agencies involved, so as to obtain desired facilities.

3. Failure of student government and student organizations to be cognizant of their latent political influence upon administrators and governmental agencies to provide facilities.

4. Failure of student government and student organizations to recognize their ability to either partially or wholly finance needed facilities.

5. Failure of student cultural programs, and departments of men and women physical education, men and women intramural sports, men and women intercollegiate sports, club sports, and recreation to *cooperatively* define a *"master"* plan for facilities.

Will demands for facilities increase to satisfy recreational activities, intramural sports, club sports, intercollegiate sports, and cultural events? Definitely YES. This assertion is based upon one or more of the following phenomena present on most college campuses:

1. Enrollments will increase.

2. Facilities will be utilized more fully throughout the calendar year; the campus is becoming an independent community, self-contained to provide basic services and social life.

3. Students have more "free" time due to general economic conditions, governmental grants, military service compensation, and a reduction in the urgency to complete college courses.

4. Students, even more so than the general populace, are becoming more "fitness" conscious.

5. There is a definite trend *away* from sports spectating *to* actual participation by men and women students through intramural sports, club sports, recreational activities, and intercollegiate sports for women.

6. An increasing number of college students seek to develop skills and knowledge through participation in "carry-over" sports, such as, bowling, tennis, golf, swimming, scuba diving, volleyball, badminton, handball, archery, dance, skiing, skating, weight training, basketball, wrestling, and soccer.

7. There is an increasing need to seek a "safety-valve" from societal pressures, namely, war, draft, atom bomb, urbanization, competition, and loss of individuality.

8. The *"new"* generation aspires to the "good, full life" to a greater degree. Sports and recreational participation are considered important to fulfilling this desire.

9. Women have adopted a *new* philosophy towards sports participation and competition. As this trend accelerates there will be enormous demands for new facilities.

10. The composition of the student body has changed. Today there are more representatives from lower economic groups attending college. In many cases, these students rely upon formal and informal sports participation as a leisure-time pursuit.

11. The campus has become a focal point for staging a diversity of activities, e.g., musical shows, exhibits, political rallies, mass meetings, and professional entertainment. Except in unusual cases, separate facilities for

Facilities

Intramural-rec sports facility planning efforts may involve innovative approaches in the future. Pictured above, a triple Geodesic Dome complex under construction at Elmira College in upstate New York. Three 232 foot clear-span aluminum domes house fieldhouse, sports arena, and regulation ice-hockey rink. (photo courtesy of TEMCOR)

207

these events are not feasible, and therefore, a well-planned multi-use unit is necessary.

12. There is a growing trend for student government to reduce or curtail funds for the support of intercollegiate sports. This shift results in an increase of available funds for satisfying *other* students needs and programs. The multi-use facility not only become more essential, but the possibilities of financing it are improved.

13. There is a clear trend toward more community use of campus sports and recreational facilities, as evidenced by the NCAA sponsored sports programs for disadvantaged youth, the Lockheed-type programs, institutionally-sponsored sports programs for youth, and community-college sports and recreational programs for youth and adults.

14. The "tight" money situation requires that more attention be given to construction of multi-use facilities that may be used *all-year* round by on and off campus agencies. This economy measure improves the probabilities that taxpayers will support the costs of such facilities.

What procedures are necessary to effect an improvement in campus sports and recreational facilities? No two campuses have identical facility needs or governing conditions. Consequently, each campus must determine its own needs and devise its own procedures to surmount specific obstacles. Nonetheless, certain basic principles, necessary for success, applicable to most cases; these are:

1. It is essential to develop simple, yet valid, indices of facility needs and interests of students, faculty, and community.

2. Under the direction of the chief executive officer, or his delegate, various departments and agencies which are involved in activities to be conducted in the proposed facilities, should be appointed to a *project committee*. Primary purposes of this committee are to:
   a. Seek input from all representatives in prescribing facility needs.
   b. Develop a comprehensive plan to include all desired facilities.
   c. Determine the total expected cost of the desired facilities.
   d. Define and coordinate the various programs of fund-raising.
   e. Define and coordinate the public relations program to support the project.

3. The committee should have representatives from all major areas interested in the project; typical of such areas are:
   a. Intercollegiate sports, women
   b. Intercollegiate sports, men
   c. Physical education, women
   d. Physical education, men
   e. Intramural sports, women

    f. Intramural sports, men
    g. Club sports
    h. Faculty senate
    i. Student government
    j. Student activities
    k. R.O.T.C.
    l. Music department
    m. Drama department
    n. Campus business or finance department
    o. Alumni association and/or fund-raising agency
    p. Architectural consultant
    q. Planning and building department
    r. Public relations department
    s. Government grants department
    t. City recreation department
    u. Community secondary schools

4. Any proposed sports and recreational facilities are more likely to be completed if details of financing the project are planned in advance. Suggested guidelines to assure this occurrence are as follows:

a. Each representative on the project committee should provide input regarding facility needs.

b. All needs should then be carefully screened with the view of combining or modifying requests in order to eliminate overlapping or excessive expenditures.

c. A tentative, comprehensive plan for *all* desired facilities should be completed, *even* if it is obvious that the entire project cannot be financed at one time. A cost estimate of the *total* project should be made.

d. If the total project, as proposed, cannot be financed at one time, then the plan should be reduced to as many phases as deemed appropriate. Each separate phase should then be assigned a priority and a date established for both its initiation and completion.

e. A master plan for financing the total project should be designed, regardless if it is to be completed in one or more phases. Details for financing the project must be spelled-out, and the financial obligations of each entity should be determined.

f. Regardless whether sufficient funds are on hand to complete the project or must be obtained in one or more ways, a carefully designed public relations program should be developed. The purposes of the public relations program should be to reveal the *needs* for the proposed facilities, the *values* to be accrued from them, how the facilities will be administered and for whom, and the methods of financing the project. The public relations program should be scheduled, detail by detail, *in advance* of any public announcement of the project. Once revealed, the public relations program should utilize effective tools, such as, news releases, artists drawings, models, photographs, charts, brochures, testimonials, posters, and a speaker's bureau.

    g. Each entity or department should develop, in detail, its plan to meet their financial obligation. Examples of general ideas how some of the entities may obtain funds are as follows:

    1) Student government may sponsor a referendum providing for the adoption of a special assessment or fee for each term for a specified length of time.

    2) Intercollegiate sports may designate a certain percentage of gate receipts, attach a special levy to admission charges, designate the income of certain athletic events to the project, campaign to solicit donations or contributions from individuals and organizations, or plan to sell preferential seats on a subscription basis. One or more of the aforenamed techniques, along with others, may be employed.

    3) Alumni contributions are a potential source of revenue. However, the success of this endeavor will depend to a large extent upon the method by which the fund-raising program is conducted. A carefully planned program is essential in order to reach those alumni other than those who are only sympathetic to intercollegiate sports.

    4) College enterprises, such as the student book store or campus shops, can consider assigning a certain percentage of sales or lump sum to the project. Goods and articles can be sold at a fractional increase with proceeds earmarked for the project.

    5) The physical education departments and intramural sports department can incorporate facility requests for those needs which are most likely to be approved from general appropriations, thereby permitting other entities to focus their financial efforts upon the remaining aspects of the project.

    6) The R.O.T.C., music, and drama departments can pursue the same track as the physical education departments.

    7) The administration should assign a liaison officer to seek federal governmental grants, particularly those available through the Departments of HEW and Interior. Areas likely to receive government funds should be identified, and thereby allow concentration upon other areas which must be funded locally.

    8) For those facilities which may be utilized by public schools, such as the football stadium, basketball pavilion, or swimming pool, a *participating* plan of financing should be structured. Contributions to the building fund may be equated through rental fee usage of the facility.

    9) The city recreation department should be considered in the same way as public schools, particularly where tennis, golf, track and field, and swimming facilities are involved.

10) *"Joint-Powers"* agreements between the college and the public schools or city should be examined for feasibility.

What should you do to obtain adequate sports and recreational facilities? Do SOMETHING. Overcoming inertia requires imagination and leadership. The lack of funds to construct sports and recreational facilities may be the *apparent* deterrent while the *real* obstacle is the lack of insight to recognize that the *whole* campus community must be made aware of its needs, how they may be met, and the values that may be obtained.

There has never been a more opportune time than the present for Intramural Sports Directors to assume the initiative on their own campuses to assure that adequate facilities will exist.

Current levels of student interest and enthusiasm are in your camp; administrators are more aware of the values of intramural sports.

What is needed, more than anything else, is a "game plan".

You are the QUARTERBACK; *you* must call the signals!

Rec-Reality 1975
Gary Colberg
(1973 NIA Proceedings, pp. 38-43)

Across the country, *recreation sport complexes, gymnasiums and geodesic athletic facilities* are presently being proposed, planned and constructed. *Life-time sport facilities is the common label now attached to such recreation structures* as assigned building committees and appointed architects are charged with the responsibility to produce innovative concepts and multi-purpose spatial designs to meet the needs of awaiting participants. Such architectural ingenuity is presently being planned in the form of a $4.4 million Recreation Hall on the Davis Campus of the University of California.

Discussion of the proposed Recreation Hall to be completed in early 1975 on the 15,000 student campus is in order at this time, but very much secondary to the issues of *need, student input, use of outside consultants and funding procedures* that have resulted from proposing and now planning such a facility. A brief description of the Hall, its areas of activity and function, however, may provide a better background to the above mentioned issues which will be dealt with later on.

Architectural Configuration

The plan and architectural form of the building evolved directly from the program requirements for four major space requirements:

1. Four basketball courts at the main floor level (level one)
2. Specialized space such as dressing rooms, offices, handball courts and weight room (level two)

3. Flexible space areas such as wrestling, volleyball, dance and badminton (level three)

4. Seating for 5,550 people initially, to be expanded to an ultimate capacity of 10,300 (all three levels)

Level 1

The minimum space has been provided at the lower level to minimize excavation, and consists primarily of the four intramural basketball courts, storage rooms, mechanical rooms and folding bleacher seating.

Level 2

The natural ground level accommodates all the specialized and non-flexible spaces, and those spaces which will be used most frequently on a day-to-day basis by the student population. These spaces include offices, handball courts, weight rooms, dressing rooms, equipment rooms, etc. It is possible to lock up these areas on the occasion of a special event to which the public is admitted.

Level 3

The upper level accommodates all the flexible areas for volleyball, gymnastics, dance, badminton, general exercise, wrestling and a jogging track, together with permanent spectator seating for 1,900 people and space for a future increment of 4,750 people in folding bleachers which will not interfere with the sporting functions of the area. Public washrooms are provided at this level.

The concrete and steel structure and exterior form of the building result from an honest expression of the function coupled with a *desire to minimize the profile of the building to retain the essentially horizontal and human scale of the Davis Campus.* Color will be introduced in the form of bold graphics and directional signs.

This *low profile has been achieved by addressing the two main areas* where height is generated, the three levels required for seating and the large span roof. The building is recessed one level into the ground and the excavated material reused to form berms around the building which provide access to the upper level, insulation to the ground level, circuit training, dry ski facilities, and spectator viewing to adjacent fields.

The problem of the large clear span required to provide column-free spectator viewing was the subject of a computer analysis, and the resultant two-way welded tube vierendeel truss system has resulted in a much shallower structure than has been used at other similar facilities. The roof form provides ideal locations for mechanical and electrical equipment and duct-work and is easily accessible for maintenance.

The building is fully air-conditioned by a flexible system which is capable of performing economically for both day-to-day recreational and intramural load, and for the special events when a large number of people will be accommodated.

Lighting will be mercury vapor for the main upper areas and economical and maintenance-free fixtures will be selected for other areas.

This building is a simple, logical, economical expression of the function and with its capability for multiplicity of use will be available for absolute maximum utilization for Intramurals, Recreational Activity, Intercollegiate Sports, and Special Events.

Need

The need for a recreation facility was dramatized this past winter term as 351 intramural basketball teams played some 1,123 games as late as 12:30 a.m. Sunday through Thursday. Fall quarter, likewise, evidenced late contests and extreme growing pains as 137 organized volleyball teams involving 1,500 participants along with the badminton, gymnastic, judo, karate and fencing clubs all bidding for the same available indoor space. Over 2,000 men were denied the privilege of checking out a locker in each of the past two quarters with the women reaching the saturation stage for the first time in their dressing quarters. The present gymnasium seats 1,500 spectators exceeded only by a nearby memorial union arena with a 2,000 seating capacity. The need for expanded space is so great that program cut backs are being considered for the first time. Use of the present gymnasium, for Intramural, instructional, and intercollegiate programs has been extended to 17 hours/day, seven days a week. Free recreation time or unstructured play is almost non-existent.

The proposed Hall has been designed with the highest priority to more fully satisfy the physical space requirements of the intramural program; second, to accommodate improved facilities for intercollegiate athletic activities insofar as this is possible *without* creating major conflicts with the effective implementation of the intramural program, and finally, to provide a facility that will be available for special events, making every effort to optimize the acoustical capabilities for such events *after* the needs for intramurals and the minimal requirements for intercollegiate athletics are satisfied. These priorities were reviewed and refined by numerous committees over nearly a decade with student input from committee members and through public hearings.

Opponents of the Recreation Hall have leveled the charge that "supporters of the project sought to quickly and quietly gain approval for it. That partial information concerning the Rec Hall was only made widely available after administrative decisions to go ahead with the project were in the final stages." Such has not been the case for as early 1960 the chancellor of the Davis Campus requested a building program for a Physical Education Complex. Students along with staff and faculty took part in the proposal which remained in limbo until 1965 when a Physical Education Facility Committee prepared a Project Planning Guide. From 1967 on, the emphasis in the program shifted to that of a recreational facility instead of a physical education complex. Student input was sought and received in the form of a questionnaire sent to members of the entire campus community. Student representation on both the Recreation and Union Advisory Board, and Intercollegiate Athletic Advisory Board plus discussions with the Associated Students Executive Committee. Discussions were also held with the Public Ceremonies Committee, Campus Recreation Advisory Committee and Registration Fee Allocation Committee, the latter two committees formed in 1969 with a student voting majority. The Recreation Hall Building Task Force included students as members as well as representatives of areas on campus that are closely related to and representative of students: For example, the Internal Affairs Commission, Memorial Union, Committee on Arts and Lectures, and Vice-Chancellor of Student Relations and Activities. Through the campus newspaper, students were invited to all Campus Recreation Advisory Committee (CRAC) and Registration Fee Allocation Committee (RFAC) meetings wherein discussions on the building program and financial outlays were held.

The Project Planning Guide (PPG) was constantly revised until the final draft submitted in February 1972 to the chancellor indicated the need to hire an executive architect to begin the development of preliminary plans and cost estimates. The architectural firm selected was that of John B. Parkin Assn., from Los Angeles, with its home base in Toronto, Canada.

Outside Consultants

The Recreation Hall Building Task Force contacted consulting architects from Washington State University (Mr. Phillip Keene), Southern Illinois University (Mr. Charles M. Pulley) and University of Utah (Mr. Bruce Jensen) to offer advice from their own experiences and respond to specific questions sent to them prior to their arrival on the Davis Campus. It was intended that the Consultant Architects be selected from varying experiences with Field House and P.E. facilities so as to provide a good mix of information, criticism and recommendations.

The major list of questions sent to the three visiting architects was prefaced by the following statement:

What recommendations or precautions would you prescribe for each of the following? (Please discuss in terms of function, aesthetics, economy, utility and maintenance).

1. Access to facility—ingress and egress
2. Types of structures
3. Seating—types, storage, etc.
4. Lighting
5. Floor finishes—anchorage of equipment, surfaces beaming slick, synthetics.
6. Considerations to minimize accidents

7. Acoustics

8. We are considering having a facility with a main floor area and a mezzanine area both to be used for activities and both to be equipped with fold-away seating. Please discuss the pros and cons of this arrangement.

9. What errors and pitfalls have you experienced during the development of your own projects that we should "lookout" for?

10. What are basic requirements for performing arts? What are the costs? Can they be planned for and added later?

The three architects met together following the two day meetings of January 5, 6, 1972 and presented a summation statement regarding the Recreation Hall Project:

1. First need is to program the first priority department (Intramurals) and arrive at net assignable areas required.

2. Apply net to gross factors and arrive at gross area for building.

3. Calculate costs on the first increment.

4. Suggestions for first increment:

a. Seek first the greatest area possible to respond to the first increment program.

b. Try in the schematic development stage to conceive a plan which makes provision for the eventual inclusion of a "non-compromise" inter-collegiate facility with seating and attendant service areas.

c. This first increment facility is not viewed as having the sophistication of acoustics, sound systems and lighting for special variety type performances. Such capability should be incorporated in the second increment.

d. Consideration in the first increment for seating (fixed or retractable should be considered as possible future inclusion. This could be bid as an alternate or separately after the basic structure is under construction contract.

e. Recognizing that the vast majority of uses of this facility will be basketball we would recommend that the floor not be the multi-use type. We recommend the least costly type floor to meet the major use be selected. This is not viewed as a street shoe type floor although we feel such a space should be provided a part of the overall facility.

Funding

Before launching into the funding details of the Recreation Hall, it might be wise to review the tuition and fee structure of the University of California. Presently, each student pays quarterly, a $100 registration fee (commonly referred to as student fees) and a $110 educational fee to enroll on a full-time basis at any one of the nine campuses throughout the state. Out of this Registration Fee comes the primary financial support for such student services as the Health Center, Financial Aids Office, Housing Office, EOP Administration, Placement Center, Black Research and Service Program,

Community Service Projects Office, Intercollegiate Athletics, Intramurals, Arts and Lectures, Dramatic Art Productions, etc. The educational fee of $110 is the funding source for such areas as laboratory expenses, some student aid and designated capital outlay. Funding for the $4.4 million Recreation Hall is to be accomplished entirely through the University Registration Fees which is limited by the UC Board of Regents "to support student services and facilities."

In 1970-71, $100,000 was set aside from the Registration Fee budget for preliminary planning to determine more precisely the architectural design and financial requirements that the Recreation Hall would assume. Another $100,000 will be used for working drawings, a $1.6 million down payment, and a construction loan of $2.6 million to be financed by bonds and retired by Registration Fees.

The annual cost of bond indebtedness for the Hall is estimated at $206,105 for thirty years. This cost estimate is predicted on an interest charge of 6 percent, but may be lower because the bonds have a tax-free status.

If the projected cost is as high as the $206,105 per year, it will commit $11.34 per year/per student, or $3.78 per quarter/per student, from the $300 per year/per student Registration Fees.

The estimated annual cost of the bond retirement for the recreation facility is based on a steady-state enrollment of 18,174 beginning in 1983-84. From 1974-75, the first year of debt payment, student population is expected to rise slowly.

Originally, the concept of a recreational facility was to be jointly used for general recreation and instruction, thereby obtaining funding from state sources and from University Registration Fees. However, as the state of California became more entrenched with the Republican party in Sacramento and national priorities changed, dependence upon state funds would have delayed or cancelled the idea of such a facility. Thus, in 1969, the campus administration explored through its numerous committees the possibilities of relying solely upon Registration Fee sources as the only avenue of funding the Recreation Hall, while not restricting the operating budgets of Registration Fee funded activities. On March 16, 1973, the UC Board of Regents approved the entire Recreation Hall Project with construction to begin by the end of this year.

How Not To Build A New Physical Education/Recreation Complex
Bernard Pollack
(1973 NIA Proceedings, pp. 15-18)

When you look around at the beautiful eleven million dollar complex here at the University of Illinois and the fine attendance at our 23rd Annual Conference, it is difficult to imagine that we are living in a financial crisis. However, when you sit at breakfast and rap with colleagues about some of today's problems, you find quite a different story. One hears echoes of: "Reductions in budgets", "Little if any building program", "No additions to staff". The list seems endless.

Recently the results of a survey by Market Facts entitled "College Athletic Facilities Survey" crossed my desk. The questions and replies asked of Intramural Directors, Physical Education Deans, and Athletic Directors are as follows:

Question No. 1: Do you feel that the *outdoor* sport and recreational facilities currently available at your campus are *adequate* to meet the present *outdoor* needs and requirements of your school's intercollegiate, intramural and physical education programs?

	Intercollegiate	Intramural	Physical Education
YES	30.6%	22.1%	28.9%
NO	69.4%	77.9%	71.1%
BASE =	1050	1065	1041

Question No. 2: If current outdoor sport and recreational facilities are *inadequate* to meet the needs of your school's intercollegiate, intramural, and/or physical education programs, is there anything being done to satisfy the increased demand for these facilities?

		Intercollegiate	Intramural	Physical Education
YES	49.4%	44.4%	46.2%	
NO		50.6%	55.6%	53.8%
BASE =		741	830	759

Question No. 3: Expansion of current facilities is limited by:

	Intercollegiate	Intramural	Physical Education
Lack of funds	88.8%	84.8%	85.1%
Land availability	36.2%	41.3%	37.3%
Other reason	5.1%	5.9%	6.3%
BASE =	605	680	606

The results were self evident!

We, at the University of Miami, have been no exception to these problems. While the University has made great strides in other areas, the recreational facilities have been sorely neglected. Except for football and softball field lights, our intramural program had had no major facilities improvements since it was inaugurated 24 years ago, except for those we could make out of our regular operating budget. This of course, limited what we could do.

After years of going through regular channels for funds, only to be refused, it seemed that the only course of action left was to approach the students with the problem. Perhaps this does not seem too unusual, but considering it occurred during student protest and student unrest, it could have been a fatal decision. However, the ability of the Intramural staff to communicate with students was great enough that we were willing to take that chance.

The idea was taken to the University of Miami's Student Body Senate which listened and then agreed to take the proposition to the student body as one item on a spring referendum. The assessment would be $1 per student per semester for all students who pay an optional student activity fee. We accomplished our first objective, that of getting the matter before our students, but we knew we had to 'sell' the idea with some good, old-fashioned grass-roots campaigning. My staff and I went to work. We approached the student newspaper and the school's radio station and both helped to bring the program before the students. We spoke to hundreds of students at dormitory, fraternity house and sorority house meetings. A poster program was inaugurated and a PA system was utilized whenever crowds attended an intramural event. We did everything under the sun we could think of and the hard work paid off.

The results of the election indicated that more people voted for the Intramural Referendum than any previous item or person since records of the elections had been kept at the University; a vote of 2-1 in favor of the assessment. The result of this election meant that we could now proceed to make a recommendation to the Board of Trustees as to how the money could be used and after extensive investigation, a recommendation was made to the Vice President of Student Affairs. The investigative committee was made up of the Director of Student Activities and Student Union, the Varsity Tennis Coach, the Director of Women's Intramurals, the Director of Men's Intramurals, the President of the Undergraduate Student Body, the outstanding female in the women's program as well as the outstanding male in the Men's program and the Director of Intramurals. After visiting a number of cities, observing the various types of playing surfaces and talking with people in the field of recreation or recreational facilities such as staff architects, Director of Planning and Design of County Parks and Recreation, and Construction Coordinator of Public Schools, a recommendation was made to the Vice President of Student Affairs who then carried on the campaign. Through his efforts the Executive Committee of the Board of Trustees approved the assessment and recommended that procedure to improve facilities be given the green light if financing could be arranged.

Through the cooperation of a local contractor and the 3M Company, financing of our projects was completed to the satisfaction of the University.

As a result of this effort, we now have six beautiful tennis courts and eight new basketball/volleyball courts which are used extensively by our student body, and we feel that our hard work was certainly worth the effort.

Why was this venture successful? Perhaps the following observations could be made.

1. A rapport is developed with all students, but especially with those who are interested in what we are doing.

2. All members of our staff get out of the office and move around so that we are aware of what is happening in the program and at the same time allowing the students to know us as individuals.

3. We have an open door policy so that students have the opportunity to rap with us when they so desire.

4. We have utilized key people.

5. We have attempted to keep abreast of the time.

6. We were able to make a thorough investigation, evaluate the facts, draw a conclusion, make a recommendation.

Perhaps most important of all, we were enthusiastic. Henry Ford is quoted as saying, "Enthusiasm is at the bottom of all progress; with it there is accomplishment. Without it, there are only alibis."

Implementation and Utilization of Intramural Facilities
Ken Droscher
(1972 NIA Proceedings, pp. 17-19)

As much common ground as we share in our intramural programs, there is an equally uncommon ground that makes each program unique in itself. It is hoped that this presentation will offer that shade of difference peculiar to the University of Arizona's program that we may share an added, if not new, insight.

Utilizing and implementing facilities has as its primary base, in most instances, a cooperative and multiple use concept. Several groups must articulate in such a manner that each group's purpose may be served without detriment to the others involved. The University of Arizona intramural program divides equipment, field and indoor space with physical education classes—both professional preparation as well as service type, the freshman and varsity athletic programs, in addition to the walk-on students from campus and individual organizations who request use of facilities. Often a scheduling conflict may be resolved by a simple determination of priorities. Facility coordinators hold the key to multiple use and it is imperative to establish and maintain lines of communication at all times. More often than not two or more people must be contacted to arrive at a confirmation of dates. It is regretfully embarrassing when two events are scheduled simultaneously and the facility can afford the time to but one activity. Intramural sports directors can assist greatly in the coordination of facilities through much deliberation and thought to the organization and scheduling to ensure administrative success. Prior to the posting of play dates, facility commitments should be finalized as early as possible and all needed staff and faculty involved in scheduling contacted. Another consideration should be the availability of buildings-maintenance personnel who engineer lining and cutting of fields, the removal of bleachers, removal of apparatus, repairing equipment, e.g. This unheralded group is, to varying degrees, a compilation of super men and extremely integral for a successfuld program. This is made mention for the fact that even though a facility is secured, the personnel may not be available to equip and maintain it. It would be prudent to notify them as early as possible in the planning phases of an activity so that they may prepare to meet your needs well within the time limits that play begins and, at the same time, suggest improvements to the administration from the equipment and maintenance standpoint.

In the preceding paragraph the general considerations of scheduling have been presented in brief. To assist in the process of better utilizing and implementing facilities I should like to offer these suggestions:

(a) The multipurpose use of a facility is universal. The gymnasium area accommodates volleyball, wrestling, badminton, basketball and the activities in your program that adapt to this indoor area. Field space supports football, track, soccer, and softball through the seasons of the year. If a facility does not conform to the official standards of a sport, then modification of the rules to the facility would allow the activity to be incorporated into the program.

(b) In scheduling:

(1) A night program will ease the congestion of an uncomfortably full schedule. At the same time, a facility may be available only during the late afternoon and evening. It is not uncommon to schedule to the 12:00 p.m. midnight hour.

(2) Selecting appropriate times for outdoor activities may increase games played by one per field each afternoon, especially during the Fall. Scheduling on the quarter hour aids the University of Arizona program by allowing two games in an afternoon per field to be played without taking students out of late classes.

(3) Intramural participants have been receptive to a Saturday-Sunday schedule. Saturdays are utilized to the fullest beginning at 9:30 a.m. and finishing at 5:30 p.m. Games are played on the hour with a ten minute allowable "grace period." On Sundays a half-day from 1:30 p.m. to 5:30 p.m.

is scheduled. Virtually one-half of all scheduled games are completed during this block segment of time. An added bonus is that referees generally favor this type of concentrated officiating time as opposed to an extended season of two to three weeks three hours per day.

(c) By taking advantage of an unexpected facility being available it is sometimes possible to schedule a one day or week-end event. It can prove to be a pleasant pause in the program especially in a close competition determining the top intramural teams. "Mini" activities can supplement a program and can satisfy the need of meeting a current popular trend. They should be well-received by a substantial number of students, have no great impact upon the intramural team championship unless otherwise agreed upon, and should be easily administered and officiated. Examples of such activities would include kite flying, football, and frisbee.

(d) Utilizing city and county facilities should be considered. The annual University of Arizona bicycle marathon is administered with assistance from the county sheriff's office. It takes place over thirty miles of scenic county road in a low-congested area.

(e) On campus, other departments as well as the student union should be contacted. It would be in the best interest to be familiar with the women's recreational program so that both departments complement each other. The result should be block periods of time available so that maximum use of facilities and field space is achieved.

(f) The proximity of the student union makes it ideal for intramural competition. Many excellent facilities are usually available among them being billiards, bowling, foosball, table tennis and, in many cases, a swimming and diving area. The one additional adjustment to be made regarding this utilization would be the determination of an entry fee.

(g) A summer program should not be neglected especially if the facilities are available. The activities should be curtailed somewhat due to the decreased summer session enrollment. Also, activities should be scheduled at an early afternoon hour and on or near the campus to accommodate commuters.

(h) Intramural competition for the handicapped should be investigated. The limitations of the participation. Primary considerations should include physical limitations of entrants, cost, proximity of facility, and modification of rules.

The intramural program should allow each intramural participant the opportunity to satisfy his recreational needs and desires. If, because of poor implementation and facility utilization, the student is not afforded this chance, then a re-examination of the program is in order.

Form Follows Function: An Overview of the
Recreation Facilities Building at SIU at Carbondale
Larry D. Schaake
(1973 NIA Proceedings, pp. 10-15)

Historical Summary

In January, 1964, the students of Southern Illinois University at Carbondale felt a growing need to expand the overall recreation facilities on their campus. In order to meet this need, a student referendum was held recommending an increase in student fees to cover the expenses involved in such a venture. With the successful passing of the referendum, the Board of Trustees of Southern Illinois University met on December 2, 1964, and established the Student Welfare and Recreational Facility Building Trust Fund. Abbreviated SWARF, such fees win the amount of $15.00 per academic quarter for each full-time student were initiated Fall Quarter, 1965. These fees were held in trust "for the purpose of future construction of physical facilities for student recreation..."

During 1964 and 1965 an interested group of students, faculty and staff met informally to begin a study of the type of recreation facilities needed on the SIU-Carbondale campus. An outside consultant was brought to the campus and a survey of student interests was conducted. In February, 1966, a formal committee was appointed jointly by the three Vice Presidents of the University and given the title "Campus Recreation Facilities Planning Committee—Carbondale". This selected group of individuals was charged with the responsibility to proceed with planning and submit a preliminary report summarizing the work of the Planning Committee to the Campus Buildings and Grounds Committee.

During the years which followed, a great deal of additional planning took place in an attempt to realize a Recreation Facilities Building Complex on the campus of Southern Illinois University at Carbondale. On May 17, 1968, the SIU Board of Trustees approved the schematic design for the project as presented by Ralph Rapson and Associates, Incorporated, the architects and planners of the proposed facility. A modified schematic design was approved by the Southern Illinois University Board of Trustees in December, 1969, along with a total project budget of $8.9 million. Of this amount, the Recreation Facilities Building was budgeted at $7 million. The remaining $1.9 million was earmarked for playfield development on a 26 acre tract of land adjacent to the building site. Part of this amount was also to be utilized in absorbing those future expenses incurred in purchasing furniture and movable equipment for the building, providing utility extensions and absorbing planning expenses.

With final SIU Board of Trustees approval for the entire project expected within the next few months, Southern Illinois University at Carbondale will begin construction on its new Recreation Facilities Building complex. By forecasting the completion date of all necessary construction work, it is anticipated that this unique facility will begin serving the campus recreation and intramural needs of Southern Illinois University at Carbondale shortly after January 1, 1975.

General Building Description

The Recreation Facilities Building at Southern Illinois University at Carbondale is an interrelated complex of indoor and outdoor recreation areas. As a year-round multi-use facility, it is planned to assist students in developing physical skills and interests for present and future leisure time enjoyment. Through a broad-based recreation program, this facility will provide greater opportunities for physical recreation and intramural athletic events. The design for the Recreation Facilities Building stems from the program statement demanding maximum functional and useable space at minimum budget. During the planning process, emphasis was placed on the total integration of the architectural, structural and mechanical systems, with the functional exposure of these elements providing the major aesthetic impact. Inasmuch as the land configuration permitted two levels of development for access and egress, the major activity areas are located at the lower level; administrative offices, lounges and observation areas are located at the upper level for maximum control. Elevator service is centered within the facility to provide wheelchair students with greater ease of movement from one level to the next. A public address system throughout the entire facility will enable a combination of audio possibilities in recreation and intramural programming.

The facility as designed contains 239,200 gross square feet, with the total building cost per square foot established at $29.00. Completely air-conditioned, except for the natatorium, the building provides separate ventilation systems for each of the main activity areas located throughout the facility.

As relates to specific activity areas, the project provides facilities for basketball, volleyball, badminton, handball, racquetball, squash, golf, swimming and diving, wrestling-judo-karate, weight lifting, fencing, dance, and other organized and individual athletics. In addition, exercise equipment, sauna baths, and lounges provide for the participants' maximum enjoyment of the facility. Ample spectator-viewing accommodations permit observation of the major activity areas within the building.

The following outline of the Recreation Facilities Building provides a brief description of each of the major activity areas housed within the facility.

Facilities

LOWER LEVEL

Gymnasia

Three separate gymnasia, each 104' x 168' provide ample space for nine basketball, twelve volleyball and thirty-six badminton courts, in addition to other related activities. Two of the gymnasia will have a hard maple wood floor, while the third "multi-purpose" gymnasium will contain an indented synthetic floor surface for greater flexibility in programming. Ceiling height in all three gymnasia is set at 30 feet in order to meet regulation volleyball specifications and prevent ceiling interference during badminton and basketball contests. Two large storage rooms, each containing 423 square feet, will be located adjacent to each of the gymnasia and permit storage of roll-away bleachers, standards, scoring tables, and other miscellaneous movable equipment when not being utilized. An observation deck at the upper level is provided for spectator viewing, thus eliminating any control problem on the playing floor.

Handball/Racquetball and Squash Courts

Sixteen handball/racquetball courts, measuring 20' x 40' each, and two regulation singles squash courts, line of the main corridors of the facility. One of the handball courts will provide for spectator viewing through a glazed side-wall, although play may be observed in each court from the open ends on the upper level. Construction will provide for poured reinforced concrete, tilt-up walls, with hard maple wood floors. Utilization of mercury-vapor lighting will allow for even distribution of light with minimum shadows to interfere with play. Each court is ventilated for maximum playing comfort.

Golf Room

This 104' x 40' room is designed to accommodate computerized golf driving stations for recreational enjoyment. A synthetic grass putting green will serve to provide for a more relaxed activity while waiting for one of the computerized stations to become available.

Dance Room

This 42' x 59' room will have a hard maple wood floor and be provided with wall mirrors and other necessary dance equipment. Exercise bars will also be mounted along one wall of the room to aid in programming flexibility.

Fencing Room

Measuring 42' x 59', this room will have a synthetic floor and provide the necessary space for most of the fencing activity. Storage space for foils and other necessary equipment will also be provided in this area.

Wrestling-Judo-Karate Room

This room is 59' x 63' and is designed to accommodate various combative activities. It will have a synthetic floor and safety mats placed on the walls and floors respectively. A sliding partition will enable this room to be utilized for additional fencing space if needed.

224

Weight Lifting and Exercise Room

The weight lifting and exercise room is 47' x 63' and contains a synthetic floor surface. Various weight-lifting and exercise equipment will be provided, along with all of the necessary mats, lifting platforms, mirrors, and other paraphernalia associated with this type of activity center.

Natatorium

The natatorium is 210' x 119' and contains a 75' x 165' (50 meter) swimming pool which can accommodate simultaneous use by some 200 individuals. Designed with the diving area centered within the pool, four 1-meter and two 3-meter diving boards are joined by a 5-meter platform tower. The natatorium ceiling height is designed at 30 feet. The maximum water depth is set at 16 feet in order to accommodate water shows, scuba, and diving events. Water depth varies from 3'6" to 5' in an area (45'9" x 75') at one end of the pool and from 5' to 7' in an area (49'5" x 75') at the competitive end. The deep water area, 83'8" x 75', in the middle of the pool recedes from a depth of 5' on one side and 7' on the other to 16' at its deepest point. Underwater lighting will enhance the recreational atmosphere of the windowless natatorium and complement the mercury vapor lamps above the pool and deck areas. An underwater speaker system will be provided for utilization in programming the natatorium during recreation and water show activities. In addition, an underwater observation room provides space for viewing underwater activities and is accessible from the pool deck. The gutter system employed in the pool is the Whitten Uniflow System. In addition, sand filters will be employed to provide for up to six months of service without backwash.

Entry of the natatorium is obtained from each of the men's and women's locker room and shower facilities. An office located on the pool deck will have direct access to a main corridor for ease of control purposes. Temporary spectator seating for the natatorium is provided on the upper level above the women's locker room area; seating for some 600 spectators is designed in the form of reverse-fold bleachers, which will provide an extra activity area 96' x 29' when not in use. The folded bleachers will also serve to provide a temporary wall structure between the natatorium and the activity area.

Locker Rooms

The Women's Locker Room measures 95' x 119' while the Men's Locker Room facilities are 157' x 119'. This accounts for a total of 29,988 square feet of locker room space, designed to serve all of the activity areas associated with the building complex. Two sauna baths are provided adjacent to each of the locker rooms, in addition to the necessary shower, drying, and toilet facilities. A towel distribution and security station is centrally located within each of the dressing room areas for locker room control and service.

Equipment Storage and Check-Out Room

Most of the recreation equipment utilized within the Recreation Facilities Building will be stored and issued from the central equipment storage and check-out room. This area is 62' x 43' and has additional repair, laundry and custodial rooms adjacent to the major equipment storage area. Separate security cages are designed for out-of-season and new equipment storage, in addition to the current equipment check-out storage racks utilized throughout the year.

UPPER LEVEL

Multipurpose Room

A large multipurpose room measuring 40' x 107' is located on the upper level and will provide space for sports club activities. This area more than likely will be schematically designed into various meeting rooms in future planning sessions.

Open Center Court

An open court is centered within the building and provides a place where students may gather for special activities. The area is 59' x 168' and also offers an outdoor lounging area for interested individuals.

Natatorium Lounges

Three separate lounges are provided on the upper level, adjacent to the natatorium, and are designed with glass walls to seal out the warm, humid air within the pool area. These particular lounge areas are each 12' x 41' and will provide a unique aesthetic quality to the building in their relationship to the natatorium and the aquatic activity which will take place below.

Main Lounge

The primary lounge within the Recreation Facilities Building is located adjacent to the administration office center and measures 33' x 83'. This area will be completely carpeted and serve as a meeting area for special events associated with the building complex. A vending room and kitchen flank the lounge and provide additional service flexibility.

Administrative Offices

The facility will house the various recreation and intramural staff offices of those individuals charged with the responsibility of administering such activities. All administrative office space is designed in an area 83' x 62' and provides for a conference room and work room, as well as ample secretarial and storage space. Central control of the public address system will originate from the administrative office area for greater flexibility in programming. A reception and information counter is located between the main lounge and administrative office complex in order to control the flow of traffic to the administrative office area.

In summary, I would like to say that we at Southern Illinois University at Carbondale are anxiously awaiting the construction and completion of the Recreation Facilities Building on our university campus. Southern Illinois

University at Carbondale, through the realization of such a facility, will be in a better position to program for, and meet the recreation and intramural needs of its student population.

Facility Consideration for Handicapped Intramural Participants
Jim McAvaddy
(1973 NIA Proceedings, pp. 5-9)

At last year's conference, I presented a paper on Adaptive Intramural Programs. I would now like to expand on that topic area and cover facility considerations for the handicapped intramural participant.

It is quite clear that the great number of disabled and/or handicapped persons are not receiving the benefits of our intramural and recreational programs. The severity of their disabilities, architectural barriers and the slowness of our professionals to adjust their programs and facilities to meet the needs have all been contributing factors.

We have certainly started to move in the right direction by adopting our programs, but now we must go even further by making sure that any future facilities that are built take into consideration the handicapped and disabled, and if possible the adaptation of present facilities to whatever extent possible.

Just to refresh your memory as to some of the many disabilities and handicaps you might encounter, let me now mention a few: wheelchair, amputees, visually impaired, perceptual-motor problems, cardiac problems and emotional problems just to mention a few.

To delve a little further into this problem, and in order to help you in your planning of any new facility, or in restructuring existing buildings, it is important that you know some of the difficulties that our impaired, disabled and handicapped people have in utilizing intramural-recreational facilities. Some of these problems are:

1. Limitation in walking
   a. difficulty in walking distances because of muscular weakness due to disease or age.
   b. difficulty in walking on non-level and non-smooth surfaces because of braces, crutches, cardiac problems, flexibility or coordination or inability to walk.
   c. inability to walk, but able to propel themselves in a wheelchair on level surfaces.
   d. inability to propel a wheelchair because of extensive disability.
2. Limitations in seeing and/or hearing
   a. difficulty in seeing and/or hearing warnings and safety hazards because of limited vision or audition due to disability or age.

b. or because of extensive disability.

3. Limitations in the use of hands and arms

   a. difficulty in opening gates, doors, manipulating equipment, etc. because of muscle and joint weakness, or because of the necessity to manipulate crutches, a cane or wheelchair;

   b. or because of extensive disability in the muscles and joints of the arms and hands.

4. Limitations in understanding information, directions and warnings.

   a. difficulty in reading printed signs because of blindness, or severe intellectual impairments:

   b. or because of partial blindness or intellectual impairment.

In general, our impaired, disabled or handicapped can and should enjoy the same basic intramural recreational experiences as do the so-called "normal" participants if the proper opportunity is provided. However, recreational facility planners too often neglect the small, but special needs of the handicapped.

Some thoughts that you should consider are:

1. The disabled should be included in existing programs whenever possible.

2. These programs should be planned for the adults as well as the children that are impaired, disabled or handicapped.

3. Facilities should be planned for year round participation.

4. Program planners and officials should consider the following three levels of intramural-recreational participation by disabled persons:

Those able to participate in activities with the non-disabled when facilities and programs are adapted for their use.

Those who for physical or psychological reasons are not ready to recreate with non-handicapped persons. Existing facilities can be reserved at certain hours for use if facilities are adequately adapted. These areas can be used for instructional periods to prepare the disabled for intramurals or recreation with the non-disabled.

Those so severely disabled or socially withdrawn that they need a sheltered environment. Special areas need be set aside for them.

5. The usual design and construction of facilities often limit or prevent handicapped people from participating in our programs. Thoughtful planning can eliminate architectural barriers.

In planning for the handicapped, the Bureau of Outdoor Recreation and most groups that work with or for the handicapped recommend that existing facilities be modified to accommodate their needs. It is urged also that maximum access be provided to all activities in which disabled persons might participate or be spectators.

The U.S.A. Standard Specifications for making buildings and facilities accessible to and useable by the physically handicapped recommends adaptations of facilities that allow disabled persons to *assist* themselves. For example, steps are augmented by ramps and paths for wheelchairs; doorways are made wider and easier to open; grab-bars are placed in rest rooms, drinking fountains are lowered, step down curbs are modified, etc.

Some of the more exacting specifications in facility adaptation and construction are as follows:

I. Information: Special signs and maps should direct wheelchair occupants and other handicapped persons to paths and facilities adapted to their use. Signs should be readable by those with impaired sight.

II. Access

a. Parking: Stalls should be made 12'-0" wide for both perpendicular and diagonal parking. Drop curbs should be provided at convenient locations for wheelchair access to walks. Avoid wheelchair circulation behind cars.

b. Walks: Should have a minimum width of 48". Walk pavement should have a hard non-slip surface of concrete, sealed asphalt, etc. Walks should blend with the adjacent ground and have a minimum gradient. Care should be taken to minimize expansion joints and expansion joint filler which expands above the walk surface. Walks which cross drives or parking areas, should blend to the level of the drive or parking area by using drop curbs. Avoid steps and sharp breaks in grade in walks.

c. Ramps: Should be provided for access to facilities when required by topography. Ramps should be constructed with a non-slip surface; 37" minimum width between railing, but 72" wide for two-way circulation. The maximum gradient for ramps should be 8.33%; a preferred grade to be 5%, with smooth transition to upper and lower levels. Platforms on ramps should be provided at the top and bottom, at 30' intervals and at all changes of direction. Handrails, preferably on both sides, should be 32" high, 2" from the wall, and extending at least 12" beyond the top and bottom of the ramp. Curbs 2" high and 4" wide made of wood or concrete should be provided under handrails and adjacent to walls to prevent wheelchair scuffing rough walls or catching railing posts. If because of extreme site conditions, the allowable maximum gradient for ramps cannot be maintained, ramps should still be constructed as a steep ramp is less of a barrier than steps, and a second party can be called for assistance.

d. Stairs: Stairs should have riser heights of standard size (6") but without having abrupt square nosing. Steps with forward sloping risers are better for physically disabled people. Railing should be set at 32" above the tread.

e. Doors and Doorways: Doors should have a minimum clear opening of 32" (preferably 36") and should be operated by a single effort. The floor, both on the inside and outside, should be level for a distance of 5 feet. As much as possible, thresholds should be flush with the floor.

f. Door hardware: Each door should have three hinges with kick plates 16" high. Door closers should be the time-delay type. Vertical bar type, pull handles should be placed 36" from floor with an additional pull handle placed near the hinge to enable wheelchair occupant to close the door, if door closers are not provided. Safety glass lights 6" x 42" high can be places 28" above floor if privacy is not required. Metal edge strips 40" high should be added to protect wood door.

III. Toilet Facilities

a. Toilet stall should be 3'-0" wide, 5'-0" deep, with a door 32" wide swinging out; handrails on each side, 33" high parallel to floor; and a wall mounted water closet 20" high.

b. Urinals should be floor mounted or, if wall mounted, the opening should be no higher than 19" above floor and should be equipped with a horizontal handrail.

c. Lavatories with narrow aprons, mounted at a height of 30" from the underside of apron to the floor. Plumbing should be placed high under lavatory to avoid legs and chair. Hot water and drain pipes should be insulated.

d. Hand dryer should be set at a 40" maximum above the floor.

e. Mirror should be set no higher than 40" above the floor.

f. Circulation in public toilets should be carefully checked for use by handicapped in wheelchairs.

IV. Swimming Pools

a. Pools can be made accessible in four ways:

1. Pool coping raised 19½" to 20" above pool deck.

2. Deck ramped down adjacent to pool coping on one side to provide a well 19" to 20" below coping.

3. A ramp provided on the inside of the pool.

4. An elevator provided in the pool.

(The most suitable method for public pools would be No. 2.) When coping is raised above the pool deck, the coping should cantilever over the deck area to provide room for wheelchair foot rest. Copings should have a smooth non-slip finish and adequate pipe handles should be provided on coping. Water level of pool should be as high as possible to top of coping (about 3" or 4"). Skimmers would enable water level to be kept at this height in the pool.

b. Locker rooms should have ample circulation space for wheelchair, and benches should be omitted in certain locations.

c. Changing areas or cubicles should be provided without benches for women and possibly for men.

d. Showers should be individual cubicles for both men and women. Benches 19½" high, faucets 36" high and hose extension for shower spray should be provided. Handrails 36" high around shower cubicle would be required. Cubicle should be large enough to permit transfer from a wheelchair to a bench by disabled persons. Shower curb should be omitted.

V. Miscellaneous Facilities

a. Public telephones should be wall mounted with acoustic side shield and should be mounted 30" above floor. (30" to underside of telephone shelf with pay phone on shelf.)

b. Food service areas should have table with height 30° from the floor to underside of table. Cafeteria self-service areas should be adapted to wheelchair use.

c. Drinking fountains of standard free-standing type can be adapted for use by wheelchair occupant by placing a side-mounted basin and bubbler 30" above grade. If wall-mounted drinking fountains are used they must be set at a height of 30". Note: If drinking fountains are adapted to the 30" height a step for children may be omitted.

The material and specific recommendations in this paper are not my own. They were taken from source materials I have gathered and proper credit should be given to everyone who has contributed towards improving the conditions for the handicapped. Special consideration and thanks is extended to the Department of Interior, Bureau of Outdoor Recreation, the Natonal Recreation and Park Association and the State of New York for its comprehensive plans for facilities.

As you can see from the previously mentioned recommendations, there is an awful lot that can be done. There is still an awful lot that needs to be done, and finally there is an awful lot of things, ideas innovations and programs that *we* as intramural-recreation directors *must* get done.

Remembers, leisure time is for everyone.

Chapter 17
Finances

Innovative Methods of Financing Your Programs
Harry R. Ostrander
(1973 NIA Proceedings, 62-66)

If one was to review past history of financing Intramural Programs the findings would not be good on the majority of our campuses. There are probably very few Directors who can say that they are receiving adequate funds for conducting their programs in a first class manner. The reasons for this inadequate funding are many but I would like to briefly discuss two major reasons. First, I believe that because traditionally most of us have been handicapped by being administratively responsible to either the Physical Education Department or the Intercollegiate Athletic Department. We have always been in a subordinate role in this situation and usually receive only minimum budget requirements while being the first to be cut when reductions are necessary. I think it is time our university administrators realize that we are in competition with the Physical Education and Intercollegiate Athletic Departments for use of facilities, equipment monies, and program monies. There is no way we can fairly compete with them while remaining in a subordinate position to one or the other.

Secondly our programs have been handicapped by the attitude of faculty and university administrators that Intramural Programs are not academic or educational and therefore they are not as important to fund as academic programs. All of us must continue our efforts to prove that our programs are every bit as important as "academic" programs and probably far more "educational" than most.

You may be wondering how these two points relate to my topic "Innovative Methods of Financing Your Program"? The point is that your chances for implementing the programs I'm about to suggest are far greater if you have a separate department from Physical Education and Intercollegiate Athletics and if you are able to change the attitudes of your faculty and adminstrators to accept your programs as educationally sound and important to the University Community.

However, before you can accept any of my suggestions for additional methods of funding your program you must also accept my philosophy that Intramural and Recreation Programs should be meeting the needs of the entire university community; to include students, faculty and staff, and families of students, faculty and staff. Students could and should retain the number one priority but programs should also be developed to meet the needs of other members of the university community.

Three years ago the University of Iowa accepted recreational responsibility for the entire University Community and it's been one of the best things that has ever happened to us. The immediate problem was how do you expand programming to include other members of the University Community when you don't even have adequate funding for your student intramural programs.

The first step is establish a policy (many universities already have such a policy) that no one may use university recreational-athletic facilities for their own private gain. Next you establish a policy that any instructional programs (other than Physical Education classes for registered students) that utilize recreational facilities must be sponsored by the Intramural Department. After these two steps are accomplished you are now ready to expand your program to include the entire University Community while at the same time generating additional income for your department operation.

This is accomplished by developing an extensive Recreational Lesson Program that will be structured to the needs of your particular campus community. The type of programs that prove successful will vary from campus to campus. Programs will have to be structured and organized around the existing Physical Education, Athletic, and Intramurals schedules. Some programs may be impossible to implement on your particular campus due to lack of facilities or lack of program time on those facilities.

The Recreational Lesson Programs are obviously a fee type program. Participants must pay for the instruction they will receive. At the University of Iowa we base our recreation lesson programs on the following criteria: (1) Programs must be professionally administered and supervised (2) Highly qualified instructors should be employed (3) Registration fees should be reasonable but must cover the cost of the program plus a margin of profit (4) Lesson programs should not be scheduled on facilities during periods of peak student use.

The University of Iowa is conducting the following types of Lesson Programs:

(1) *Gymnastics*

Method: Seven week session. Participants may register for once or twice a week.

Available to: Pre-school through adult (Release form required)

Registration Fee: $13.00 for those coming once a week and $20.00 for those coming twice a week.

Instructors: There are ten instructors and wages vary between $3.50-$5.00 per hour depending upon experience. The Director of the Program is paid $10.00 per hour

Number of Participants: Approximately 400 per session. We conduct four sessions per year.

(2) *Yoga*

Method: Conducted on a semester basis. Classes meet twice a week.

Available to: Family oriented activity. Youth must be at least 10 years of age.

Registration Fee: $10.00 for individual registration, $15.00 for two from the same family, or $20.00 for all members of a family.

Instructor: One instructor—instructor receives 2/3 of registration fees—intramural office 1/3.

Number of Participants: Approximately 15-20 per session.

(3) *Women's Self-Defense*

Method: Eight week session meeting twice a week.

Available to: Women 10th grade and above (Release form required).

Registration Fee: $10.00 per person.

Instructor: Instructor receives 2/3 of registration fees (two instructors) and intramural office 1/3.

Number of Participants: Approximately 15-20 per session.

(4) *Karate:*

Method: Conducted on a semester basis with participants meeting twice a week.

Available to: Students (university), Faculty and Staff (Release form required).

Registration Fee: $25.00 for all new participants and $15.00 for anyone enrolled in any of our previous sessions.

Instructors: Instructors (5) receive 2/3 of registration fees and intramural office 1/3.

Number of Participants: Approximately 50 per session.

(5) *AIKIDO:*

Method: Conducted on a semester basis with participants meeting three times per week.

Available to: Students, Faculty and Staff (Release form required).

Registration Fee: $25.00 for new participants and $20.00 for anyone enrolled in any of our previous sessions.

Instructors: One instructor who receives 2/3 of the registration fees and intramural office receives 1/3.

Number of Participants: 10 to 15 participants per session.

(6) *Scuba-Diving:*

Method: Classes meet once a week for ten weeks. Classes include one hour of lecture and two hours of pool time.

Available to: Sixteen year olds and above.

Registration Fee: $50.00 per person which includes tank, regulator and air.

Instructor: Instructor receives 2/3 and intramural office 1/3.

Participants: Approximately 50-75 per session.

(7) *Tennis:*

Method: Tennis is offered on three levels (A) group lessons meeting twice a week for four weeks (B)individual instruction of which participant may register for any number of lessons and (C) on a clinic basis.

Available to: Third grade and above.

Registration Fee: $5.00 per person for group lessons, $3.00-$4.00 per half hour lesson for individual lessons, and $10.00 per person for clinic instruction. Three group sessions are conducted—May, June, July.

Instructors: Instructors receive $5.00 per hour for group lessons $2.50-$3.50 per half hour (intramural office receives .50 cents of each individual lesson) for individual instruction, and 2/3 of clinic registrations and intramural office 1/3.

Number of Participants: There are approximately 100 participants per group session, over 700 participants enrolled in individual lessons, and approximately 60 in clinic instruction.

(8) *Golf*

Method: Gold is offered both on a group and individual basis. Group lessons meet twice a week for four weeks. Participants may register for any number of lessons for individual instruction.

Available to: Third grade and above.

Registration Fee: $5.00 per session for group lessons, $3.00-$4.00 per half hour lesson for individual lessons. Three group sessions are conducted—May, June, July.

Instructors: Instructors receive $5.00 per hour for group lessons and $2.50-$3.50 per half hour (intramural office receives .50 cents of each individual lesson) for individual instruction.

Number of Participants: There are approximately 100 participants per group session and about 50 enrolled for individual lessons.

The establishment of an extensive lesson program cannot be accomplished without problems. You can anticipate there will be some resentment on the part of the Physical Education Department because you are becoming involved in an instructional program. However, Recreational Lesson Programs are primarily for the non-student, participants receive no academic credit, and in many cases your lessons may be at a more convenient time for the participant (evening or late afternoon). In addition to this they are paying a fee to register for your program.

You can also anticipate that some individuals will express concern that Recreational Lesson Programs are taking facilities that should be available for open recreation. As long as this is not abused you can put up a good argument when you show that the lesson programs are paying for themselves and in fact making a profit which is being used to increase student intramural programs and to purchase additional equipment which is available for everyone's use.

In conclusion I can only say that the University of Iowa has found that the Recreation Lesson Programs are an excellent way to reach *all members* of the University Community while at the same time generating additional revenue for the operation of the Intramural Department.

Commercial Involvement in Intramurals: McDonald's Restaurant Involvement in Intramural Sports Publicity at Iowa State University
Gerry Maas
(1974 NIA Proceedings, pp. 68-70)

Publicity for Intramural Programs can be a problem if the student newspaper or local paper gives most of its coverage in sports to intercollegiate athletics. Good coverage in the student or local newspaper can mean much to the intramural program, especially if it appears on a regular basis, as intramural participants then begin to count on and look for program information and stories. At Iowa State University, the student newspaper was virtually not covering intramural sports at all, but rather concentrating on intercollegiate athletics. This was quite disappointing as Iowa State has a very fine Intramural Program that involves 61% of the male and female students on campus, but the University community knew little of its scope and student involvement.

Initially, representatives of the Intramural Program, both students and staff, made a number of overtures to the student newspaper staff hoping to convince them to cover intramural sports. When these attempts failed, it was evident that if we were to get intramural publicity a different approach to the problem would be needed.

My experience in the Intramural Program at the University of Minnesota during my graduate work there introduced me to the concept of involving private commercial business in sponsoring an intramural sports page in the student newspaper. This involvement at Minnesota was with the Theodore Hamms Brewing company and consisted of the buying of one full page space each week in the student newspaper with Hamms appearing only in the title of the page and with the Hamms Cartoon Mascot. (Hamms had other intramural program involvements besides the page.) The entire page was filled with intramural sports information. The page was also blown up to poster size (26" x 20") for placement in local business establishments and campus buildings. With this background with the Hamms Program at the University of Minnesota, I hoped to find a sponsor for a similar page in the Iowa State student newspaper.

The search for a sponsor for such a page in our student newspaper began in an informal intramural staff meeting. A number of possibilities were discussed. We looked for a business that did extensive advertising in the student paper and for some hint of a connection with sports, especially the intramural program. An early suggestion was McDonald's Restaurant as one of the intramural student staff members knew the owner personally. Along with advertising heavily in the student newspaper, the owner of McDonald's also was an avid jogger and supporter of intramural sports and informal recreational pursuits. It was agreed that McDonald's would be a good potential sponsor of this type of advertising program.

The approach used in the meeting with the McDonald's owner was as an *innovative* approach to advertising. I took a poster with a blow-up of the Hamms page from Minnesota to the meeting. This was a big help as the potential advertiser had something to look at and could visualize his business in the place of Hamms. Needless to say, McDonald's gladly accepted the proposition. Another big selling point was the tremendous participation we have at Iowa State University. We could indicate that our constitutents (over 12,000 students) would be looking for the page if it appeared on a regular basis.

The details of the McDonald's Intramural Highlites page included the following:

1. Each page costs $100.00 and would appear on a bi-weekly basis with two pages on successive weeks during the last two weeks of each quarter to wrap up championships, etc. We attempt to have it on the same day (Tuesday) when it appears. Tuesday was selected as we have entries due on many occasions on this day.

2. The title of the page is McDonald's Intramural Highlights and includes the cartoon character Ronald McDonald.

3. The page is boxed in and labelled "Advertisement" and "Sponsored by McDonald's."

4. A box appears on each page that explains the page indicating that it is sponsored by McDonald's in conjunction with the Iowa State Intramural Program.

5. The cost of putting the page together and providing photographs is supported by the Intramural Program.

6. The Iowa State Daily provides a sports staff writer to put the page together with help from an intramural student staff member.

7. A recent addition to the McDonald's program has been a poster blow-up of the page. This is done by a local printer and costs approximately $30 per 100 copies of the page (size 20" x 25"). These posters are put up all over campus and in the community to give another dimension to our publicity.

8. The Intramural Program has total freedom in what appears on the page concerning the intramural program.

9. The "advertising" by McDonald's is "low key" by association only— nowhere will you see "Eat at McDonald's," coupons, etc.

10. A banquet for all members of Intramural championship teams will be held near the end of spring quarter with McDonald's serving that world renowned food.

The McDonald's Intramural Highlites page has been very well received by the entire University community. The McDonald's staff and the Iowa State Intramural staff has had many fine comments concerning the involvement in intramural publicity. The publicity has given the Iowa State Intramural Program the exposure it both needs and deserves. This has also spurred interest on the student newspaper staff at Iowa State to reconsider its present coverage of intramural sports and give us some room on the sports page. They are finally recognizing the scope of the Intramural Program.

In summary, if your intramural program has a problem with publicity you might consider the involvement of local private businesses. If you would want poster-size blow-ups of the Iowa State McDonald's page to aid in your search for a sponsor for a similar involvement, please contact me at Iowa State as we would gladly help in this endeavor. Again, the way to sell this concept of advertising is to stress the following two points: (1) It is an *innovative* method of advertising along with being *soft-sell* and (2) you can show *solid readership interest* in the ad through your *intramural participation records*.

Chapter 18
Handbooks

The Intramural Handbook — Its Purpose, Function, and Assets
William T. Odeneal
(1967 NIA Proceedings, pp. 16-19)

The intramural handbook is a necessary and indispensable resource of every intramural director. It is as important to him as a hammer is to a carpenter, for it is a source of referral, of information, of reference, of public relations, of direction, of purpose and of function.

Direction

Webster defines a handbook as a book capable of being conveniently carried as a ready reference: a concise reference covering a particular object.

A student defines a handbook as a quick guide to find out a particular thing he wants to know.

A chairman of the physical education division defines a handbook as a set of policies and activities of a segment of the total physical education program.

A director in intramurals defines a handbook as a Bible of the intramural program.

Purpose

Webster defines purpose as something that is set up as an object or an end to be obtained — an object or result aimed toward. The aim of the intramural handbook should be to provide a variety of activities which will develop skills, interest and enjoyment for the present and in later life. The handbook should include objectives and outcomes desired which spell out briefly these desired aims. These objectives and outcomes should include the following:

1. Development of coordination, strength and endurance.
2. Development of an improved cardiovascular system.
3. Development of an improved nervous system.
4. Development of such personality traits as perseverance, courage, and confidence.
5. Development of desirable standards of conduct, sportsmanship and honesty.
6. Development of leadership, followship, group spirit and better understanding of one's own capabilities.
7. Knowledge of rules and techniques of play.
8. Pleasure and fun derived from engaging in activities.
9. Widespread acquaintanceship for the present and in later life.

239

Statements from the President of the institution, the chairman of the physical education division, and the intramural director should stress the physical and social opportunity for participants both individually and collectively. These should relate how recreational activities and competitive sports provide a healthy use of leisure time, a sound outlet of physical energy, and a means of informal contact and friendship.

Function

Webster defines function as the action for which a thing exists. The function of an intramural handbook is as follows:

1. To inform the student body of all the physical facilities available to them in the area of physical education.

2. To explain the general operational policy of the intramural program.

3. To explain the administration and control of intramural activities.

4. To list the operating hours of the gymnasium.

5. To list the general regulations of the physical education facilities.

6. To explain the rules governing intramural competition; eligibility, how to enter competition, forfeits, protests, postponements, health regulations, list team and individual events, officiating procedures, publicity, awards, various league competition and club information.

7. To list the seasonal sports and the rules governing these activities.

8. To list the past champions, using pictures if possible.

9. To list the constitution of an intramural council if one is used.

Assets

Assets are defined as advantages or resources. There is no doubt that the handbook is a portable source of information to the director and the participant. Most handbooks can be carried in the pocket to the playing field or on the court. In addition to this, other assets are:

1. It is an excellent teaching aid and study guide for the rules of the contests.

2. It relates the facts pertaining to rules governing intramural competition.

3. It is a record which can be used to compare reports and programs of other institutions for the improvement of one's own.

4. It is an excellent public relations media and source of information that creates interest. Students are stimulated to participate in a well-organized and publicized activity.

5. In most cases it is the only source which acquaints the student with various activities in which one may participate.

Overlook

Excellent examples of the ideas presented here are shown in handbooks of schools throughout the country. Oswego and New Paltz in New York have a separate section for aim and purpose of the intramural program. Under the items listed for function; Purdue has maps and instructions showing how to get to various facilities, The University of Michigan has an attractive and descriptive section on operating policy, West Point has a very good section on administration, the University of Minnesota lists hours when the gymnasium will be open and telephone numbers and names to contact people, The University of Denver has a section on general regulations, The University of Illinois has a section printed on colored paper which contains eligibility rules, The University of South Florida has good photographs of all activities, The University of Buffalo and the University of Louisville handbooks contain good constitutions.

Unusual features are presented in some handbooks. The University of Iowa has a section called "hints from has-beens", which helps future team representatives. UCLA includes a calendar of monthly activities in the handbook to be inserted as they are issued. The University of Texas has a detailed section on recreational hours and a faculty staff program. The University of Virginia has an attractive front cover which advertises its program.

Suggestions

Some suggestions that are offered to the prospective director of intramurals and to those who would strive to improve their own handbook are as follows:

1. Develop a handbook that is attractive inside and outside by using drawings, colored paper and unusual layouts.

2. Organize the handbook so that it lists briefly and completely all the important aspects of the program.

3. Make the handbook pocket size so it may be carried in the hip pocket size so it may be carried in the hip pocket.

4. Include pictures and names of past champions or winners.

5. Since it is impossible to make a standard handbook, each institution should strive to utilize its uniqueness.

6. The cost of printing the handbook dictates the possibility of scheduling events with dates on a two or more year basis. Another possibility is to use inserts, listing the events offered with entry and first contest date and another insert listing names or pictures of past champions.

7. A suggested format for a typical handbook is as follows:
   a. sports calendar with dates
   b. Aims and purpose of the program
   c. General information section
   d. Rules governing intramural competition
   e. Records section
   f. Recreational information section.

Conclusion

In order for the Intramural Director to attack his privilege and restore equal rights to his program he must challenge the pretensions of plutocracy of the hierarchy of sports. This is done in part by the development of an intramural handbook. The administration of an institution will not overlook the promulgation of a program well-conceived, well-organized and well-directed.

Handbooks—Are They Worth the Effort?
Larry Fudge
(1969 NIA Proceedings, pp. 13-14)

Handbooks—Are they worth the effort? Is the cost prohibitive? Today, the role of an intramural handbook is more significant than ever. With the rapid growth of most universities and the larger flux in enrollment, it is becoming increasingly more difficult to communicate with the student body.

Webster defines handbook as "a book, especially a reference book, that can be easily handled or consulted; a manual." What better way is there of promoting your program? A handbook is most beneficial in providing the individual with essential and pertinent information which will enable him to become better acquainted with the various activities and many services that are offered by the Intramural Department.

What constitutes a good handbook? How elaborate should it be? Should it include pictures? Will a mimeographed book be as effective as something more elaborate? Should a handbook be a joint effort with the women's program? Should the faculty-staff program be included? How much money should you allocate for a book? Is it necessary to print a handbook each year? Several factors are involved, but probably the most significant one is cost. What is a reasonable price for printing a book?

On a random sampling of intramural handbooks the cost of printing ranged from 15¢ per copy to as high as $1.10. The average cost was approximately 30¢ per copy with the average number of pages 36. The cost ratio for the larger colleges per unit was lower with a larger volume of books printed. Are there advantages of mimeographing as compared to other methods if the same content is involved? Mimeographing would most likely be more reasonable, but the attractiveness would be less desirable than offset or other means of printing.

What items should be included in a handbook? This book should be geared solely to the freshmen and transfer students and should include the following items: purpose of the program, rules governing intramural competition, staff members, intramural calendar, intramural sports constitution, health regulations, facilities—their location and hours, protests, postponements, forfeits, free play, university point system and champions of individual and team sports. I feel that a handbook of this nature in essence will provide the individual with the necessary information. A more elaborate publication would involve pictures of staff, individual and team champions, officials and athletic chairmen and action shots of the program.

Handbooks are more beneficial to some schools than others. A book for a commuter college can be considerably more important than to a resident college. Communication is a greater problem at a commuter school and you cannot depend entirely on bulletin boards, school newspapers and P.A. systems, although they too are very important to your public relations problem. Does this mean that a commuter college without a handbook cannot conduct a successful program? Obviously not; but it stands to reason that several of these students are not informed and therefore do not participate in the program because they are unaware of what is going on.

There is a question whether it is necessary to print a handbook each year. If funds cannot be attained each year, would it be realistic to put out a publication in large volume and insert a center page on the two non-printing years? There are two ends of the spectrum, and in between there is something for everyone.

Evaluating a handbook must be done from a realistic approach. If the above questions can be answered, then I feel that it warrants the effort, time and cost, providing that cost does not exceed 40¢ per copy.

Handbooks—Are They Worth The Efforts?—
The Negative Side
Peter Steilberg
(1969 NIA Proceedings, pp. 11-12)

Gentlemen, as administrators of intramural programs we must progress in all phases of the program. By this I mean not simply by updating sports programs, but also by updating awards programs, and by finding new methods for disseminating information. In my opinion the effort most of us devote to publishing handbooks can better be spent towards improving or inventing other types of printed information which would be more effective in providing relevant information than the average handbook. I am unable at this point to describe what an average handbook looks like; however, I would say that handbooks fall into the following four descriptive categories:

1. Those which generally outline the sports offerings, and include rules, regulations, a constitution, and lists and photographs of defending champions. These are usually printed on 8½" x 11" paper, and then folded.

2. Those which include only rules, regulations, records, and a constitution. These are usually pocket size.

3. Those which contain brief intramural information and many action photographs. These are usually printed on unfolded 8½" x 11" paper.

4. Those which contain the intramural information as a part of a larger section dealing with all campus sports-oriented activities. These are generally very large and comprehensive.

Since I volunteered to take the con side of the discussion, I would be neglected if I failed to at least constructively criticize existing handbooks. Here are some criticisms: Group pictures are old hat. Most students do not seem to want to read small printed pamphlets. Intramural offerings can easily be overlooked if they are included as a part of a large bulletin type handbook. Action photographs are great, but the captions are seldom read. Handbooks still cater to campus residents, thus ignoring the commuter students who comprise increasingly larger percentages of the total enrollment. The cost is probably far too prohibitive to justify the use by major colleges, and smaller colleges would do far better by utilizing other techniques. Of course my case is based on the premise that at least one of the purposes of the handbook is to advertise the program, and because of the prohibitive cost of publishing a handbook this purpose can not be satisfied. If a department is overstaffed and/or overbudgeted, then effort spent on publishing handbooks is acceptable.

I have no cost figures for handbooks on a national, or on a local scale; however, I was able to determine that the last thousand handbooks which we published at our school cost in the neighborhood of $1.00 per copy. For our school this means that 14,000 male students could not obtain a copy of the handbook if they asked for one. In the case of our school this is an important point because one of our goals is to interest the commuter students who comprise about 80% of our enrollment. We cannot possibly print enough handbooks to provide every male student with a copy; therefore, only those who participate usually obtain copies. What can we do? Our efforts should be directed towards finding new ways to print the information which we want distributed. This year at the University of Washington we began experimenting with the Itek process of duplicating, and found it to be very successful and superior to ditto and to mimeograph.

I am in favor of printing separate fliers for every phase of—for every sport in—the intramural program. When an inquiry is made concerning a specific activity, the individual making that inquiry should be given the specific information for which he has asked. Handbooks usually do not go into detail concerning specifics of each activity offered.

Chapter 19
Point Systems and Awards

What's the Point of Points?
Nancy L. Curry
(1972 NIA Proceedings, pp. 59-63)

This position paper is based on the following premise: Play for it's own reward should be the major philosophical structure supporting any college intramural program.

The major purpose of college intramural programs is to provide as many kinds of activities as needed so that students have the opportunity to participate, and do participate because of their honest pursuit of play. Play for any reason other than play is not play, but work.

I appeal to you. Let us examine thoroughly our basic philosophies regarding intramural sports and determine their relation to point systems.

History is quick to disclose many doctrines which have been accepted and practiced because of the inherent values or disvalues which are obscurely hidden by a superficial covering of lesser goals.

The purpose today will be to attempt to expose some of these values and disvalues that have been obscurely hidden by time-honored practices. I fully realize that many of the suggestions that follow are in direct opposition to those practices which are currently utilized on many of our college campuses. It is not the intent to offend or criticize but rather to explore. Let us now examine the pros and cons of point systems in college intramural programs.

In Rodney James Grambeau's thesis, "A Survey of the Administration of Intramural Programs for Men in Selected Colleges in North and South America", he found that "80.06% of the schools in the United States" responding to his questionnaire used a point system in their intramural sports program. (3:108) That's a tremendous percentage. With so many colleges utilizing a point system, then it must be the thing to do. But is it? Does utilization of point systems foster our basic philosophic structure — play for it's own reward, or our current practice, play for points?

Art Endres stated at our meeting in Blacksburg that he found there to be as many point scoring plans in existence as there are schools using them. (1:103)

Does one then assume that because point systems exist and are widely used that they are indeed a necessary element of all successful college intramural programs? The premise of the paper is that a well planned opportunity for play makes a successful program, not a well planned system for obtaining points. Some of the well known leaders in our profession and long time proponents of the point system have their justifications. Let's look at them now. Norma Leavitt and Hartley Price state, "interest in intramurals is created and maintained" through point systems. (5:245) This is indeed true. Many teams are formed in the fall and stay together throughout the entire intramural activity schedule. However, quite often a major purpose for the cohesiveness of that team is that of trying to amass the greatest total points usually toward a championship trophy rather than playing for the sake of play.

Participation is increased and recognized through the awarding of points. Mueller states that "many additional participants are included as a result of a little incentive and it encourages those who would perhaps not otherwise participate. Giving participation points helps get people started in new activities being offered." (6:182-183) However, very little, if any mention, is made of the increase in the number of forfeits which occur after participation and entry points are obtained.

"Points offer a system of giving awards." (1:103) In order to fully understand this rationale, we must first differentiate between award and reward. Webster defines award as "a prize which is conferred or bestowed" while a reward is "something given in return for a service." This service may be "good or evil." We must then ask, "Do our points serve as a system of awards or rewards?" In a buzz session with a colleague, I was informed of a situation in which a student organization on his campus approached him requesting that he give intramural points to students for donation of their blood to the Red Cross drive. He refused to do so because he felt that the people who gave blood had done so altruistically and needed no reward. Likewise, people who participate in intramural activities should do so as a result of intrinsic motivation, the joy of play, play for its own reward.

Another argument for point systems is that offering points will draw participants into the less popular sports. It is a commonly accepted premise that individuals participate in those things that they know and do best. It would seem much more philosophically sound to offer clinics in those so-called less attractive sports to familiarize students with activities. This idea would seem to have more merit than the mere offering of points for participation.

Mueller states, "If participants obtain valuable experience from intramural participation, a motivating device is not only helpful but necessary." (6:183) But is it really necessary? Points tend to make play more like work. Play itself is the reward. One works for an end production, but play is both a process and a product—fun.

What would happen without points? Do our programs really have merit to stand alone without enticing gimmicks to increase participation numbers? Yes, I think they do. Hall states, "It is possible to develop a good intramural program without benefit of either awards or point systems." (2:102) There is some research which indicates support for the philosophical structure offered earlier in this position paper. When point systems are a part of the program, quite often participants cease to enter for the fun. Many enter strictly for the points. Terry Lynn Weatherford, in his masters thesis at the University of Illinois in 1966, discussed the history of intramural sports at the University of Illinois. He stated that one of the major changes in their intramural program was to stop awarding points for individual and dual sports. "This action was taken to eliminate a large number of forfeits due to participants entering in sports only for participation points and not for active competition." (7:22)

To further elaborate on this point, I would like to share some personal experiences. Three years ago, on our campus in Springfield, one of the intramural swimming teams entered four men in a relay. Of these four men, only three were even deep water swimmers. The fourth individual had to be pulled from the water before the relay was over. When asked why he entered, he stated, "To get the points for my team." In affect, he was making a mockery of the men's program by endangering his life for points.

In 1966, at Raytown High School in the greater Kansas City area, a well meaning young teacher of girl's physical education initiated a point system in her high school intramural program. A highly skilled group of young girls formed a team in the fall and stayed as a unit throughout the academic year. This team built a tradition of winning first in every activity they entered. They had amassed such a large total of points that no one threatened their championship. By the time the softball season rolled around in the spring, this team (which had captured so many intramural championships throughout the year) was the only team to enter girl's intramural softball. The team that played only for points found that all they had was points. No one would play them.

On our Springfield campus, we initiated a point system for Women's Intramural Sports in 1970. The rationale for starting the point system was to encourage more participation in the life-time sports area. There had been so few entries in the past, that at times it had been impossible to hold competition. All of the points were to be amassed toward the all-college championship team to be named at the end of the academic year. As the academic and intramural year progressed, we could see our purpose being fulfilled. Women were entering many of the life-time sports areas; however, they were doing it purely for the sake of points. At the same time, we began to notice friction developing between old friends and competitive teams. It appeared to us that they were out after the points at any cost. A basketball, a volleyball, or a powder puff football championship lost its true meaning. They failed to appreciate the experience of playing equally skilled opponents. Students were seeking championships for points which could go toward the intramural all-college trophy. Informal interviews were arranged with a cross section of the women who were representatives of the various teams participating in the point program. The following results were obtained: many stated that (A) "winning a basketball championship is unimportant. We are happy about it only because it gets us a few more points closer to the intramural all-college trophy"; (B) "our team has had several arguments triggered mainly because we failed to earn any points toward the all-college trophy. We never had those disagreements before, when we were playing just for the fun"; (C) "we probably won't enter any more because everyone knows who is going to win the championship"; (D) "it's just not any fun any more. It seems that people are playing for blood or points."

Leavitt and Price in their rationale against points stated that "students may tend to enter an activity in which they can get the most points rather than entering activities that would provide them with immediate enjoyment and would be of value later." (5:246) A sports manager from one of the fraternities on our campus entered my office to inquire as to whether men's badminton would be played for points or not. When told that it was a first year activity and it was going to be played for fun, he stated, "I guess that I had better not enter our fraternity. We're a small fraternity and we don't have enough men to enter anything that is not for points." Participation becomes forced instead of voluntary action. (6:183) This, in itself, violates one of the basic philosophic values of intramural activities. The spirit of play is often lost in the mad rush to gain points. Motivation is extrinsic. Students are participating for the reward of points. At this very conference last year, in a conversation with a gentleman, he stated, "You have to give points. They won't come out if you don't." I challenge that statement. "Administrative time to record points and keep totals updated is needed." (6:182) It would appear that this administrative time spent on point keeping could be better spent on devising new and different activity opportunities so that one's program would have a broader appeal and fulfill more student interests. The men's student advisory councils for the intramural programs on our Springfield campus voted this year to do away with the point systems in the men's program. It was felt that the true meaning of intramurals had been lost. Play for the sake of play.

Perhaps we are afraid to allow our programs to stand on their own merit. Participation would not decrease. Last spring, the women voted to do away with the point system. Intramural participation in the women's program has increased this year without points.

It is very easy to use massive statistic charts on participation numbers to impress our peers as to the worth of our program. This is perhaps one of our weaker attributes.

The gauntlet is down. Let's evaluate the motives underlying our point systems. We must examine our philosophies. It is conceivable that the importance of intramurals will increase to the extent that there will be an activity for everyone and everyone in an activity without enticement of artificial rewards such as points. Play itself will then be the process and the product: play for fun and fulfillment.

BIBLIOGRAPHY
1. Endres, Art. "Intramural Point Scoring System." *Conference Proceedings, National Intramural Association.* Blacksburg, Virginia, 1971.
2. Hall, J. Tillman. *School Recreation: Its Organization, Supervision and Administration.* Dubuque, Iowa: Wm. C. Brown, 1966.
3. Grambeau, Rodney James. "A Survey of the Administration of Intramural Sports Programs for Men in Selected Colleges and Universities in North and South America." Doctoral Thesis, University of Michigan, 1959.
4. Kleindienst, Viola K. and Arthur Weston. *Intramural and Recreation Programs for Schools and Colleges.* New York: Appleton Century Crofts, 1964.
5. Leavitt, Norma M. and Hartley D. Price. *Intramural and Recreation Sports for High School and College,* Second Edition. New York: The Ronald Press Company, 1958.
6. Mueller, Pat. *Intramurals: Programming and Administration.* New York: The Ronald Press Company, 1971.
7. Weatherford, Terry Lynn. "A History of the Intramural Sports Program at the University of Illinois, 1903-1965." Master's Thesis, University of Illinois, 1966.

Point Systems, Awards, and Records
Edsel Buchanan
(1963 NIA Proceedings, pp. 50-53)

The purpose of this address is not to fully cover the large areas indicated in the title, but simply to cover in specific detail these three areas as regards Texas Technological College of Lubbock, Texas, and to explain to a brief extent why our practice is what it is, what is being done and how it is done.
Point Systems

The Washington Conference Report of 1955 sponsored by the AAHPER, NAPECW, CPEA, had the following to say regarding point systems:

"Some institutions have been able to promote a successful intramural program without a point system. Other institutions have found that the point system has helped to make the program more successful.

Point systems generally serve two functions: (1) to determine winners in each activity and winners in the year's programs, and (2) as a means of motivating participation in activities.

If a point system is desired or deemed necessary, it is suggested that it be set up in such a manner that it will be simple to understand, that additional work will not overburden the staff, and that it will take into consideration for winning, losing, and forfeiting."

There are probably no two colleges or universities who use the identical point system. Most intramural directors will agree that a sound point system will help motivate the total program, stimulate constant and varied interest, and induce greater participation in a wider choice of activities. A sound point system will also serve as an excellent basis for specific awards. At Texas Technological College our Intramural Point System is a device for the stimulation of widespread participation in all phases of the program. As you will discover from the detailed discussion of our actual point system later on, little emphasis is placed upon winning. A provision is made to meet the demands of the students who feel that winning is important, however. Just as many other intramural directors feel, full and spirited participation rather than an emphasis upon winning will best meet the objectives of any sound program. A good point system will include provisions for scoring both individuals and groups. In studying point systems in the available literature, a person will soon discover that many different types of point systems are possible and in use. Point systems should be constantly studied, evaluated, and revised where necessary. As in every phase of intramural activity, application of procedure should be designed for the local situation. It is readily admitted that a great deal of detail work is involved in point systems. However, the results derived therefrom usually outweigh the drudgery of the work involved. In discussing the point system as used at Texas Tech, I would ask that you turn to page 18 of the Intramural Athletic Handbook so that you may follow along with me as I elaborate upon the various aspects of the point system.

Awards

The Washington Conference Report also has the following statement to make regarding awards:

"Every institution should establish a sound educational policy relative to awards.

1. Awards should not serve as the primary motive for participation.
2. Awards should not have little intrinsic value.
3. Awards should be a symbol of recognition of achievement.
4. There would be a time and place for presenting the awards which will serve not only to recognize the winners, but also as a further means of publicizing the program. Awards may be presented at an appropriate assembly such as a banquet, convocation, or an intramural carnival or

festival. An invitation to faculty members representing other departments on the campus to attend the event serves to promote good relations with the faculty and administration as a whole."

No one will argue that the fun of play and competition should be the primary incentive for intramural and recreational participation. However, no one can logically deny that awards are a tremendous motivating force in intramural sports. Achievement is recognized at all levels and in virtually all areas. Academically we still recognize outstanding achievement through our grading system, through certificates, diplomas, and scholarships. Business and government recognizes achievement through various types of awards and financial incentives. There is no reason why achievement cannot be recognized also in a sound program of awards.

It is extremely difficult to offer almost any type of award today that has little intrinsic value. Any school with a large program recognizes the fact that the total awards to be presented for the entire year represent a substantial financial layout. Naturally, if awards are used in a program, there should be a suitable time, place, and method for presenting the awards. Our individual awards consist of trophies of the Dodge Z-11, Z-60, or the Noble 799 triangular type. These are small awards which cost very little and which can be presented in quantity almost as economically as medals. For other type activities where individual awards are made, we use the Owens #972 and #973 with an appropriate trophy and engraving. For individual awards in our annual track meet, ribbons are used. Our other awards such as League Champions, All College Champions, Special Recognition, Rotating Trophies, and the like, are all special type and more distinctive in design. We realize that we are extremely fortunate to have a budget which will support these types of awards. This has presented a problem, however, as the number of activities has been expanded and participation increased. One factor that will help our program, budget-wise, starting in the 1964-63 year will be the elimination of some duplication. Specifically we will no longer offer both singles and doubles competition in our individual sport activities each semester. We will then offer doubles competition in the fall and singles competition in the spring. This will serve our program in a number of ways but specifically regarding awards, it will eliminate 50 per cent of the individual awards that we have presenting to date. Here on the table before you, I have examples of the awards which I have mentioned previously. At the conclusion of this meeting, you are welcome to take a look at these awards and I will endeavor to answer any questions you may have regarding them.

Records

Regarding records the Washington Conference Report has these following comments to make:

"Records which clearly indicate student participation in the program should be kept for the following reasons:

1. To justify each activity offered in the program, and to determine future growth of programs and the interests of participants.

2. To evaluate the program and to show need for increased facilities, equipment, staff, budget, and program.

3. To show the relationship of intramural participation to the total recreational experiences of the student.

4. To recognize team and individual achievement.

5. To determine eligibility

6. To serve as public relations instruments."

Just as many other programs do, Texas Tech maintains a separate card on file for each individual who participates in the intramural program and a record of his participation is posted on the card each time that he takes part in any phase of the program. A sample of the actual card which is used will be discussed later on so that it will point out specifically how our card system works for us.

I personally feel that correct and accurate record maintenance is one of the most significant things that any director can do in providing a basis for justifying his program and for making reasonable requests which lead to the growth, development, and expansion of a strong sound program. Record keeping is probably one of the most unpleasant chores that any of us face; however, when the records are maintained, analyzed and used in the many different ways which they can be used, then we truly realize that the drudgery was extremely worthwhile.

Record maintenance involves many things and I would like to discuss a few of those with you. At this time we will discuss the participation record cards which each of you should now have in your hands.

You will notice that on pages 6, 7, and 8, of the Texas Technological College Handbook of Intramural Athletics for Men, the participation records and point total records are recorded so that this information can be made available to all people concerned. Many of you will probably notice that our participation multiple is calculated somewhat differently from that which many departments use. Our participation multiple calculations produce a lower total than do other multiple calculations; however, for our purpose at Texas Tech, this total and its interpretations suffice excellently. I would like to comment briefly on each of the various phases of the participation records so that you will have an understanding of how they function for us. Also on page 8 you will notice that our top ten (10) teams all have a point total which is less than 1,000 points. One of the aims of our point total program is to keep points at a low level, thereby making them much easier to work with. Fortunately our goal was achieved in that our first place team still fell short of the 1,000 point total. We feel that this is a workable plan because when points run over the 1,000 points, this does increase bookkeeping chores, in my opinion.

You do not have this information available to you regarding participation costs, attendance data, and graph records; however, I would like to discuss these briefly with you as they are used at Texas Tech. I am not proposing that any of these be implemented on your program; however, I feel that they will stimulate some thinking and that there may be some possibility that you could use something like this. Copies of these are here at the desk and you are welcome to take a look at them at the conclusion of this meeting. Please do not, however, take any of these copies with you for they are withdrawn from my permanent files and I would like very much to retain them in my permanent file records.

In concluding this brief address, I want to emphasize that record keeping, along with a reasonably successful program, has been one of the primary reasons for the growth and development of our program. I find, personally, that when you have a good program in operation, your superiors are aware of this. If you can follow this up with an annual report reflecting a healthy situation statistically, I find that this is your surest guarantee of having your requests for increased budget, facilities, time, space, etc., being honored by your supporters. People who run colleges must deal with facts and figures which we call statistics. If your statistical program impresses them, you will have little need to worry about your actual program of activity.

Awards, Their Value and Meaning
Joseph M. Sullivan
(1969 NIA Proceedings, 231-233)

Awards are tangible symbols of achievement or accomplishments and take a variety of forms and sizes. Honoring successful and outstanding performance is a mode consistent with American culture. Awards, used as incentives, are practiced in all fields of endeavor.

In education, diplomas, honors, certificates, pins, rings, and "Professor of the Year" are all signs or symbols of outstanding academic achievement. In industry, awards take the form of Group Bonuses, watches, pins and certificates, including various tangible awards given to safety campaigns. The business world gives their recognition of an achievement in the forms of vacations, holidays, foreign trips, and merchandise bonuses. The armed services have their "Man of the Month" to stimulate achievement.

If we, as intramural directors, would ever hope for some type of revision of this practice, then it would have to be started in infancy, carried through Little League Baseball, pee wee football, and biddy basketball; then through the complicated varsity athletic award program; and continued through all phases of life. Otherwise, little would be accomplished if awards were abolished solely in the intramural program.

If we are to defend awards as part of the American way of life, and if the material values are made the desired end, the participant may be more concerned with the award itself, rather than the manner in which it was achieved. Therefore, to be educationally sound, awards must be a means to an end—rather than ends in themselves. The love of the activity, the benefits gained toward physical and mental health, and the desire for competition must be the primary purposes for participation.

Awards are secondary; they should be simple, intrinsic in nature, and of little monetary value. In studying early Greek history, we find the most coveted award was the crown of olive branches placed upon the head of an Olympic champion.

Further study indicates the harm over-emphasizing the awards can do. The policies governing the types and cost should be set by each educational institution. The NCAA, AAU, NIAA, and various state athletic associations regulate what monetary value may be placed on the awards given to varsity athletes. Intramural awards should be so regulated. Finances should be so provided.

As each day passes and costs increase, awards become smaller and fewer in number. Demands on the budget increase, and it becomes necessary to seek more creative and imaginative ideas for awards.

I hope I can give a few suggestions that may be of value to you. Some of the most beautiful awards I have ever seen were made by the students in one or more of the departments within the school.

In the art department, ribbons, silk-screening, tooling and copper and aluminum have produced most desirable awards. The woodshops have always produced outstanding trophies in the forms of lathe turning and wall plaques.

The printing department, with its offset press, can produce almost any type of certificate desired. Metal shops have contributed their fair share of trophies toward the intramural program.

The photography department or the school photographer can photograph the winning intramural champions. Each member of the team can in turn be awarded an autographed copy. Framed, this makes a simple but attractive award.

You might investigate the possibilities of an occupational lab in your school system, or similar programs where students are given additional training in industrial techniques. These students possess a great degree of skill and are constantly searching for projects. One example I know of: A local sporting goods dealer filed for bankruptcy. His stock was sold at public auction. The entire silk screening supplies and the engraving machine were purchased by a private individual and donated to the local occupational laboratory. These students today produce a considerable number of awards for the entire school system.

On the university level I would like to call the attention of the intramural directors to the fact that each August most trophy manufacturers close out the previous year's stock. Considerable bargains are available at this time if you are willing to purchase large quantities.

In conclusion, I would like to point out that a very worthwhile self-satisfying intramural program designed to meet the needs of all students can be administered successfully without awards, but a superior program is one conceived and planned in accordance with the accepted cultural practices of the American way of life.

REFERENCES

Beeman, Harris F. and Humphrey, James H., *Intramural Sports, A Text and Study Guide*, Wm. C. Brown Company, Dubuque, Iowa, 1960.

Kleindienst, Viola K. and Weston, Arthur, *Intramural and Recreation Program for School and Colleges*, Meredith Publishing Company, New York, 1964.

Means, Louis E., *Intramurals, Their Organization and Administration*, Prentice-Hall, Inc., Englewood Cliffs, New Jersey, 1963.

Mitchell, Elmer D., *Intramural Sports*, A.S. Barnes & Company, New York, 1938.

Points for Participation
Bob Dalrymple
(1974 NIA Proceedings, pp. 73-77)

As a result of having reviewed many intramural brochures from many institutions, I find that most schools have some sort of an all-sports, all-events, end-of-the-year, or some comparable award; the winner of which is determined by the organization which accumulates the most points from entering, winning, placing, and/or non-forfeiting in the several activities which are conducted throughout the school year.

Although it is recognized that there are many valid reasons for *not* using a point system and even using one has some inherent disadvantages, nevertheless, the question of whether to use a point system or not to use a point system is one which can only be settled by each of you on the basis of the circumstances under which you function. I plan only to direct my remarks to those of you who now use such a system or who may be contemplating establishing one in the future.

When I arrived at the University of South Carolina there was a point system in effect which had been in use for several years. The first year I was there I used it. As a result, I discovered that while it looked good on paper, experience showed that it had many shortcomings.

Entry points were given to an organization when they submitted an entry in team sports or when they entered a set number of individuals in individual competition. Entrants, both individuals and teams participated in all of their scheduled competition, some participated in some of their matches, and some never showed up at all. Of course, points were deducted for these forfeits. This not only entailed a lot of bookkeeping, but resulted in a failure to effectively utilize facilities which were already in short supply. Further, deducting points did not serve as a deterrent to forfeits. Since most of the individuals who forfeited were from organizations which weren't in contention for the all-sports trophy anyhow, the loss of 10, 20, or 30 points didn't mean anything to them.

The next year we instituted a system whereby each organization was required to pay a one dollar forfeit fee for each individual whose name they entered. This dollar was returned if the individual played all of his matches. This didn't work, either. Most of the time the organization paid the fee from money available to it. Since it didn't come out of the individual's pocket, the incentive to get it back was lost. Therefore, we had to try something else.

Another portion of the system that had been included was that of using a set number of points for major sports and a set number of points for minor sports. The major sports didn't seem to present much of a problem, but we discovered a wide variation of interest in minor sports. For instance, one season we had 20 for squash and 140 for tennis. It was our feeling that an individual who was the best of 140 people should get more credit than one who was the best of 20. Thus we decided that some system was needed to accommodate to this variation. We therefore developed a sliding scale of points for participation—as you can see on the first page of the handout.

First—please notice in particular that the basis for points is *not* the number of entrants nor the number of matches scheduled, but the number of matches actually played. This means that in a double elimination tournament, the byes and forfeits are not counted.

There's nothing sacred about the breakdown in the "Matches" column. With fewer competitors involved, you might want to consider a spread of only five, for instance. With more, a spread of 20 or 25 might be more appropriate. Any of this can, of course, be tailored to fit your specific program.

We use a double elimination competition for all our individual sports and keep our records like I have shown on the second page of the handout.

My thanks to Pat Mueller for his convenient list of symbolic names from his book on Intramurals.

You may notice that even though this is a double elimination tournament, those individuals who forfeit in the winners bracket do not appear in the losers bracket. We discovered that, habitually, individuals who forfeit once, will more than likely forfeit again. Therefore, we have established a rule that one forfeit=elimination. This way we can more effectively schedule our limited facilities and save other contestants the inconvenience of showing up for a match and then not getting to play because their opponent forfeited. Further, to earn points for their organization they must participate in at least one match in the losers bracket. Thus, in the example, Edd, Ken, Lew and Jon would not earn any points.

The little "x's" on the chart are merely a convenience feature. When a match has been played and the scores or results turned in, we mark the chart with one of those Hi-Liter pens (the ones that leave a mark that you can read through) in the appropriate bracket. Then, when the tournament is completed, all you have to do is count the marks and refer to the chart to determine the place points.

Please notice the statement concerning the number of points that an organization may earn. For awhile we functioned on the basis that an organization could only earn points for their individual who finished in the highest position. This had a tendency to discourage people from entering when there was an individual entering from their organization whom they knew was more talented and would undoubtedly finish higher in the standings. Next we considered giving them points for all the places they earned. Without even testing this premise, we could readily see that an organization could possibly get more points for having several people earn a placing in a minor sport than they could earn for winning football which involved hundreds of people in extended league play. Now this may not be bad in all instances, but we felt it wasn't desirable for us. As a compromise solution we decided everyone who placed should get something. Thus the 1/5th factor. Under this system—if there were 22 matches played, for instance, and fraternity XYZ had members who finished 2nd, 3rd, and 4th—they would earn the 35 points for 2nd, 5 for 3rd, and 4 for 4th for a total of 44.

In the sports of Swimming, Track, Softball, Football and Basketball we restrict entries to one team per organization for points. Thus, these points are not on an incremental basis.

In Bowling, Golf, Putt-Putt and Volleyball each organization may enter as many teams as there are individuals interested in participating. Like the individual sports, however, a forfeiture eliminates a team and they must be in the competition at the end in order to earn points.

I don't really anticipate that the USC Point System is going to be adopted universally across the country as a result of this meeting. However, I do feel that it is sufficiently different from any I have seen and that by sharing it with you there might be some elements of it that might be beneficial to your program.

POINT SYSTEM
DOUBLE ELIMINATION TOURNAMENTS—
Count the number of matches PLAYED.

Matches	Places							
	1	2	3	4	5	6	7	All others
1-15	30	25	20	15	10			5
16-30	45	35	25	20	15	10		7
31-45	60	50	40	30	20	15		10
46-60	75	60	45	35	25	20	15	12
61 or more	90	75	60	45	30	25	20	15

A single organization may earn their best finish plus 1/5 of any other places.

Bowling, Golf, Putt-Putt and Volleyball—Number of teams finishing.

	1	2	3	4	5	6	7	All others
1- 8	60	50	40	30	20	15		10
9-16	75	60	45	35	25	20	15	12
17 or more	90	75	60	45	30	25	20	15

Swimming and Track

1	2	3	4	5	6	7	All others
75	60	45	35	25	20	15	12

Softball

1	2	3	4	5	6	7	All others
90	75	60	45	30	25	20	15

Football and Basketball

1	2	3	4	5	6	All others
125	100	80	60	40	25	20

Chapter 20
Injury Prevention and Treatment

Intramural Injuries: Your Responsibility
George M. MacDonald
(1966 NIA Proceedings, pp. 131-132)

Intramural injuries are your responsibility. You, as the director of the program, have a moral and sometimes legal responsibility of providing a safe, sound and prudent program of intramural sports and activities in which your students may participate with a minimum expectation of injury.

"Accidents are unplanned." Are you ready? Have you eliminated all hazards to health and safety from the playing area? Do you have a plan for accident prevention? Do you have a plan of action when injury does occur? These are some of the questions that we will explore in this presentation.

The most important phase of our program is the student participation. It is not the buildings, the brochures, the glossy handbooks and all the rest of the paraphernalia, that we sometimes spend too much time upon, that is most important, but rather the health and safety of our participants. We have a moral as well as a legal responsibility to each of our participants to provide him with a program in which his health and safety is paramount. To do this, we must have an accident prevention plan. What are the ingredients of such a plan?

1. We must make certain that the activity to be offered is a prudent activity and that it is reasonably safe for participants.

2. We must be sure that the playing area and equipment are free of all hazards to health and safety.

3. We must make certain that all participants have received clearance from the health service to participate and that each participant is covered by some insurance plan.

4. We must be sure that all participants have undergone a pre-conditioning or training program for strenuous activities.

5. We must see that competent officials are secured, and that they conduct the contest in a safe, sane manner according to the rules.

6. We must see that official personnel, trained in first aid procedures, be present at the contest to render such first aid as is necessary, to insure the health and safety of the participants and also to determine if the participant may continue in the contest.

7. We must educate the participants to the fact that they must abide by the decision of the first aid person.

8. We must notify the health service immediately so that medical personnel will be available if necessary.

First, I should like to convey the thought that I am fully cognizant of how dull and uninteresting a safety topic can be made when the speaker approaches the negative concept implications in the term of safety. From the negative side, "Safety" immediately suggests a multitude of restrictions that do not conform to the adventurous, vigorous and stimulating activities that make up a qualitative Intramural Program. As I see it gentlemen, the nature of your business is such that it provides for greater adventure to life on a college or university campus. This is the positive approach and the avenue which I desire to pursue in addressing you on the occasion of your national meeting.

It is reasonable to assume that certain intramural activities involve certain movements and exposures that might be considered to be hazardous, however we cannot overlook the fact that much of the value, pleasure, and popularity of these activities lies in this fact. The complete removal of these hazards would be to remove a great portion of their participation appeal. Physical Educators, Intramural Athletic Directors and Varsity Coaches would not have it otherwise, for the very element of a calculated risk makes the participation a stimulating adventure and satisfies a young man's desire for competition, joyous effort, and creative activity. A safety program in Intramurals is not established merely to eliminate hazards. The primary purpose of motivating safety in the Intramural program is to intelligently regulate and control the activities so that injuries can be reduced to an absolute minimum. The safe way of participating in any type of an athletic activity is the most efficient way. Therefore, we might think of safety as a primary contributor to an efficiency program.

Many of the hazards in the Intramural Program can be eliminated:

Faulty equipment and supplies
Unsafe play spaces
Lack of space
Too many participants
Poor supervision

These are factors which the Intramural Director can eliminate or at least reduce to a minimum. Such deficiencies jeopardize the value, pleasure, and popularity of the program, and are largely responsible for a considerable number of accidents.

Let us not overlook the fact that a mounting toll of injuries and accidents can produce moral problems and bring about public disapproval which may possibly lead to curtailment of certain Intramural Activities.

It is the responsibility of the Intramural Director to provide a complete accident prevention program that will provide for the maximum of safety for all participants.

The problem of accident prevention should be approached with the following factors being seriously considered:

9. There must be a means of, or a plan for, transportation to the health service after medical diagnosis has indicated need for further medical treatment or observation.

10. There should be a filing of complete accident reports by officials and witnesses to the accident in which injury occurred.

11. There should be communication and follow-up with the health service upon the disposition of all injuries.

12. A written release, from the health service or doctor, must be presented in all cases before further intramural participation is permitted.

If such procedures are known, posted and are carefully followed, the health and safety of participants will be prudently and reasonably handled. Legal liability and negligence suits will be kept to a minimum. Liability laws are designed to protect the innocent through:

1. Promotion of safe activities.

2. Establish fault and most important, the cause of accidents.

3. Provide financial payment to innocent victims.

M.K. Strasser, et al, in their test *Fundamentals of Safety Education* state that, "in all except nine states, school districts and state governments have retained their historical immunity against law suits and cannot be held liable for accidental injury." The net result, liability and negligence suits against individuals. These nine states have waived school immunity through enactment of legislation. Each state law is different, but each of these nine have accepted the responsibility for answering claims resulting from school injury. The law requires that the person bringing suit against a teacher must show that the teacher failed to take action that a prudent teacher would have taken to avoid the accident...a teacher is liable for a school accident when it is proven that he is legally responsible for the occurrence of the accident.

What is the law in your state? You should find out if you don't understand your legal position in cases of accidental injury. After all, INTRAMURAL INJURIES ARE YOUR RESPONSIBILITY.

Motivating Safety in Intramural Competition
Bernard I. Loft
(1958 NIA Proceedings, pp. 29-32)

Thank you Mr. Chairman for the very kind introduction. I am somewhat apprehensive of complimentary introductions—the reason for this can best be told by the following experience—ROTARY INCIDENT—Seriously, gentlemen, I am indeed pleased to have this opportunity of participating on your program, particularly being assigned the all-important topic, namely, that of Safety. Although it does not appear on the program this way, I have entitled my discussion with you this morning, "Motivating Safety In Intramural Competition."

1. Identification of the possible hazards or risks involved in each activity.
2. Removal or reduction of these hazards, if possible.
3. Methods of compensating for those risks which cannot be removed.
4. Avoidance of new and unnecessary hazards.

To accomplish these four major premises let us take a look at some of the factors that we must consider in establishing an Intramural Program that will adequately provide for accident prevention. This of course precludes that accident prevention is not something in addition to the Intramural Program, but is a definite part of the total program:

Go through the following steps:

Application of remedy

Selection of remedy

Analyses

Fact Finding

Organization

Basic Philosophy

This plan for years has been used most advantageously in business and industry, where such factors as moral, income, absenteeism, and increased production are paramount. Management literally spends hundreds of thousands of dollars for safety because of its relationship to efficiency which in turn culminates in increased production. Many of those same business principles are applicable to the Organization, Administration and Supervision of a sound Intramural Program.

I am certain that everyone present today is greatly concerned about some mishap which has possibly taken place on your own campus in the intramural program. Where accident prevention is a consideration, there are two major concerns—

1. Those accidents that have happened.
2. Those accidents that have not happened.

The following accident sequence which I will illustrate may possibly give us a more distinct picture of the accident prevention problem:

Use blocks — go through Accident Sequence

Invariably the application of this accident sequence will provide a clear understanding as to the contributory causes of most accidents. For the most part 85% of the accidents will have been brought about by the human element.

I don't feel that my presentation this morning would be complete unless some mention was made of the Legal Liability for Athletic Injuries—

A jury in California recently awarded a 17 year-old high school football player $325,000 in his damage suit against the school district for which he played, the student alleged he had been paralyzed as a result of injuries suffered in a contest. Ultimately he received an award of $206,804 as a result of the decision of the trial judge. This illustrates that school districts and persons connected with sports activities are subject to legal liability under certain circumstances for incurred injuries.

It is imperative the individuals responsible for the administration of intramural activities be familiar with what lawyers call "TORT" liability; that is, liability for personal injuries caused through the defendant's negligence. To succeed, any cause of action, in TORT involves proof of four essential elements. They are:

1. That the defendent owed a duty to avoid unreasonable risks to others.
2. That the defendent failed to observe that duty.
3. That failure to observe that duty caused the damage which occurred.
4. That damage in fact occurred to plaintiff, together with proof of the nature and probable extent of the damages.

In setting this standard of conduct for Intramural Directors, Physical Education Instructors and Coaches, the law does not in effect intend to make them guarantee that no injuries will occur, rather it requires them to act as a "reasonable man" would in the circumstances. Hypothetically, the "reasonable man" is a person endowed with normal intellect, normal perception, and normal experience. The all important consideration for us to keep in mind is the necessity for taking every conceivable precaution to eliminate any possibility of contributory negligence by personnel affiliated with the Intramural Program.

This can be accomplished by the Intramural Director assuming responsibility for maintaining an accident prevention program through—

1. Facility and equipment controls
2. Leadership controls
3. Program controls
4. Participant controls

We could very easily spend several hours discussing each one of these areas. Since, I am aware of other important business that you will transact this morning, it is best that I bring this presentation to a conclusion. I was once told by a very wise old professor that, if you want to be heard you must speak up, if you want to be seen you must stand up and if you want to be appreciated—it is best to be seated.

I have certainly enjoyed the opportunity of meeting with you today. In concluding, I would urge you to remember that—Safety conserves manpower; manpower builds the future.

Chapter 21
Research

A Model for Intramural Research
K. Nelson Butler
(1971 NIA Proceedings, pp. 111-113)

It has been characteristic of the biological sciences to conduct research studies on a scale often times irrespective to the theoretical structure of those sciences and, in some degree, irrelevant to the purposes of science itself. Likewise, the social sciences have embarked on studies not aligned to any "grand design" or even fairly refined conceptualized models of issues they purport to understand.

The professions of physical education and recreation, while only relatively new in their research endeavors, have been guilty also of rushing pell-mell into research studies which ultimately yield very little in conclusive results. Inconclusive results often occur simply because of poorly constructed research designs. However, by and large the most significant factor resulting in "much ado about nothing" is the lack of a theoretical base of which the hypothesis should be attempting to substantiate or refute. Theoretical structures are, in and of themselves, not too difficult to come by if one is predisposed toward a little bit of dreaming and a great deal of reflective thinking which hopefully would result in an articular presentation of some ideas. Given the time element it is probably more practical to think in terms of conceptualized models than about broader theoretical bases.

With this consideration in mind the following is an attempt to provide a conceptual model for study of many if not most, of the issues and concerns facing the IM director. The model is based on the presupposition that the purpose and function of intramural is to *provide opportunities*, ensure *use* of those opportunities, encourage whatever *meaning* a participant may attach to that use to flourish, and realize the *modification* that is inherent in the three preceding steps.

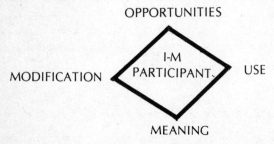

The above model brings to mind immediate questions about IM and

264

recreation programs which could lead to a plethora of hypotheses but still aligned to a central theme providing answers to the fundamentals of which we are concerned.

For example:

Opportunities. The whole idea of the structure of individual as well as collective organization providing opportunities for the IM participant is in question here. Who is providing? What is being provided? When? To whom?

Use. How are the opportunities used? Who uses it? When is it used? Are there patterns to use? By whom? How much time is available for use? How is the use related to the distribution of demographic variables and changes in these distributions?

Meaning. What does it mean to use the opportunities available? In other words—Why? Are there different meanings per the individual? The group meaning? The idea proposed here is one of a social-psychological nature. This area can be the real crux as well as the crucial area of concern.

Modification. How is our IM participant affected by whatever it means to him or her to use the opportunities we have provided. Have we made a contribution to his or her life? Have we not?

A sample run through—Touch Football. Most everyone provides the opportunity of touch football. Could somebody dare ask the question should we all do the same thing by providing touch football. Or, are we *really* providing *everybody* a chance to play touch football. Don't we have exclusionary procedures in our program whereby some people couldn't take part if they really wanted to.

Does everyone utilize (use) the opportunity to play touch football? Do we exclude the girls in using this opportunity? Can we provide more time so more people can use this opportunity?

What does it mean to the boy or girl to play touch football? Health and fitness? Broken legs? Increased self image? Cathartic relief? An opportunity to belong?

What effect did playing touch football have on a boy or girl? A group of boys and girls? Are they better for it? Are they not?

Some of these simple, off-the-top-of-the-head questions which may or may not lead to valid hypotheses. However, the point is made that there is a continuity; a contingency of and an understanding the whole and not just an isolated part.

If we are going to conduct meaningful research we must begin to conceptualize our problems around significant themes which can be analyzed and understood. I offer this as one example. My hopes are that many more will be forthcoming.

Investigating the Behavioral Consequences of Participation in Intramural Activities: A Changing Emphasis for Intramural Research
James A. Peterson
(1970 NIA Proceedings, pp. 75-80)

At our last N.I.A. convention, I, like many of you, was a member of the audience that listened to Dr. Bruce Ogilvie's presentation of the "Mental Ramblings of a Psychologist Researching in the Area of Sports Motivation."[1] Delineating a somewhat controversial viewpoint on the values of physical education, this noted psychologist from San Jose St. College urged his audience to reconsider the validity of several popularly held notions concerning the value of individual participation in highly competitively-structured activities. No longer, he surmised, should physical educators espouse to the educational communities they serve the empirically unsubstantiated hypotheses of the past: physical education builds character; sports participation reinforces the American value system in individuals; competition is the purest expression of democracy; and so forth.

In short, Dr. Ogilvie presented to the membership of the National Intramural Association a manifesto of inquiry. The essence of his manifesto was to challenge each of you to reject the babbling rhetoric of glittering generalities and to accept the responsibility of providing a legitimate, empirical base by which to analyze the behavioral consequences of participation in your intramural programs. Why, he asked, in the light of its extreme relevance to the discipline of physical education, does the matter of the relationship between sports participation and human development remain a relatively untapped area of study? What, he asked, is the relationship between sports participation and social and psychological variables.

I realize, of course, that there are some of you who believe that such a viewpoint is merely an exercise in oral defecation. To you, my answer would be that the inquisitive, volatile, and demanding student bodies of today's world are no longer unique to the Berkeley or Columbia campuses. Time and again, intramural departments are being asked to justify their programs, justify their expenditures, and in some cases, justify their very existence. The intramural administrator on today's campus is becoming increasingly aware of the fact there is a growing hesitation on the part of the college administrator and university student to accept the expenditure of state or student funds on a program that is justified by such vague statements as: "it builds character" or "people who participate in our programs get better grades."

A few years ago, I had the opportunity to review Ben McGuire's anthology of all the research completed in intramurals.[2] From the more than 250 studies abstracted in that thesis, no more than two of those research endeavors concerned themselves with the behavioral implications of participation in intramural activity. Without reservation, I contend that the functional importance of doing historical investigations, participation surveys, and equipment inquiries is subject to serious value limitations. Certainly, one can find substance in Dr. Ogilvie's implied manifesto that a critical need exists for intramural people to examine the effects of their programs on people. As a body of professionals, the message for us is clearly: the research emphasis of the membership of the N.I.A. must be focused on the individual, not the inanimate objects which are the tools of our trade.

For the past two years at the University of Illinois, I have been a co-director of a research project which has endeavored to provide information on the effects of participating in an intramural activity. Supported by a University grant, this project investigated the antecedents and consequences of a cohesiveness of sport groups—specifically intramural basketball teams. Group cohesiveness has been defined by Festinger, Schacter, and Back[3] as the resultant of all forces influencing members to remain in the group. Included in the problems investigated in this project were: (1) the effect of success and failure of group cohesion; (2) the motivational basis for affiliation with sport groups and its relationship with group cohesion and team performance; (3) the factors affecting the social structure of basketball teams (e.g. success and failure); (4) group cohesiveness as a determinant of success and member satisfaction in team performance; and (5) individual and group aspiration levels and their relationship with performance and cohesion.

What, many of you now ask, is the relevance of psychological constructs—such as cohesiveness—to the intramural administrator? The study of social and psychological variables is a tool—a tool that can be used by intramural administrators to determine such matters as: why do people participate in our programs; what are the consequences to those who do participate; and what knowledge about behavioral dimensions can be gained to be used to functionally modify existing intramural procedures and practices to better meet the needs of the students. In short, the information gained from behavioral research can aid each of you in the performance of your specific responsibilities. In the cohesiveness study, cited earlier, it was found in a number of cases that an individual's motivation to participate in an activity and belong to a group changed over the course of the season as a function of the number of games won by his team. This discovery has relevance to those intramural administrators who debate the merits of a highly competitive versus a low-key type of intramural program. Too much emphasis on winning, the point system, and other rewards can have a detrimental effect on student participation.

As an example of behavioral research, I cite my master's thesis.[4] Written on one phase of the group cohesion project, this study investigated the degree to which the post-season cohesiveness of intramural basketball teams could be attributed to a team's residential affiliation or to a team's relative degree of success. One thousand two hundred sixty-two male college students, members of 144 intramural basketball teams, were used as subjects. Each individual responded to a questionnaire instrument designed to measure cohesiveness. The questionnaire was administered to each subject pre-season (before his first league game) and again, post-season (after his last league contest). The questionnaire assessed various components of cohesiveness such as interpersonal attraction and power, and also asked for member's direct evaluations of the group's teamwork and closeness. The teams participated in 24 leagues in three divisions based on their residential affiliation: fraternities, dormitories, and cooperatives. Team achievement was trichotomized into three levels—successful, moderately successful, and unsuccessful—according to the number of games won.

Statistically, a 3 x 3 factorial design was used. The data, treated by the appropriate univariate and multivariate techniques, yielded the following results:

1. Fraternities were found to be initially more cohesive than either dormitories or cooperatives. The wide latitude of opportunities for membership interaction by fraternities provides one of the more logical explanations for this condition. Obviously, on many campuses, the fraternity system is one of the more stable bases of the competitive program. This cohesion data provides an empirical insight into one of the reasons for the strong participation by fraternities.

2. An individual's residential affiliation was found to have no significant effect on his post-season level of team cohesiveness. With initial pre-season differences covaried out, there were no post-season differences in team cohesiveness levels that could be attributed to residential affiliation.

3. Successful teams were more cohesive than moderately successful or unsuccessful teams after a season of competition. This data lends credence to the general premise that the warm and relaxed elements associated with successful situations provide a more desirable setting for interpersonal interaction than do unsuccessful situations, which are usually replete with tension and anxiety. It substantiates the belief that the circumstances surrounding the ease and amount of interaction between group members do either facilitate or hinder the cohesiveness of that group.

I am hopeful that this brief discussion of the methodological, procedural, and result dimensions of this one phase of a larger research project will provide each of you with a thought provoking look at an example of behavioral research. From a research standpoint, intramurals are an untapped reservoir of investigative potential.

Twelve months after Bruce Ogilvie's manifesto of inquiry, each of you continue to stand on a threshold of challenge. As professionals engaged in the task of providing quality programs of service and leisure opportunities, your research efforts can either be founded on the traditional tools of logical observations, intuitions, and over-generalizations or on the granite foundation of empirical evidence.

Your choice of research emphasis will be the significant factor in whether or not we continue to grow as a profession or we degenerate to be nothing more than a fraternity of technicians.

I contend that there are a number of relevant questions that can be answered by research investigation either by professional intramural people or by cooperative arrangements between intramural people and trained researchers. Such questions would include:

— *What's the nature of inter-group conflict?*

1. How do you solve inter-group conflict?

2. What are the factors which initiate inter-group conflict?

3. If you can determine the causes, what steps can you take to minimize inter-group conflict?

— *What type of leadership styles facilitate satisfactory and effective participation in intramurals?*

1. How do different styles of leadership behavior influence the action of groups? (Authoritarian, democratic, and laissez-faire),

2. What effect on the students' motivation to participate does the leadership style of the intramural administrator have?

3. How do leadership patterns affect the integration of student help into the intramural organization?

— *What is the nature of prejudice?*

1. What dimensions of prejudicial attitudes are relevant to your programs?

2. What effect does competition and interaction have on prejudicial attitudes?

— *What application do attitude theories have in explaining the motivational basis of intramural participation?*

— *Does intramural participation influence individual personality?*

1. Are there activities which attract unique types of dispositions or personalities?

I am aware that for most of you in this room, the nature of your responsibilities is such that you have little time to spend on research and still maintain your high levels of programming. I am also aware of the fact that many of us have had a limited exposure to the highly intricate and complex research techniques—such as multivariate analysis—which are an integral part of behavioral research.

The point that I would like to emphasize is that through an interdisciplinary approach—by working with other departments—we can meet the challenge of identifying the behavioral consequences of participation in intramural programs. I believe that on most campuses the departments of sociology, psychology, and the related social sciences have interested people who *have* the time, *have* the expertise, and *have* the desire to collaborate with intramural personnel to do the kind of research that will yield a much needed insight into the behavioral implications of participation in intramural activities.

I would like to close with a statement from the 1964 N.I.A. Proceedings in an address by the presiding president of that conference, Dr. David Matthews:[5]

"Let us dedicate ourselves to something besides the everyday humdrum of administering traditional or perhaps outdated programs. Let us dedicate ourselves to discovering truth through research."

BIBLIOGRAPHY

1. Ogilvie, Bruce, "Mental Ramblings of a Psychologist Researching in the Area of Sports Motivation", *20th Annual Conference Proceedings of the National Intramural Association: 1969.* pp. 173-193.
2. McGuire, R. J., "A Retrieval of Selected Intramural Research and Literature". An unpublished master's thesis: University of Illinois, 1966.
3. Festinger, Schachter, and Back, *Social Pressures in Informal Groups: A Study of a Housing Project;* (N.Y.: Harper and Brothers) 1950.
4. Peterson, James A., "Success and Residential Affiliation as Determinants of Team Cohesiveness". An unpublished master's thesis: University of Illinois, 1970.
5. Matthews, David O., "President's Address: What about our Constitutional objectives", *15th Annual Conference Proceedings of the National Intramural Association: 1964.* pp. 6-8.

Chapter 22
Sport Clubs

Intramural Sport Clubs at Purdue University
George W. Haniford
(1972 NIA Proceedings, 64-67)

The Purdue intramural philosophy incorporates the concept that all students be provided opportunities to enjoy satisfying experiences related to their particular needs. The Intramural Staff realizes that the needs of all students can not be met in a stereotyped competitive type of program. The competitive activity program is extremely important and serves as the nucleus of the Purdue intramural sports program; however, in an attempt to provide all students with opportunities to engage in wholesome recreational activities the total sports offering has been enlarged to include sports clubs. These sports clubs are known as "Intramural Sports Clubs."

For the past twenty-five years the personnel of the Purdue Intramural Department has been actively engaged in providing all types of assistance to the student sports clubs organizations. The clubs have been given professional guidance, facilities and financial support. Many of the present Purdue intramural sports clubs were initiated under the administrative responsibility of the Intramural Department. The others were organized prior to their decision to petition the Intramural Department for acceptance as intramural sports clubs.

Within the Purdue sports clubs activity program the members have an unlimited number of opportunities to express themselves and to become involved. They collectively have the responsibility for: the writing of their constitution and by-laws, the determination of their membership requirements, the establishment of their dues schedule, the selection of their faculty advisor, the establishment of the duties of their officers, the selection of their volunteer coach and/or assisting in the selection of their paid coach, and the development and administration of their budget.

Early in 1960 the expenditure of departmental funds for the support of the sports clubs was questioned. On August 18, 1960 at a meeting called by the President of the University and attended by the Vice President and Treasurer, the Vice President in charge of Student Services, the Director of Athletics and the Intramural Director, an official University policy was established to govern the supervision of the sports clubs. The provisions of the policy are as follows:

1. The Clubs receiving financial support from the Intramural Department (Recreation Gymnasium funds — student fee income) will be known as Intramural Sports Clubs. They will, after having their constitutions approved by the Dean of Men's and Dean of Women's Offices, be under the direct supervision of the Intramural Director.

2. Intramural Sports Clubs will be required to have a staff member (full time or graduate student with staff appointment) accompany them on all of their out of town meets or tournaments.

3. A staff member desiring membership in an Intramural Sports Club must pay the Recreational Gymnasium Facilities Fee ($7.00 per semester). The faculty advisor of an Intramural Sports Club will not be required to pay the fee.

4. A graduate student desiring membership in an Intramural Sports Club must possess either a student passport that has been validated by the Bursar or the Recreational Gymnasium Management, or a Recreational Gymnasium Facilities Fee Card.

5. Within current budget allotment financial support to the Intramural Sports Clubs may include:

a) Game supplies and equipment.

b) Wages covering: game officials, supervision and instruction and maintenance and care of equipment.

c) Maintenance and upkeep of sport clubs grounds and buildings.

d) Travel—University automobiles to be driven by staff members. Travel assistance to be dependent upon budget approval.

e) Transportation charges for capital items.

In a later meeting, the Vice President in charge of Student Services informed the Dean of Men and the Dean of Women of the new policy to be followed in supervising the Intramural Sports Clubs. Both philosophy and budget limitations have determined the number of clubs the Intramural Department has accepted to become Intramural Sports Clubs.

Currently the student organizations desiring recognition as Intramural Sports Clubs must satifsy several requirements before their acceptance. They include:

1. Written constitutions approved by the Intramural Director and the Dean of Men's and Dean of Women's Office.

2. Submission and approval of a budget to the Intramural Director and the auditor of student organizations.

3. Selection of a faculty advisor.

4. A written indication of their desire to become an Intramural Sports Club.

Once accepted as intramural sports clubs they then are governed by the several rules and regulations established by the University and the Intramural Department.

Many sports clubs require little financial assistance once they are organized and in operation for a year or two. The initial expense comes from developing the facilities and in purchasing the necessary equipment. Financial support for the Purdue intramural sports clubs is budgeted under the Recreational Gymnasium.

The current Recreational Gymnasium budget allotment provides $300.00 in wages for sports club supervision and $625.00 for sports club supplies and expenses. The members of the Purdue intramural sports clubs share in the financial support of their clubs through the payment of individual annual dues, fund raising projects, and special assessments to cover extramural competition expenses.

Most of the Purdue intramural sports clubs participate extensively in extramurals under the governing hand of the Intramural Director.

In most instances when an intramural sports club makes a trip for extramural competition they receive little or no financial assistance from the Intramural Department. They pay for their own meals and lodging. The extramural schedules for the intramural sports clubs are set jointly by the officers of the individual clubs, faculty advisors, and the coaches. A requirement is that all schedules must be approved by the Intramural Director. In addition, where there are game or meet contracts to be signed the only official signer for the Purdue intramural sports clubs is the Intramural Director.

The Soccer Club and the Crew Club are coached by graduate assistants employed by the Intramural Department. The coaches of the women's extramural teams are normally volunteers from the professional staff of the Department of Physical Education for Women. The other intramural sports clubs have as their coaches student members of their clubs.

The Purdue intramural sports clubs determine their own membership. However, due to the financial assistance that is given the clubs from Recreational Gymnasium funds the graduate students and staff of the University accepted for club membership must have either a validated passport or a validated Recreational Gymnasium facilities fee card.

Even though all IM sports clubs are under the direct supervision of Professor Haniford, it is recommended to each club that they select a staff members (Professorial rank) to serve as their faculty advisor. The faculty advisor is not required to pay the Recreational Gymnasium facilities fee.

Travel and other specifications of sports clubs are governed by both the sponsoring Intramural department and student organization regulations. Thus, the handling of forms for the scheduling of their functions and approval of trips involves the offices of the sponsoring Intramural Department, the Dean of Men and the Dean of Women. Specific policies and procedures that have been established include:

1. The provision of a standard form for use in securing approval for sports clubs trips and off-campus functions.

2. The determination of responsibility for signing the trip request forms.

3. The establishment of requirements governing the accompaniment of students on their sports clubs trips to out of town meets or tournaments.

The standard form used by the sports clubs in securing approval for their trips and off-campus functions answers the questions of who, what, where, why and when and also provides the following information: a list of the club members making the trip, signatures of the faculty advisor and club president, mode of travel, housing accommodations, date and time of departure and return, trip leader's name, name of staff member accompanying the students, signature of the Intramural Director and the representatives from the Office of the Dean of Men and Dean of Women. The signature of the Intramural Director indicates his approval of the activity from the standpoint of its being a legitimate activity within the sports club program. The signature from the Dean of Men and/or Dean of Women's Offices indicates approval from the standpoint of appropriateness and compliance with student organization regulations.

The President of the University set the general policy that is used to govern the accompaniment of students on their sports club trips to out-of-town meets or tournaments. He has ruled that all Intramural Sports Clubs must meet the minimum requirement of a staff member (full time or graduate student with staff appointment) accompanying them on all of their out-of-town trips, meets, tournaments or extramural matches.

At present, the sports clubs that are known as intramural sports clubs are: Archery, Canoe, Crew, Cricket, Fencing, Figure Skating, Ice Hockey, Judo, Lacrosse, Gymnastics, Outing, Rugby Football, Sailing, Soccer, Squash, Weight Lifting, Handball, Triton, Volleyball and the Women's Extramural and Performance Club. The majority of the clubs are open to both men and women students.

The Impact of Sports Club Growth on Intramural Programs
Michael J. Stevenson
(1971 NIA Proceedings, pp. 35-39)

Much has been written in recent years covering the various aspects of sports clubs and their operation. After giving you a thumb-nail sketch of what has been written concerning sports clubs, I will touch on two areas of current interest; first, the effect that expanded sports club programming is having on existing intramural programs, and secondly, the Sports Club Federation, a new innovation at The University of Michigan.
Definition
Haniford[6] defines sports clubs as a group of student organizations that have been established to promote and develop the interests and skills of their members in particular sports activities emphasizing the student organized concept.

Phelps[9] sees a sports club as a group of individuals organized for the purpose of furthering their interest in a common sport through participation in intraclub and/or interclub competition. This second definition highlights what would appear to be the two major areas of club emphasis; one being the recreational-instructional emphasis, the other being the more highly structured, interclub, competition oriented emphasis.

Historical Background

Both sports clubs and intramural programs in this country are outgrowths of European sports clubs which developed toward the close of the nineteenth century.[6] In the U.S.A., Stanford's Crew Association dates back to 1905,[4] while Purdue has been providing professional guidance, facilities, and financial support for clubs since 1944.[6]

In most schools, however, the sports club impetus began in the early 1960's[4] and it would appear in the 70's to be a major trend on most of the nation's campuses.

Why So Popular?

Fehring attributed the growth and popularity of sports clubs to the following factors: younger people in graduate schools; more single students; more scholarship assistance giving students more "free" time; more students with athletic backgrounds in high schools who are not selected for intercollegiate varsity teams or who themselves choose not to participate in intercollegiate programs; more overseas study where students are exposed to foreign clubs and who bring back ideas to their own campuses; desire for "outside" competition not offered by intramurals; dissatisfaction with existing intramural programs; and exchange programs in which foreign students implement their club sports on our campuses.[4] It would also seem that the desire of most students to "do their own thing" without being highly restricted by the sometimes rigid structure of existing intramural programs has had some effect on the growth of sports clubs on campuses throughout the country.

What Sports are Involved?

A recent survey by Jamerson[7] found some seventy-five different sports have club status with the number in any single institution ranging from zero to forty. The majority of the institutions have from three to eight clubs. Soccer and karate appear to enjoy the greatest popularity with sailing, skiing, judo, fencing, gymnastics and rugby not far behind. He found that there is a wide variety of sports interests among students; interests he feels that are influenced by past experiences, geographical location of the institution, availability of enough students with similar interest in forming a club, a fad of the times, or simply a desire to play and participate as a group with equally interested, skilled and socially acceptable individuals at a time suitable to those involved.

Club Administration

It is not the purpose of this presentation to discuss sports clubs administration in depth. However, it would seem appropriate to highlight the administrative areas of concern to the intramural administrator.

Sports clubs, as student organizations, are usually recognized as such by offices of student affairs within institutions. Financial support for the clubs can come from this area, but generally comes from areas such as intramural departments, physical education departments, or in some cases, athletic departments.

Grambeau[5] has listed the following as some possible requirements for university recognition of the club: a written constitution; elected club officers; a faculty advisor; an established method of acquiring necessary funds whether through membership fees, through the intramural department, through fund raising projects, through intercollegiate fees, or the like; a yearly calendar of events; equipment and facility needs; and an established procedure for maintaining continuity of the club.

Whoever is responsible for extramural administration will have to consider the following administrative details: transportation; eligibility; insurance; housing accommodations; equipment; food; facilities; medical protection; supervision; reciprocal institutional agreements for contests; and officials.[5]

Now that we have covered the general background of club sports, lets direct our attention to the impact this trend of sports club growth will have on existing I.M. programs.

In my opinion, two recent trends, first the rapid growth of sports clubs, and secondly, the trend for students to become more and more engaged in non-structured, free play type activities, will require a possible reordering of existing priorities within intramural programs throughout the nation.

Historically, the competitive program has held a first priority in scheduling, and in time spent in the administration of intramural programs. Now two other phases of the program, club sports, and informal free time recreation are placing tremendous demands and pressures on programs in many schools.

Administrators must now decide which of the three areas will get equipment, facilities, budget expenditures, and administrative time; and in what priority, and in what proportion.

I am not prepared to suggest an ordering of these priorities, but it is obvious to me that this ordering will have to be made by most of us in the future, if in fact we have not already had to meet this challenge.

Since part of the program is addressed to new innovations, I would like to briefly discuss a new innovation at The University of Michigan, the Sports Club Federation.

The Michigan Sports Club Federation was formed one year ago as a merger of the Women's Athletic Association and the Michigan Sports Club Association. With a membership of seventeen clubs, out of thirty sports clubs on campus, the Federation functions on the premise that sports clubs share common problems which can best be solved through a collective organization.

Over the past year the Federation has touched upon problems related to facilities, scheduling, transportation, and coaching among others.

The Federation's most pressing concern is for funding. It is hoped that by working collectively, the Federation will be able to initiate fund raising projects which will be of a permanent nature. The Federation also works together on club publicity, scheduling, and travel.

Membership in the club is presently held by the Women's Basketball Club, the Equestrian Club, the Field Hockey Club, Women's Gymnastics, Handball, Judo, Lacrosse, Michifish, Paddleball, Rugby, Women's Tennis, Women's Swimming, Tae Kwon Do, Men's Volleyball, Women's Volleyball, Weightlifting, and Soccer.

Clubs must pay dues of $10.00 each year to become members of the Federation and must fulfill the Student Government Council's regulations for club status. Activities for the club must also be competitive in nature and must require and promote skilled athletic development.

It is obvious that Sports Club programs are rapidly becoming areas of considerable concern to Intramural administrators throughout the country. It is hoped that this discussion will cause the administrator to consider carefully some of the areas which must be accounted for when programming for the future needs of all the students on our campuses.

SELECTED REFERENCES

1. Bankhead, William H., "Club Sports Program at L.S.U.", Eighteenth Annual Conference Proceedings of N.I.A., pp. 58-61, 1967.

2. Barnes, Samuel E., "Sports Clubs, A Rapidly Growing Pattern of Participation in Sports Activities at the College & University Level," Journal of Health, Physical Education & Recreation, March, 1971, pp. 23-24.

3. Bulger, Howard J., "Athletic Clubs," Nineteenth Annual Conference Proceedings of the N.I.A., pp. 100-101, 1968.

4. Fehring, William P., "Club Sports," Twentieth Annual Conference Proceedings of the N.I.A., pp. 49-52, 1969.

5. Grambeau, Rodney J., "Encouraging the Development of Intramural Sports Clubs," Seventeenth Annual Conference Proceedings of the N.I.A., pp. 115-117, 1966.

6. Haniford, George W., "Pros & Cons of Sports Clubs," Proceedings, Annual Meeting, National College Physical Education Association for Men, pp. 49-54, 1969.

7. Jamerson, Dick, "Pros & Cons of Sports Clubs," Proceedings, Annual Meeting, National College Physical Education Association for Men, pp. 49-54, 1969.

8. Johnson, W. P., "The Club Approach to Intercollegiate Athletics in a New Community College," Journal of Health, Physical Education & Recreation, March, 1971, p. 25.

9. Phelps, Dale E., "Current Practices and Recommended Guidelines for the Administration of Sports Clubs in Selected Four-Year Midwest Colleges & Universities," Twenty-First Annual Proceedings of the N.I.A., pp. 32-26, 1970.

10. Stevenson, Michael J., "Outrigger Canoeing," Twenty-First Annual Conference Proceedings of the N.I.A., pp. 23-25, 1970.

Sport Clubs—You Gotta Believe
Norman C. Parsons, Jr.
(1975 NIRSA Proceedings, pp. 162-165)

One of the most difficult challenges about making a presentation at a National Conference is getting one's point or message to the audience. The difficulty is further demonstrated in that the success or failure of that message, being received by the audience, will be measured perhaps many months later as each of the program participants return to his or her respective campuses to implement the idea of the presenter.

Programs vary on campuses in numbers, types, and qualities. None of us expect a program at a campus of 500-600 students to have the same quantities as a program at an institution with 40,000-50,000 students. However, the qualities of the program should be similar.

This morning I want to share with you some thoughts and concepts regarding sports clubs. Some thoughts and concepts that I hope will be meaningful to you, if not this morning, at some point during the next few months after you return to your campus.

What are sports clubs? What are the characteristics of sports clubs? Perhaps the greatest characteristics of sports clubs is that they are composed of an extremely captive audience. One which is completely engrossed with the subject matter—whatever recreational sport they happen to be pursuing. Students, faculty and staff that are members of sports clubs are tremendous people with which to work. They possess an unequaled enthusiasm for their endeavors. Nowhere on the college campus will an administrator or faculty person have the pleasure of working with people who are more totally enthusiastic about their activity than members of sports clubs. Perhaps the reason for this is that each individual in the club, male, female, faculty or student is involved for a singular common interest, the particular activity in which they are pursuing. That singular activity is one of many different recreational sport activities which are participated in during their leisure time.

Sports clubs are unique and extremely exciting in that they are totally participant oriented. They are maintained by the students, administered by the student, and should succeed or fail based upon the competency of the students involved. The students face societal decision making processes while involved with sports clubs. The students, whether leaders or individual members, will be faced with decisions which may eventually lead to the stability or the fall of the club.

Sports clubs provide unlimited opportunities for social development by the members. The members are placed in a non-academic, social atmosphere in which they succeed or fail based on their personality and social attributes. This of course, leads to some tremendous leadership opportunities and it gives the students an opportunity to test their leadership ability in various situations.

Each sports club is sort of a mini-society with leadership and follower roles in which everyone takes part in a majority of the decision making processes. The procedure that the administrator uses in dealing with this mini-society is extremely important. In reviewing the literature and talking with Intramural and Recreational Sports Directors around the nation, it seems that we can classify this administrative procedure into a liberal or conservative approach.

The liberal approach would as the name implies, allow the student to do what they want as they want. Some of the principles of this approach would be as follows:

1. Although the University assumes no responsibility for their organization or operation, the activities of a number of sports clubs were coordinated by the Recreational Sports Department.

2. An Intramural Staff member directs this phase of the programs to assist in scheduling the use of facilities and in procuring equipment.

3. The sports clubs arrange the competitive schedule as they deem necessary and coordinate all travel arrangements.

Those utilizing the conservative approach may list their guidelines as such:

1. The sports clubs will be under the direct supervision of the Recreational Sports Director and have their constitutions approved by him or the Dean of Men's or Dean of Women's office.

2. The Recreational Sports Clubs will be required to have a staff member (full-time or graduate assistant) accompany them on all of their out-of-town meets.

3. It is recommended that each sports club select a staff member to serve as their faculty advisor.

4. All sports clubs will complete, as appropriate, the following forms which must be approved by the Intramural Director. The list of club membership, student release forms, parent release forms, competitive schedule approval, application for home meets, travel request forms,

officers list, and application for social function.

The conservative approach directly involves the Recreational Sports Department and the University in every phase of the sports club program. Because of this, the possibility of legal vulnerability has increased many times.

In my opinion, the real secret of a successful sports club program is for the administrator to allow the clubs to function as independent student oriented, student controlled, social organizations with a recreational bond. We must allow them to make decisions and learn to live with the consequences.

I must hesitate at this time and say that, if you select this (liberal) route, each of you, when you return to your campus, must coordinate this approach with your legal and/or insurance offices to insure that you are not overstepping the university guidelines with reference to student organizations. You should pay particular attention to the liability statutes of your state and your campus to insure that you are doing what is necessary to prevent any cases of negligence being brought against you.

I would also suggest you attempt to, if you have not already done so, organize your clubs in some sort of a federation or alliance. Offering minimal administrative help, one will find this federation can work to solve many of the common problems that face the clubs (i.e.) travel, insurance, and publicity, etc. A survey of the Mountaineer Contingency reveals the following current issues in Sports Club Administration:

1. Fund raising—utilize the student club members as fund raisers. You will never find a more energetic group of young people to sell a product.

2. Campuses are finding that Sports Clubs are getting involved as a unit in Intramural competition, student activities and other campus related functions.

3. Utilize your Sports Clubs to supplement a leisure education or recreational sports education teaching program. The clubs will teach the courses for you for a minimal fee and provide quality instruction.

4. Clubs are getting involved in the community with demonstrations and other activities which will enhance the rapport with the University and the community.

5. The development of the World's Sports Club Association which is an attempt to unit sports clubs and provide necessary services to them, shows the impetus behind clubs.

I guess if we have one thing to remember about Sports Clubs and the enthusiasm of the students, it's to never say no to them, to work as hard as we can to develop as many different Sports Clubs as there is a demand for on our campuses. It's quite a challenge to nurture a program and see it grow and work diligently to increase its growth, but yet not get involved except when absolutely necessary. I encourage you to nurture the programs but yet stay away and give the students a chance to "do their thing."

Chapter 23
Student Leadership

Student Input: It Makes The Program
William R. Zimmer
(1974 NIA Proceedings, pp. 41-43)

Universities and colleges throughout this country are experiencing a great change in student attitudes and awareness. Students are no longer carrying placards into the streets in order to accomplish change. They are, however, becoming active in numerous areas of concern, and interest. Students are now working within the "system" to generate change. Recreation and Intramural Sports must conform to this movement or be lost, for without student participation, we would be without intramurals.

There are a great number of ways in which students may become actively involved in intramural programming. The most obvious and most common are in the areas of supervising, officiating and managing. These are necessary tasks that require competent students to make the program a smooth-running operation.

At West Virginia, we have found that there are basically two types of student workers, who are interested enough to actively take part in an intramural program. We classify the supervisory, official and managerial jobs as jobs for "doers." The other type of student usually begins with this job, but soon grows stagnant. He needs something more and begs to contribute. This student is the one that can change an intramural program from mediocre to excellent. We classify this student as a "thinker."

How can these "thinkers" be channeled to make the most for a program? Avenues are countless. Executive intramural boards or councils can be formed to make rule changes and constitutional amendments. Project committees are essential. Students from nearly every major field can be utilized to make your program better.

As mentioned earlier, special men's or women's intramural councils could be established. These could have any number of duties from protest ruling to disciplinary problems to constitutional revisions. Obviously, this would be a vital service that active students could perform.

Another very helpful avenue could be in student government. If your program is funded through student fees, a voice inside the student administration could do wonders. At West Virginia intramural workers are presently serving on the Bureau of Finance (the committee which allocates all student fee money), the Board of Directors (the governing body of student administration), the Planning Council (a faculty-staff committee which plans future facilities), and Student Foundation (a student fund raising organization). With their help and help from others like them, West

Virginia's budget has increased nearly 50% in four years; and facilities have more than doubled in this time.

All intramural programs work in some degree with the Athletic Department and/or the School of Physical Education. Most schools have Athletic Councils on which students are represented; and many Physical Education Departments have student advisory boards. A student, knowledgeable in intramurals could have a great impact on these councils. Through West Virginia's student members on the Athletic Council, we were able to conduct the championship flag football game as a preliminary game to the WVU-Tulane contest!

Finally, the backbone of a good Recreation-Intramural Department must be a Recreation-Intramural Student Committee. This should have each area of programming represented with the top student in that area (Men's Intramurals, Women's Intramurals, Co-Recreation, Arts and Crafts, Sport Clubs, etc.). These students, when integrated with student administration, can make or break the program. This committee could become a meeting of the most innovative thinkers within the intramural program, indeed the university. This is the committee that has the knowledge, powers and drive to make change.

These students do not, by any means, do the job of the men's or women's intramural coordinator or the director; but work in conjunction with them in all areas of concern. Oftentimes, situations arise which could make a director extremely vulnerable, if he were to speak up. Naturally, students have no worry—they can not be fired!

With this confidence, an informed student can make the university hierarchy aware of a difficult situation—in fact, may even change it. West Virginia University's intramural basketball courts are monuments to this philosophy. They were doomed to become an indoor track until demanding students became concerned and met with the University president. The track was not built and the building was remodeled. This is just one example of the weight the student voice carries. It shows that if students get behind a cause and create enough controversy—something will be done!

The student voice carries power. Hard workers and innovative thinkers are essential for it to be heard. But all of the "doers" and "thinkers" work will be futile without the support of you, the director, and your staff. These workers will only become figureheads for dictatorial administrations, unless they are given an active and powerful voice. Only you can give them that voice and that voice must be heard! To paraphrase *Hotting Carter,* "Little good is accomplished without controversy, and no intramural injustice is ever defeated without publicity."[1]

The power, the voice, and the changes, derive from students. Get them the opportunity to make your program—SOMETHING FOR EVERYONE!

---

[1]Carter, Hotting "Where Main Street Meets the River."

The Extent and Effectiveness of Student Involvement In The Administration of the University Intramural Program
Don Poling
(1972 NIA Proceedings, pp. 165-172)

Student involvement in the administration of the university intramural program has received administrative support during the past decade (Steckbeck, 1965; Matthews, 1966; Townes, 1966). Inspection of recent professional literature reveals a number of articles which specifically emphasize the values to be derived from student involvement (Clegg, 1966; Pollack, 1969; Anderson, 1970; Colgate, 1970; McGuire, 1970).

While there is increasing evidence that individual intramural administrators stress the importance of student involvement, little attention has been directed toward the general philosophy of the intramural profession regarding student participation in the administration of the university intramural activity program.

Purpose of the Study

The purpose of this study was to investigate student involvement in the administration of intramural activity of randomly selected North American universities. The study was specifically concerned with: (1) the relationship between departmental allocation of faculty and student involvement; (2) the extent of student assignment to permanent intramural committees; (3) the methods employed for determining student committee membership; (4) the effectiveness of committees which involved students as members; and (5) the participating intramural director's perception of the role of student involvement in the administration of the campus intramural program.

Procedure

An initial random listing of 16 North American public universities whose intramural activity programs indicated a variety of individual, dual, and team activities was obtained from the National Collegiate Athletic Association Handbook. Intramural directors from each university were contacted and requested to participate as study respondents. Administrators of intramural activity programs from 12 American and two Canadian universities agreed to take part in the survey.

A questionnaire designed to solicit the necessary data while maintaining respondent anonymity was completed by each student participant. While detailed statistical analysis of the data was not attempted, the tabulation of item responses and subsequent rankings facilitated comparisons and the formulation of conclusions regarding the extent and effectiveness of student involvement in the administration of the contemporary campus intramural activity program.

Results and Discussions

To examine whether the extent of student involvement depends upon the degree of faculty allocation to the intramural department, each study respondent was requested to indicate the amount of full teaching equivalency (FTE) received for the administration of his program.

As revealed in Table 1, intramural director assignments ranged from full assignment (1.00 TE) to one-half assignment (.50 FTE) with an average of .75 FTE allotted the director for the administration of the intramural program. Assistant director assignments were reported by eight departments with time allocation for faculty members in this position ranging from 1.00 FTE to .40 FTE, including graduate assistants, averaged 1.57 FTE, with a high of 2.90 FTE reported.

To determine the extent of student committee participation, study respondents were requested to indicate the degree they involved students as committee members. A numerical scale from five (indication of always involving students) to zero (indication of never involving students) was developed for respondent consideration. The study respondents reported student committee participation in the areas of policy making, judicial review, research, communications, and social events.

The total extent of student involvement within each committee area was determined by multiplying each selected numerical value by the total number of responses. Final committee rankings were obtained by assigning the highest rank to the area receiving the greatest number of points.

While Table 2 indicates general student involvement in each area under investigation, greatest student participation was reported in judicial review and policy making—those aspects of the intramural program which most directly affect the student athlete.

The study respondents listed and evaluated all permanent administrative committees which included students as members. Information relating to the committee composition, the method of selection of student members, and the administrator's subjective appraisal of committee effectiveness was also reported by the participants. Those permanent committees (judicial review and policy making) identified by survey respondents as *most valuable* to the administration of their intramural program were selected for further analysis.

According to the respondents, *judicial review committees* decide the validity of protests involving interpretation of rules and investigate the eligibility of teams and individuals. As indicated by Table 3, administrative appointment and peer selection were the most common procedures employed for the selection of student committee membership.

Administrator comments revealed that judicial review boards organized through student peer selection generally functioned as advisory committees and forwarded suggestions and conclusions to the faculty intramural director for final decision and implementation.

Student-administered judicial review committees which initially excluded

TABLE 1
FULL TEACHING EQUIVALENCY OF RESPONDING INTRAMURAL DEPARTMENTS

Position	FTE	Number	Position	FTE	Number	Position	FTE	Number
Director	1.00	4	Assistant Director			Graduate Assistant		
	.90	1		1.00	2			
	.85	1		.60	2		.50	2**
	.83	1		.50	3		.30	3 (10 GAs)
	.75	1		.40	1*		.25	3** (6 GAs)
	.60	3		none	6		none	7
	.50	3						
Totals	10.63	14		5.90	14		5.50	14 (18 GAs)
Average/ Dept.	.75			.42			.39	
Total FTE (all dept.) 22.03								
Average/ Dept.	1.57							

* 3 assistant directors (total of 1.20 FTE)
** 1 reporting department grants .50 and .25 FTE graduate assistantships

TABLE 2

TOTAL EXTENT OF STUDENT INVOLVEMENT ON INTRAMURAL COMMITTEES

Committee Area	Always Involve (5)	Most Often Involve (4)	Frequent Involve (3)	Infrequent Involve (2)	Never Involve (0)	Total Points	Committee Ranking
Judicial	11(55)	1(4)	—(0)	2(4)	—(0)	63	1
Policy	7(35)	3(12)	1(3)	3(6)	—(0)	56	2
Research	5(25)	4(16)	3(9)	—(0)	2(0)	50	3
Special Events	6(30)	3(12)	2(6)	—(0)	3(0)	48	4
Communications	5(25)	2(8)	3(9)	2(4)	2(0)	46	5

faculty participation were reported by the respondents to exhibit greater effectiveness than faculty-administered boards. These findings reinforce the empirical observation that peer-oriented judgments regarding protests and eligibility are more readily accepted by the student participant (McGuire, 1970).

The study respondents agreed that *policy making committees* should establish and coordinate intramural activity in accordance with departmental rules and regulations.

As indicated in Table 4, student membership on policy making boards was accomplished through administrative appointment, peer selection, and student volunteering. Although most administrators utilized administrative appointment or peer ballot selection techniques to accomplish student committee membership, a combination of selectional procedures was reported by several directors.

Faculty-directed policy making committees with student membership determined through administrative appointment were generally rated as exhibiting greater effectiveness than boards which were student-directed. Respondent evaluation relative to the composition of effective policy-making committees appeared to identify with the philosophical position described by Anderson (1970) which recognizes the value of student membership on advisory boards providing the administration maintains control over the final decision.

Opportunity to relate personal opinions regarding the role of student involvement in the administration of the intramural program was provided each study participant. Advocates of student involvement stressed: (1) the student is a "consumer" and should be afforded some responsibility for the administration of "his" program; (2) the student committee members possesses insight relative to the needs and interests of his peers, thereby providing the intramural department with current "student pulse" regarding recreational desires; and (3) the intramural program becomes more meaningful to the student if he is allowed to take part in the decision making process.

Of concern to the study respondents, however, was the practicality of involving students in the administration of extensive programs since students often dislike the concept of administering intramural activity through committees. Student attendance at regularly scheduled meetings provided an additional source of concern. Directors faced with this situation emphasized the value of daily, informal student contact as the most effective method of obtaining relevant student recreational interests.

Conclusions

For purposes of this study, the analysis of data facilitated formulation of the following conclusions regarding student involvement in the administration of the present university intramural activity program:

TABLE 3
JUDICIAL REVIEW COMMITTEES

Committee Size		Student Membership Procedure			Committee Effectiveness		
Fac.	Student	Appoint	Vote	Volunteer	Superior	Excellent	Good
—	5*	X			X		
1	2	X	X			X	
—	7	X				X	
1+	9		X			X	
—	4		X			X	
—	7		X			X	
1	3	X	X				X
—+	4		X	X			X
3+	4	X					X
1+	6		X				X
—	3	X					X
2	5		X				X

+ dual purpose (judicial review and policy making) committee
* graduate assistants

TABLE 4
POLICY MAKING COMMITTEES

Committee Size		Student Membership Procedures			Committee Effectiveness		
Fac.	Student	Appoint	Vote	Volunteer	Superior	Excellent	Good
1	40-	X	X	X	X		
—	5*	X			X		
4	5	X			X		
1+	9		X			X	
2	3	X				X	
1	49-	X		X			X
—+	4	X	X	X			X
1	3		X				X
—	4			X			X
3+	4	X					X
1+	6		X				X

+ dual purpose (police making and judicial review) committee
* graduate assistants
— intramural managers

288

(1) the full teaching equivalency (FTE) alloted the intramural department often determined the type and extent of student involvement. Departments with greater FTE were better able to solicit suggestions from students through informal, personal contact, while intramural staffs operation with minimal FTE structured student involvement through committee assignment;

(2) student involvement was included in *most areas* of the administration of the intramural program. Greatest student participation appeared in the areas of judicial review and policy making;

(3) the administrative committee composition generally determined the committee effectiveness. The majority of effective judicial review committees displayed student membership and excluded initial faculty participation while effective policy making committees were faculty-directed and composed of student-faculty membership;

(4) the method employed in student selection to intramural committees appeared to influence the committee effectiveness. Committees receiving superior or excellent administrator-ratings generally were composed of student members selected by administrative appointment or peer ballot;

(5) the respondents of this study generally support the moderate or practical philosophical position regarding student involvement—a position which recognizes the values of providing extensive opportunity for student participation in all aspects of the intramural program while stressing the importance of maintaining faculty guidance of the decision-making process.

REFERENCES

Anderson, Bruce D. "Student Power-Student Policy Boards and Advisory Committees, "National College Physical Education Association for Men, 73rd Annual Proceedings (Chicago, Ill., 1970), pp. 19-20.

Clegg, Richard. "Methods of Involving Students in College Intramural Programs," National Intramural Association, 17th Annual Conference Proceedings (Norman, Okla., 1966), pp. 87-90.

Colgate, John A. "Student Power and Student Administered Program," National College Physical Education Association for Men, 73rd Annual Proceedings (Chicago, Ill., 1970), pp. 23-24.

Grambeau, Rodney J. "A Survey of the Administration of Intramural Sports Programs for Men in Selected Colleges and Universities of North and South America," unpublished doctoral dissertation, University of Michigan, 1959.

Matthews, David O. "Intramural Administration Principles," Athletic Journal, Vol. 46 (1966), pp. 82-85.

McGuire, Raymond J. "Student Power in a Positive Direction—A Student Manager Program," National College Physical Education Association for Men, 73rd Annual Proceedings (Chicago, Ill., 1970), pp. 21-22.

Pollack, Bernard. "Student Involvement in the College Intramural Program," *Journal of Health, Physical Education and Recreation,* Vol. 40, (March, 1969), pp. 36-37.

Steckbeck, John. "The Architecture of Excellence," *National College Physical Education Association for Men, 68th Annual Proceedings* (Minneapolis, Minn., 1965), pp. 73-74.

Townes, Ross E. "Student-Interest and Student Involvement," *National Intramural Association, 17th Annual Conference Proceedings* (Norman, Okla., 1966), pp. 91-93.

Student-Administered Intramural Programs
Harvey Miller
(1972 NIA Proceedings, pp. 120-121)

Student help and student workers play a vital role in the organization and administration of intramural activities. Student administered Intramural programs can be detrimental or advantageous to the program depending upon the students in charge or the group sponsoring the activity. Student-administered intramural programs are sponsored in whole or in part by a club, organization or fraternity.

The major reason for this type of program is to utilize outside facilities in which the college or university does not have access, i.e. bowling alley, golf courses and race tracks. Many advantages are found concerning these types of programs which can be as follows:

(1) More students and organizations are given the opportunity to share the responsibility of preparing and arranging necessary guidelines, rules and regulations within the activity.

(2) Administrative work load for the Intramural staff is lowered when outstanding student helpers share responsibilities.

(3) A variety within activities and more activities within a program can be offered.

(4) Expenses are reduced within the intramural department (awards, officials, etc. are furnished by sponsoring group).

(5) Clubs and organizations concentrate on this particular activity for several months—"It may be come a yearly tradition for that group."

(6) Facilities can be utilized off-campus.

(7) Knowledge and recognition is gained within the organization.

(8) Students take a more active role in the intramural program.

(9) Brings recognition to the intramural program through different organizations on campus.

Some of the disadvantages given for student-administered programs:

(1) Professionalism is lacking due to inadequate knowledge and foresight of organizational procedures.

(2) Experience is gained at the expense of the intramural department.

(3) Sponsoring groups may be given advantages. Careful checks have to be made before events take place.

(4) Entry fees may be set at a high level.

(5) Highly organized groups such as fraternities could sponsor more activities than independent clubs.

(6) Rules and Regulations must be carefully checked and communicated to all interested participants.

(7) Facilities may not be acquired at proper time and date to coordinate schedule of the intramural department.

(8) Rental fees on facilities are very expensive.

(9) Conflict in scheduling campus-wide activities.

Methods and guidelines to follow to initiate student-administered programs.

(1) Student interest must be present in that activity.

(2) Select activity that necessitates off-campus facilities primarily.

(3) Assign the group members the entire preparation of the activity.

(4) Before rules and regulations are made public, intramural director and staff must check for errors, corrections, or advantages given to a team or person.

(5) Checks must be made for conflict of campus activities, schedule of events and entry fees.

(6) After final corrections are made distribute material by the sponsoring groups to all concerned by utilizing all facets of news media.

(7) Conduct activity and have intramural personnel available for supervision.

(8) Presentation of awards are made immediately after activity and results reported to intramural office for final standings.

(9) Evaluation sheets are recorded by participating teams—constructive criticism is made and ideas for improving the activities are initiated for the following year.

Chapter 24
Professional Preparation

In Search of Leadership
Clifford Trump
(1970 NIA Proceedings, pp. 61-64)

My contention here today, in reference to the theme, "Professional Preparation," is that most intramural administrative careers begin somewhat accidentally, a result of fortuitous circumstances rather than the result of a methodical self-directed career planning. This assumption is not a condemnation. However, perhaps the time has come to examine our traditional theories and practices.

When considering the topic of "Professional Preparation," for the first time, my inclination was to make an impassioned plea for a high level, specialized, course of study for prospective intramural directors without regard for any other considerations. This was my idea approximately four years ago when the program at Ohio University in Athens, Ohio, first came to my attention. Ohio University offers the Master's Degree in Athletic Administration. On further examination I found that several schools were already doing this very thing in the field of intramurals.

Continued reflection on just what type of preparation would be most meaningful for a person desirous of the ultimate in intramural leadership suggested that a course of study does not contain all the answers. There are many other skills necessary that may be acquired or as some suggest are either part of your psychological make-up or they are not and no amount of preparation will be sufficient.

Joseph Joubert,[1] an early French educator once said, "It is better to stir up a question without deciding it than to decide it without stirring it up."

Relatively little information is available in the current literature to describe the career patterns and attitudes of administrators of intramural programs. That is, a study which would trace empirically the career patterns and attitudes of individuals now holding intramural posts and to examine some of the forces that influenced their commitment to this type of work.

David Uhrlaub,[2] in a study entitled, "The Qualifications and Status of College Men's Intramural Directors," which was presented last year in Los Angeles makes an excellent start in this direction.

The intramural director is constantly confronted with the necessity for making choices and finding valid answers. Theoretically, if we wanted to plan a good professional experience for developing intramural personnel, we would find out how intramural directors spend their days.

In such an undertaking, we would have them indicate the percentage of time spent discharging their various duties and have them give some rating as to the degree of importance for each task. After analyzing 200 or more directors the items could be ranked in terms of frequency with which these duties have to be performed and in terms of their importance. We could then simply set up learning experience for teaching students to do well those items highest in frequency and importance.

According to Kleindienst and Weston,[3] the list of duties of an intramural director is a formidable one. The numerous aspects of the program impose many duties and functions. These are carried out with varying degrees of success according to the authors and include such things as the following:

1. Interpret philosophy and purposes to students, staff, administrators, and the public.

2. Interpret the program master plan to staff and students.

3. Assist other leaders within the organization and administration problems.

4. Coordinate all levels of administration including school, department, and the community.

5. Ensure good practices and observation of standards in all aspects of the program.

6. Free leaders' time and provide enough help so that the responsibilities of the job can be carried out without undue pressures.

7. Point out ways for developing the program without the possibilities of the local situation.

8. Make recommendations for activities and program content.

9. Direct activities and planning schedules.

10. Develop a workable schedule for use of facilities and equipment.

11. Suggest means of obtaining qualified leadership assistants.

12. Arrange for in-service leadership training.

13. Assign staff responsibilities.

14. Involve and train student leaders as effective administrative personnel and benefactors of leadership experience.

15. Help with student classifications for units of competition and tournament plans.

16. Point out dangers and values of a points and awards system and help to develop a plan for the particular situation.

17. Indicate sources for official rules and help to develop necessary local regulations.

18. Help to investigate possible sources for financial support.

19. Assist in developing a plan of evaluation.

20. Ensure that all departmental staff members give positive vocal support to the program.

21. Develop public relations and functions of the organization that will ensure continued growth and development.

A curriculum which could aid in the development of these various functions would necessarily have to be a series of rich and guided experiences with some definite order of priority (progression) and directed toward the achievement of certain objectives. Once we decide on what directions we want to change people the curriculum then becomes the medium for consciously controlling or purposefully directing the process designed to produce the desired changes in behavior.

In discussing preparation for intramural directors with several individuals in the field, most as a matter of conviction, favor direct experience over any formal program in intramural administration. In fact, Uhrlaub's study points out that directors now in the field recognize this as important but as a matter of fact, his study so distinctly points out, intramural internship is very seldom available. This experience dictum is based on the succinct observation that if one possesses the ability—the drive, the vision and the force of character—he can learn the perfunctory details of administration but without these qualities, no amount of facility with these details can make a person a good administrator.

John McConnell[4] says that, "Administration is a skill—a form of artistry which does not lend itself to scientific analysis. Administration can be studied and certain techniques identified, but these become part of a complex and unique pattern of behavior in the actions of a single administration."

Regardless of our treatment of the design of the training, cruder limits of error will be prevalent. Human behavior is complex and so few of its elements clearly isolated that while the training goes on there is constant change in the human materials. Therefore, even if a curriculum covered all of the efficiency variables mentioned thus far, it would still not necessarily produce an accomplished administrator.

There are many noncongruent personality dimensions and patterns that must be dealt successfully also. Rosenblum,[5] suggested several intangible characteristics that are pertinent: For instance, how do you keep the lines of communications open? Are you able to say no when it is necessary? Are you honest and consistent in your administrative philosophy and behavior? Have you developed a sense of humor or do you take yourself too seriously? Do you fit the needs of your constituency, that is meet the needs of your particular institutions and none else? Do you establish and perpetuate credibility with those whom you serve? Do you practice the 'art of the possible'; are you reality based even though your tendency to dream is strong? Do you know and understand human behavior? Do you use tact in dealing with others? Can you accept criticism constructively? Do you keep your eye on the larger objective at all times? Do you leave subordinates room for error and abide weaknesses in others?

Maybe the teaching of such things is an impossible task as some suggest. Perhaps leaders are born and not made. I subscribe to the notion that leadership can be improved. Maybe a course in the psychology of administration which dealt with communicating, listening and hearing, encountering, helping and consulting, confronting, accommodating and collaborating is the answer.

The challenge to do better is here. The road is unclear. What may seem idealistic may be realistic in the future. I would like to close with a quote by Ordway Tead[6] in his book, *The Art of Leadership.* "Leaders are known by the personalities they enrich not by those they dominate or captivate."

REFERENCES

[1]Joubert, Joseph, *Pensees et lettres,* Paris: Grasset publishers, 1954, p. 7.

[2]Uhrlaub, David, *National Intramural Proceedings,* "Qualifications and Status of College Men's Intramural Directors," Dubuque: Kendall/Hunt Publishing Company, 1969, p. 82.

[3]Kleindienst, Viola and Arthur Weston, *Intramural and Recreation Program for Schools and Colleges,* Appleton, Century Crofts, 1964, p. 93.

[4]McConnell, John, *Law and Business,* New York: McMillan, 1966, p. 44.

[5]Rosenblum, Sidney, et al, *College and University Journal,* "The Academic Administrator", 1968, pp. 35-42.

[6]Tead, Ordway, *The Art of Leadership,* New York: McGraw Hill, 1935, p. 3.

Preparing The Intramural Director: A Practical Approach
Joseph Johnson
(1976 NIRSA Proceedings, pp. 109-111)

One of the major criticisms in the past decade by students in intramural classes has been the dryness of the course in terms of the content of the material presented. Being an Intramural Director at both the college and high school level, and having the responsibility for teaching the course at the University of Colorado, I must admit that to a certain extent the students have been correct in their analysis of the course. However, in the area of intramurals, we are dealing with a set body of knowledge that must be comprehended by the future intramural directors if they are to be successful in the field. It was through this criticism by the students and the need for a more practical approach to training intramural directors that gave rise to the *practical approach for training the intramural director* at the University of Colorado.

At the University of Colorado, due to insight of students, the recreation department staff, faculty and staff, one of the best laboratories for preparing the new intramural director is located. Blessed with a new 4.5 million recreation building that possesses two swimming pools, ice skating rink, ten handball courts, two squash courts, a large multi-purpose gymnasium, a combative gymnasium, exercise room, first aid and therapy room, excellent administrative offices and a very competent recreation staff, the opportunity for providing practical experiences for intramural directors is immeasurable.

The class (administration of intramurals) has been broken down into two phases: theory and practical. This has been done in order to provide students with the necessary knowledge as well as experience to deal with the intramural program.

In the theory phases of the class, those topics that are necessary for handling the basic program are covered, along with an extensive knowledge of the field of administration. These basic topics we feel are necessary to gain this knowledge are:

a. Historical perspective of Intramurals
b. Finances, facilities and equipment
c. Units of preparation
d. Scheduling and Structuring tournaments
e. Rules and regulations
f. Publicity for IM program

To back up to the area of administration, I feel that any person with the responsibility of dealing with large numbers of people should be people oriented, and if the IM director does not possess those qualities needed for dealing with people, then it is obvious he or she will not be successful in the field. We therefore attempt to focus on preparing the potential IM director in those areas of administration we feel are vital for continued success in the field. Mueller best described the purpose of administration when he stated: "The basic purpose of an administration is to be of service to those whom it is supposed to serve."

Due to the many challenges thrust upon us by the automated society in which we have to work, it becomes imperative that students intent on becoming intramural directors conceptualize that not adequate but superior administration of IM programs is necessary if it is to exist, produce and compete with other programs on campuses for the few dollars that now exist on college campuses throughout the country. Therefore, how these IM programs run, how successful the results of these programs, will be determined by how well they are administered.

The most important basic skill that is emphasized in the theory phases of the program is that of understanding the purpose of organizing your IM program for success. In teaching students how to organize, it therefore becomes necessary for them to understand the specific steps of the IM director in organizing are thus:

1. Defining and describing the tasks to be accomplished and grouping these actions into duties.
Example:
a. Scheduling of IM fields and courts
b. Dissemination of IM information to participants

c. Scheduling of leagues, individuals or team
d. Issuing of equipment to participants
e. Training of Officials

2. Systematically separating the duties and forming them into jobs or positions.
Example:
a. Facilities coordinator
b. Clerical help
c. IM coordinators
d. Equipment or service manager
e. Supervisors of Officials

3. Arranging jobs into groups, functions or specializaton.
Example:
a. Scheduling of facilities without conflicts
b. Publicity—Radio, newspaper, IM packets, eligibility forms
c. Hiring of personnel for programs
d. Equipment check out procedure
e. Supervision of Officials—ratings, clinics, meetings, etc.

4. Assembling the functional areas into a unified organization.
Example: The complete IM program
a. Programs
b. People
c. Facilities
d. Equipment
e. Finances

In the area of practical work, the students are involved in a wide variety of IM activities ranging from keeping scores to working as assistant to the IM director. It is felt that these opportunities to become a practicing practitioner enhance the knowledge of the students by making them a part of the actual IM program. The students are required to put in 30 hours in different phases of the IM program on a rotating base. Example—5 hours officiating, 5 hours as programmer, 5 hours as assistant to IM administrator, 5 hours clerical, etc. We feel that with the students involvement in such a wide variety of activities they are being provided with a look at the big picture in IM or even better a complete knowledge of the program.

In conclusion, it would be safe to say from the responses we have received from students by way of evaluation of their participation in the program, this has truly been a valuable part of the preparation as an IM director.

Professional Preparation
Jim Wittenauer
(1970 NIA Proceedings, pp. 65-68)

My interest in professional preparation stems from experiences with student leaders and providing student leadership opportunities as an Intramural Director, and also from being involved in a physical education teacher preparation program. What I say this morning reflects my personal views and not necessarily those of my University or anyone else.

My interest is a deep concern for the professional preparation of intramural and school recreation leaders for the secondary and elementary schools. Professional preparation of baccalaureate degree candidates seeking certification to teach at these levels are the eligible candidates. My partner, Cliff Trump,[1] last year at UCLA asked the question, "How many intramural specialists did your school turn out last year?" I have been Intramural Director at our school for ten years. My first three undergraduate student assistants were granted graduate assistantships at our school to continue their study and service in our intramural program. Two of the three were appointed college intramural directors for their first job. The third is teaching physical education and is supervisor of intramurals and recreation at a junior high school in Los Angeles County, California.

As College and University Intramural Directors you men motivate, train and develop potential intramural and school recreation leaders through various media in your programs. Perhaps some of these potential leaders are physical education majors who use this experience as supplemental training, or as a part-time job. Perhaps, there are those who would like to pursue intramural leadership as a profession. There are a very few who are fortunate to have the opportunity to continue in this profession at the college level. There are still others who desire this opportunity, but are discouraged partly because there are not enough intramural job opportunities each year due to the near absences of intramural and school recreation programs at the secondary and elementary levels.

One of the most obvious forces creating a need for an Intramural/Recreation program is the overwhelming increase in school populations caused by consolidation. This factor alone has created unbelievable changes in the types of facilities and equipment for these facilities. Recently a consolidated one County unit, junior and senior high school not far from Purdue University, included space for unlimited outdoor programming. Indoor facilities include a swimming pool that permits family recreation swimming. A circuit trainer is also available to students. This rather progressive community employed college students during Christmas Vacation as supervisors in order to keep the gyms open for free play in the three or four small towns in the system. Bermingham, Michigan in the early

1960's made provisions for intramural opportunities in each of the elementary schools in the system.

These things are not just happening in one place, but nationwide. Hardly a year goes by that I do not hear about a school system that has abolished interscholastic competition below the high school level in favor of competitive intramural and free play recreational programs. I am of the opinion that this is true exclusively in Los Angeles County, California in the junior high schools. Recently, I heard of similar proceedings for the Louisville, Kentucky area. It is this type of program development that will motivate school boards to begin looking for one person to coordinate the intramural/recreation program.

Is Physical Education Getting the Job Done?

Last summer a graduate student who was a Site leader in the Task Force R (recreation) program in Indianapolis reported that the kids would come to his park and huddle in small groups, and smoke or what have you. He remarked that they did not know who to play, and therefore did not want to get involved except with switchblades and rocks. Wayne Wiemer,[2] New Trier High School East, in his presentation at UCLA said, "Perhaps part of the college campus unrest is a result of no or poor recreational services at the high school level...Perhaps these students who have not participated in high school intramurals do not avail themselves of the opportunity in college and their excessive energies explode into questionable activities."

If education for leisure is important, perhaps we as a society should be educating for the wise use of free time in the hub of all education—OUR SCHOOLS!! What is the most frequent constructive way that people use their free time? Recreation, isn't it? Recreation is more than participation in traditional sports that are emphasized in our competitive intramural sports programs. Recreation includes hobbies, handicrafts, and other constructive forms of amusement. These areas provide opportunities to learn new skills and to meet new people, while renewing energy spent in routine living. J. Tillmore Hall[3] in his book *"School Recreation"* says that schools should devote additional time to organizing and administering a dynamic educational recreation program by increasing the amount and quality of leisure-time leadership at all school levels. The ASHPER in 1959 sponsored a national conference on school recreation. Significant recommendations evolving from the conference were (1) Schools should educate for the worthy use of leisure (2) Maximum articulation should be achieved between school instruction and recreation, (3) Schools should interpret recreation to the people.

Why doesn't physical education instruction include bait casting, game hunting, archery, et al? The standard answer is time allotment. Perhaps physical education instruction can be supplemented with sports clubs in the high schools. The sport club programs at the college level are an excellent example of educating for leisure. Students can select activities of their choice for the purpose of learning new activities for leisure time pursuit. Who administers the sports club program at the college level? In most cases the Intramural Staff. We are witnessing an overwhelming increase in the demands for free play time at the college level. Below college level, perhaps free play time could be directed to insure constructive development of wholesome free play habits. Undoubtedly, secondary and elementary schools will pattern such programs after the colleges. This creates a need for professionally trained intramural and recreation leaders, that is if the program is going to have a real professional purpose.

What should the qualifications be for a professionally trained intramural and school recreation leader? The School of Health, Physical Education and Recreation at Indiana State University offers a specialization in Intramural Sports for undergraduate men. The specialization is a series of courses designed to afford students desirous of becoming leaders in intramural sports and school related activities, an opportunity to learn the basic knowledge and concepts necessary for effective leadership. The major objectives of the specialization are to prepare and train leaders. Students who subscribe to this specialization experience gain many leadership opportunities in the Men's Intramural Sports Program. Also, the young men who serve as student leaders in the ISU program can receive special recognition for their service and achievement. The courses prescribed for the Specialization are:

COURSE TITLE	HOURS—CREDIT
Leadership In Intramurals	2
First Aid	2
Recreation Leadership	3
Reports and Newspaper Writing	2
Preparation of A-V Materials	3
Sports and School Related Activities	2

The University of Illinois offers a Masters Degree in Physical Education with a specialization in the administration of intramural activities.

The charge I am making to the membership is to consider a resolution providing for the appointment of an ad hoc committee to recommend minimum standards and qualifications for certification by the National Intramural Association for a professionally trained intramural leader. The National Trainers Association has a similar certification with five or six different ways to become certified. The first one is the Grandfather Clause which includes all those currently in the field by a certain cut off date; the second is issued to undergraduates who complete 1800 hours under a qualified trainer; the third way is for undergraduates to complete an approved curriculum which by the way is only currently offered in four colleges; the fourth method to become certified is to complete a Masters Degree with a specialization in Athletic Training. The latter three include the requirement of passing a National Trainers Association test.

Perhaps, a certification program would add prestige to our profession as well as provide an excellent service to the high schools and enhance the Association's placement service. To quote Wayne Weimer[4] again, "Is this organization willing to dedicate itself to the leadership necessary to provide direction to this sorely neglected activity in the high schools throughout the nation?"

REFERENCES

[1]Trump, Clifford M., "National Intramural Association's Responsibility to the High School", *Proceedings — National Intramural Association,* March, 1969, pp. 153-156.

[2]Weimer, M. Wayne, "High School Intramurals: The Need, and Meeting It", *Proceedings — National Intramural Association,* March, 1969, pp. 156-159.

[3]Hall, J. Tillman, *"SCHOOL RECREATION: Its Organization, Supervision and Administration",*W. C. Brawn, Dubuque, Iowa, 1966.

[4]Ibid. p. 17.

The Achievement of True Professional Status for Intramurals
Raymond J. McGuire
(1969 NIA Proceedings, pp. 199-206)

Today is the era of specialization. Furthermore, we as a society have become very status conscious. Never before has so much emphasis been placed upon the achievement of recognition by different occupational groups. This universal desire for recognition is an objective of the vast majority of such groups, whether they try to identify themselves as professions or not. It is the key word "professional" that seems to signify the achievement of the ultimate in recognition, whether it refers to a doctor, athlete, lawyer, or nurse.

Intramurals is one of the occupations that is attempting to improve its image and elevate its status to a more prominent position in society. Is intramurals a contender for the status of a profession? This question is a source of interest to many intramural directors. The directors' attitudes vary on this subject, falling roughly into three groups. The first group wonders if intramurals is a profession; the second is sure it is; and the third doesn't much care.

This paper is primarily directed to the skeptics who ponder over such things as status. These people must have wondered why intramural directors often occupy the lower end of the scale in rank and salary within the various administrative structures in which they operate. It could be argued that this is caused in part by a lack of professional status, and also because they perform mainly a service instead of an educational function. However, a movement toward more research, writing, and teaching (i.e., a movement to more professionalism) could soon improve the status of the intramural director within his college or university.

From another standpoint there is a human relations factor which must be considered in most situations. How does the dean or director to whom the intramural director is responsible influence the intramural program? What does this person think about the worth of intramurals? If he sees it as making a valuable contribution, then the status of both the director and the intramural program itself will most likely be elevated.

. Certainly, some will say, "What difference does it make whether or not intramurals is labeled a profession?" Many reasons could be cited to account for this difference. Bucher possibly best summed them up in three points when he stated that being part of a profession: (1) means public recognition; (2) indicates that the professional person is placed above the rank and file workers who do not possess specialized knowledge and skill; and (3) identifies an individual as a member of a group with such special qualifications as knowledge, skill, and intellectual competency for rendering a particular specialized service. (1:43) The time seems especially appropriate for an investigation to discover if intramurals is becoming a profession and to what extent people in this occupational group can be called professionals.

I. WHAT IS A PROFESSION?

Good defines a profession as an occupation involving relatively long and specialized preparation on the level of higher education and governed by a special code of ethics. (2:42) Often it is difficult to distinguish a profession from a non-profession. The following definition is offered for your consideration:

> A profession is a vocation whose practice is founded upon an understanding of the theoretical structure of some department of learning or science, and upon the abilities accompanying such understanding. This understanding and these abilities are applied to the vital practical affairs of man. The practices of the profession are modified by knowledge of a generalized nature and by the accumulated wisdom and experience of mankind, which serve to correct the errors of specialism. The profession, serving the vital needs of man, considers its first ethical imperative to be altruistic service to the client. (2:49)

Other definitions of a profession that were examined tended to be less complex and are much more general in meaning. Some of them referred only to an occupation requiring advanced academic training, while others defined a profession as a specialized activity engaged in to earn one's livelihood. With such broad statements being given, it was apparent that deeper investigation had to be undertaken in order to obtain the more specific elements which could be used to define a profession.

II. ATTRIBUTES OF A PROFESSION

Carr-Saunders of England was perhaps the first social scientist to analyze the process of professionalization systematically. He defined professionalization in terms of specialized skill and training, minimum fees or salaries, formation of professional associations, and codes of ethics governing professional practice. He mentioned that all special interest associations are not necessarily professional in character. Professional associations according to Carr-Saunders are distinguished by the degree to which they (1) seek to establish minimum qualifications for entrance into professional practice or activity, (2) enforce appropriate rules and norms of conduct among members of the professional group, and (3) raise the status of the professional group in the larger society. (7:2-3)

Bucher believes that in order to achieve professional status a field of endeavor must: (1) render a unique and essential social service; (2) establish high standards for the selection of members; (3) provide a rigorous training program to prepare its practitioners; and (4) achieve self-regulatory status for both the group and the individual. (1:43)

Lee, writing in the *Journal of the American Institute of Planners,* delineated five characteristics of a true profession as follows:

1. A professional maintains confidential loyalty to the client.
2. Professional work is intellectual and varied in character.
3. It involves consistent exercise of discretion and judgment.
4. It must be public spirited and not monopolistic.
5. A professional must possess recognized skill. (4:26-27)

The question can well be: What common components do these professional occupations possess which distinguish them from the non-professional ones? After a careful canvas of the sociological literature on occupations, Greenwood was able to list the following five elements as constituting the distinguishing attributes of a profession. Succinctly stated, all professions seem to possess: (1) systematic theory; (2) authority; (3) community authority; (4) ethical codes; and (5) a culture. (7:10) It is interesting to note, as one attempts to identify the attributes of a profession, that the only occupations that were listed in the professional category of the United States census Bureau were: accountant, architect, artist, attorney, clergyman, college professor, dentist, engineer, journalist, judge, librarian, natural scientist, optometrist, pharmacist, physician, social scientist, social worker, surgeon, and teacher. (6)

It should be pointed out that the true difference between a professional and non-professional occupation is not a qualitative but a quantitative one. Strictly speaking, these attributes are not the exclusive monopoly of the professions; non-professional occupations also possess them, but to a lesser degree. Similar to most social phenomena, the construct of professionalization cannot be explained in terms of clearly defined classes. Rather, the occupations in a society must be though of as distributing themselves along a continuum. At one end of this continuum are bunched the well recognized and undisputed professions (e.g., physician, attorney, professor, scientist); at the opposite end are bunched the least skilled and least attractive occupations (e.g., watchman, truckloader, farm laborer, scrubwoman, bus boy). The remaining occupations, less skilled and less prestigious than the former, but more so than the latter, are distributed between these two polarizations. The occupations bunched at the professional pole of the continuum possess to a maximum degree the attributes of a profession as surmised by Lee. However, as we move away from this pole, the occupations possess these attributes to a decreasing degree. (7:10-11)

A description of these five attributes is as follows:

1. *Systematic Body of Theory.* The skills that characterize a profession flow from and are supported by a fund of knowledge that has been organized into an internally consistent system, called a body of theory.

2. *Professional Authority.* Extensive education in the systematic theory of his discipline imparts to the professional a type of knowledge that highlights the laymen's comparative ignorance. The professional dictates what is good or evil for the client, who has no choice but to accede to professional judgment.

3. *Sanction of the Community.* Every profession strives to persuade the community to sanction its authority within certain spheres by conferring upon the profession a series of powers and privileges, both formal and informal (e.g., control over its training centers, legal protections for its title and skills, control over admission into the profession).

4. *Regulative Code of Ethics.* Through its ethical code the profession's commitment to the social welfare becomes a matter of public record, thereby insuring for itself the continued confidence of the community. Advance in theory is disseminated to all.

5. *Professional Culture.* Every profession operates through a network of formal and informal groups. These interactions of social roles required by these formal and informal groups generate a professional culture consisting of its values, norms and symbols. (7:11-18)

The picture of the professons just unveiled is an ideal type. One function of the ideal type is to structure reality in such a manner that discrete, disparate, and dissimilar phenomena become organized, thereby bringing order out of apparent disorder. The ideal-type model of a profession is much sharper and clearer than the actuality that confronts us when we observe the occupational scene.

Of all the analyses of the components of a profession considered, Sorenson's list of criteria seems to be the most comprehensive. The major factor which, in the writer's opinion, sets this description of the attributes of a profession above the others is the specific mention of a body of knowledge as one criterion for a profession. Granted, an occupation could be analyzed to see if it meets the requirements of a profession outlined by Greenwood, Carr-Saunders, or Lee, but for the remainder of this paper the present status of intramurals will be related to the criteria established by Sorenson for a profession.

III. AN EVALUATION OF INTRAMURALS

The field of intramurals will now be briefly assessed according to these criteria established by Sorenson:

Criterion #1: A profession serves a distinctive and permanent social function in the community.

Evaluation: Intramurals is expanding to new areas to upgrade and enlarge the social functions which it performs. Its aim is to provide for the physical, mental, social, emotional and recreational well-being of the community which it serves.

Criterion #2.: A profession has a specialized body of knowledge, complex enough to require special education and a technique.

Evaluation: Intramurals has a rather small, limited body of knowledge consisting of over twenty doctoral dissertations, one hundred and sixty masters theses, and thirteen hundred articles and unpublished reports. However, the intramural occupation is far from research conscious. Serious questions about the quality and scope of intramural research can be raised. Very little investigation has been conducted in conjunction with such fields as psychology, philosophy, sociology, and administration. Information concerning new developments in intramurals is not readily disseminated. In addition, very few intramural administrators devote an adequate amount of time for writing or research. *The Proceedings of the National Intramural Association* is the major source of information concerning intramural research and ideas. At the present time intramurals do not reflect sufficient knowledge and technique to meet this requirement of a profession.

Criterion #3: Professional preparation must precede entrance.

Evaluation: Coherent preparation is lacking. Intramural administrators usually have a physical education background with some people entering the occupation from recreation. There is not a consensus among the leaders in intramurals as to the best method of academic preparation. A number of institutions of higher learning offer a specific course in intramurals. However, with the exception of the University of Illinois, which offers a specialized Master's Degree program in intramurals, no other course of study aimed specifically toward preparation for a position in intramural administration is offered.

Criterion #4: A Profession organizes into guilds or societies to improve the profession.

Evaluation: It was not until 1950 that intramurals organized itself into a major guild, the National Intramural Association. Prior to that time the only guild of its type was the association of the Western Conference (Big Ten) Intramural Directors which was organized and has been in operation since 1920.

Criterion #5: A profession is identified around a social function rather than an institution or agency.

Evaluation: Intramurals is organized around a social function, that of providing for the well-being of the community it serves. It is identified with society, be it in a college, high school or community setting.

Criterion #6: A profession develops standards: Standards of training and admission, codes of ethics and conduct toward those served, toward others in the profession and toward the general public.

Evaluation: Intramurals has moved toward training in the area of providing graduate assistantships in intramurals and various student managers positions. However, intramurals has not yet developed standards of admission and codes of conduct. Intramural administrators have an excellent rapport with each other and have displayed a cooperative attitude with the public.

Criterion #7: A profession is characterized by professional behavior, attitudes, and workmanship of those who make it up.

Evaluation: Intramural administrators have to acquire more professional awareness towards the value of research and communication. They have not fully developed their professional maturity and concepts of the future direction of intramurals.

IV. THE STATUS OF INTRAMURALS

In reviewing the definition of a profession as related to a subjective evaluation of intramurals in connection with the attributes of a profession, it can be concluded that intramurals has not achieved the status of an established profession. *The major obstacle confronting intramurals in the achievement of professional status seems to lie in the fact that it has a very limited body of theoretical knowledge upon which it is based.* The occupation of intramurals is not research conscious, and it is oriented mainly towards service. However, with the growth of the scope of intramural repsonsibility and the accompanying complexity, intramural administrators will be forced to turn to research increasingly in an effort to solve the perennial problems which occur in the field. There is also a great need for interdisciplinary research in intramurals. Intramurals is directly concerned with the well-being of people, yet, there have not been any studies conducted in the area of sociology and psychology and their relationship to the experience one receives while participating in intramurals. Furthermore, much of the knowledge associated with the intramural occupation is taken from the physical education and recreation curricula, and it is unlikely that intramural administrators will be trained by their own curriculum in the near future. *In addition, the knowledge of intramurals is not complex and it can generally be absorbed by the average layman without much difficulty.* Thus, intramurals appears somewhat distant from the goal of becoming an established profession.

V. THE FUTURE

Being an optimist, I can't help but believe that the future can be bright. There is now within the field of intramurals a new awareness of the need for better communication and research. This new awareness is the result of an extensive effort on the part of some intramural directors to foster the growth of the body of knowledge within the field. It has also been caused by the establishment of a research committee within the National Intramural Association whose purpose is the encouragement of research pertaining to intramurals. In addition, it is becoming standard that a person have at least a Master's Degree in order to operate within the intramural occupation. In some cases a doctorate degree is required. This points up the fact that more extensive professional preparation is now taking place. The National Intramural Association has become a dynamic force in the intramural movement. It should consider establishing standards and a code of ethics for intramurals. These conclusions, in addition to the fact that intramurals is now spreading out to cover all aspects of campus recreation, show that Intramurals has become a dynamic and exciting occupation. Now it is up to the intramural administrators to formulate and implement the ideas and plans which will bring it close to the established professions.

REFERENCES

1. Bucher, Charles A., "Physical Education An Emerging Profession;" *J.O.H.P.E.R.,* Volume 29, No. 7, September, 1968.

2. Cogan, Morris L., "Towards a Definition of Profession." *Harvard Educational Review;* Volume 23; 1953.

3. Good, Carter V., *Dictionary of Education.;* New York and London: McGraw-Hill Book Company, Inc., 1945.

4. Lee, James; "Planning and Professionalism,"; *Journal of the American Institute of Planners.;* Volume 26; No. 1; February, 1960.

5. Sorenson, Roy; "Professional Maturity."; *American Recreation Society Bulletin.;* Volume 5; No. 1; May, 1953.

6. United States Bureau of Census; *1960 Census of Population: Classified Index of Occupations and Industries.;* Washington, D.C.; Government Printing Office, 1960.

7. Vollmer, Howard M. and Donald L. Mills; *Professionalization;* Englewood Cliffs, New Jersey; Prentice Hall; 1966.

Chapter 25
Affirmative Action

Affirmative Action: Its Effects Upon Intramural-Recreational Sports Department Employment Policies
Peter J. Graham
(1976 NIRSA Proceedings, pp. 29-42)

Affirmative action was enacted to provide a tool for tapping the wealth of human resources that either have not been utilized or have been under-represented. Affirmative action is a concept that allows for the development and implementation of programs designed to assist the entry of identified non-utilized and under-represented segments of the population into the employment market e.g., educational institutions.

Affirmative action was also designed to help eliminate discrimination based upon sex, race, color, national origin and religion. In certain instances, affirmative action has been the evaluative criterion selected to measure the success or failure of a program's compliance with the equal employment opportunity legislation—laws proposed, enacted and instituted for the express purpose of systematically shattering the shackles of prejudice that for so long have hampered and stymied the employment progress of certain segments of society.

Historically, most intramural-recreational sport programs were developed to promote sport activities primarily directed toward the male population. The number of women's programs, until recent years, was virtually insignificant. Those that did exist were, for the most part, administered and conducted separately from the men's programs. Women's programs were frequently instituted under the auspices of agencies such as the women's athletic association.

Relatively few female professional personnel are found in intramural-recreational sport administrative capacities. This small representation, in some measure, may be attributed to the lack of emphasis focused upon the women's programs. Glaringly evident also is the under-representation of minority administrators. For many institutions of higher learning, situations of this nature have resulted from discriminatory practices related to student admissions and employment of professional personnel.

How might affirmative action be introduced into intramural-recreational sport department employment policies? This question has generated a multitude of responses and suggestions. However, for purposes of this paper, just four areas will be addressed: (1) recruitment and hiring, (2) interviewing, (3) contracts and (4) career advancement.

RECRUITMENT AND HIRING

The Department of Health, Education and Welfare requires that recruitment and hiring standards be "reasonably explicit" and that they be accessible to employees and applicants (Varner, 1975, p. 264). Under Executive Order 11246, new recruiting practices must be developed whenever evidence indicates that the old methods have resulted in the attraction of a low representation of women and minority applicants.

How then, to comply with affirmative action regulations, should intramural-recreational sport department recruitment and hiring policy procedures be structured? Usually, the initial step involves a review of the existing employees. Such an examination should reveal the status of women and minorities within the organization—status with respect to the number employed, the types of jobs and the organizational level of employment.

To determine whether the minority group members and women are under-represented, the following factors must be considered (Bulwik and Elicks, 1972, pp. 6-7):

1. The percentage of minority and female work force as compared with the total work force in the immediate area.

2. The general availability of minority group members and women with requisite skills in the immediate work area.

3. The availability of members of minority groups and women with requisite skills in an area in which the contractor institution can reasonably recruit.

4. The availability of women and minority groups seeking employment in the labor or recruitment area of the contractor (institution).

5. The availability of promotable or transferable minority group and female employees within the contractors (institutions) organization.

6. The existence of training institutions capable of training members of minority groups and women in the requisite skills.

7. The degree of training which the contractor (institution) is reasonably able to undertake as a means of making all job classes available to women and members of minority groups.

If, as a result of this review process, a deficiency is detected i.e., none or too few women and/or minorities are employed or those employed are assigned to departments and functions below their capabilities, the next step requires the construction and implementation of an operational plan designed to reduce (and eventually to eliminate) the identified problem(s).

New intramural-recreational sport administration positions have been created by some institutions as a means of attempting to eliminate inequities. Whenever new positions of this nature are created, intensive campaigns are usually launched to attract and identify qualified minority and women applicants. Most colleges and universities, on the other hand, have been forced to maintain a posture of financial constricture due to the sagging national economy. Consequently, institutions suffering from this affliction have found that new positions are nearly impossible to generate.

Under current circumstances, two possible options remain as vehicles to bring more women and minority group members into intramural-recreational sport department administrative positions: (1) to terminate some current employees (usually white males) and fill the vacated slots with women or minorities; or, (2) to employ affirmative action candidates whenever replacement positions become available through normal turnover. In reality, neither method is desirable. The former is unjust to the terminated employees, whereas the latter is much too slow and unpredictable in accomplishing the necessary and required remedy.

Yet, when positions do become available, regardless of the source, the job description assumes extreme importance. Typically, at least two types of job descriptions need to be developed to fill a professional vacancy: (1) the official job description, and (2) the announcement job description (University of Massachusetts, 1974, p. 4). It is critical that the announced job description be carefully examined to ascertain that it has not been written in such a manner that would inhibit or exclude qualified potential candidates from submitting applications.

In certain professions, a "bona fide occupational qualification" may be established and justified for a particular position (Griggs, 1971). However, for intramural-recreational sport department administrative positions, it would be almost impossible, under most conditions, to defend the inclusion of such a restriction; especially if the restriction were in any manner related to sex or race. Therefore, it is strongly recommended that all intramural-recreational sport department administrative positions be described and advertised in such a manner that the widest possible spectrum of qualified candidates are attracted. It should be noted that,

> The affirmative action concept does not require that any employer employ or promote any persons who are unqualified. The concept does require, however, that any standards or criteria which have had the effect of excluding women and members of minority groups be eliminated, unless the employer can demonstrate that such criteria are conditions of successful performance in the particular positions involved (Higher Education Guidelines, Executive Order 11245, p. 4).

Only when a position and the accompanying job descriptions have been firmly established should an announcement be issued. Applicants, in the past, have been recruited through use of personal contacts, written notices distributed among program directors and NIRSA Newsletter announcements. More recently, position advertisements have been appearing in athletic, coaching and physical education journals and publications. Nonetheless, under the present guidelines, such recruitment methods are no longer considered sufficient. It has been contended (and probably rightfully so) that the use of these methods have failed to disseminate the announcement information to a significant number of qualified potential applicants (specifically women and minorities).

Nevertheless, traditional vacancy announcement channels may continue to be employed as long as the announcements are also made available to institutions of higher learning composed primarily of women and/or minorities. Additionally, advertisements should appear in publications commonly read by minorities and women. For example, vacancy announcements should be sent to Smith College and Texas College for Women as well as Howard University and North Carolina State University. Advertisements should appear in *The Chronicle of Higher Education, Atlanta World, Brooklyn New York Recorder, The Black Scholar Classified, Ms.* and *WomenSport.*

Prior to or immediately following the dissemination of job announcements, a search committee or interview team should be constituted. No matter which committee form is selected, a valid attempt should be made to include, whenever possible, female and minority representatives.

When should a search committee or interview team be employed? Are there instances when the establishment of such committees are not necessary? Under normal circumstances, search committees (interview teams are not commonly used in higher education) should be constituted and required whenever a full-time professional position is to be filled. Search committees are usually considered optional with respect to the filling of part-time or one year terminal positions.

Although there are no rigid requirements concerning the length of an affirmative action search, most searches are conducted for a period of three (3) months. There are situations, however, when this guideline may be either reduced or extended dependent upon the particular set of circumstances.

The scope of the search usually depends on the nature of the position to be filled. Local searches are normally used to recruit applicants for part-time professional slots or to fill temporary full-time professional positions (terminal appointments of one year or less). In the recruitment of professional persons to fill full-time professional positions with an annual salary or less than a predetermined amount (a commonly used figure has been $14,000 or less) a regional search should be undertaken. National searches should be conducted when attempting to recruit individuals to fill professional vacancies in situations other than those identified under local and regional searches.

An affirmative action statement should be developed once a position has been announced, applications received, candidates reviewed and interviewed, and the successful applicant identified. The statement should include the following (University of Massachusetts, 1974, p. 18):

A. Nature of the position

B. Dates indicating the commencement and termination of the search

C. List of search committee members including sex and race

D. List of vehicles used to announce position vacancy which were directed at generating minority and/or female applicants.

E. A breakdown of the actual number of applications received in terms of race and sex.

F. A brief description of the screening process employed

G. A breakdown by race and sex of the candidates interviewed.

H. The name, race and sex of the individual ultimately selected to fill the vacant position.

INTERVIEWS

Although interviewing is a widely used technique for employee selection, surprisingly few interviewers are able to extract the information necessary to avoid inaccurate decisions. Svetlik (1973) suggested that one reason for such problems concerned the fact that interviewers really do not allow the candidate to do much talking. He contended that interviewers talk more than half the time, thus leaving less than 50% of the interview for the candidate to communicate. Yet, merely providing the candidate more time to respond to questions will not necessarily guarantee a fruitful interview.

Serafini (1975) felt that the interviewer must develop specific listening skills to properly evaluate the candidate's responses. These skills which Serafini labeled as "active listening" require a fundamental openness toward the other person. The active listener must reject preconceived ideas and stereotypes. Unless the interviewer truly respects the applicant's beliefs and uniqueness, his/her own biases and prejudices will invalidate the interview. Thus, simply listening to the candidate is not, in and of itself, sufficient to insure an effective interview.

With respect to affirmative action, it is of the utmost importance that an interviewer look at the applicant with an open mind and without any bias or stereotyping. This concept is critical for as Blodgett (1972, p. 139) puts it, "It is a natural facet of selective perception to prefer people like oneself". If preconceived ideas are allowed to contaminate an interview, it then becomes an impossible task for the interviewer to objectively judge the applicant's ability, background and motivation to effectively perform in a given position. The exclusion of bias is easier said than done. In many instances an interviewer is not aware of personal bias, of equating certain applicants with selected stereotypes or of placing too little or too great an emphasis on selected portions of the interview. Thus, before an attempt is made to suggest remedies for biased interviews, identification of the bias source must first be made.

Webster (1964) in a classic monograph on interviewing found that a bias was established early in the interview and this tended to be followed either by a favorable or unfavorable decision. It was believed that early impressions—impressions based upon quickly assessed material—played a dominant role in determining the final outcome of the employment interview (this phenomenon is referred to as the halo or gate effect).

Hakel and Schuh (1971) recognized the existence of this early stereotyping resulting from first impressions. They concluded, however, that such a problem could be partially alleviated by identifying a core of applicant attributes that were judged to be important to many occupations. As a result, they developed a set of twenty-two (22) statements descriptive of job applicants' attributes that were found to be important in each of seven diverse occupational areas. They believed that these specific items would assist in the reduction of the halo effect applicant stereotyping because of the statements suggested the content that should be covered in the early stages of the interview. This method would capitalize on the interviewer's urge to jump to conclusions by assuring that his/her first experience with the applicant would provide the types of information believed by other professional interviewers to be of importance.

In a later study, Schuh (1973) reported that although a well constructed rating form might play a role in breaking down the halo effect, it should also be anticipated that, whereas, a novice interviewer might fall victim to either a rating form that led away from important information or to an interview in which irrelevant information occupied the early portion of the interview, an experienced interview would not. Schuh designed an experiment to test this hypothesis. From the results, he concluded that the content of the rating form did indeed effect the novice interviewer's impressions and decisions, whereas experienced interviewers arrived at the same decisions regardless of the content of the rating form. Consequently, it becomes evident that a rating form, especially a poorly designed document, will not automatically release the novice interviewer from formulating a bias due to the halo effect. As a matter of fact, a bias of this nature may possibly be augmented by irrelevant information obtained from a poorly designed instrument.

Aside from the bias of emphasizing information obtained early in an interview over that received at the later stages, there also exists a bias related to the type of information available and its weighting. In a study, Hollmann (1972) found that interviewers were biased by the fact that they gave too much weight to negative information reflecting the applicant's suitability for employment, at the expense of positive information. The net result of such unbalanced weighting was a disruption in the efficiency (and presumably the accuracy) of the interviewer's information processing. Hollmann hypothesized that because interviewers received only negative feedback from their superiors—feedback concerning previous employee situations (i.e., criticism when an employee failed to meet the test)—they lacked knowledge of the criteria associated with a good employee.

Consequently, interviewers set up a stereotype based upon the character-istics that a model applicant should *not* possess. In the interviewing process, the interviewer then compares negative information received from the applicant with the negative stereotype.

Shaw (1972) asserted that negative feedback from superiors played a large role in interviewers developing a negative stereotype. Yet, he also believed that if an interviewer was provided with an increasing number of specific job parameters with which to match the applicant's credentials, there would tend to be less reliance upon the interviewer's personality theories. He subsequently hypothesized that occupational categories (such as intramural-recreational sport administration) which rely upon the interviewer's own personality theories, are more influenced by traits associated with negative applicant stereotyping than are occupational categories that require specialized and readily identified skills (such as scientific research and engineering).

Shaw's study supported a hypothesis concerning the sex of an applicant. His data indicated that when the experimental variable was the applicant's sex, the bias (in this instance, toward women) was less when the job qualifications were not as clearly defined. In addition, the findings indicated that a female applicant's sex was perceived (by some women as well as men) as being a negative trait and therefore could have a differential effect for certain occupational categories.

When job information is inadequate, even experience may not be of value in attempting to overcome the tendency towards bias. A study conducted by Langdale and Weitz (1973) indicated that even experienced interviewers were not in agreement on the suitability of most candidates when insufficient job information was provided. Thus, it appears that interviewers, experienced or not, when supplied with inadequate job information tend to rely upon their own personality theories and are influenced by traits associated with negative stereotyping. Since many interviewers (both male and female) perceive a female's sex as a negative trait for certain jobs, they immediately form a negative stereotype of the female applicant.

A similar bias against women was also evidenced in a study by Rosen and Jerdee (1974). The study examined sex stereotyping in the many phases of personnel decisions. They found that subtle forms of sex discrimination occurred in the formulation of decisions to employ, develop and promote employees. Significant among their work was one survey which indicated that when job requirements were exact and the applicant's qualifications failed to match them, the respondents rejected both male and female applicants. Similarly, when the applicant's and job qualifications matched, both males and females were evaluated highly. On the other hand, it was found that in situations where available information was ambiguous or contradictory, there was a larger number of positive evaluations for males than for females. This result led Rosen and Jerdee to conclude that it may be relatively easy to arrive at unbiased decisions when a candidate's qualifications are either clearly acceptable or unacceptable. But when information is scant and the position ambiguous, decision-makers tend to rely upon preconceived attitudes (in this particular instance, sex-role stereotyping) to arrive at their ultimate decision.

The availability of sufficient job information and the use of a relevant rating form does not fully guarantee that stereotyping will not occur. In this regard, Wiener and Schneiderman (1974) discovered that under such conditions stereotyping did, in fact, occur, although of a positive nature. Their results indicated that when interviewers were supplied with a complete job description in addition to rating sheets designed to measure relevant characteristics, agreement among interviewers was far superior to that evidenced when the interviewers were supplied with very little job information and irrelevant rating forms. Data of this sort suggests that, under ideal conditions, interviewers are able to reduce their biases through the use of objective job requirements and rating sheets relevant to desired applicant characteristics.

Another method for inhibiting the halo effect was proposed by Farr (1973). He contended that interviewers should be required to formulate repeated judgments of an applicant. This could be accomplished by structuring a rating form in a manner that necessitated the use of information normally attained well into the interview. The construction and use of such an instrument would then force the interviewer to attend to information presented throughout the interview—not just information obtained during the early stages.

Regarding the availability of job information, Langdale and Weitz (1973) evidenced that by providing the interviewer with extensive information about the job to be filled, the reliability of employment selection decisions could be increased. However, interviewer bias problems go beyond that of merely making decisions based upon limited information. If this were not the case, the above recommendations would be sufficient to eliminate such bias.

The Rosen and Jerdee study (1974) also indicated that bias, especially against women (and probably against other minorities as well), runs much deeper. In many instances, an individual's biases become an ingrained form of behavior and can not be alleviated by the technical recommendations made thus far. The only way to eradicate biases of this nature is to make the interviewer aware of his/her bias and then to work at correcting it.

To this end, Gery (1975) has suggested that interviewers stop imposing their own values and generalizations developed from past negative experiences with women (or other minority groups). Driscoll and Hess (1974) made even stronger suggestions. They proffered that, in order to eliminate bias, programs should be offered to foster interpersonal relationships and to develop sensitivity to the needs of others. Seminars for recruiters should be conducted and should include practice interviews as well as formal and informal discussions with groups composed of men, women and minority group members. In addition, Gery (1974) realized that despite all these efforts, individual biases might still remain. Therefore, he further suggested that to increase interview objectivity, several people should independently interview and evaluate the candidate. Moreover, he posited that, whenever possible, minority and female representatives should be included in the candidate selection process.

Drake (1972, p. 59) proposes some basic informational areas that an interview should cover: "college and other studies, military experience (when applicable), summer and full-time work experience, attitude towards job(s) and employer(s), aspirations and goals, and a self-assessment of candidate's strengths and limitations." In a well-organized, planned interview each of these informational areas may be covered within a reasonable period of time. It is advisable, however, to develop an interview format that will assist in providing each candidate an equal opportunity. Failure to afford equal interview treatment could (and probably should) be construed to be a violation of affirmative action and equal employment opportunity legislative mandates.

Each member of the search committee (or the interview team) should be provided with the interview plan prior to actually conducting the candidate interview. If such a plan were to be used, the probability of affording an equal opportunity for each candidate would be greatly enhanced. "Much of what is covered in the interview should be developed by the applicant under the control and direction of the interviewer (Drake, 1972, pp. 58-59)". The planned interview provides for such control and direction.

The primary purpose of any interview is to gain as much information as possible about the candidate's ability to successfully fulfill the responsibilities of the position sought. Generally, the types of decision-making information required by interviewers can be categorized as: (1) knowledge and experience factors, (2) intellectual factors, (3) motivational factors and (4) personality factors (Drake, 1972).

Planned interviews may be developed by focusing on each of these informational categories. Specific information required to properly evaluate an applicant's suitability for employment can be listed in a format similar to that displayed in Figure 1. The use of a Position Specification Guide helps to assure that all candidates received equal interview treatment.

How, then, when seeking intramural-recreational sport administrative personnel, may search committees (or interview teams) eliminate personal stereotypes and biases from entering the interview process? The fact of the matter is that there is no single prescription that, if adopted, would resolve

316

the problem. Nonetheless, if search committee members institute some of the following suggestions, the probability of contaminating the interview and selection process through the introduction of bias and stereotyping should be significantly reduced:

A. All search committees should have female and minority representation

B. Novice committee members should receive interview training and practice prior to serving on the search committee.

C. Committee members should possess a knowledge of the responsibilities of the position to be filled.

D. Specific skills and knowledges necessary to successfully function in the position should be identified.

E. A Position Specification Guide should be developed and instituted as a part of the interview process.

F. Committee members should not make decisions on the candidate until all of the necessary decision-making information has been obtained

G. Committee members should possess "active listening" skills

H. A well designed rating form should be employed

I. The interview should be conducted according to a planned procedure, and the same procedure used for all candidates

J. Candidates should be judged strictly on their qualifications and abilities, not upon their sex or race

K. Committee members should formulate their evaluation of the candidate independent of one another

L. Committee members should not compare the candidate to either a positive or negative "ideal" model.

CONTRACTS

Individuals possessing equal qualifications and employed in the same or similar roles within a given institution or agency should receive the same contract. For example, if a college or university intramural-recreational sport department were to recruit and hire two assistant directors, one female and one male, each should receive the same contractual conditions. Affirmative action and equal employment opportunity legislation prohibits the awarding of differing contracts to equally qualified individuals employed at the same or approximately the same time for the same or similar function. Therefore, in the above example, if the male assistant director were to receive a contract calling for an annual salary greater than that offered the female, charges of discrimination could be leveled, and probably substantiated.

Contracts usually contain a number of specific conditions of employment. From an affirmative action and equal employment opportunity perspective, some of the contractual considerations that should be reviewed for equality of application include the following areas:

Length and renewal — Employees hired at the same time for the same or similar function should receive contracts of equal duration and which also contain the same renewal stipulations. It would not be acceptable for one individual to receive a five-year contract renewable annually when others receive a three-year contract that is renewable only at the end of the third year.

Salaries and source of funding— Employees with equal service, responsibilities, performance evaluations and qualifications should receive the same salary. In addition, the salary funding for such employees should be generated from the same source, be it "soft" or "hard" monies.

Fringe benefits — Employees in the same or equal job classification should receive the same fringe benefits. Benefits of this nature include, but are not limited to: paid vacation, paid sick leave, health insurance, payroll deduction plans, tuition benefits and training opportunities. Fringe benefits must be provided for all employees in the same classification without regard to race or sex (Frontiero, 1973).

Tenure— In recent years, tenure has become very difficult to obtain primarily due to the high percentage of faculty already tenured. Nevertheless, when faculty are eligible for tenure consideration, the criteria used for denying or awarding such status must be the same for all candidates. Such criteria should be established, published and made available to employees at the time of their hiring. In addition, individuals employed at the same time with the same rank should collectively be either eligible or ineligible for tenure consideration. For example, if two assistant intramural-recreational sport directors were to be employed at the assistant professor rank both should be either eligible or ineligible for tenure consideration. To do otherwise would constitute a violation of affirmative action and equal employment opportunity mandates.

Task assignments and support services — Individuals employed in like or similar positions should be assigned equal job responsibilities and provided with the necessary support services. Equated work loads should be developed and support services such as office space, office equipment, clerical and secretarial assistance, telephone, postage, travel and reproduction monies, etc., should be provided at the level necessary for the employee to successfully fulfill the task assigned.

All employees (black and white, male and female, majority and minority) should maintain a continual evaluation of the benefits they receive as compared to those received by others in the same or similar employment classification. Whenever suspected instances of discrimination are detected, the employee should immediately bring the matter to the attention of the employer. If after a reasonable period of time the situation is not corrected, the employee should then proceed to file a formal complaint with the appropriate governmental agency. On the other hand, the employer should institute an ongoing evaluation process designed to detect unequal employee treatment. If and when such a practice is evidenced, the management should seek to introduce corrective measures.

CAREER ADVANCEMENT

In the world of work, most professional employees harbor a variety of career advancement aspirations. To put it another way, most individuals anticipate an opportunity to advance within the organizational structure, to move vertically from their point of entry position. Yet, knowing where one wants to go, and actually arriving at the destination are two entirely different matters.

Yeager and Leider (1975, p. 34) state that, "...the individual should be the manager of his own career". Unfortunately, no matter how strong the aspiration for vertical mobility is possessed by an individual, not all persons will be provided an equal opportunity for advancement. Women and minority group members tend to encounter greater difficulty in achieving upward mobility than do their male and majority counterparts. A study by Rosen and Jerdee (1974, p. 53) revealed that:

1. Male employees are expected to give top priority to their jobs when career demands and family obligations conflict. On the other hand, female employees are expected to sacrifice their careers to family responsibilities.

2. If personal conduct threatens an employee's job, employers make greater efforts to retain a valuable male employee than the equally qualified female.

3. In selection, promotion and career development discussions, employers are biased in favor of males.

Factual research discoveries such as the above prompted enactment of affirmative action and equal employment opportunity legislation, and only through application and enforcement of such prohibitions will discrimination by sex or race by eliminated.

Several areas of career advancement should be independently examined (especially by women and minorities) to ascertain that intramural-recreational sport departments and/or institutions of higher learning are complying with and promoting affirmative action and equal employment opportunity regulations. Key areas to examine include:

Promotion—Affirmative action calls for equal treatment of all like or similar categorical personnel when promotions are being considered. Race or sex can neither be used as an asset nor a liability in the promotional process. Intramural-recreational sport department employees of the same rank or status should be treated equally in terms of promotion consideration. Standards and qualifications established for promotion must not be applied differently for any group or individual. Additionally, the criteria used to qualify or disqualify an individual for promotion must be relevant to the position under consideration (Griggs, 1971). Finally, it should be understood by both administrators and employees that not all employees will continually receive vertical promotions. Consequently, consideration should be given to developing lateral promotions. Lateral promotions can be used to satisfy career expectations, and as Walker (1973, p. 70) states, "...we need individuals who are committed to lateral careers simply because there is limited room at the top."

When promotions are awarded, it is important that the "Peter Principle" is not invoked. To promote in such a method is neither beneficial to the individual nor to his/her subordinates or associates. "The way we match interests and talents of employee with opportunities needs to be attuned to both the career expectations of the individual and to the (institutions) staffing needs (Walker, 1973, p. 70)".

Educational opportunities — College and university intramural-recreational sport departments have numerous opportunities to provide professional personnel means to enhance their educational background. Inservice training programs, released time for attending academic classes, tuition waivers, sabbatical leaves and general leaves of absence each represent methods of providing employees with an opportunity to further develop their professional expertise. It is extremely important that the availability of these opportunities be made to all employees on an equal basis.

Professional growth opportunities — For intramural-recreational sport department personnel, professional growth opportunities might include such things as allowing employees specific time within the work schedule to engage in research projects, providing released time (and possibly finances) to attend professional meetings and extending encouragement for professional personnel to produce journal articles and text materials for publication. As with each facet of career advancement, all employees must be allowed to engage in professional growth projects on an equal basis.

Career opportunities — Internal and external career advancement opportunities should be brought to the attention of each intramural-recreational sport department employee. Administrators should continually encourage employees to seek better job opportunities, when and if they occur, and should provide equal support services to those subordinates actively pursuing career advancement opportunities. It is important that the top administrator provide an equal and adequate degree of counseling to subordinates with respect to their growth prospects within the organization, the advisability of their seeking advancement opportunities elsewhere or the possibility that they should pursue professional careers in another area of endeavor.

Each intramural-recreational sport department employee concerned with career advancement should be familiar with the quiz designed by Edith M. Lynch and contained in her book, *The Executive Suite — Feminine Style*. The quiz is quite useful in determining one's assets and liabilities as they relate to career motivation. Here's the quiz (Higginson and Quick, 1975, p. 5):

1. What do I really think of my own talents?

2. Am I willing to make the most of my talents?

3. Do I resent the fact that men seem to have the best jobs, the best chances for promotion, and the most exciting challenges?

4. How am I trying to improve my own position—more study, new research, better attitude?

5. Do I look at everything realistically instead of making poorly thought-out plans?

6. When did I last read a book pertaining to the job I'd like to hold?

7. Do I continually think of myself as limited to being a lady, a helper, a crutch instead of being a person doing higher level work?

8. Do I put the blame for not having a good job on someone else—my parents, the boss, the school I attended and so on?

9. Am I willing to do the hard work necessary to hold a responsible position?

10. Am I willing to work as a member of a team to accomplish a worthwhile project?

11. Am I willing to help others on the way up, particularly other women?

12. Am I willing to fight for my rights on equal ground and on the basis of what I have done and can do in the future?

Obviously, the answers are going to be somewhat prejudiced, but they can still provide a good deal of objective information. With the quiz information in hand, an individual should be able to gain with the "big picture" about him/herself. This "picture" can be developed by a three part process: (1) a determination and examination of your failures, (2) a review of your triumphs and (3) a determination and analysis of your assets. The processed information should subsequently enable the individual to establish his/her career plans with a greater probability of success.

Finally, intramural-recreational sport department personnel should periodically review both their department and institution to determine whether a proper climate for personal growth is maintained. Henry (1974, p. 25) provides the following growth climate guideline:

No matter how well you develop your counseling techniques, you won't be able to help upgrade subordinates if the atmosphere in your department or institution is not conducive to their career growth. What kind of atmosphere nurtures development? Here are some characteristics of a true growth climate:

1. The institution is profitable or successful.

2. The institution is expanding.

3. There is a formal system for developing people.

4. There is a policy for promotion from within and identification of outstanding employees.

5. The subordinate is supervised by a boss who is growing him/herself.

6. Administrators are not promoted unless they have successfully trained a subordinate to take over.

7. The work experience itself becomes a form of training.

8. The administrator expects a lot of his/her people.

9. Competence rather than seniority alone is rewarded.

10. The administrator puts a high premium on originality, resourcefulness, creativity and innovation.

11. Subordinates have an opportunity to share in decision making, planning and problem solving.

12. Each subordinate knows where he/she stands (how he/she is doing) and what is required to progress.

13. Employees are not exploited or deprived of rewards for work above and beyond that normally expected.

Adapted from Machine Design (Vol. 42, No. 17) Copyright 1970 by The Penton Publishing Company, Cleveland, Ohio.

After such a review, if the results indicate that the department or institution has failed to provide an adequate "growth climate" for all employees on an equal basis, the proper administrative authorities should be appraised of the situation so that they make take immediate corrective action.

Professional Opportunities for the Qualified Minorities: Some Affirmative Approaches to Action
Charles Espinosa
(1976 NIRSA Proceedings, pp. 44-45)

One important objective of any conference is to provide an opportunity for professionals in a specific field to meet, exchange ideas, discuss problems and propose possible solutions. The annual NIRSA conference has always succeeded in fulfilling this purpose and more. I am always surprised and somewhat comforted to find that we all generally share similar problems in our programs and institutions.

A realization related to one such problem remained on my mind from last year's conference because its solution was sought by many directors. The problem dealt specifically with the need for better recruitment of qualified minority applicants in the field of intramural recreational sports.

To date, this task of recruiting qualified minorities faces many administrators throughout most institutions or higher education. The task has, in many cases, become a "problem". Recruitment of minorities has taken the connotation of "quota systems" because of enforcement to compliance by the federal government through HEW and the Department of Labor.

I will not expound on the justification of such legislation as Title VII or IX, or the Affirmative Action Program. However, it should be noted that "legislation and commission action have been considered to be major instruments in bringing about fair or equal employment opportunity".[1] To say that such legislative action will eventually "flood" all professions with "unqualified" minorities (including women) would place the situation completely out of perspective. As Casper Weinberger remarked, "one might get the impression that the campuses are reeling under the onslaught of hordes of "unqualified" minorities and women, aided and abetted by the merciless minions of the Department of Health, Education, and Welfare (HEW). The reality of the situation is quite different. In 1966, women and blacks made up, respectively, 19.1 percent and 2.2 percent of college faculties; by 1972, the figures were, respectively, 20 percent and 2.9 percent. The numbers have not changed appreciably, in the last 3 years and thus would hardly constitute a mass invasion."[2]

Many institutions and professionals should take a more favorable attitude by taking the initiative review, evaluate, and improve recruitment policies rather than prolong the situation with frustrating litigation. This would, in my view, facilitate the whole process of affirmative action. This approach would indeed improve the state of confusion and befuddlement over the question of affirmative action that is prevalent in many institutions of higher education.

Putting further comments aside, pro and con, I contend that the task may hinge on devising or implementing approaches to make employment opportunities more accessible to the qualified minorities. Many approaches have been developed by colleges and universities since the inception of affirmative action. Some have worked through the process of trial and error. Some are the results of intense study and evaluation between E.E.O. affirmative action officers, faculty and administrators in an attempt to deal with specific circumstances at various universities and colleges. The effectiveness of these techniques or approaches are as yet unknown since there is little research that has been conducted in the area. However, the following approaches represent how the situation has been dealt with at some institutions.

1.) Participation by the Minority Faculty "Caucus" in Recruitment—Such groups on many campuses can serve as excellent sources of information in recruitment of qualified minority candidates. They can serve in an advisory capacity for various search committees in all disciplines.

2.) Job Vacancy Advertising Through the Offices of Ethnic Programs—Advertising job opportunities through the ethnic programs on campus is a logical alternative since most of these offices are very much involved in job placement for minority students.

3.) Minority Faculty Participation in the "Search Committee"—

Involving the minority faculty or staff member in the search can be a positive step in improving the recruitment and promotion requirements in higher education.

4.) Active Recruitment of Minority Graduate Students for Graduate Assistantships—Although a more long range remedy to the situation, this technique has great potential in developing more qualified minority professionals (The Educational Testing Service) (ETS) has an extensive program to assist universities in locating minority graduate students through the *Minority Locator Service.*

5.) Announcing the Job Vacancy Well in Advance—Allowing for sufficient time in filling a staff position will insure a more effective search of qualified applicants and increase the "applicant pool."

6.) Making Job Qualifications Relevant to the Position—Job qualifications should be carefully reviewed and compared with the responsibilities the job entails. Over-qualification requirements can have disparate effects on minorities. This approach would concur with the fact that many standards that are used for qualifications are as yet invalid. Advocating that the standard of publishing, for example is a valid predictor of future job performance, has *not* been proven. There are other facets (such as teaching and counseling) involved in being a "qualified" faculty member.

These approaches are by no means the answers to providing minorities access to employment opportunities. Every institution and department will have their own unique situation to deal with. However, I feel that any group of professionals, be it in chemistry, math, or intramural recreational sports, who are sincere in searching for the qualified minority, will indeed succeed in the task. The initiative must come from within the profession.

The need for such action is evident in intramural recreational sports. It is time to devise, modify, and implement such approaches to determine employment opportunities in this dynamic field before it becomes more central to our society. Developing approaches to make professional opportunities more accessible to the qualified minority in intramural recreational sports would be an expedient effort in keeping ahead of the times.

Sexism, Discrimination, and The Laws
Hazel Varner
(1975 NIRSA Proceedings, pp. 262-268)

Sexism refers to all those attitudes and actions which relegate women to a secondary and inferior status in society. Sexism further indicates a preference, by society, for one sex over the other. Society then attributes to that selected sex various preferred qualities and attitudes at the expense of the other sex. According to Thomas Boslooper and Marcia Hayes, authors of *The Feminity Game*, "The qualities necessary to success in today's culture — competitiveness, agressiveness, the desire to achieve — are considered unwomanly. Femininity is defined as passivity, as emotional dependence and physical weakness, as reaction instead of action; the portrait, in short, is a loser."[1] Audrey Van Deren states, in "Tonka Toys for Boys", "A female is born into a pre-determined existence — the student, wife, mother, grandmother syndrome. This is beginning to change, but it takes a gut-level change of consciousness concerning what being a human being is all about, to end the conditioning of females and males. Males, too, are channeled into roles and ways of behavior which need not be. Too long the "masculine" and "feminine" mystique has determined how one must behave and what one must do if one wishes to "fit in" to society as it has been predetermined."[13]

Sexism, as practiced in its every day form, may be conscious or unconscious. It may take the simple form of sexist language which demeans, ignores, patronizes or puts women in a special class. For example, to say:

"Arthur Ashe is one of the best tennis players in American, and Billie Jean King is one of the best women players" is sexist. An alternative would be to say "Arthur Ashe and Billie Jean King are among the best tennis players in America Today."

Sexism, in one of its most blatant forms, appears as discrimination in the professional career world when women work for less pay and are still unlikely to be promoted to positions of authority.

Sexist attitudes and discriminatory practices must be changed if we are to have a society in which both sexes can derive pleasure from all the roles human beings can play, a society with sufficient flexibility to allow both men and women full expression of their talents.

Attitudes are best changed by a process of education whereby each person reaches a state of awareness.

Disciminatory practices can be changed by legislation: the passing of laws which forbids discrimination on the basis of race or sex.

Many federal laws and regulations speak to discrimination. There are four federal laws which are the most important ones that affect the operating policies of educational institutions in the area of employment.

Title VII of the Civil Rights Act of 1964, as amended by the Equal Employment Opportunity Act of 1972, prohibits discrimination in employment (including hiring, upgrading, salaries, fringe benefits, training and other conditions of employment) on the basis of race, color, religion, national origin, or sex. It is administered by the Equal Employment Opportunity Commission, Washington, D.C. and regional E.E.O.C. offices.

Executive Order 11246, as amended by 11375, prohibits discrimination in employment by institutions with federal contracts of over $10,000. It is administered by the office for Civil Rights, U.S. Department of Health, Education and Welfare, Washington, D.C., 20201, and regional HEW offices.

Equal Pay Act of 1963 as amended by the Education Amendments of 1972 (Higher Education Act) prohibits discrimination in salaries, including almost all fringe benefits, on the basis of sex. It is administered by the Wage and Hour Division, Employment Standards Administration, U.S. Department of Labor, Washington; and Regional Wage and Hour Division Offices.

Title IX of the Education Amendments of 1972 (Higher Education Act) covers the employment practices of education institutions. It is adminstered by the office of Civil Rights, U.S. Department of Health, Education and Welfare and Regional offices.

In addition, there are many state and local laws and regulations which prohibit discrimination. These should be reviewed with state and local authorities. Complaint procedures are inherent within each of the federal laws and regulations. Procedures for filing complaints may be obtained from the specified agencies.

Today, there are many affirmative action issues being faced by administrators on our campuses. We should be aware of the major issues:

"1. *Affirmative Action Plans:* Required of all institutions with federal contracts totaling $50,000 or more and having 50 or more employees. The plan must be written and Revised Order No. 4 details what these plans must cover.

2. *Numerical Goals and Timetables:* Required of all institutions with federal contracts covered by the Executive Order. The institution must document its "good faith" efforts; such as what it did to recruit women and minorities, were they interviewed and what was the decision, etc.

3. *Salary Equalization:* Women and minorities cannot be paid less because of their sex and/or race. Criteria for raises must be applied equally. Numerous institutions have set aside specific sums for "equity adjustments."

4. *Back Pay*

Title VII—Allows up to two years, but not prior to date of coverage for professional staff—March 24, 1972.

Equal Pay Act— Allows up to two years for unwillful violation, three for willful violation—July 1, 1972.

Executive Order—Time limit not clear.

5. *Pensions such as T.I.A.A.:* which pay women less on a monthly basis because of actuarial differences. Under Executive Order, employers make either equal contributions or provide equal benefits. Under Title VII, equal benefits must be provided regardless of contribution.

6. *Nepotism:* Under Title VII and the Executive Order policies or practices which restrict the employment of spouses are prohibited.

7. *Maternity Leave:* Both Title VII and the Executive Order apply:

Childbearing leave—Title VII guidelines require that the part of pregnancy and childbirth, when a women is physically unable to work, be treated like all other temporary disabilities in terms of sick leave, health insurance and job retention.

Childbearing leave—Under HEW guidelines, this leave should be granted if leave is available for other personal reasons.

8. *Internal Grievance Procedures:* HEW does not require this but recommends that there be written procedures whereby individuals who feel agrieved because of sex or racial discrimination can ask for an investigation and if necessary, redress.

9. *Child Care:* Not required by any of the laws, but recommended by HEW guidelines.

10. *Recruitment and Hiring:* HEW requires that standards and criteria be "reasonably explicit" and be accessible to employees and applicants. Under the Executive Order, new recruiting practices must be developed if old methods result in low representation of women and minorities in the applicant pool.

11. *Affirmative Advertising:* All job notices should indicate that applications from women and minorities are sought. Employers cannot state that only members of a particular sex or race will be considered.

12. *Policy Statements:* Under the Executive Order institutions are required to have in writing a policy of non-discrimination in employment. This statement must be disseminated throughout the campus.

13. *Conditions of Employment, Salaries and Benefits:* Federal regulations require that there be no discrimination in all conditions of employment, including:
   —recruiting, hiring, lay-off, in-service training
   —opportunities for promotion
   —participation in training programs
   —wages and salaries
   —sick leave time and pay
   —vacation time and pay
   —overtime work and pay
   —medical, hospital, life and accident insurance

14. *Search Committees:* HEW recommends that all search committees, whenever possible, should include minorities and women.

15. *Marital and Parental Status:* Discrimination on the basis of marital status is forbidden by Title VII when applied to only one sex. Criteria concerning parental status would also be a violation if applied to one sex.

16. *Monitoring and Accountability:* System required by Executive Order.

   A. There must be an institution wide office that maintains records and monitors individual departments and units and reports annually.

   B. Individual departments and units are required to maintain records of applicants and hires, as well as records to recruit women.

17. *Job Analysis:* Under Executive Order all job classifications must be reviewed in order to identify "underutilization" of women and minorities.

18. *Work Assignments:* Teaching load, research responsibilities, etc. cannot be assigned on the basis of sex.

19. *Termination and Reduction in the Work Force:* Termination is prohibited unless the employer is able to demonstrate reasons unrelated to race, sex or national origin. Lack of seniority cannot be used as a reason for termination when the person laid off has been found to have less seniority because of previous discrimination."[6]

Dr. Bernice Sandler, director of the project on the status and education of women, states "Many of the issues now being debated, somewhat ex post facto in the Halls of Ivy, have already been decided in the courts." Among those likely to have the most impact are the following:

The existence of intent to discriminate is irrelevant. The effect of a policy or practice is what counts.

Statistics can be used to document a pattern of discrimination. Institutions cannot simply say no women or minorities applied. An institution may have a reputation as discriminatory which has a "chilling" effect on applications.

Any individual, including a third party, has standing to raise class allegations, and charge a pattern of discrimination, using statistics as evidence. Persons can make a general allegation without having to name names and incidents. The appropriate agency then investigates to see if the charges are substantiated.

All hiring and promotion policies must be based on objective, job-related criteria. A policy implemented by predominately white males using subjective opinions can be held to be discriminatory.

If an administrator ends up with only white males, when there is a pool of qualified women and minorities available, the institution may well be discriminating and may be called upon to prove it is not.

Any policy or practice that has an adverse or disparate effect on a protected class (e.g. women) and cannot be justified by business necessity is considered discriminatory. (Enunciated by Supreme Court Decision, Griggs vs. Duke Power Co.)

Seniority systems, such as tenure, which have been previously discriminatory, may come under review. Termination of women who do not have tenure because of prior discrimination may well be illegal.

Equal pay for equal work does not necessarily mean identical work, but only substantially equal work. Women may not be paid less simply because they often command a lower market value.

The law does not prohibit bona fide differences in pay based on merit or seniority.

Numerical goals have been upheld and ordered by the courts in numerous discrimination cases. Goals are set after there has been a finding of discrimination. Goals are not punitive; no one is required to be fired. Goals are an attempt to remedy present discrimination and give relief to a specific class that has been discriminated against in the past.

The courts have also maintained, clearly, that affirmative action and goals are not preferential treatment when undertaken to remedy past discrimination.

What is *not* at stake is the hiring of lesser qualified persons or reverse discrimination. A very real economic threat is present: for every women or minority person that is hired, it means that one less white male is hired. If affirmative action were to be enforced, it would become more difficult for white males to get jobs (meaning they wouldn't automatically get the job as in the past), but it cannot be called "reverse discrimination."

There has been a great deal of "flack" recently by the white male establishment, causing HEW to issue a new directive stating that universities may not discriminate against white males, or lower standards, to attract women or minorities, advertise specifically for women or minorities, or create minority slots. We should keep in mind that the opponents of affirmative action are the same tenured white male professors directly responsible for the unjust and discriminatory hiring system in academia.

Washington Post columnist William Raspberry comments that "the HEW memo sent to 3,000 college and university presidents by Peter Holmes, tells them they can hire anybody they damned well please, as long as they make it look good." Raspberry concludes that "Affirmative action quotas and the rest don't make any sense if you assume a rational, fair world to begin with. But they make a good deal of sense if you assume that bigotry, conscious or otherwise, is a fact of American life, and that we ought to do what we can to overcome it."[14]

James A. Harris, President of the N.E.A., states that "complaints of reverse discrimination against white men reveal a peculiarly ingrained type of prejudice" indicating that some people "simply can't bring themselves to believe that white males aren't always more qualified." He warned that we must now allow the HEW statement to be used as a new defense for the old bigoted thinking."[14]

Looking to the future, Sandler sees increased litigation. Women's groups can be expected to use the courts with increasing frequency. The EEOC can take to court employers who are found to be in violation of Title VII and Under the Executive Order, hundreds of institutions have been charged with pattern and practice of sex discrimination. The Equal Pay Division of the Department of Labor expects to file suit against at least ten universities this year.

As of now, the financial crisis is the first issue of concern on most college campuses. Sex discrimination is the second largest issue. "Women are the fastest growing and potentially the largest advocacy group on campus. They are challenging policies and practices, and using the law to its full extent. The hand that rocked the cradle has learned to rock the boat!"[10]

In conclusion, sexism and discrimination will vary in amount and degree from one institution to the next, and within universities, from one department to the next. Some colleges and universities started to take steps to improve equality as soon as the laws were passed; others still have done nothing. According to Dr. Sheila Molnar, sociologist and educator, "Discrimination is no longer simply a moral issue—It is a legal issue. The only remaining question is: Will the institutions make the necessary changes themselves, or will they wait for someone else to force them to do it?"

BIBLIOGRAPHY

1. Boslooper, Thomas and Marcia Hays. *The Feminity Game.* Stein and Day Publishers, New York, 1973.

2. Bird, Caroline, *Everything a Woman Needs to Know to Get Paid What She's Worth.* David McKay Co., New York, 1974.

3. Emma William Task Force (Ed.). *Sexism in Education.* Box 1429, Minneapolis, Minnn. Revised, 1973.

4. Epstein, Cynthia Fuchs. *Woman's Place.* University of California Press, Los Angeles, 1971.

5. Gornick, Vivian and Barbara K. Moran (Ed.) *Woman in Sexist Society.* Basic Books, Inc. New York, 1971.

6. *Journal of Law and Education.* Volume 2, Number 4, October 1973. National Press Building. Washington, D.C. Reprint Appendix II.

7. Molnar, Sheila. *Ending Sexual Discrimination in the Schools.* Unpublished paper.

8. Norton, Eleanor Holmes (Ed.). *Women's Role in Contemporary Society.* The Hearst Corporation, New York, 1972.

9. Sandler, Bernice and Dunkle, Margaret; et al. *What Constitutes Equality for Women in Sport?* Project on the Status and Education of Women, Association of American Colleges, Washington, D.C.

10. Sandler, Bernice. "Sex Discrimination, Educational Institutions, and the Law: A New Issue on Campus," *Journal of Law and Education,* Vol. 2, Number 4, October 1973. Washington, D.C.

11. Roche, John. "Reverse Discrimination Stymies Merit" *Democrat and Chronicle.* December 23, 1974.

12. Scott, Foresman and Company, "Guidelines for Improving the Image of Women in Textbooks." (Available from the company.)

13. Van Deren, Audrey. "Tonka Toys for Boys." *Sexism in Education.* (Emma Willard Task Force).

14. *Women Today.* Washington, D.C. Vol. V., No. 1, January 6, 1975.

Chapter 26
Liability

Liability—The Real Nitty Gritty
E. Moses Frye
(1975 NIRSA Proceedings, pp. 75-79)

The purpose of this presentation is to explore the meaning and scope of public liability. At the outset, it will be imperative for us to confine ourselves to the nature of Public Liability that more closely touches those of us here present. Liability is properly defined as the state of being bound or obliged in law or justice to do, pay, or make good something. Now, having refreshed our memories as to what liability actually means, let us take a further step and properly clarify liability for our purposes.

Remember, liability only attaches when damages have resulted. In order for liability to attach herein, there must be some type of injury. In most cases damages are physical in nature. There are or there is contractual liability which may arise solely from the nonperformance by one party to a contract more commonly referred to as contractual liability. By-and-large, contractual liability has become set over the years in case by case interpretation of contract law; however, tort liability is an entirely different subject. The word tort means literally wrong or injury, the opposite of right. In modern practice, the word tort is constantly used to denote a wrong or wrongful act for which an action will lie as distinguished from a contractual right. So, a tort is a legal wrong committed upon the person or property independent of contract. It may either be a direct invasion of some legal rights of individual or the infraction of some public duty by which special damage accrues to the individual. In the former case, no special damage is necessary to entitle a party to recover, however, in the latter two cases, damage is necessary. It should be apparent that the great body of law having arisen concerning liability is due to the development of tort liability. Since tort liability can vary appreciably while contractual liability is more confined, contractual liability does arise the manner in which it is handled is more established and well said.

So, let us begin a discussion of liability and its aspects and in more particular, tort liability. The liability of the state in its ordinary affairs is somewhat different from that of a private individual. Under ordinary circumstances, it can sustain a liability only by reason of a contractual obligation. It is not liable for the tortess acts of its officers, and where a governmental duty rests upon a state or any of its instrumentalities, there is an absolute immunity in respect to all acts or agencies. There is no moral obligation upon the part of the state which can be enforced upon equitable principals alone. That the state is not liable as an individual or private corporation may be on the ground that its agent acted upon an apparent authority which was not real. It is not bound to compensate an individual employee for injuries sustained while in its service. And no right of recovery in favor of such employee exists by inference or legal construction or otherwise than by statute. It is not the policy of state to indemnify persons for loss either from lack of proper laws or administrative provisions or from inadequate enforcement of laws or the inefficient administration of provisions which have been made for the protection of persons and property. Thus, while the state is not liable in tort for the acts of its officers, agents, or servants, it may assume such liability by statute in the absence of any prohibition in the constitution of the state. The state may recognize the liability for payment of moral or equitable obligations when not restricted by constitutional limitations and the legislature may properly appropriate public funds for the payment thereof. The state can adopt whatever mode or method it elects to determine whether it shall become liable and discharge a given obligation. It can select whatever agency it sees fit and proper to pass upon the question and provide that upon the determination of such agency, the claim shall be paid and the inquiry conducted by such agency may be administrative or judicial as the legislature so elects.

Having addressed ourselves to liability generally, it is important that we discuss two fundamental aspects of public liability which are necessary for an understanding of public liability. The first fundamental that we will discuss is known as sovereign immunity. Our legal history, sounded in Anglo-Saxon law, of necessity came on with the implication that the king can do no wrong. Early on in American jurisprudence, it became well established that the sovereign can not be used in its own courts or in any other court without its permission. It is inherent in the nature of sovereignty not to be amenable to the suit of an individual without its consent and this principle applies with full force to the several states of the union. Subject to some exceptions, which we will discuss at a later point, it has long been established that an action for tort is not maintainable against the state, either in its own courts or the courts of the sister state by its own citizen, the citizens of another state, or the citizens of subjects of a foreign state, unless by statute it has consented to be sued, or has otherwise waived its immunity from suit. On the other hand, it should be noted that in many instances, the immunity of a state from liability for tort has been held to be depended upon the governmental or proprietary nature of the function of the state in connection with which the alleged tort occurred which brings us to the next fundamental concept that must be understood in a discussion of public liability, the proprietary versus governmental dichotomy.

If I might digress for just a moment, it must be apparent from the foregoing that the legislative branch of government is the proper body to authorize suits against the state. The distinction that has been bond between governmental versus proprietary type functions is also an outgrowth out of the idea of sovereign immunity. Inherent in the reasoning behind the dichotomy between governmental and proprietary functions, is the recognition of a cause-effect relationship. In other words, in looking at the distinction between governmental and proprietary functions, one must look at the reason behind the function. If the state or municipality or educational institution or public body must of necessity perform that function, then it is a governmental function. On the other hand, if the function is solely one which is ancillary to proper exercise of governmental functions, then the governmental function may be more properly classified as proprietary. For instance, the leasing by a high school of a football stadium to another school district has in some jurisdictions been held to be proprietary in nature. The line between public operations that are proprietary and therefore, the proper subject ot suits and those that are governmental and therefore immune from such suits, is not clearly defined. Powers and functions held to be governmental or public in one jurisdiction are sometimes held to be corporate or private in another, and it has often been said that it is impossible to state a rule sufficiently exact to be of much practical value in deciding when a power is public and when it is private. As stated, the underlining test is whether the act performed is for the common good of all. It has been advocated that a governmental duty is one which involves the exercise of government power and is assumed for the exclusive benefit of the public. Perhaps I should point out that in a discussion concerning public liability as it pertains to public entities conceptualization of the levels and strata of government must be maintained. In other words, in thinking about liability, it is important to remember that it has been shaped by the established levels of government. Therefore, governmental immunity from suit may be different at different levels of government. For example, some jurisdictions recognize the proprietary versus governmental function dicotomy and the courts in those jurisdictions hold that a government agency in performance of a proprietary function is amenable to suit for tort liability. However, that same jurisdiction may well hold that a doctrine of absolute immunity applied regardless of the character of the function at the state level. Therefore, it is important to recognize of the manner and way in which the courts of that particular jurisdiction handle and deal with governmental immunity.

Having laid the ground work and background behind public liability and tort liability in regard to public liability, let us now consider a few of the exceptions and limitations on the doctrine of government immunity. Initially, of course, we must recognize that legislative abrogation or modification of the doctrine of immunity is the foremost method by which the state becomes amenable to suit and I think it has become apparent from our previous discussion that judicial abrogation of immunity also exists. That is, the judicial branch of government itself, the courts, in defining what governmental immunity is, and in recognizing the governmental proprietary distinction, also define the scope of governmental immunity. Thus, the courts in the past have found that the doctrine of immunity from liability for injuries occurring in connection with the exercise of governmental functions is subject to certain exceptions and limitations. For instance, it does not apply where injury complained of is the taking or damaging of private property for public use without compensation. The doctrine of immunity has frequently been denied application also where damage or injury has been occasioned through the establishment, maintenance, or permission or a nuisance. In some instances, in the cases of injuries from acts of negligence with respect to duties of an absolute or mandatory character. It must also be remembered that the issue of immunity and the issue of liability are two complete and distinct issues. The removal of governmental immunity in a specific area of tort actions does not impose absolute liability in the place of immunity. It only makes a governmental entity subject to the same rules which apply to nongovernmental immunity.

Heretofore, we have not mentioned constitutional implications, the first of which is the state constitution. State constitutions could very well speak to certain individual specific instances in which liability shall not be imposed upon the state. In such a situation, the state legislature, for instance, could not abrogate the grant by the constitution upon itself of sovereign immunity. Therefore, in connection with that specific activity, the legislature could not make the state amenable to suit. It should be apparent from the foregoing discussion that what the legislature giveth, the legislature can taketh away. Therefore, where the legislature grants or denies to individuals the right of action against a government entity for injuries resulting from negligence of persons and their employees or from defective condition of places and structures which they are bound to keep in repair, the general rule is that it may grant the right of action upon any condition which it chooses to prescribe.

Now, let us discuss the procurement of liability or indemnity insurance. How does it affect immunity? There is a seemingly growing trend by the courts to adopt the view to the extent that a liability insurance policy protects a government unit against tort liability, the otherwise existing immunity of the unit is removed. Nevertheless, the prevailing view still seems to be that the immunity from tort liability of a political subdivision is unaffected by its procurement of insurance which purports to protect it from such liability. Moreover it has been held that the fact that a government unit in procuring insurance against tort liability has acted pursuant to statutory authorization does not require the conclusion that the unit's immunity from liability has been abrogated in whole or in part so long as the authorizing statute contains no expressed waiver of immunity. And it is patent that a governmental unit's immunity from tort liability continues to exist notwithstanding its procurement of insurance against such liability where the statute authorizing it to procure the insurance expressly provides for continuation of the immunity. Often state constitutions have an effect on the desirability of indemnity insurance. For instance, in my home state of Oklahoma, there is a constitutional prohibition against the state indemnifying any party with which the state deals. In this case then, the state simply by constitutional fiat has envoked its sovereign immunity and will not allow any governmental subdivision to acquire or bear the expense of acquiring an indemnity insurance contract or acquiring indemnity insurance for any other contractual party.

Before I conclude, I should make mention of some of the modern tendencies in this area of the law. Often in the past, in fixing liability for tort there has been a blind adherence to the proprietary governmental distinction without real consideration of the reasons which gave birth to that doctrine and whether in the light of the general expansion of governmental activity, the doctrine has not outlived its usefulness. At present, the modern tendency is to restrict rather than to extend the doctrine of governmental immunity. However, the courts generally take the view that not withstanding the obvious justice of compensating the plaintiff for his injuries, the contrary doctrine as to governmental functions is so well established that the overwhelming weight of authority is that the law must be considered settled until altered by the legislature.

In conclusion, let me say that it is well established that by consenting to be sued, the state does nothing more than waive its immunity from action. It does not thereby concede its liability in favor of another party or create a cause of action in his favor which did not theretofore exist. Thus, liability of the state for tort cannot be predicated upon the fact that the state has entered its general statutory consent to be sued or directing the manner in which suits may be brought by those having claims against the state. Neither does a special statute permitting suits on particular claims concede the justice of the claim and in some states, Oklahoma for instance, there exists a constitutional prohibition against special statutes granting permission to sue the state.

It must, therefore, be kept in mind that statutory consent to be sued merely gives a remedy to enforce a liability and submits the state to the jurisdiction of the court subject to its right to interpose any lawful defense.

Liability Insurance: Pros, Cons, and Availability
Gene G. Lamke
(1975 NIRSA Proceedings, pp. 80-82)

Before I enter into a discussion about liability insurance, a few funda-mental concepts about liability in general should be emphasized that have a direct effect on whether or not insurance is an advantageous alternative for you, your department, or your school.

The first concept has to do with the phrase "the king can do no wrong," the concept of sovereign immunity. This statement implies a legal immunity for governmental entities against most liability judgments. This is a fading concept today and in many court cases throughout this country, governmental entities are being sued for injuries where negligence can be established.

A second point concerns joint power agreements. Many of us allow our functions to be carried on by someone else other than our own hired personnel (i.e., sports club), without really realizing the extent of our liability. For instance, many departments believe that since some other entity is responsible for supervision of a given program, only that entity can be held liable for negligence. Well, in joint powers agreements, all parties that enter into the contract are jointly and severally liable. They all share the liability if accidents occur. Also, governmental entities cannot delegate functions to another organization in hopes of escaping liability. The courts are clear and concise in this area. Most of us claim sports clubs as parts of our program and advertise for them, but believe only the club itself is liable for its negligence. It is simply not the case.

Dealing with a slightly different area is the concept of "deep pockets." This refers to the ability of those named in a lawsuit to pay large sums of money. Juries seem favorable to granting large awards. Litigation today is producing bigger and bigger awards because lawyers will generally only tackle cases where deep pockets exist. Also, injuries in our programs involve young adults who have rarely begun to work for a living. Disabling accidents to students therefore cause courts to grant higher awards because they have built up less capital and will have longer lives.

Now, on to the topic of whether or not you need insurance and what it is going to cost. The first thing you should ask yourself is, do I need insurance? This question, in itself, involves three variables.

First of all, is someone else covering you. The possibility exists that your institution may already have insurance which covers all of its employees. You can check with your school's director of business affairs to secure this information. Find out whether or not you are covered and to what extent (amount of dollars) you are covered. The fact may be that the school has insurance to cover its acts, but may not cover you personally. And the courts are clear that, although presidents, directors, school board members, and trustees are not personally liable for negligence while acting in their official capacities and within the scope of their authority, individual teachers and school employees may be held personally liable for their acts if negligence can be clearly established.

Now, if your institution is a state supported college or university, the school might be "self-insured." This is to say that the state will review each claim made against it for accident, injury, or loss, and then award or deny damages based on the merits of each individual case. Most states have set limits for claims (i.e., California — 2 million dollars). But the ironical fact here is that the state may disclaim any liability and then you might still be held personally liable. Or, if you have insurance, the state might pay amounts above your liability limits.

The second variable relating to, do I need insurance? is "What do I give up if I buy comprehensive personal liability insurance?" If I am immune, do I forfeit my protection of immunity as a legal defense? Does this create a deep pocket from which I might invite greater numbers of, or larger, lawsuits? The best possible way to answer the previous questions is expressed in the phrase, "nothing to lose, but everything to gain." In most states, the purchase of liability insurance has no effect upon the immunity of school districts or its institutions. And deep pocket, although it may exist, should not be a deterrent, as your company, and not you personally, will have to pay if you are found negligent. Also, deep pockets in itself will not create a greater number of suits or larger suits.

The final variable concerned with, do I need insurance? is "what can it do for me?" The answer to this is obvious. If it can't do me any harm, and the cost makes it feasible, it can only afford me the protection against expenses incurred in defending suits and cover the judgments if any. Having liability insurance from a reputable company immediately supplies you with the finest of legal counsel trained in tort liability. And also, the funds to pay if the jury so decides. In summary then, each and every one of us should possess liability insurance to some extent, because we give up no rights or privileges and gain needed protection from possible legal action.

Let's now examine the types of coverage available to us and their cost. First of all, there's the school's policy. In most cases, we are insured under its policy at no cost to us. School insurance is a costly item. Policies involving A.S.B. activities will vary with the activities that student bodies offer and also the number of people involved. But, just to give you an example, at San Diego State University (30,000 students and a broad program of activities, IM Sports, 30 Sport Clubs, outdoor programs, etc.) the yearly cost is $3,750 for policies up to 3 million dollars.

If the school will not or cannot include teachers or administrators in its liability insurance, it will often allow the teachers to be named as additional insureds if they pay the premium charge themselves. These premiums will generally range from five to ten dollars per year for similar coverage to that of the school.

Probably the best way to cover ourselves is by the purchase of personal liability insurance available under an Owners, Landlords, and Tenants Comprehensive Personal Liability, Homeowners, or Farmers Comprehensive Personal Liability policy. A "business pursuits" clause can be tacked on one of your existing insurance policies for a minimal yearly cost. Below are some charts indicating yearly costs for some of the more popular insurance companies.

Amount of Insurance	Firemen's Fund (Homeowners)	All-State (Auto Policy)	Safeco (All Policies)	State Farm (Home Owners)
25,000 CPL	$3.00	$9.90	$5.00	$5.00
50,000 CPL	3.00	10.70	5.00	5.00
100,000 CPL	4.00	11.50	6.00	6.00
200,000 CPL	5.00	12.60	8.00	7.00
300,000 CPL	6.00	13.60	10.00	8.00

In most instances, you can obtain additional personal liability coverage on your existing policy for an approximate cost of five to ten dollars a year (up to 300,000 CPL).

A slight possibility exists that you may have to submit a cover letter to your company stating your occupational duties and asking them for a rating. Generally, this exists only when the company cannot write your business pursuits endorsement under one of the existing teacher classifications. This sometimes happens when an employee's chief duties are administrative in nature. Even if you must submit your risks to the company, it will most likely still insure you on one of your existing policies, although the cost might range from two to five dollars per year more than the normal cost.

It's time to buy. Protect yourself and/or your employees.

Liability: Preventive Practices Concerning Facilities and Equipment
Patti Holmes
(1975 NIRSA Proceedings, pp. 82-84)

I.   *Fieldhouse*
    A.   Unstructured Use
        1.   Gym area—never unsupervised
            a.   Keep floor area clean.
            b.   Make sure baskets are secure.
            c.   All hazards are kept off floor area: wrestling mats, gymnastic equipment etc.

    d. Fighting should occur—always supervision, so if tension mounts, can be controlled (campus police contacted if necessary!)

    e. Injuries—constant supervision, phones available to supervisor or any student, first aid equipment close in activity area.

    f. Lighting—set numbers of lights are turned on—very adequate

    g. I.D.'s checked always—Private School

2. Weight room (Olympic Weights)

    a. Attendant in room at all times

    b. Buddy system is used

    c. Control the numbers in room

    d. Checking weight equipment, benches etc.—students normally tell us this

B. *Structured Use*

1. *Intramurals*—(gym area)

    a. Floor area is kept clean.

    b. Equipment is checked constantly for damage.

    c. Hazards are cleared before activity starts—activity specialist check this.

    d. Two activity specialists are assigned to each specific game—officials work with them but activity specialists have final say.

    e. Injuries—first aid available, most students have taken 1st aid at University in Physical Education program. Report must be filed regarding injury.

    f. Activity Evaluation Forms are filled out after each supervisor has worked an activity. Forms have area for listing *conditions* of *activity area*—gym floor clean, baskets in good condition, handball walls need repair, check holes in field, lights out in softball field, etc. Taken from this form, if a situation needs to be remedied it is acted upon immediately by Intramural Staff and maintenance personnel.

2. *Special Events*

    a. Personnel involved in the event are required to hire: security if necessary, proper personnel, building personnel must be hired for the evening.

    b. All equipment brought in for events must be checked out for safety.

    c. Any equipment belonging to the University is constantly checked and repaired if necessary—stands

        structure, fields etc. Work closely with maintenance
        department.

    d. All events not connected with the University, the personnel in charge must take out public liability insurance.

II. *Baujan Stadium, Tennis Courts — Playfields*

  A. Unstructured Use

    1. All areas are supervised and checked periodically for any needed repairs — fields, stands, nets, lighting, etc.

    2. Phones in area are available and campus police found in area to assist can generally be if necessary.

  B. Structured Use

    1. *Always* supervise.

    2. Activity evaluations and reports used for feedback on condition of activity area and also personnel involved in any injury.

    3. Follow up on both reports.

    4. Equipment is checked constantly.

    5. *Rentals* — security must be hired if necessary, public liability attained.

In conclusion, there is a tight watch on all equipment and facilities at the University of Dayton. Since the Intramural Director is in charge of these facilities at our school, he coordinates along with his staff strict measures to maintain equipment and facilities in top order. All precautions necessary are taken to ensure the safety of all involved.

Chapter 27
Contemporary Issues

Gay Liberation in Intramurals
Lawrence S. Preo
(1974 NIA Proceedings, pp. 65-66)

Kent State University has become synonymous with student unrest in this country. The killing of four (4) students on our campus on May 4th, 1970, will long be remembered as one of the greatest tragedies of the student movement.

Prior to my going to Kent State as its intramural director in 1972, I read all that I could get my hands on relative to the school, its administrators, its programs, and, of course, its students. As you can well guess, since 1970 there have been reams and reams written about the institution. I looked forward to my involvement with great excitement and anticipation. The prospect of becoming a significant part of that student culture really turned me on. It was to be a real challenge. Most of what I read about the student body indicated that they were a politically aware, suspicious group. They were reputed to look beyond simple acts to search out the "hidden motivation" and were an interesting and volital group. I was led to believe that they were angry and uptight and would protest and picket at the slightest injustice or suspected injustice.

They weren't gonna get me tho. No sir. I was ready. I came prepared to beat them at their own game. I felt I had done my homework well and after having been associated with two great intramural men, Dr. G. W. Haniford of Purdue and Dr. D. O. Matthews of Illinois, how could I go wrong?

I began my first year at Kent determined to put into practice all the innovative programming and plans possible. For example, I actively recruited black program supervisors, actively recruited black gym supervisors, I actively recruited black officials, actively recruited women refs for mens intramurals, created a Student Protest Board, created a Student Advisory Board, created a Student Review Board, created a co-rec program, created a F-G-S program, established the open door policy, established a suggestion box, created a handicapped students recreational program, created an international students night in one of the gyms on a weekly basis. I was determined to meet the needs of all the students and be responsive to their wishes. After six months on the job I thought I had been relatively successful. Things seemed to be running smoothly. But alas, I had made on major mistake. I had not anticipated the KGLF—which is of course, the Kent Gay Liberation Front.

I didn't realize at the time, but, I was running a sexist program! At least that is what the KGLF thought. It didn't matter that we had every possible division for competition—men, women, co-rec, open leagues, F-F-S, handi-capped—the KGLF said we were sexist!!! So...

Well—before I knew it, I had a major—or at least *the makings* of a major—incident on my hands. It all happened during the first week of basketball play. Unknown to me, there was an NBC-TV camera crew hidden in the parking lot behind the gymnasium. They were waiting for the signal which would bring them into the gym to record another student protest at the infamous Kent State University. Needless to say, the media is always quick to respond to trouble or suspected trouble at Kent.

What happened next was soon to be known as the "Lavender Menace" incident. A mixed team, males and females, had signed up under the team name of Lavender Menace to play in the men's basketball league. As the players went out on the court to warm up, I realized that I had a real zoo here. Up to that point, I had no idea that something was underfoot. I then took a close look at the players, coach, scorekeeper and fans. A good number of them were in cosmic drag (define the term). I approached the captain and informed him that this was the night for mens league basketball play and that the co-rec teams played the next night...I was under the impression that they had made an honest mistake and were looking for the co-rec league. No way! The Menace's captain informed me that they refused to play co-rec basketball because its rules discriminate on the basis of sex and that was a no-no for them (a female's basket scores 4 points whereas a male's basket scores only 2 points). He went on to say that the co-rec rules would be impossible for his team to interpret because of the sex thing...some of the players were males "physiologically" but females emotionally and psychologically.

At this point the news crew came in. The Lavender Menace began to sit down on the court and the team captain began to read a prepared statement about the ridicule, repression, and non-responsiveness of the KSU adminis-tration. They were very surprised when I interrupted the captain and informed them that they could compete in the men's basketball league. They were prepared for a lot that evening except the prospect of actually being allowed to play basketball!!!!

They played.

They scored 2 points.

They scored 12 points in five games.

The campus accepted them.

Great crowd reaction.

Great P.R.

The KGLF has since become a regular competitor in the co-rec division. They also speak, on a regular basis, to my classes on the whats and whys of their competition in the intramural program.

What was learned from this incident? For one, we now understand what the word flexible means—what was unheard of before is now commonplace.

We must respond to the changing needs of our students. After all, that's what we're all about.

Credit for Intramurals
Paul Gunsten
(1974 NIA Proceedings, pp. 61-62)

During my seven years as director of intramurals and extramural sport clubs at Virginia Tech, my teaching load has been reduced from three-quarters to one-quarter to provide time for administration and organization of the programs. Under the Virginia Tech policy for computing faculty loads and additional faculty positions, there was no existing formula for the Division of Health and Physical Education to receive credit for this release time. This meant that the release time given for intramurals and extramurals had to be absorbed by other faculty members in the Division, in turn creating an overload on several faculty members.

Virginia Tech computes faculty load in two ways. First a full teaching load is considered being twelve didactic hours based on:

1 didactic hour for each hour of a lecture class per week

1.6 didactic hour for each three hour laboratory class per week

New faculty positions are created by WSCH's (Weighted Student Credit Hours). One thousand fifty hours equaling a faculty position. These hours are credited as follows:

Freshman & Sophomore Classes—One hour for each hour of credit

Junior & Senior Classes—1.3 hours for each hour of credit

Graduate Classes—1.5 hours for each hour of credit

Due to the inequality of faculty load, as a result of state policy, a system was needed to provide administrative credit for faculty involved in the intramural and extramural programs. Two years ago a plan was presented to the administration to create Student Credit Hours. Basically, the plan was:

To allow one hour credit for a student who participates in 27 hours of intramurals or extramurals, the usual amount of time spent in a one hour lab class.—Said credit to be non-degree and a grade of pass. To provide state recognition, a course number and title was assigned and the course listed in the University Catalogue.

To procure recognition of the course the normal channels of administrative procedure were followed:

1. approval by the Division of Health and Physical Education

2. approval by the Curriculum Committee of the College of Education

3. approval by the University Undergraduate Commission
4. approval by the College Deans
5. approval by the University Administrative Committee
6. approval by the State Council of Higher Education

Upon final approval, the course was listed in the University Catalogue and students are receiving non-degree credit this school year (1973-74).

Based upon the participation records over the past seven years, it was anticipated there would be an accumulation of enough hours during the school year to justify four or more faculty positions for intramural and extramural programs.

A program of credit for intramurals, has merit in junior and senior high schools, either for part or full credit towards the required physical education program. This type of credit could alleviate a part of the physical educator's trouble with the problem child that does not want to participate in scheduled classes. It could also be a culmination of an instructional program for the skilled student providing more time for the physical educator to work with the unskilled and/or handicapped student. This does not mean a special class for handicapped.

With the large number of students being assigned to physical education classes in many school systems, a program of this type through testing programs to determine skill level and/or competency could also be an aid in reducing class size.

As a result of this presentation it is hoped that some individuals have received information that will help with the present emphasis on "Accountability." The Virginia Tech plan or an adaptation of it, that would fit other situations, could provide schools with additional assistance in the administration of their programs. The implementation of "Title IX," in the near future will place greater demands on already expanding intramural and extramural programs. Intramural Directors need to prepare for these demands and have sufficient staff to continue to run quality programs.

Suggested Administrative Approaches for Solving Racial Tension in College Intramural Programs
William Manning
(1971 NIA Proceedings, pp. 62-65)

I am presently located in an area that has had its share of student unrest. I was an undergraduate student at Berkeley in 1964 which you will recall was the year of the 'free speech' movement, the initial major incident of campus unrest. Though Berkeley was first, it did not take long for the movement to spread cross-country. In the last few years I doubt that more than a handful of colleges have escaped the turmoil, violence, and destruction often accompanying student unrest.

As we are all aware, there are aspects of such a complex problem which appear beyond the limits of administrative control. Berkeley's People's Park incident in 1966 and last spring's Cambodian Moratorium are two good examples. During the spring strike our program came to a standstill as the majority of the students refused to go on with 'business as usual.' Participation dropped over 10,000 man-hours during this period. Though there does not appear to be much that we as administrators can do in certain situations, there are other aspects of student unrest over which some degree of administrative influence can be exercised.

One such problem which we have encountered at Berkeley is that of racial tension; more specifically, the recurrence of explosive black-white confrontations. In the past few years this problem has manifested itself in numerous ways: fighting, threats (including on the life of the Director and Assistant Director at Berkeley), and frequent claims of prejudice by our black participants. This is, and has been, no easy matter to cope with, being white and as an authority figure representing white middle-class establishment.

I think we have made progress towards harmony at Berkeley. This morning, I would like to share with you some of my ideas concerning methods in dealing with these problems, as well as several ideas of ten of our colleagues as expressed through a questionnaire I distributed to the administrators of ten major universities at last year's convention.

Copies of the results of this questionnaire have been distributed amongst you. The numbers to the left indicate the number of responses for that particular answer. The purpose of this study was to determine if other intramural programs were experiencing the same kinds of problems with racial tension that have occurred at the University of Illinois and at the University of California at Berkeley. And if so, how were other administrators dealing with these problems?

Since most of us use student help either as supervisors, officials or student managers, the first few questions were designed to determine whether they were given any special training or instructions in the handling of problem situations.

Seven administrators indicated some type of special student training in this area, primarily conducted by a professional staff member. In general, the student is instructed to arbitrate disputes and disruptions on the court or field in an attempt to make an immediate settlement of differences. If this approach is unsuccessful, the following procedures were to be taken:

Threaten with game forfeiture or expulsion from program (2 responses).

Call police if order not restored (3 responses)

Call on-duty staff member (2 responses)

Two respondents indicated that it would be desirable for one of the professional staff to be summoned immediately to handle the problem. Only one indicated a preference for immediately calling police in potentially explosive situations.

Six of the ten respondents indicated some specific problems with black participation. A seventh was obviously anticipating trouble as evidenced by his 'not yet' response to the question. These problems were the same that most of us have faced: threats of physical violence, fights, and claims of prejudice. Only two administrators indicated the use of campus police to quell the situations. The concensus was that use of police curbed only the immediate problem and did nothing to prevent similar recurrences.

The methods indicated most effective in dealing with these situations were:

Employment of black professional staff members (3 responses).

Use of black student employees (3 reponses).

Threats of game forfeiture or expulsion from program (3 responses).

Meeting with black groups and leaders (3 responses).

Inclusion of blacks on student protest and policy boards (1 response).

To eliminate claims of prejudice and insure equal treatment of all participants the following procedures were preferred:

A firm stand behind existing *written* program policies (7 responses).

Employment of black professional staff members (6 responses).

Employment of black students (5 responses).

Consultation with blacks concerning policy changes if needed (5 responses).

Black representation on all student boards (4 responses).

With the next few questions I attempted to find out how many blacks were employed at these institutions; in what capacity; and whether or not they were effective in lessening potentially tense racial situations. As is evident, of the thirty-seven professional staff members only one was black. Four of the forty-two graduate assistants were black, and sixty-two of sixteen hundred-thirty student employees were black.

Perhaps one of the reasons for the small number of black employees is their reluctance to place themselves in a position which might conflict with loyalty to peer groups. Recently I feel that my efforts to recruit black employees at Berkeley have been thwarted by this problem.

Five administrators thought that black student employees were of help in dealing with these problems. Only three, however, indicated that they actively recruited black employees. It is interesting to note that although five administrators indicated that black representation on all student boards would be of positive value, only one of the five institutions with a student policy or protest board indicated black representation. Since the number of black participants is usually small in relation to total participation, the chances of their election to these boards is questionnable. One positive approach is for the administrator to appoint black representatives.

The responses to the next to last question suggest that the racial problem ranks low in terms of administrative priority when compared with acquisition of facilities, finance, growth of program, and supervision of student employees. Two conclusions can be drawn from this evaluation: perhaps this problem is not really of major consequence, or as one administrator responded, "all of these problems should be ranked number one." Regardless of its priority ranking, the problem is of such nature that it should warrant a great deal of administrative attention.

When I attempt to interpret the administrative implications of the findings, a few ideas stand out. Written program policies or guidelines appear to be a must. In addition, it is imperative that students be given an active voice in the decision-making process that determines these policies and guidelines. Whether this be a student policy board or student representation on a faculty board makes little difference. The important thing is that today's students must be consulted and that we, as administrators, must listen to them with an open mind. We must also make certain that there are frequent reviews of these policies to insure that they are both current and relevant.

I have found that black employees help to bridge the communication gap between the director and black participants. In addition, they help immeasurably in meeting the needs of minority group participants by providing an open line of information to and from the black student community. In working to insure a fair, harmonious program, I think that we as intramural directors have an administrative responsibility to actively recruit black employees. In a somewhat similar vein, I feel that we must also greatly increase our efforts to encourage more blacks to join our professional ranks and must provide the avenues by which this can be realized. I feel that by adopting many of these actions we can not only demonstrate our good faith, but make positive steps toward needed change.

We have found a few other methods to be somewhat effective at Berkeley. Some of our football games are played at night on poorly lit fields. After a few unfortunate incidents, anticipated problem games are no longer scheduled during these time periods. An effort is made to have a staff member present at all games where trouble of this nature may occur. We have also found it good policy to make sure our best referees are schedule for these games. We try to meet informally with black participants to gain their confidence as well as establish lines of communication. The problem has certainly not disappeared from our campus, but I feel our efforts are being rewarded in a lessening of the number as well as the intensity of racially tense situations.

In conclusion, I would like to propose a few guidelines for dealing with this problem. One is to be completely frank and honest in discussions, 'lay all the cards on the table', so to speak. Never promise anything you are not sure you can deliver or back-up, don't try to placate or patronize, and never equivocate. Stand firm on existing written policies while still remaining open for change if change becomes necessary.

We are charged with the responsibility of meeting the needs of all our students; therefore, we must make every effort to insure that maximum benefit is accessible to each individual who participates in our program.